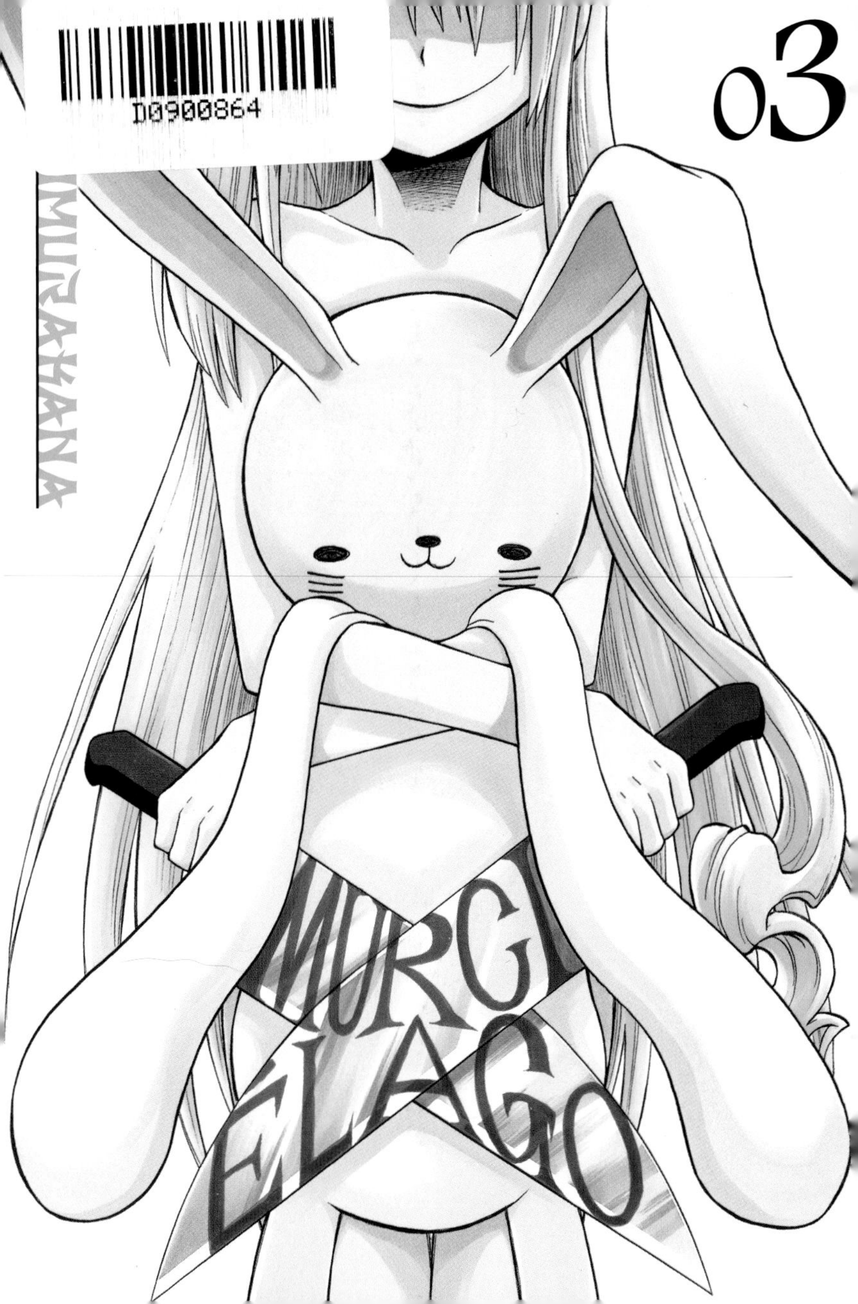
03
MURAKANA
MURCI
ELAGO

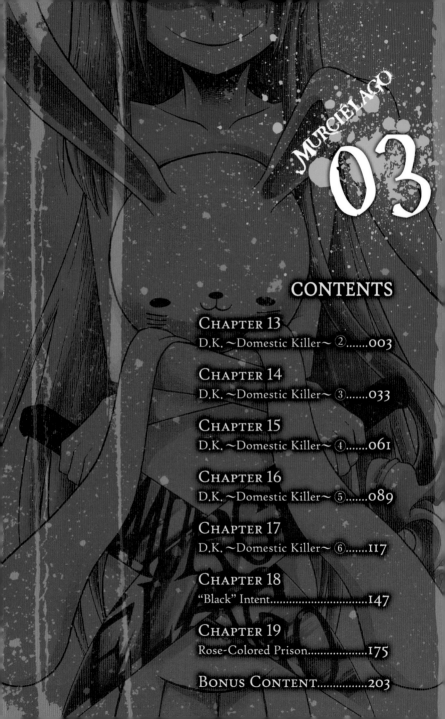

MURCIÉLAGO

03

CONTENTS

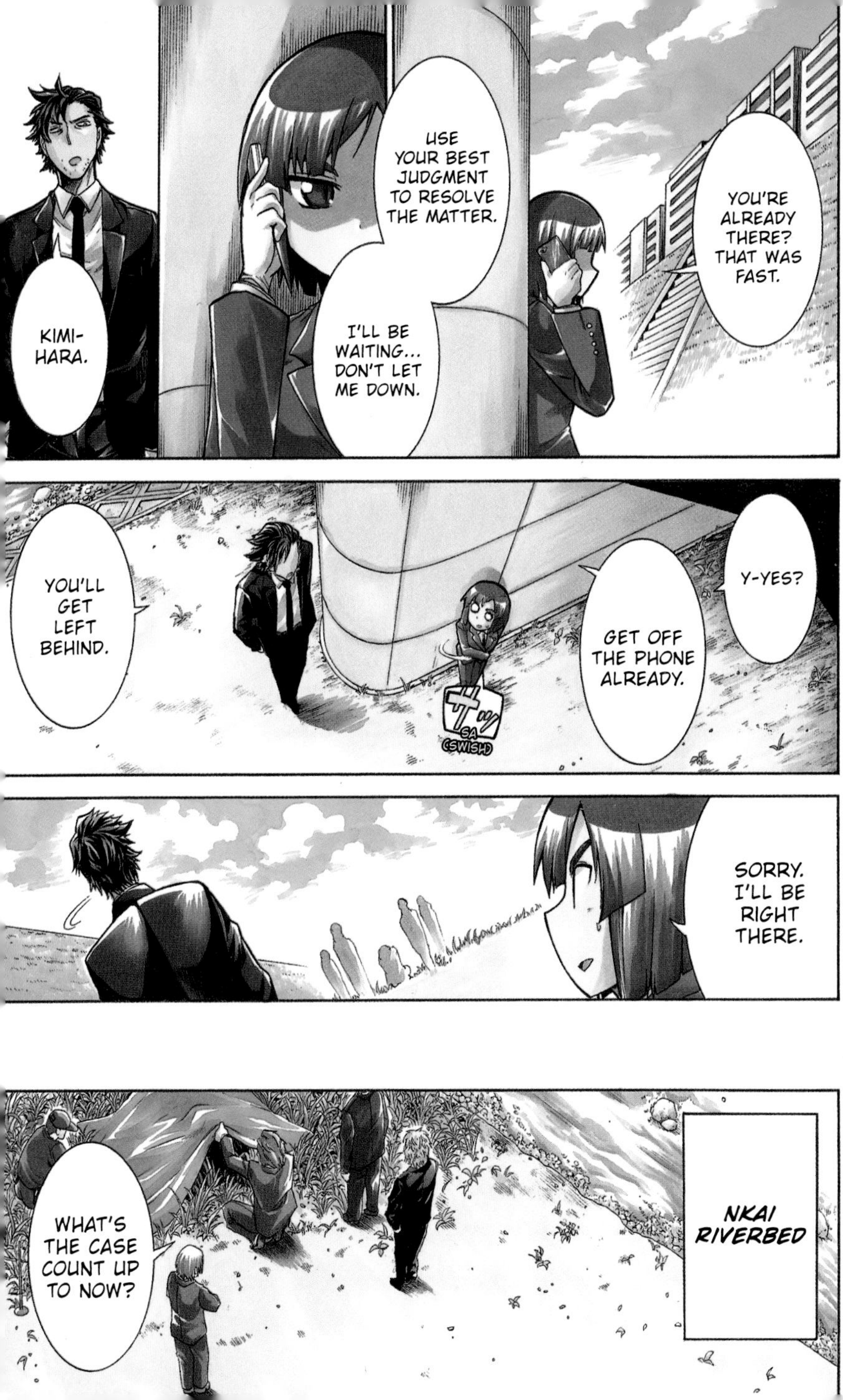

YOU'RE ALREADY THERE? THAT WAS FAST.
USE YOUR BEST JUDGMENT TO RESOLVE THE MATTER.
I'LL BE WAITING... DON'T LET ME DOWN.
KIMI-HARA.
Y-YES?
GET OFF THE PHONE ALREADY.
SA (SWISH)
YOU'LL GET LEFT BEHIND.
SORRY. I'LL BE RIGHT THERE.
NKAI RIVERBED
WHAT'S THE CASE COUNT UP TO NOW?

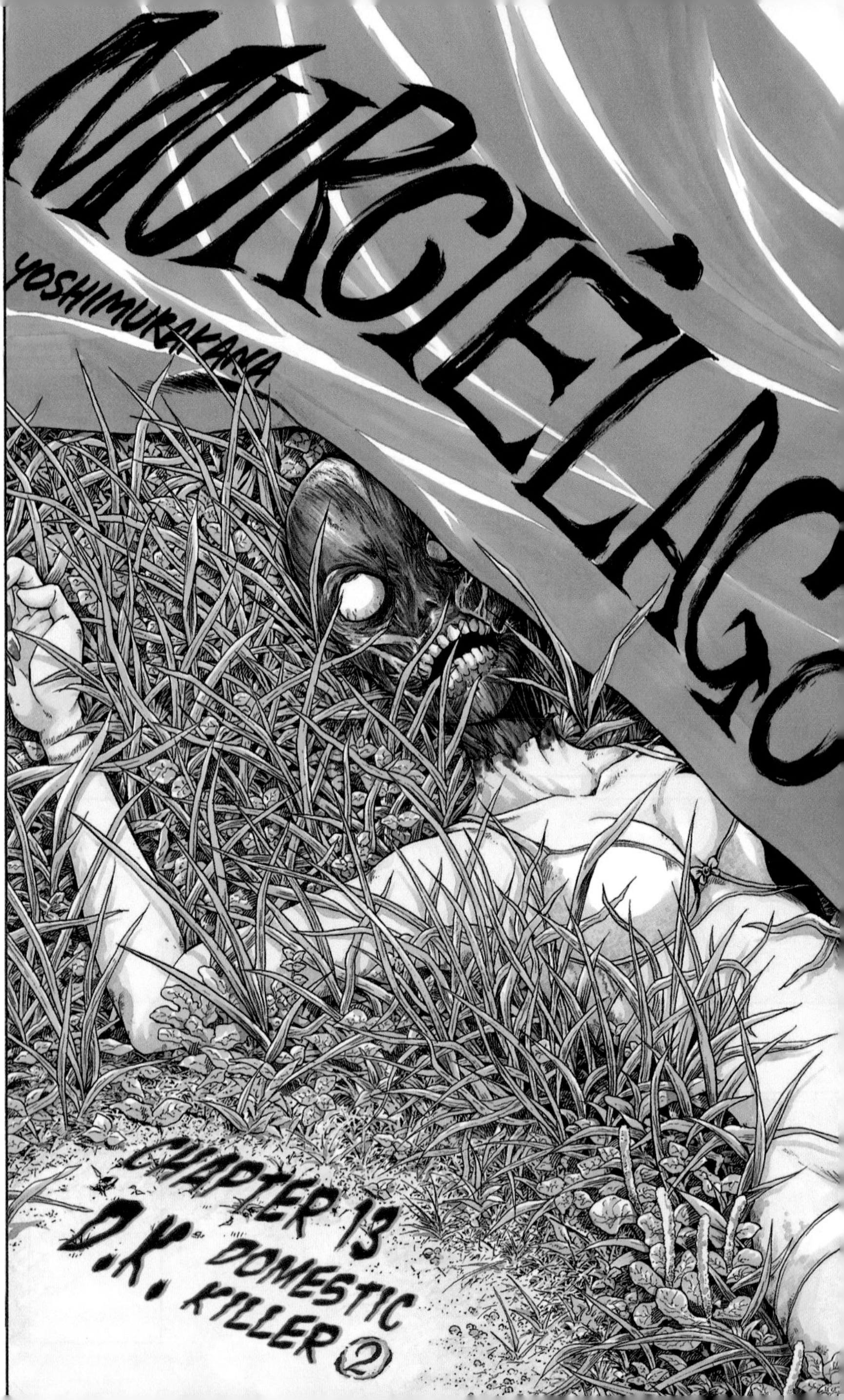
MURCIÉLAGO
YOSHIMURAKANA
CHAPTER 13
D.K. DOMESTIC KILLER ②

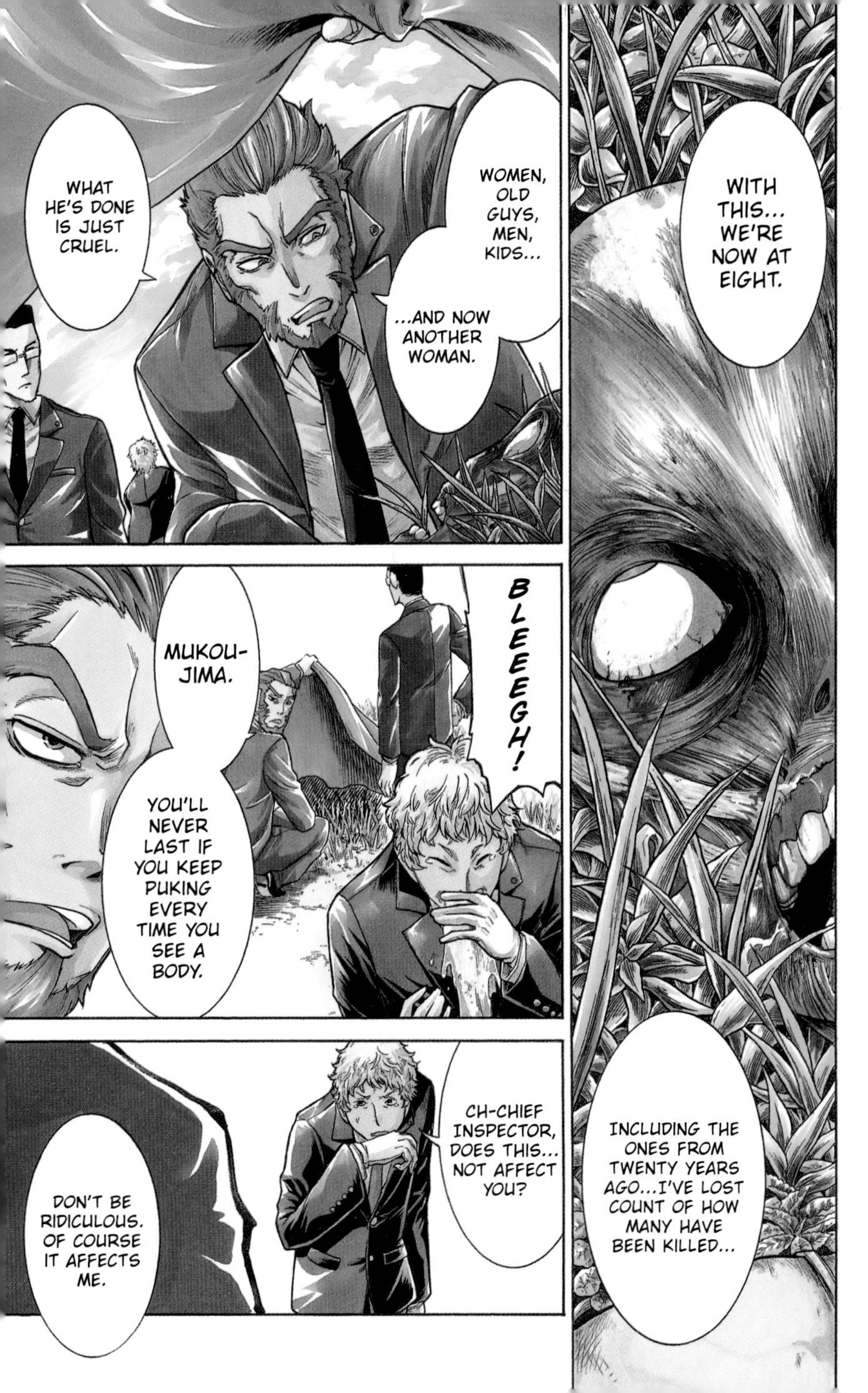
WITH THIS... WE'RE NOW AT EIGHT.
INCLUDING THE ONES FROM TWENTY YEARS AGO...I'VE LOST COUNT OF HOW MANY HAVE BEEN KILLED...
WOMEN, OLD GUYS, MEN, KIDS...
...AND NOW ANOTHER WOMAN.
WHAT HE'S DONE IS JUST CRUEL.
BLEEEEGH!
MUKOU-JIMA.
YOU'LL NEVER LAST IF YOU KEEP PUKING EVERY TIME YOU SEE A BODY.
CH-CHIEF INSPECTOR, DOES THIS... NOT AFFECT YOU?
DON'T BE RIDICULOUS. OF COURSE IT AFFECTS ME.

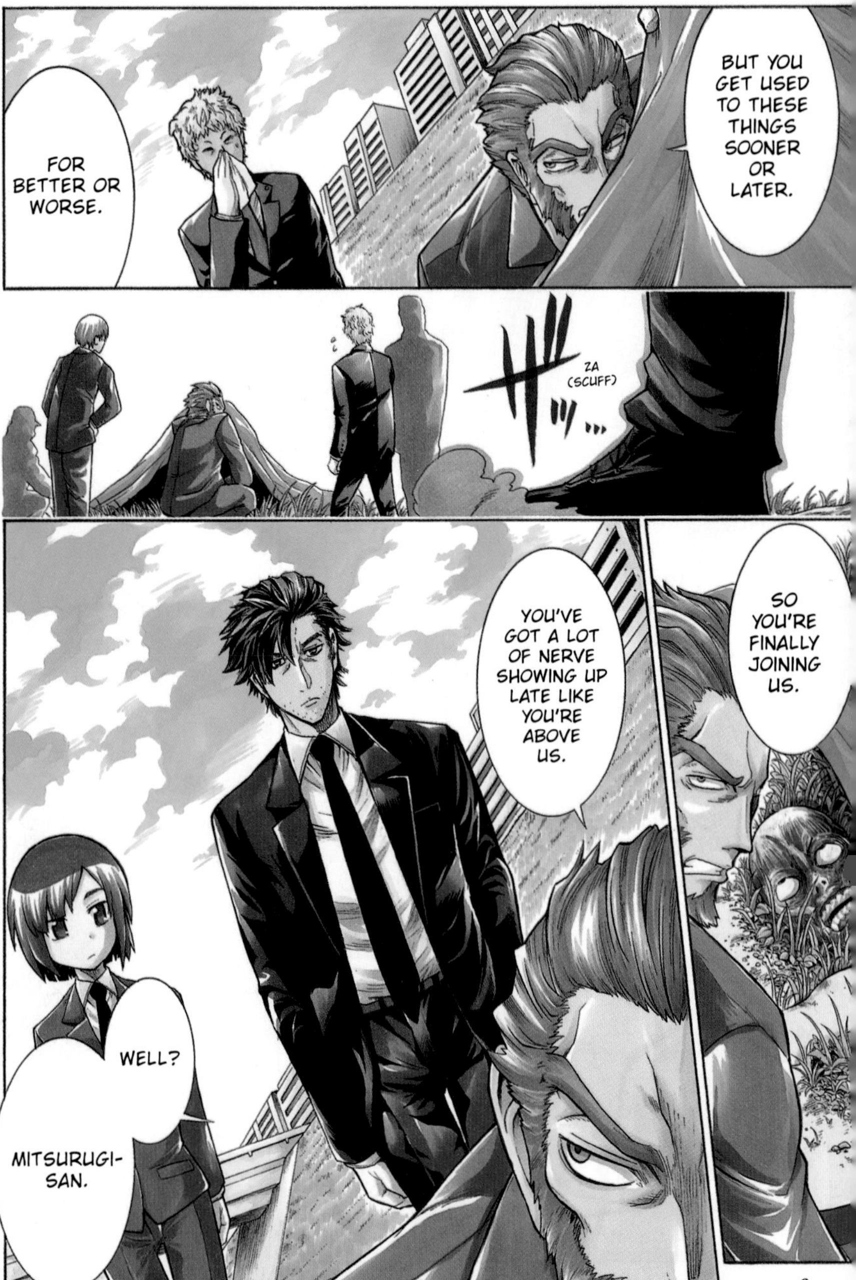
BUT YOU GET USED TO THESE THINGS SOONER OR LATER.
FOR BETTER OR WORSE.
ザッ…
ZA (SCUFF)
SO YOU'RE FINALLY JOINING US.
YOU'VE GOT A LOT OF NERVE SHOWING UP LATE LIKE YOU'RE ABOVE US.
WELL?
MITSURUGI-SAN.

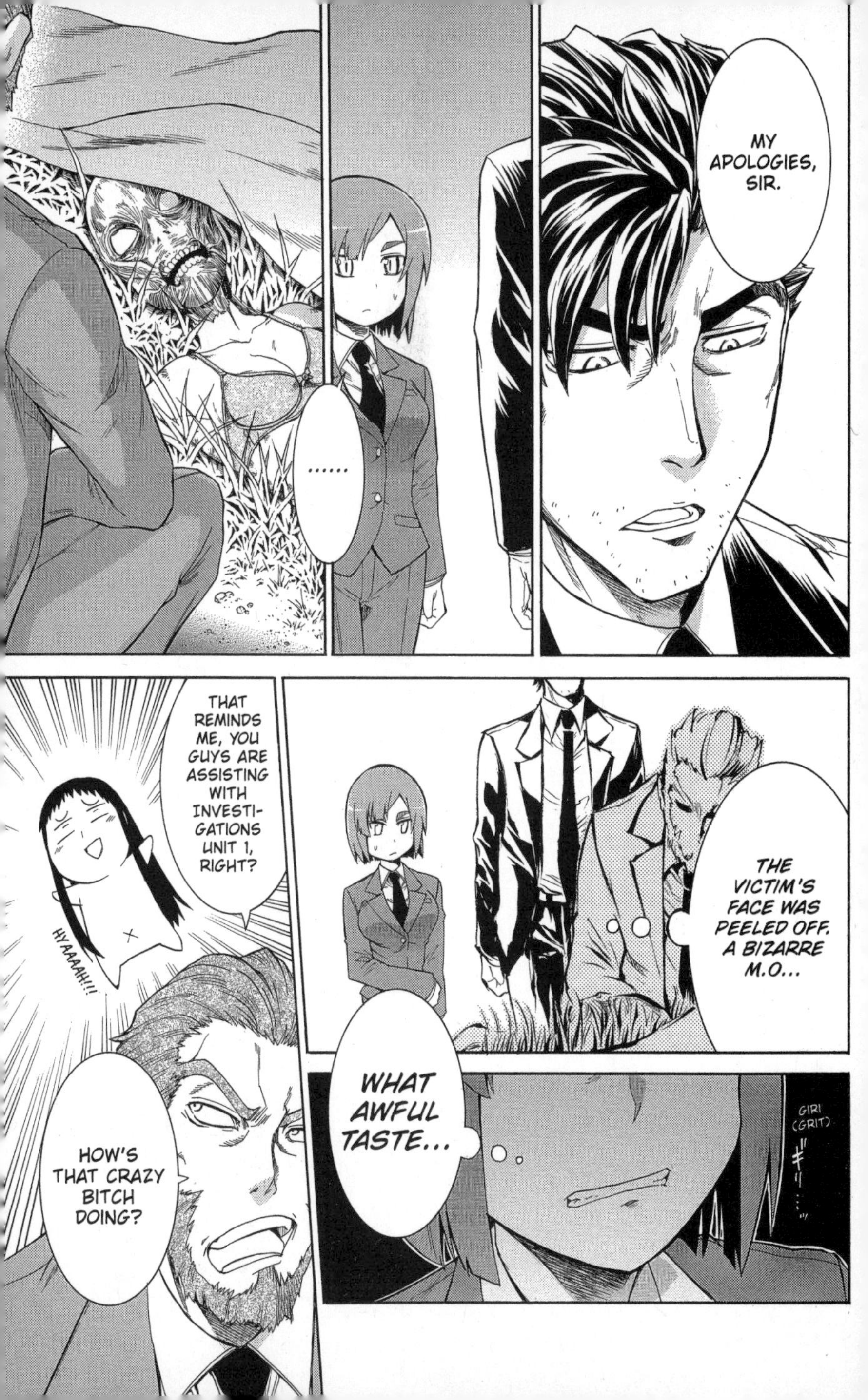
MY APOLOGIES, SIR.
......
THE VICTIM'S FACE WAS PEELED OFF. A BIZARRE M.O...
WHAT AWFUL TASTE...
GIRI (GRIT)
ギリ…
THAT REMINDS ME, YOU GUYS ARE ASSISTING WITH INVESTI-GATIONS UNIT 1, RIGHT?
HYAAAAH!!!
HOW'S THAT CRAZY BITCH DOING?

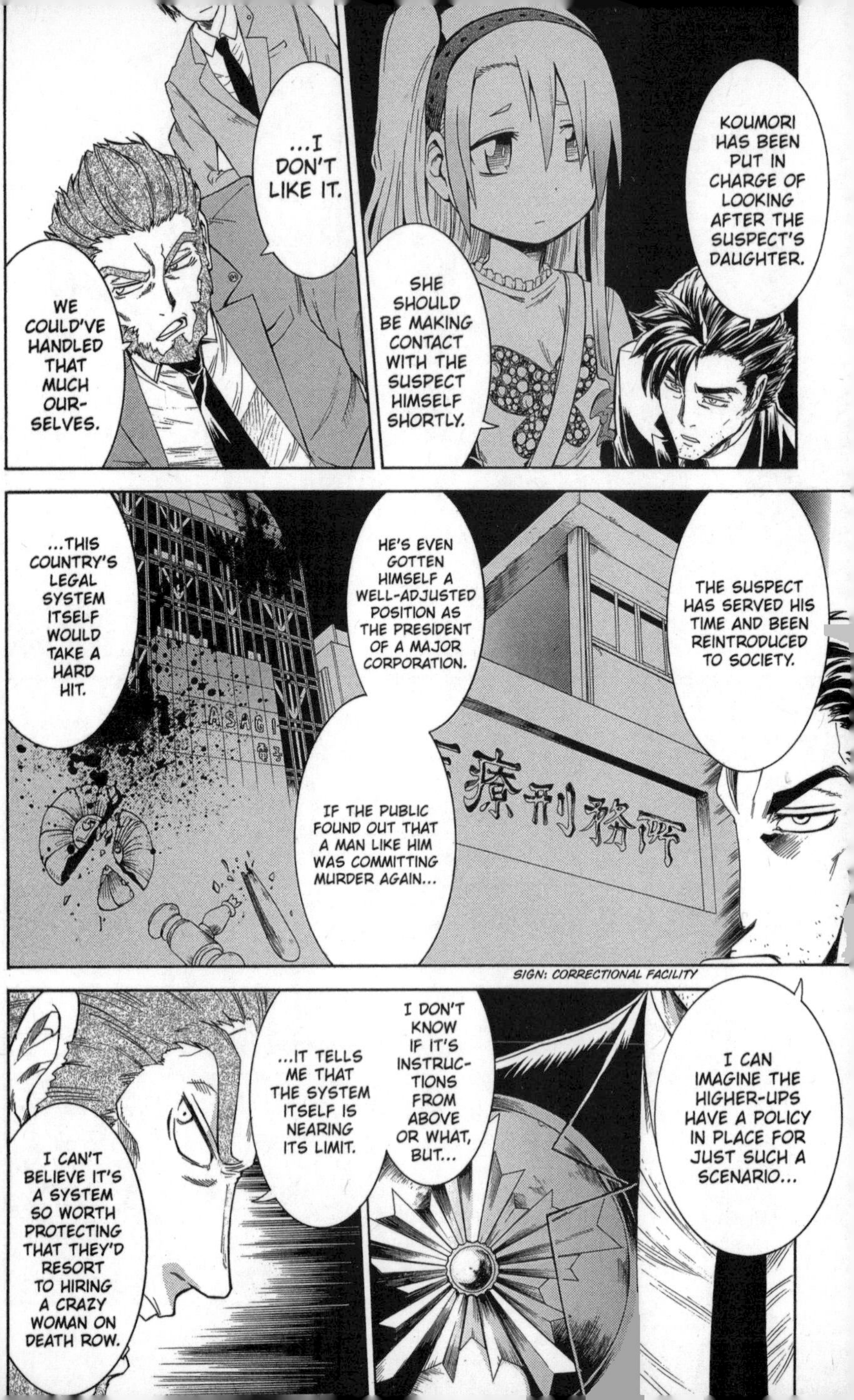
KOUMORI HAS BEEN PUT IN CHARGE OF LOOKING AFTER THE SUSPECT'S DAUGHTER.
SHE SHOULD BE MAKING CONTACT WITH THE SUSPECT HIMSELF SHORTLY.
...I DON'T LIKE IT.
WE COULD'VE HANDLED THAT MUCH OURSELVES.
THE SUSPECT HAS SERVED HIS TIME AND BEEN REINTRODUCED TO SOCIETY.
HE'S EVEN GOTTEN HIMSELF A WELL-ADJUSTED POSITION AS THE PRESIDENT OF A MAJOR CORPORATION.
IF THE PUBLIC FOUND OUT THAT A MAN LIKE HIM WAS COMMITTING MURDER AGAIN...
...THIS COUNTRY'S LEGAL SYSTEM ITSELF WOULD TAKE A HARD HIT.
ASAGI
SIGN: CORRECTIONAL FACILITY
I CAN IMAGINE THE HIGHER-UPS HAVE A POLICY IN PLACE FOR JUST SUCH A SCENARIO...
I DON'T KNOW IF IT'S INSTRUCTIONS FROM ABOVE OR WHAT, BUT...
...IT TELLS ME THAT THE SYSTEM ITSELF IS NEARING ITS LIMIT.
I CAN'T BELIEVE IT'S A SYSTEM SO WORTH PROTECTING THAT THEY'D RESORT TO HIRING A CRAZY WOMAN ON DEATH ROW.

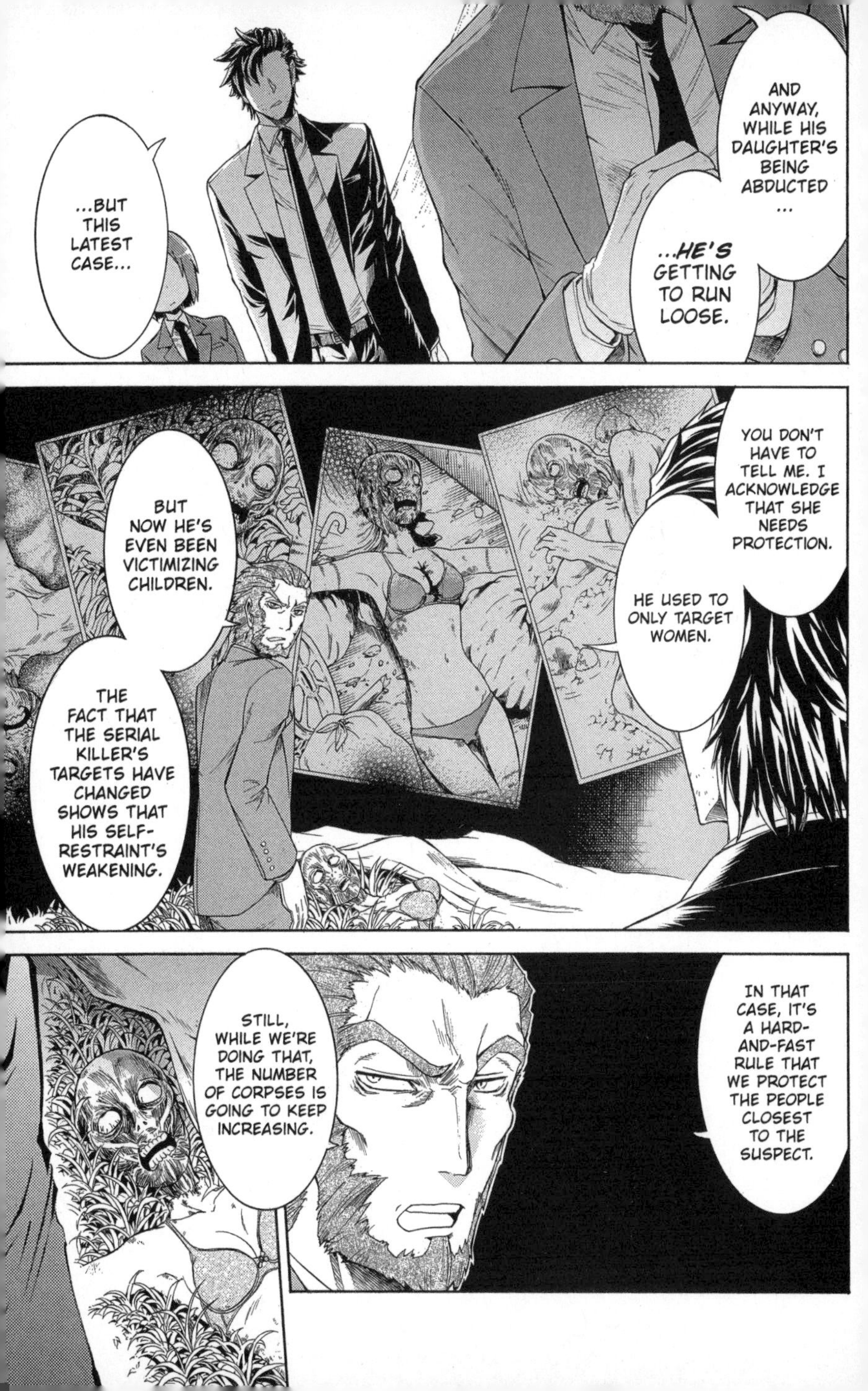
AND ANYWAY, WHILE HIS DAUGHTER'S BEING ABDUCTED...
...HE'S GETTING TO RUN LOOSE.
...BUT THIS LATEST CASE...
YOU DON'T HAVE TO TELL ME. I ACKNOWLEDGE THAT SHE NEEDS PROTECTION.
HE USED TO ONLY TARGET WOMEN.
BUT NOW HE'S EVEN BEEN VICTIMIZING CHILDREN.
THE FACT THAT THE SERIAL KILLER'S TARGETS HAVE CHANGED SHOWS THAT HIS SELF-RESTRAINT'S WEAKENING.
IN THAT CASE, IT'S A HARD-AND-FAST RULE THAT WE PROTECT THE PEOPLE CLOSEST TO THE SUSPECT.
STILL, WHILE WE'RE DOING THAT, THE NUMBER OF CORPSES IS GOING TO KEEP INCREASING.

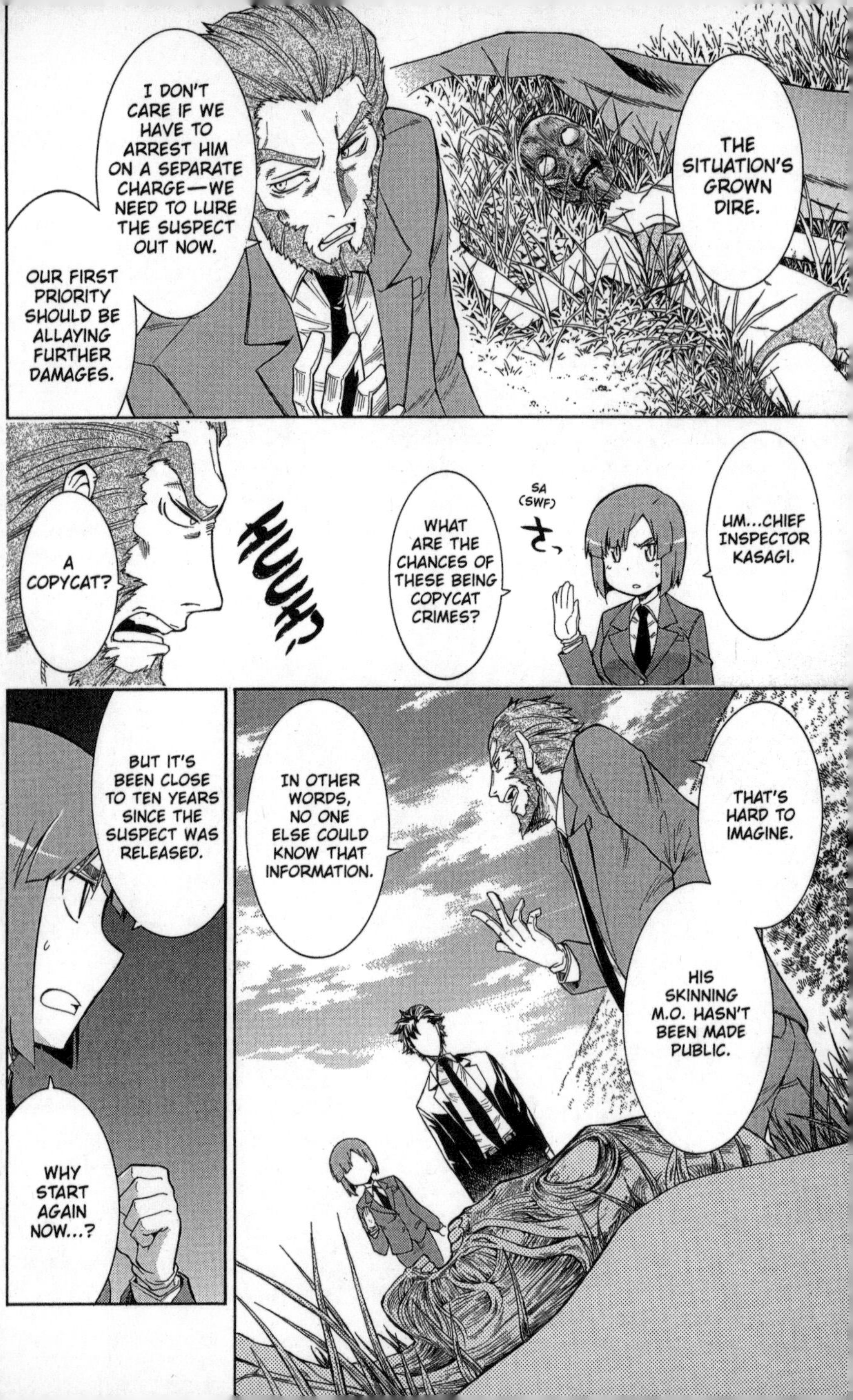
THE SITUATION'S GROWN DIRE.
I DON'T CARE IF WE HAVE TO ARREST HIM ON A SEPARATE CHARGE—WE NEED TO LURE THE SUSPECT OUT NOW.
OUR FIRST PRIORITY SHOULD BE ALLAYING FURTHER DAMAGES.
UM...CHIEF INSPECTOR KASAGI.
さっ
SA (SWF)
WHAT ARE THE CHANCES OF THESE BEING COPYCAT CRIMES?
HUH?
A COPYCAT?
THAT'S HARD TO IMAGINE.
HIS SKINNING M.O. HASN'T BEEN MADE PUBLIC.
IN OTHER WORDS, NO ONE ELSE COULD KNOW THAT INFORMATION.
BUT IT'S BEEN CLOSE TO TEN YEARS SINCE THE SUSPECT WAS RELEASED.
WHY START AGAIN NOW...?

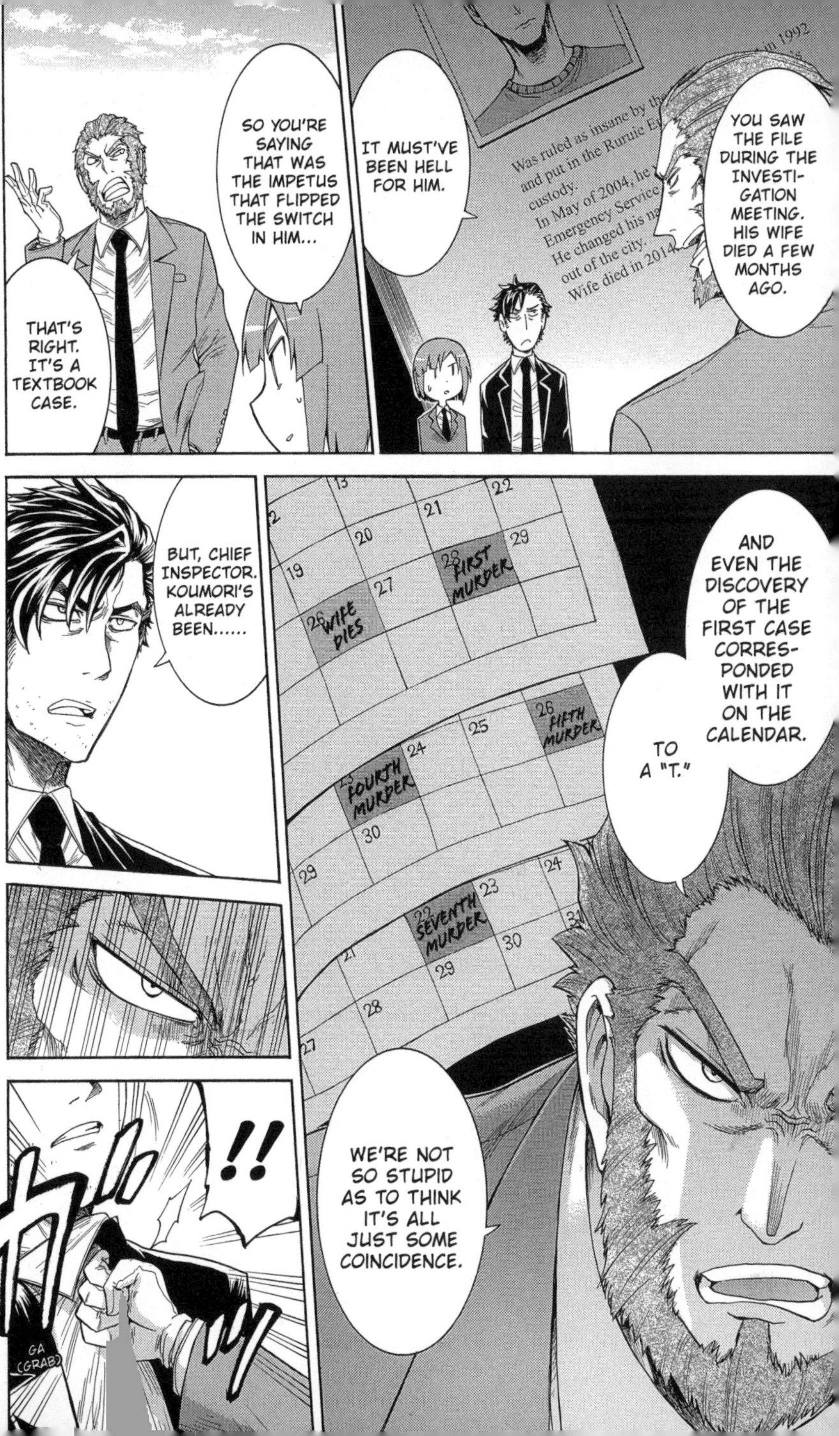
Was ruled as insane by th
and put in the Ruruic E
custody.
In May of 2004, he
Emergency Service
He changed his na
out of the city.
Wife died in 2014
YOU SAW THE FILE DURING THE INVESTIGATION MEETING. HIS WIFE DIED A FEW MONTHS AGO.
IT MUST'VE BEEN HELL FOR HIM.
SO YOU'RE SAYING THAT WAS THE IMPETUS THAT FLIPPED THE SWITCH IN HIM...
THAT'S RIGHT. IT'S A TEXTBOOK CASE.
AND EVEN THE DISCOVERY OF THE FIRST CASE CORRESPONDED WITH IT ON THE CALENDAR.
TO A "T."
FIRST MURDER
WIFE DIES
FIFTH MURDER
FOURTH MURDER
SEVENTH MURDER
WE'RE NOT SO STUPID AS TO THINK IT'S ALL JUST SOME COINCIDENCE.
BUT, CHIEF INSPECTOR. KOUMORI'S ALREADY BEEN......
!!
GA (GRAB)

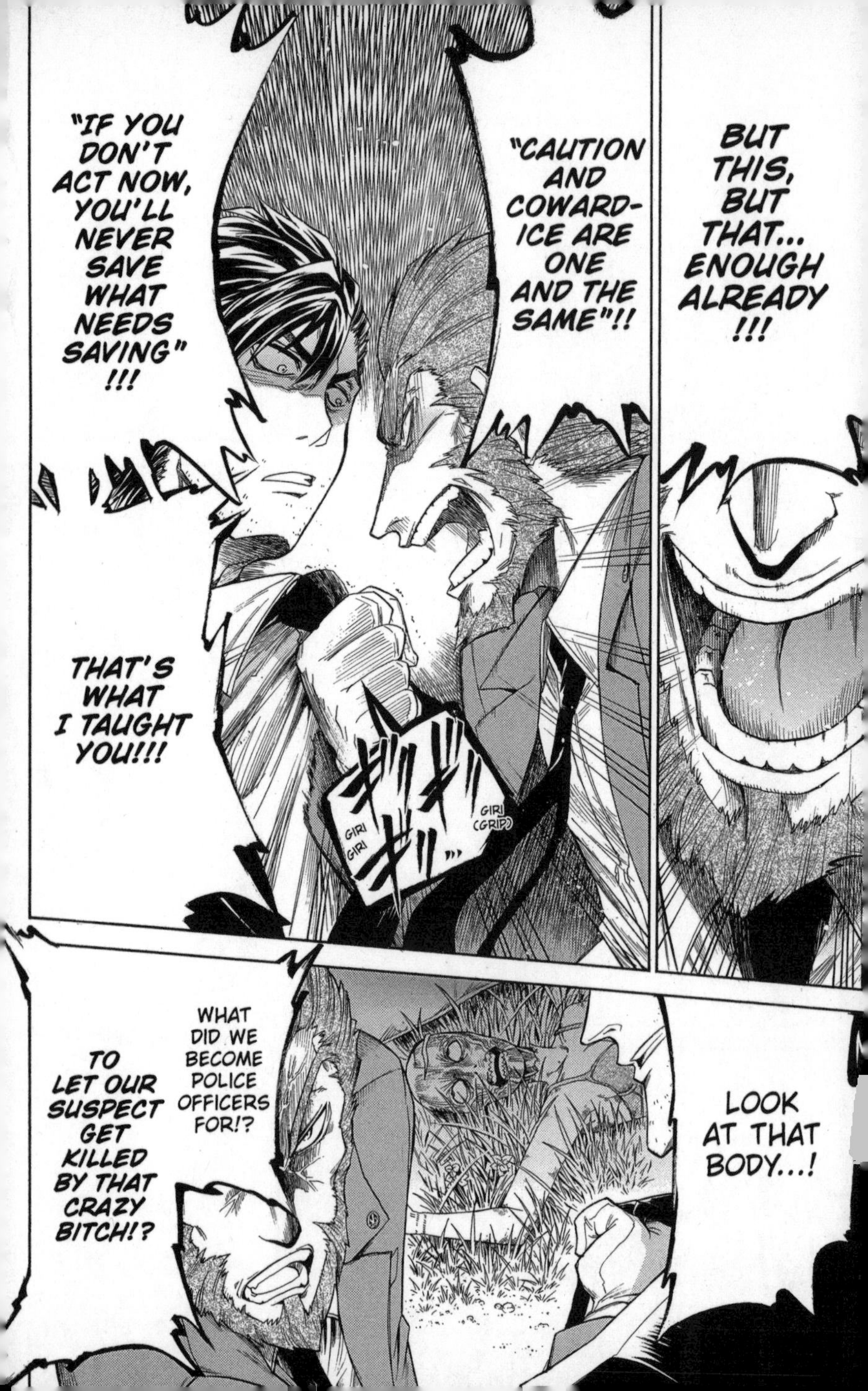
BUT THIS, BUT THAT... ENOUGH ALREADY!!!
"CAUTION AND COWARDICE ARE ONE AND THE SAME"!!
"IF YOU DON'T ACT NOW, YOU'LL NEVER SAVE WHAT NEEDS SAVING"!!!
THAT'S WHAT I TAUGHT YOU!!!
GIRI (GRIP)
GIRI GIRI
LOOK AT THAT BODY...!
WHAT DID WE BECOME POLICE OFFICERS FOR!?
TO LET OUR SUSPECT GET KILLED BY THAT CRAZY BITCH!?

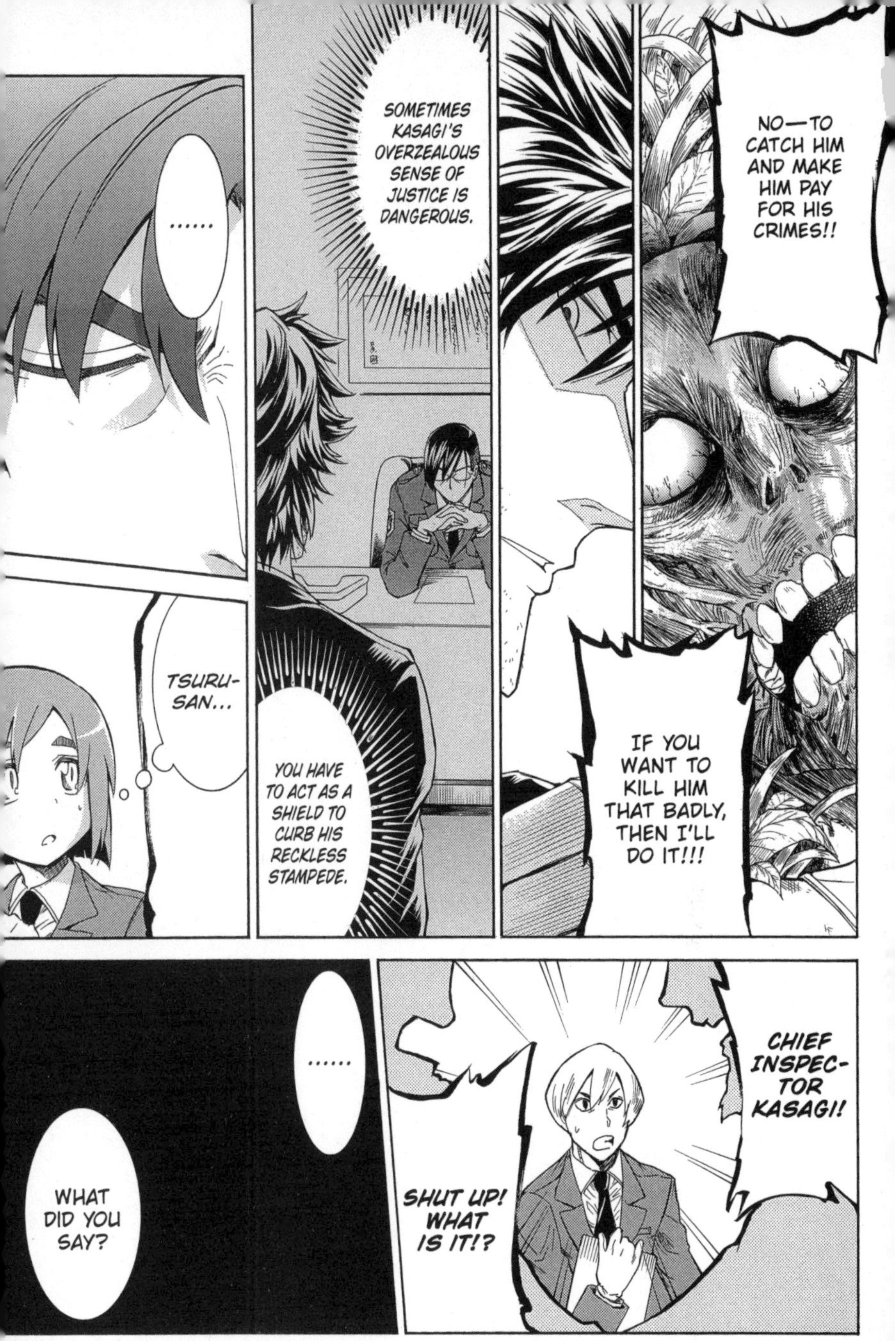
NO—TO CATCH HIM AND MAKE HIM PAY FOR HIS CRIMES!!
IF YOU WANT TO KILL HIM THAT BADLY, THEN I'LL DO IT!!!
SOMETIMES KASAGI'S OVERZEALOUS SENSE OF JUSTICE IS DANGEROUS.
YOU HAVE TO ACT AS A SHIELD TO CURB HIS RECKLESS STAMPEDE.
......
TSURU-SAN...
CHIEF INSPEC-TOR KASAGI!
SHUT UP! WHAT IS IT!?
......
WHAT DID YOU SAY?

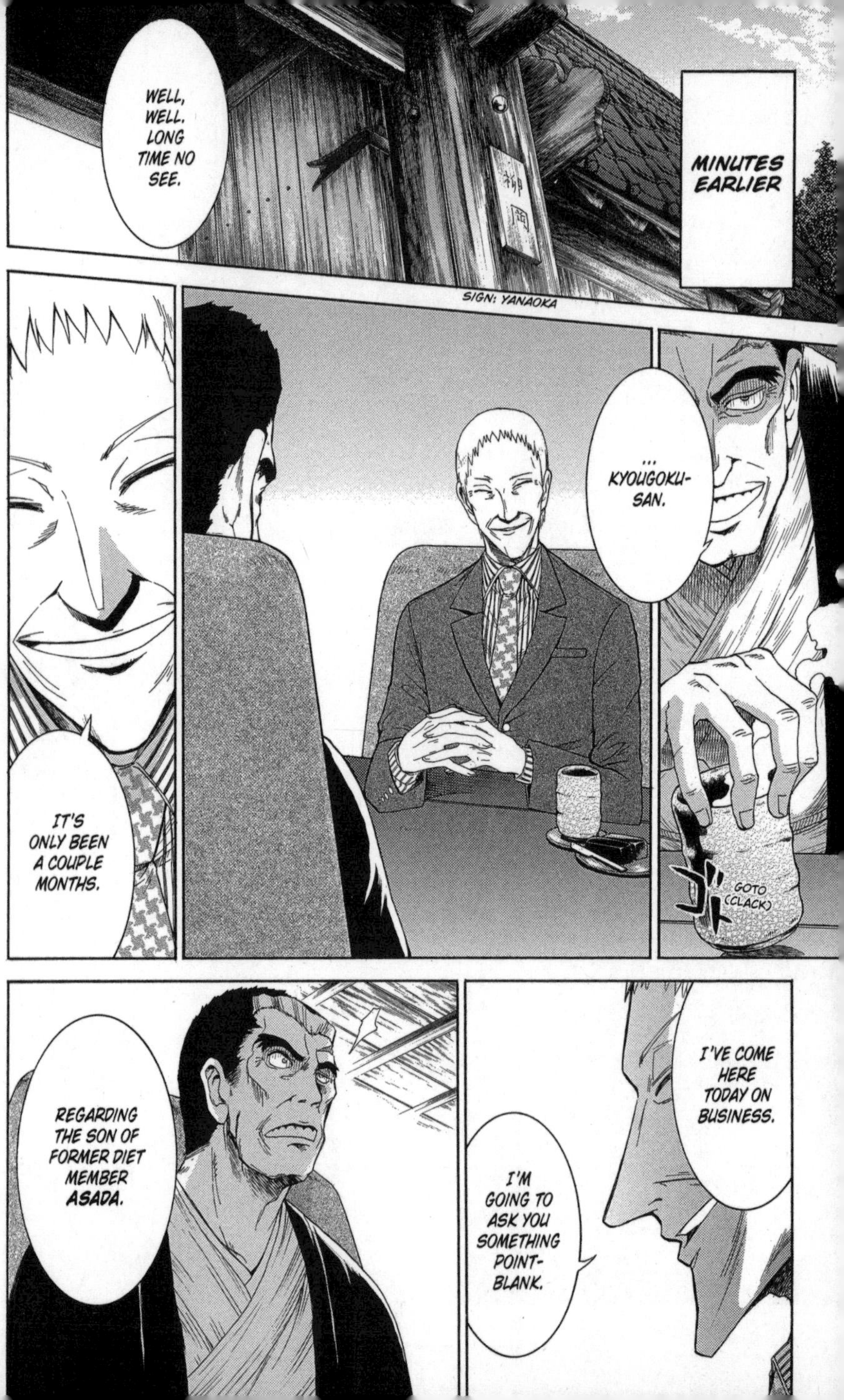
MINUTES EARLIER
WELL, WELL. LONG TIME NO SEE.
SIGN: YANAOKA
... KYOUGOKU-SAN.
GOTO (CLACK)
IT'S ONLY BEEN A COUPLE MONTHS.
I'VE COME HERE TODAY ON BUSINESS.
I'M GOING TO ASK YOU SOMETHING POINT-BLANK.
REGARDING THE SON OF FORMER DIET MEMBER ASADA.

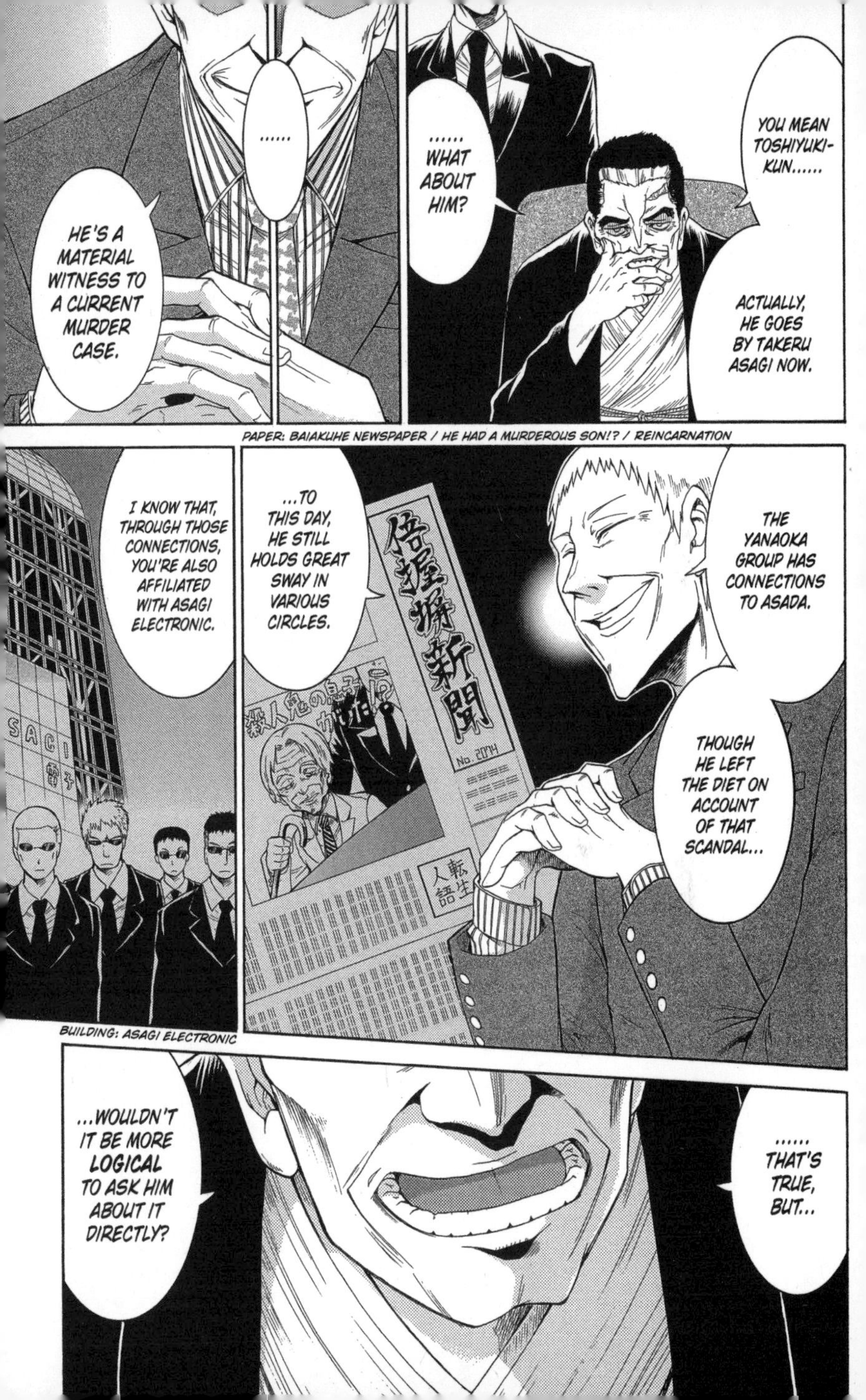
YOU MEAN TOSHIYUKI-KUN......
ACTUALLY, HE GOES BY TAKERU ASAGI NOW.
......WHAT ABOUT HIM?
......
HE'S A MATERIAL WITNESS TO A CURRENT MURDER CASE.
PAPER: BAIAKUHE NEWSPAPER / HE HAD A MURDEROUS SON!? / REINCARNATION
THE YANAOKA GROUP HAS CONNECTIONS TO ASADA.
THOUGH HE LEFT THE DIET ON ACCOUNT OF THAT SCANDAL...
...TO THIS DAY, HE STILL HOLDS GREAT SWAY IN VARIOUS CIRCLES.
I KNOW THAT, THROUGH THOSE CONNECTIONS, YOU'RE ALSO AFFILIATED WITH ASAGI ELECTRONIC.
BUILDING: ASAGI ELECTRONIC
......THAT'S TRUE, BUT...
...WOULDN'T IT BE MORE LOGICAL TO ASK HIM ABOUT IT DIRECTLY?

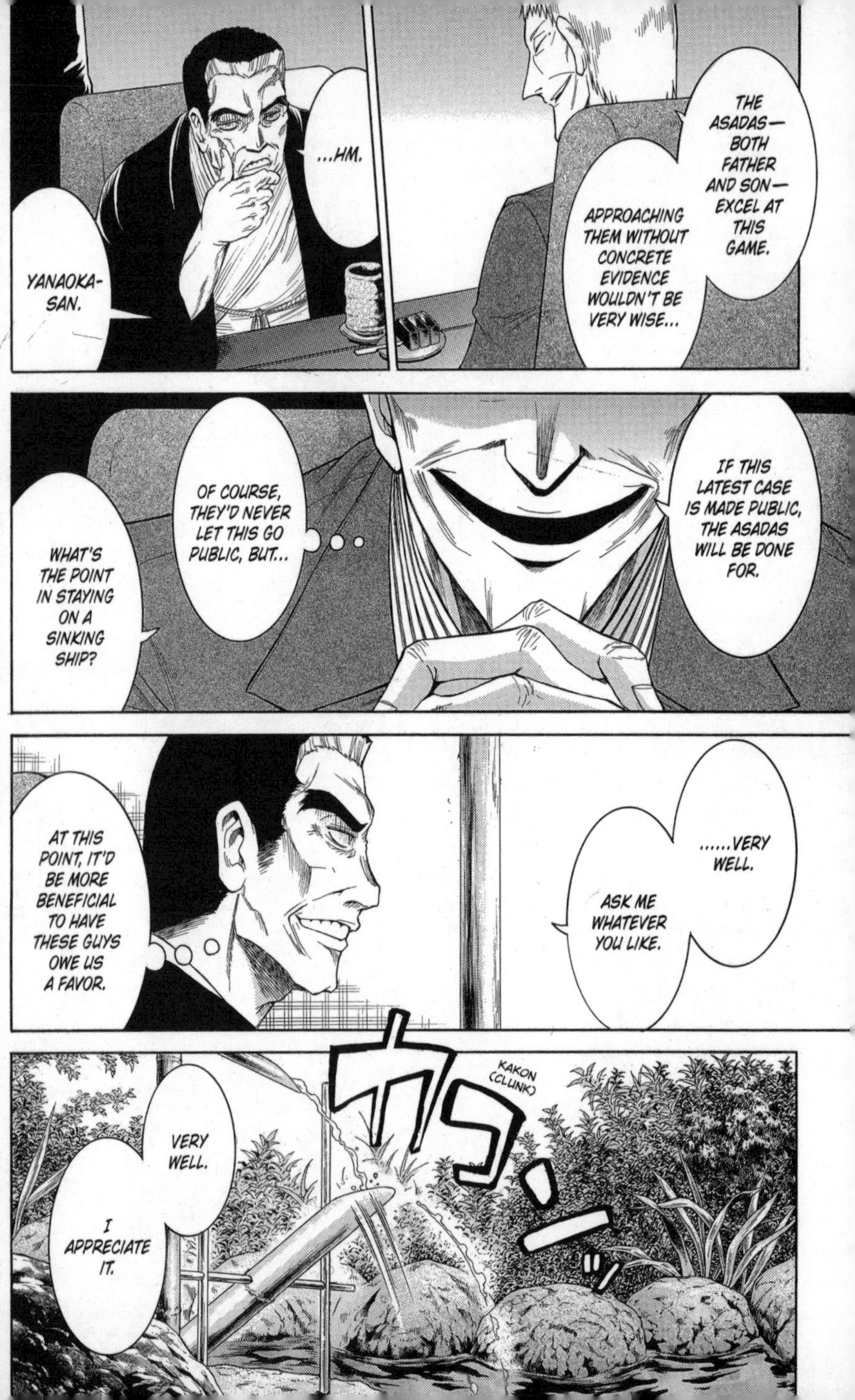
THE ASADAS—BOTH FATHER AND SON—EXCEL AT THIS GAME.
APPROACHING THEM WITHOUT CONCRETE EVIDENCE WOULDN'T BE VERY WISE...
...HM.
YANAOKA-SAN.
IF THIS LATEST CASE IS MADE PUBLIC, THE ASADAS WILL BE DONE FOR.
OF COURSE, THEY'D NEVER LET THIS GO PUBLIC, BUT...
WHAT'S THE POINT IN STAYING ON A SINKING SHIP?
......VERY WELL.
ASK ME WHATEVER YOU LIKE.
AT THIS POINT, IT'D BE MORE BENEFICIAL TO HAVE THESE GUYS OWE US A FAVOR.
KAKON (CLUNK)
VERY WELL.
I APPRECIATE IT.

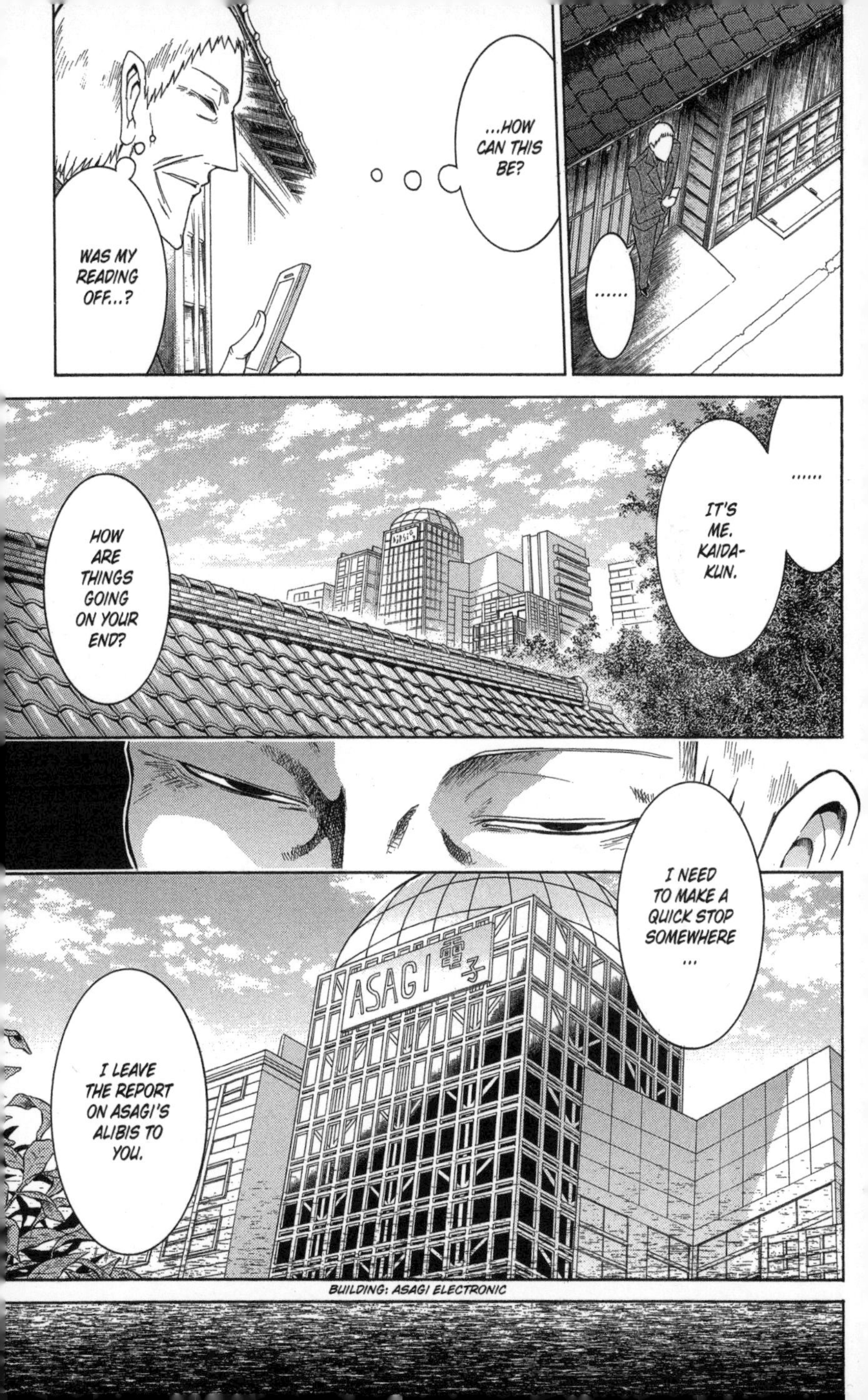
......
...HOW CAN THIS BE?
WAS MY READING OFF...?
......
IT'S ME. KAIDA-KUN.
HOW ARE THINGS GOING ON YOUR END?
I NEED TO MAKE A QUICK STOP SOMEWHERE...
ASAGI 電子
I LEAVE THE REPORT ON ASAGI'S ALIBIS TO YOU.
BUILDING: ASAGI ELECTRONIC

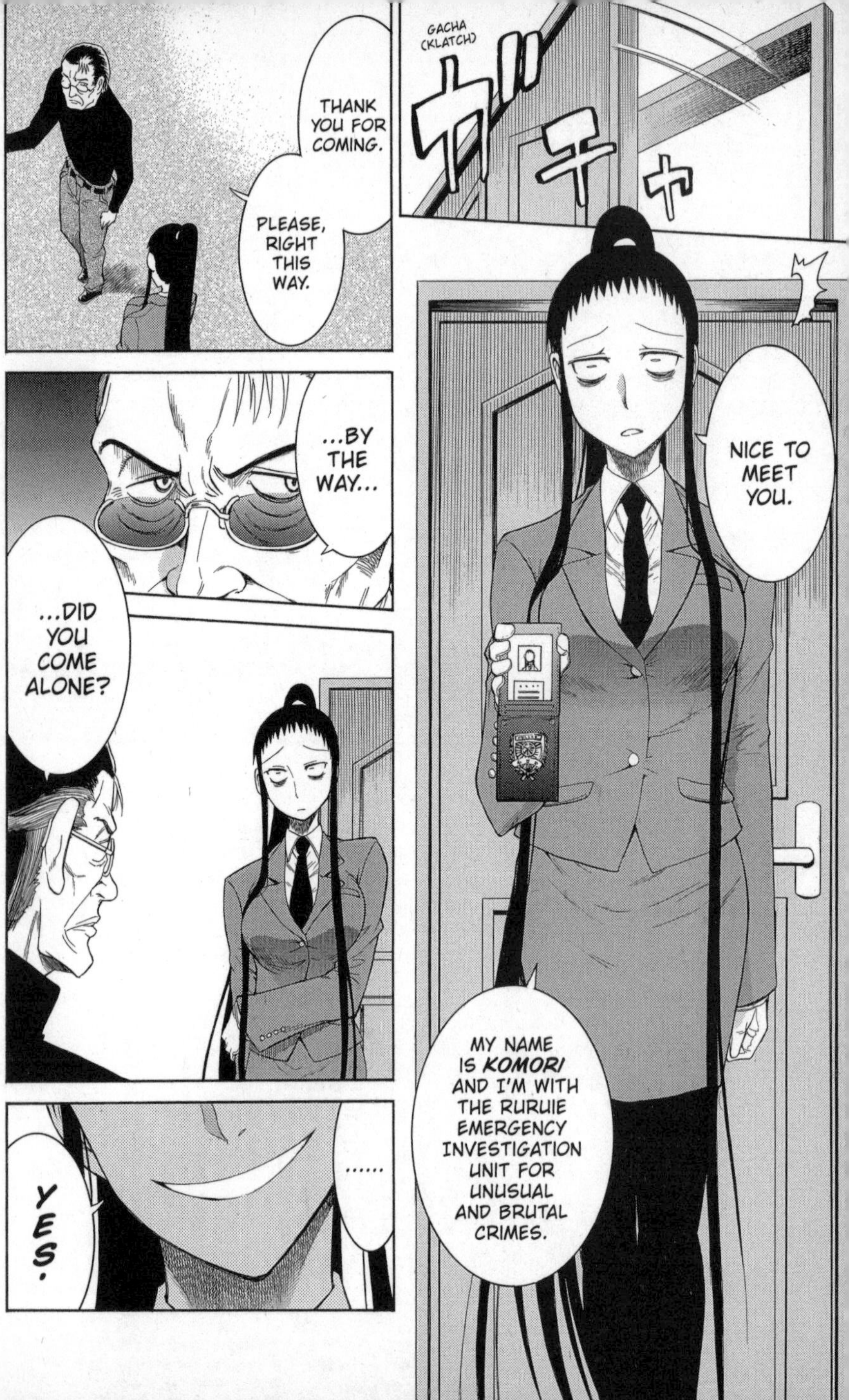
GACHA (KLATCH)
ガチャ
NICE TO MEET YOU.
MY NAME IS *KOMORI* AND I'M WITH THE RURUIE EMERGENCY INVESTIGATION UNIT FOR UNUSUAL AND BRUTAL CRIMES.
THANK YOU FOR COMING.
PLEASE, RIGHT THIS WAY.
...BY THE WAY...
...DID YOU COME ALONE?
......
YES.

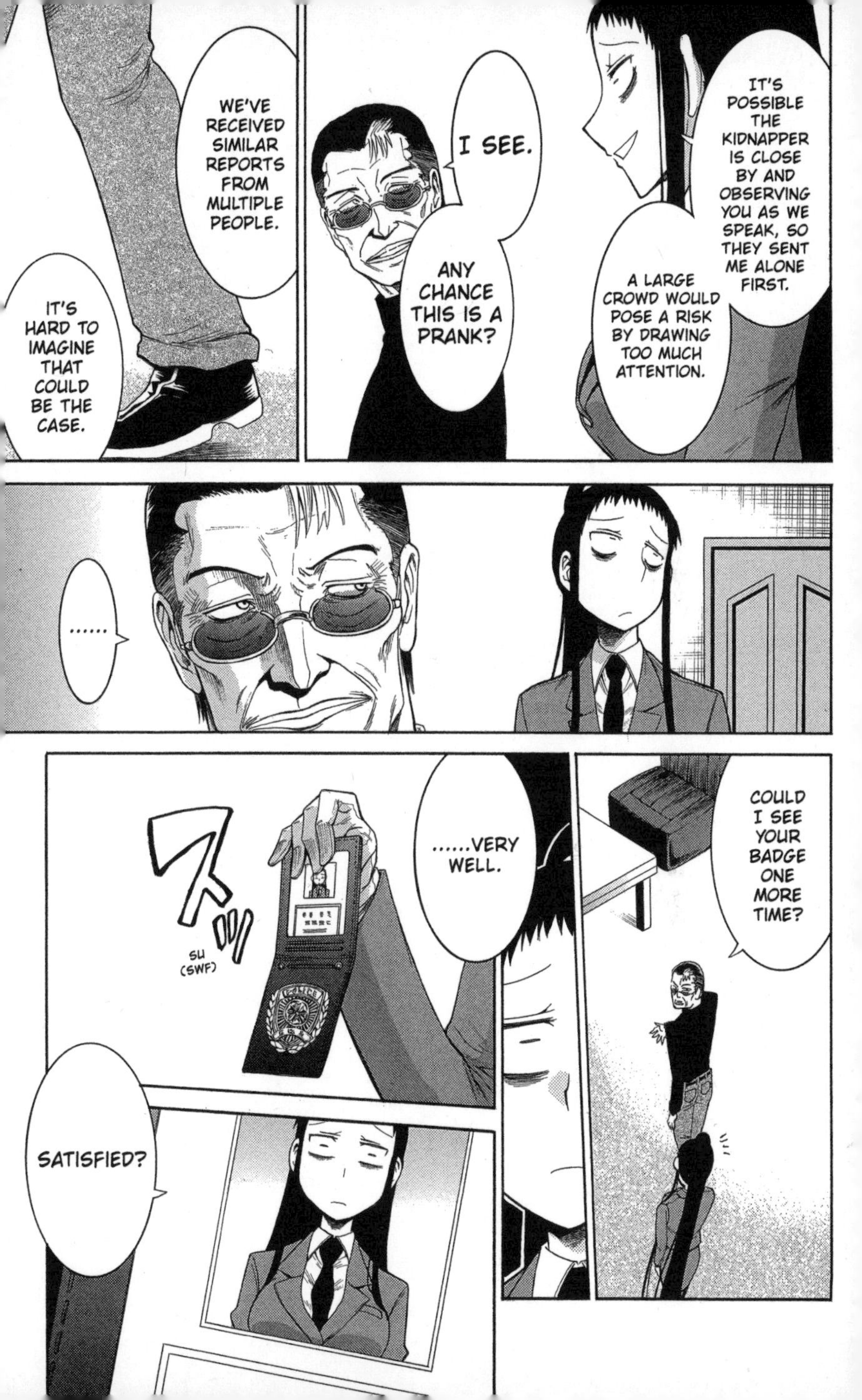
IT'S POSSIBLE THE KIDNAPPER IS CLOSE BY AND OBSERVING YOU AS WE SPEAK, SO THEY SENT ME ALONE FIRST.
A LARGE CROWD WOULD POSE A RISK BY DRAWING TOO MUCH ATTENTION.
I SEE.
ANY CHANCE THIS IS A PRANK?
WE'VE RECEIVED SIMILAR REPORTS FROM MULTIPLE PEOPLE.
IT'S HARD TO IMAGINE THAT COULD BE THE CASE.
......
COULD I SEE YOUR BADGE ONE MORE TIME?
......VERY WELL.
SU (SWF)
SATISFIED?

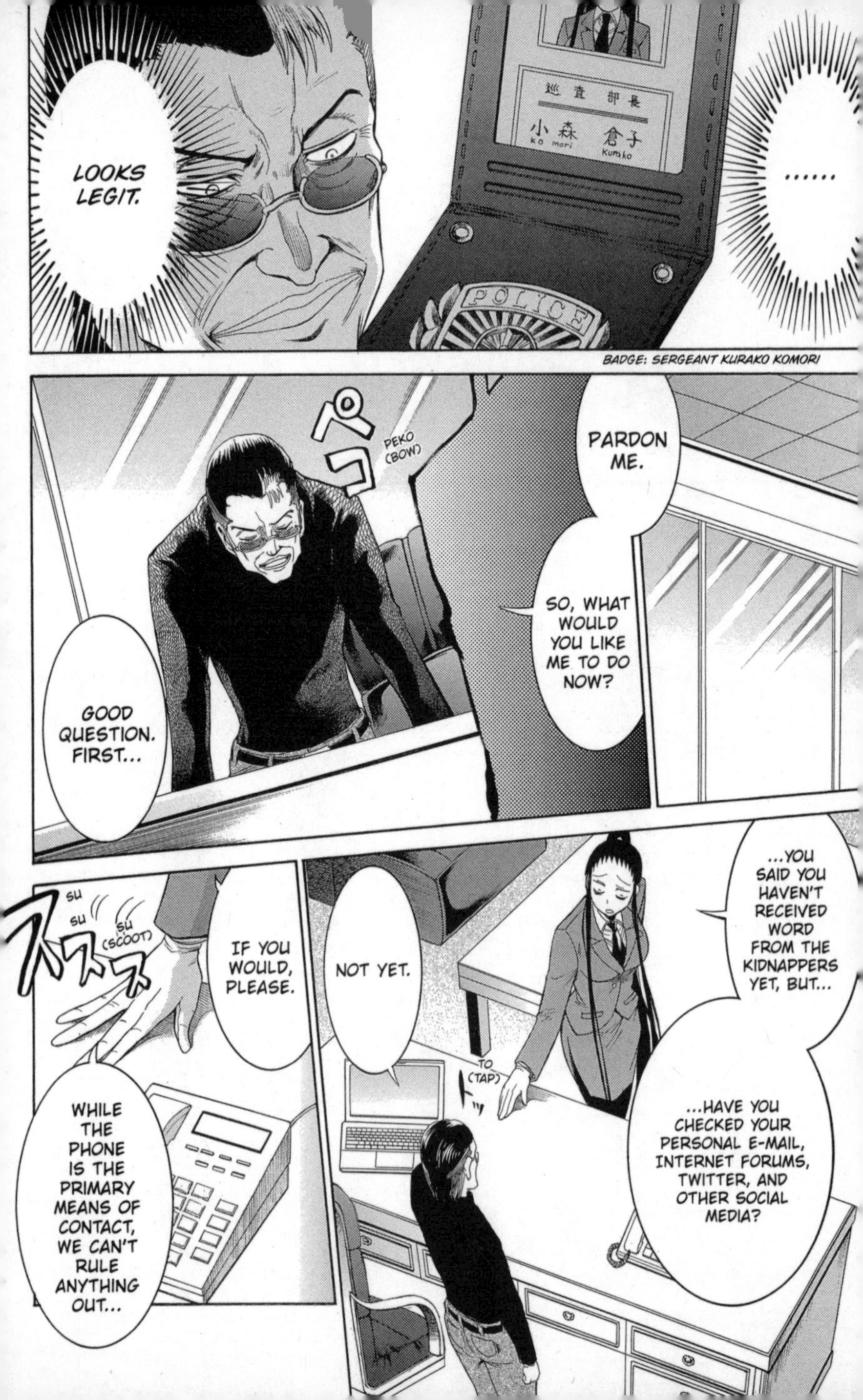
......
LOOKS LEGIT.
巡査部長
小森 倉子
ko mori Kurako
POLICE
BADGE: SERGEANT KURAKO KOMORI
PARDON ME.
ペコ
PEKO (BOW)
SO, WHAT WOULD YOU LIKE ME TO DO NOW?
GOOD QUESTION. FIRST...
...YOU SAID YOU HAVEN'T RECEIVED WORD FROM THE KIDNAPPERS YET, BUT...
TO (TAP)
...HAVE YOU CHECKED YOUR PERSONAL E-MAIL, INTERNET FORUMS, TWITTER, AND OTHER SOCIAL MEDIA?
NOT YET.
IF YOU WOULD, PLEASE.
ススス
SU SU SU (SCOOT)
WHILE THE PHONE IS THE PRIMARY MEANS OF CONTACT, WE CAN'T RULE ANYTHING OUT...

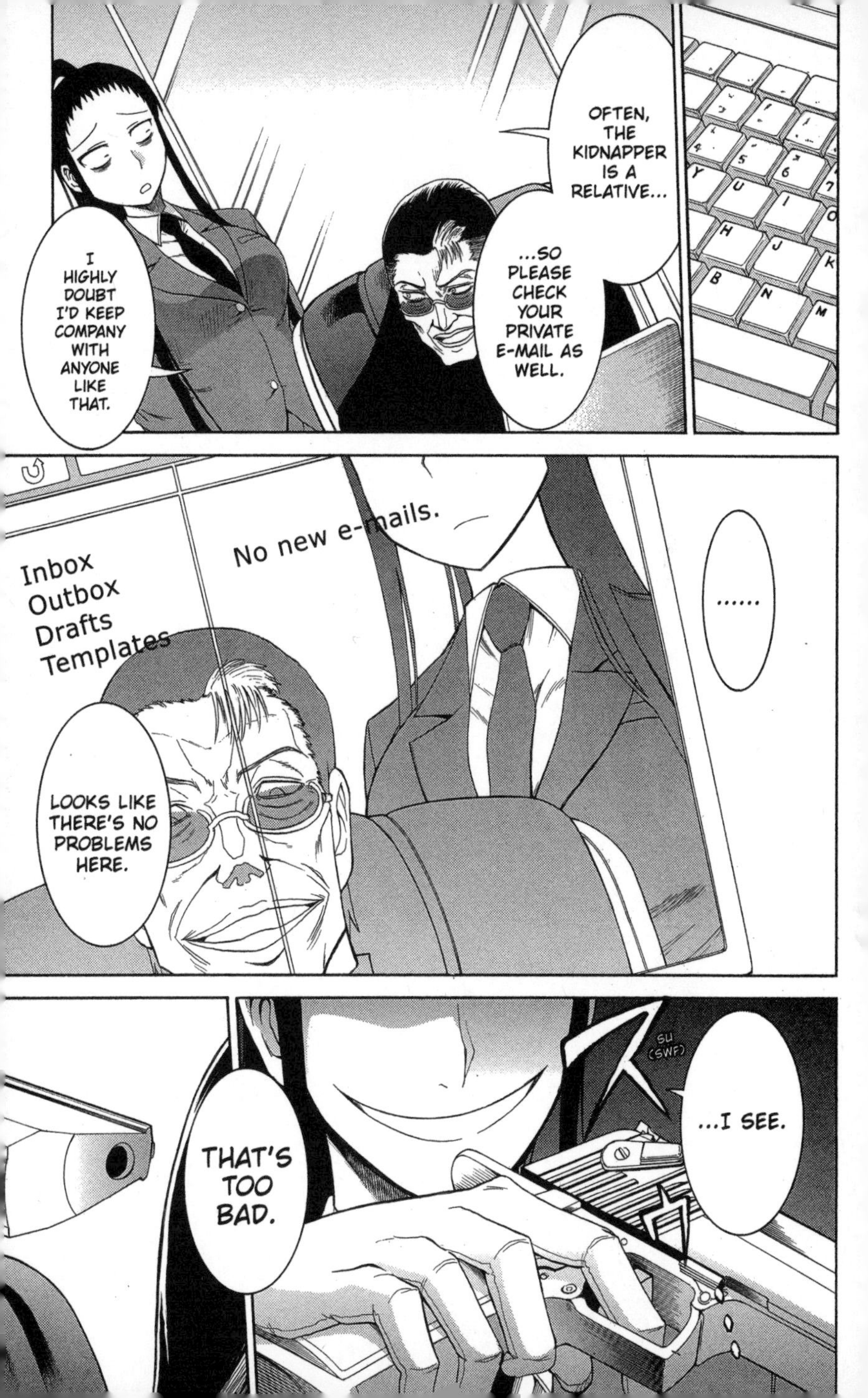
OFTEN, THE KIDNAPPER IS A RELATIVE...
...SO PLEASE CHECK YOUR PRIVATE E-MAIL AS WELL.
I HIGHLY DOUBT I'D KEEP COMPANY WITH ANYONE LIKE THAT.
......
No new e-mails.
Inbox
Outbox
Drafts
Templates
LOOKS LIKE THERE'S NO PROBLEMS HERE.
SU (SWF)
...I SEE.
THAT'S TOO BAD.

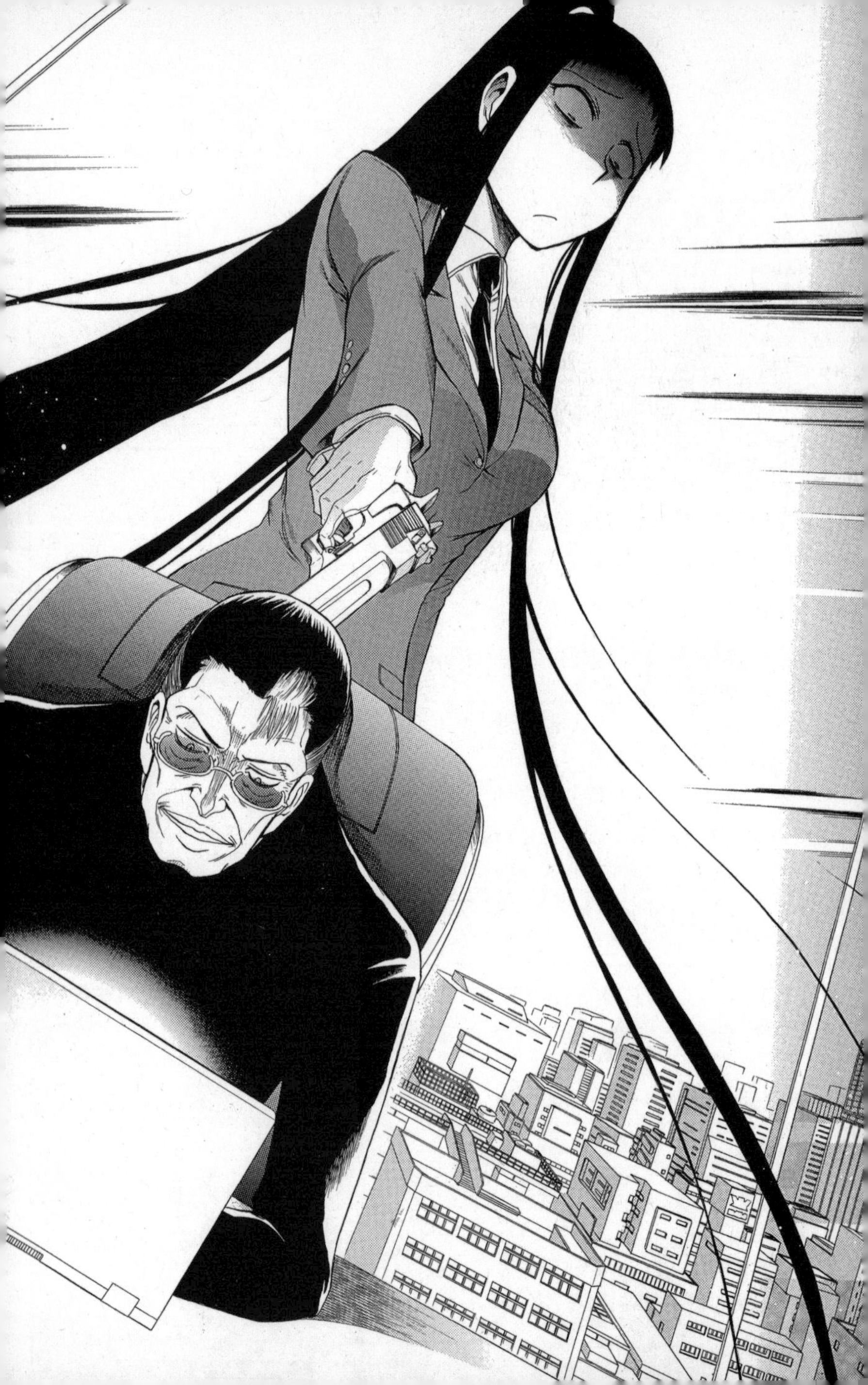

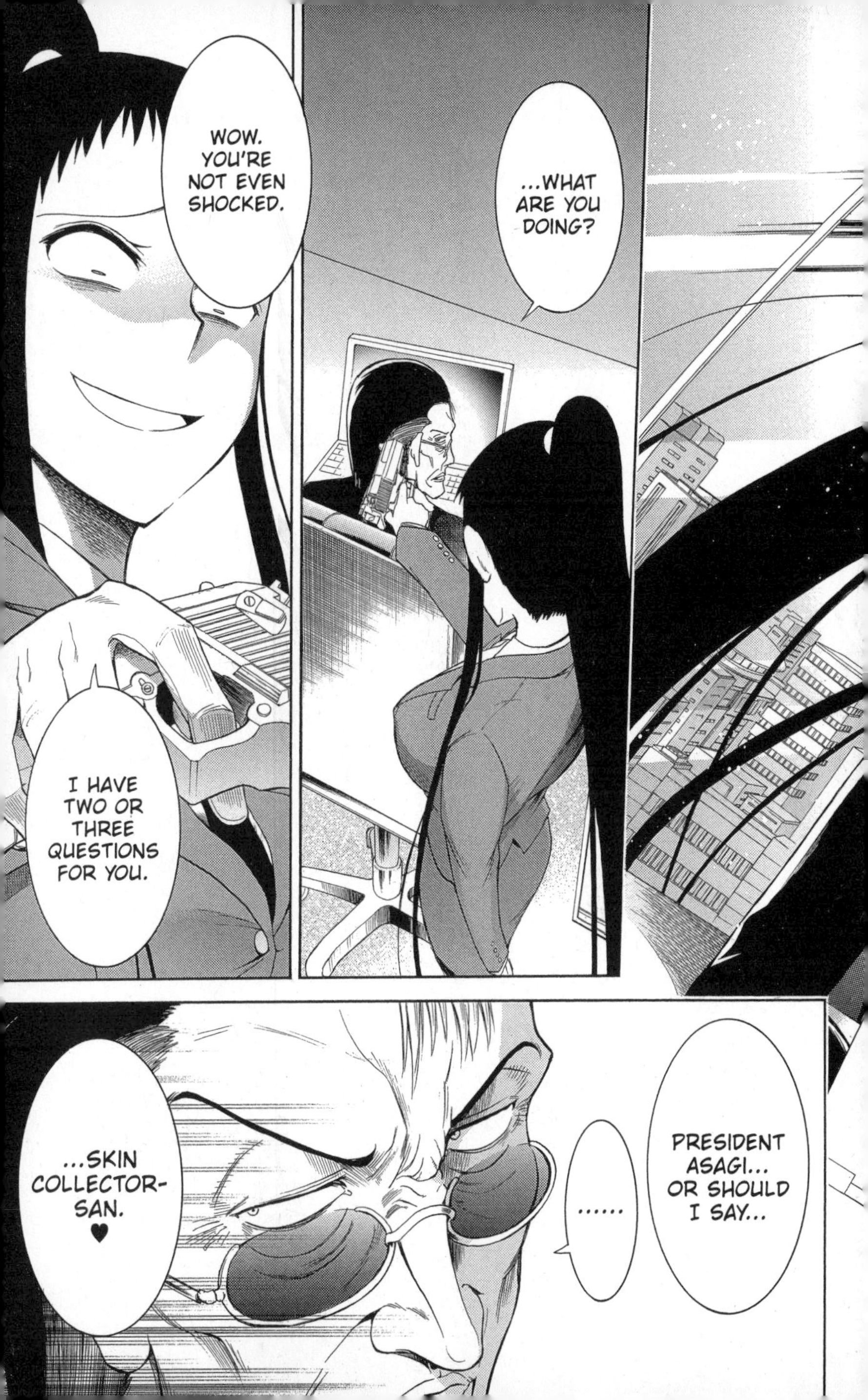
...WHAT ARE YOU DOING?
WOW. YOU'RE NOT EVEN SHOCKED.
I HAVE TWO OR THREE QUESTIONS FOR YOU.
PRESIDENT ASAGI... OR SHOULD I SAY...
......
...SKIN COLLECTOR-SAN. ♥

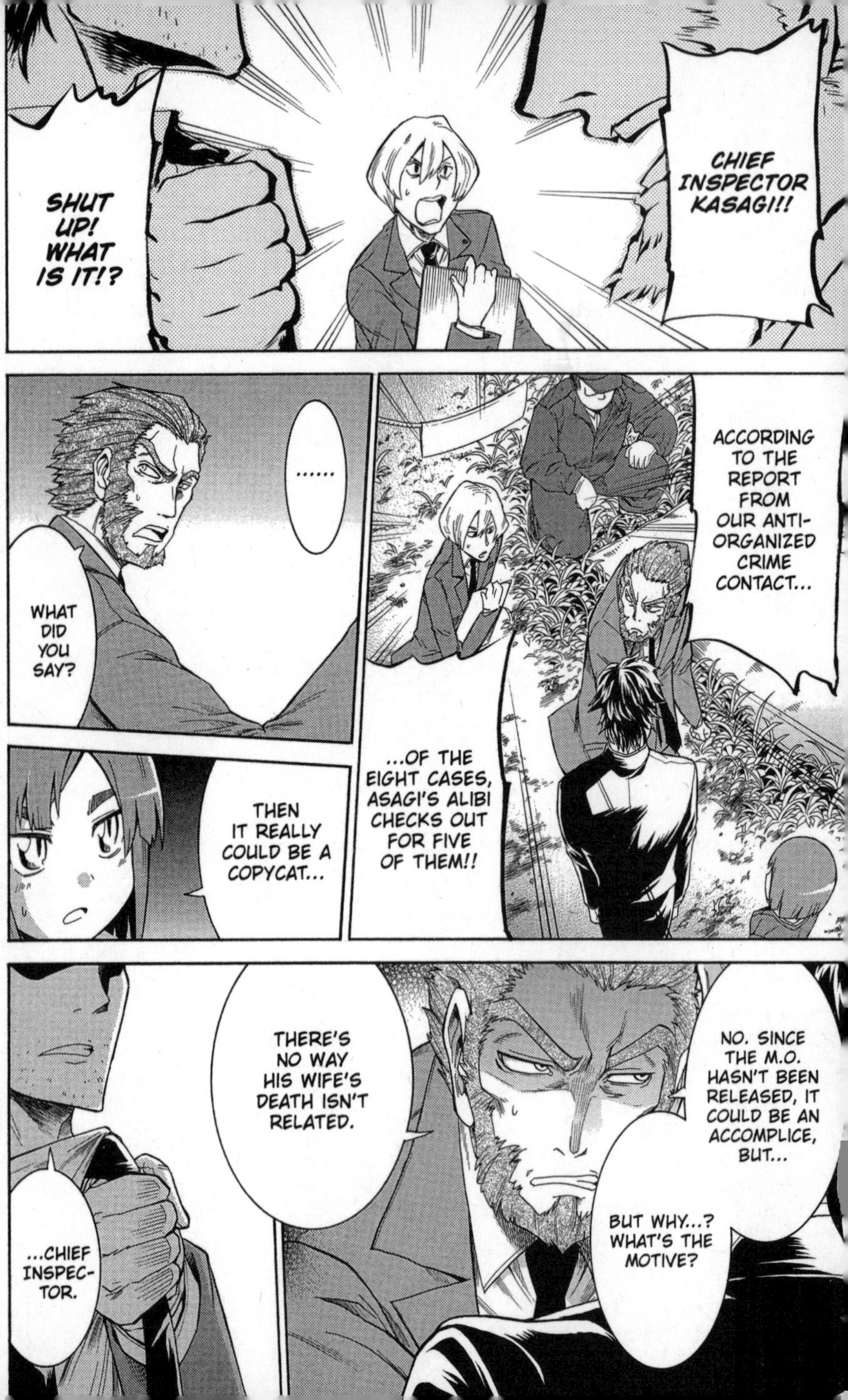
CHIEF INSPECTOR KASAGI!!
SHUT UP! WHAT IS IT!?
ACCORDING TO THE REPORT FROM OUR ANTI-ORGANIZED CRIME CONTACT...
...OF THE EIGHT CASES, ASAGI'S ALIBI CHECKS OUT FOR FIVE OF THEM!!
......
WHAT DID YOU SAY?
THEN IT REALLY COULD BE A COPYCAT...
NO. SINCE THE M.O. HASN'T BEEN RELEASED, IT COULD BE AN ACCOMPLICE, BUT...
BUT WHY...? WHAT'S THE MOTIVE?
THERE'S NO WAY HIS WIFE'S DEATH ISN'T RELATED.
...CHIEF INSPEC-TOR.

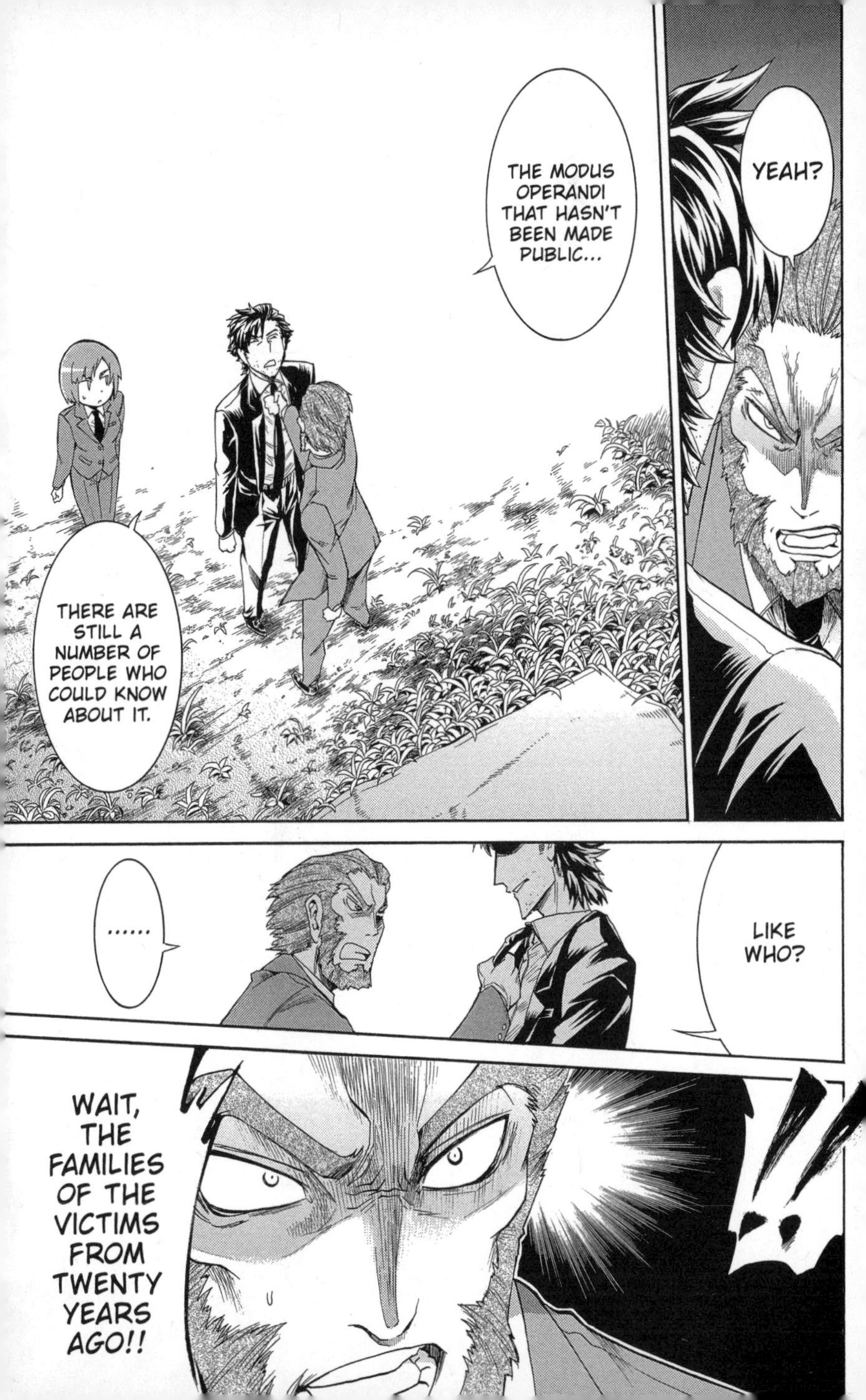
YEAH?
THE MODUS OPERANDI THAT HASN'T BEEN MADE PUBLIC...
THERE ARE STILL A NUMBER OF PEOPLE WHO COULD KNOW ABOUT IT.
LIKE WHO?
......
WAIT, THE FAMILIES OF THE VICTIMS FROM TWENTY YEARS AGO!!

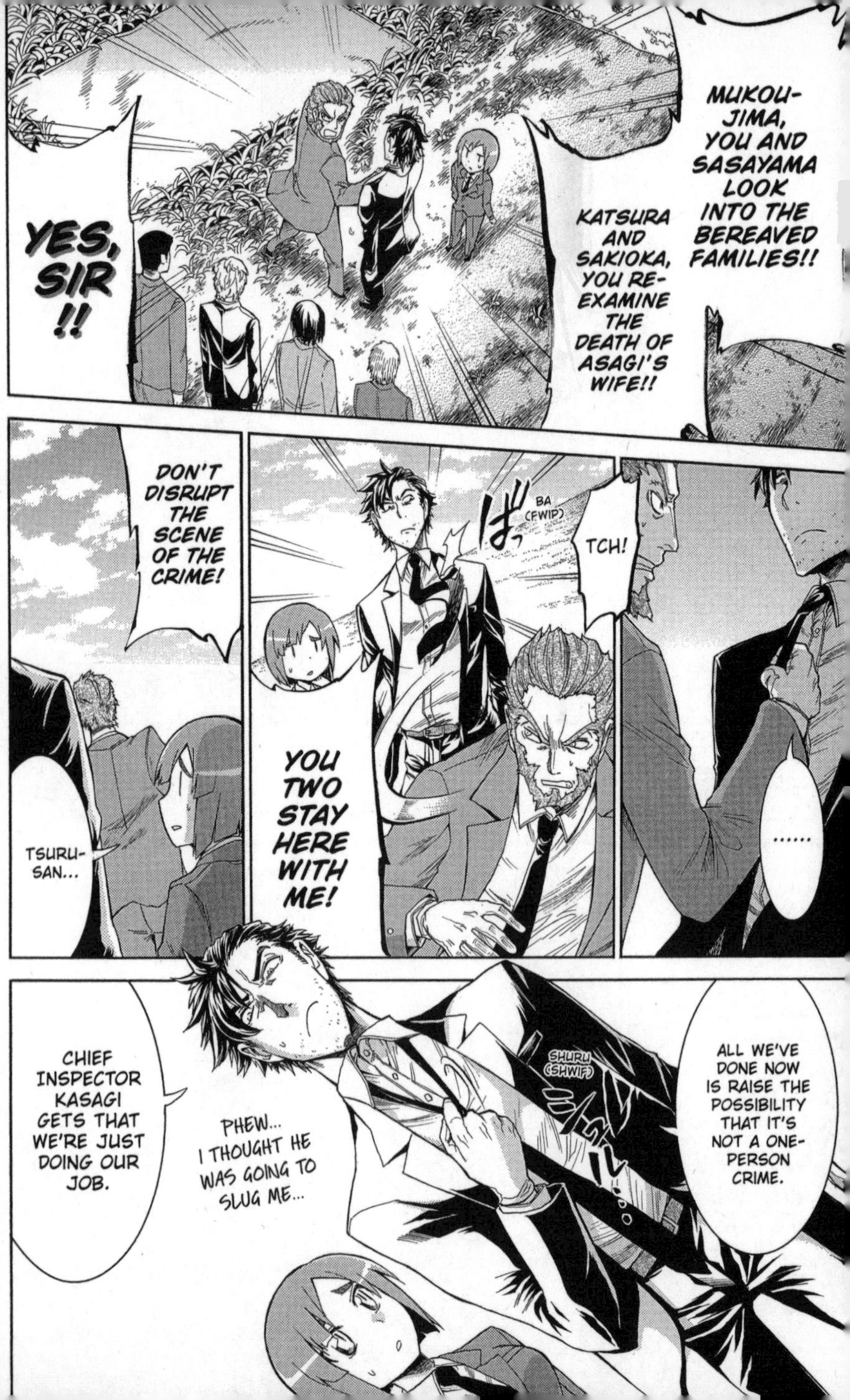
MUKOU-JIMA, YOU AND SASAYAMA LOOK INTO THE BEREAVED FAMILIES!!
KATSURA AND SAKIOKA, YOU RE-EXAMINE THE DEATH OF ASAGI'S WIFE!!
YES, SIR!!
......
TCH!
ば
BA (FWIP)
YOU TWO STAY HERE WITH ME!
DON'T DISRUPT THE SCENE OF THE CRIME!
TSURU-SAN...
ALL WE'VE DONE NOW IS RAISE THE POSSIBILITY THAT IT'S NOT A ONE-PERSON CRIME.
SHURU (SHWIF)
PHEW... I THOUGHT HE WAS GOING TO SLUG ME...
CHIEF INSPECTOR KASAGI GETS THAT WE'RE JUST DOING OUR JOB.

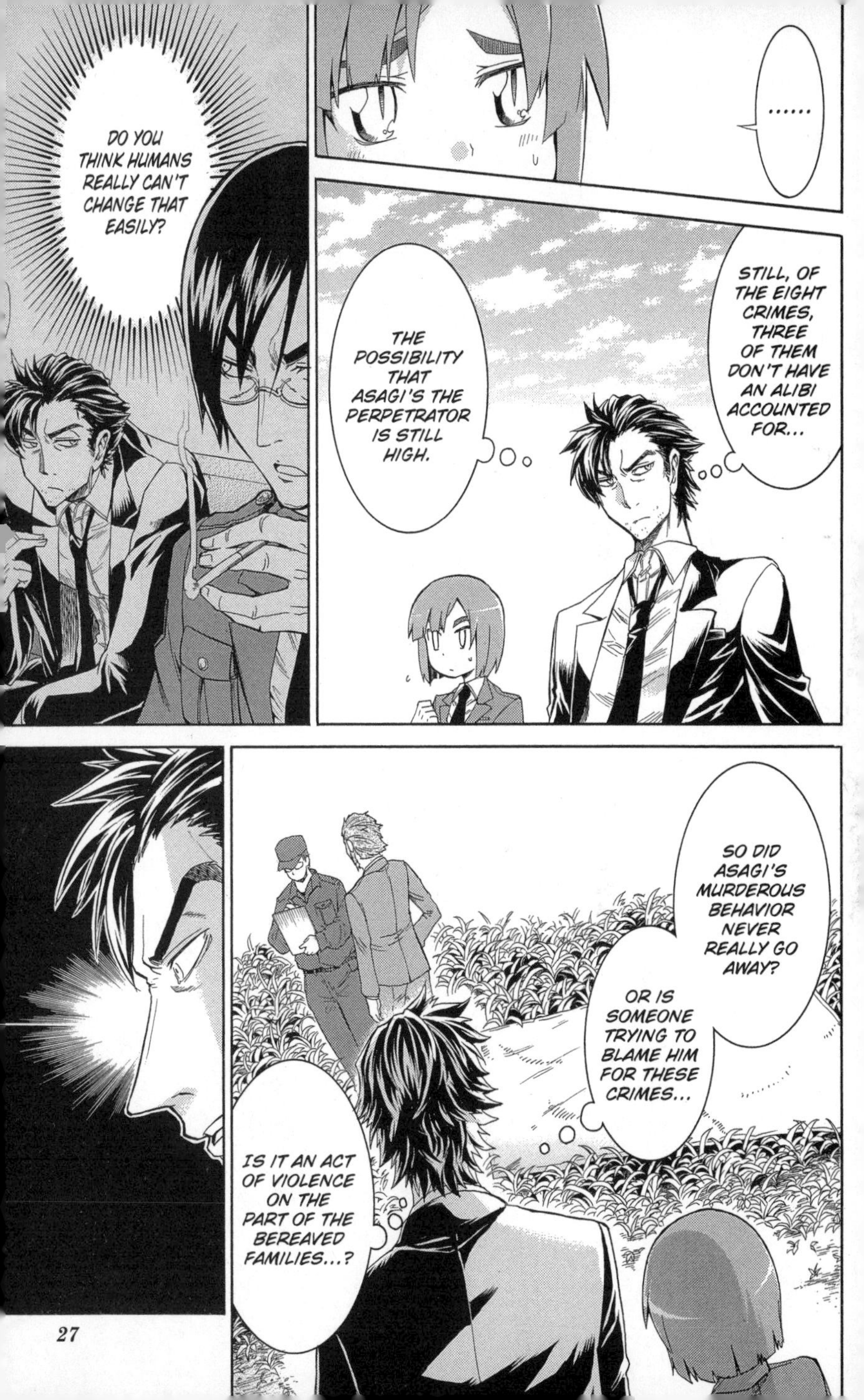
......
STILL, OF THE EIGHT CRIMES, THREE OF THEM DON'T HAVE AN ALIBI ACCOUNTED FOR...
THE POSSIBILITY THAT ASAGI'S THE PERPETRATOR IS STILL HIGH.
DO YOU THINK HUMANS REALLY CAN'T CHANGE THAT EASILY?
SO DID ASAGI'S MURDEROUS BEHAVIOR NEVER REALLY GO AWAY?
OR IS SOMEONE TRYING TO BLAME HIM FOR THESE CRIMES...
IS IT AN ACT OF VIOLENCE ON THE PART OF THE BEREAVED FAMILIES...?

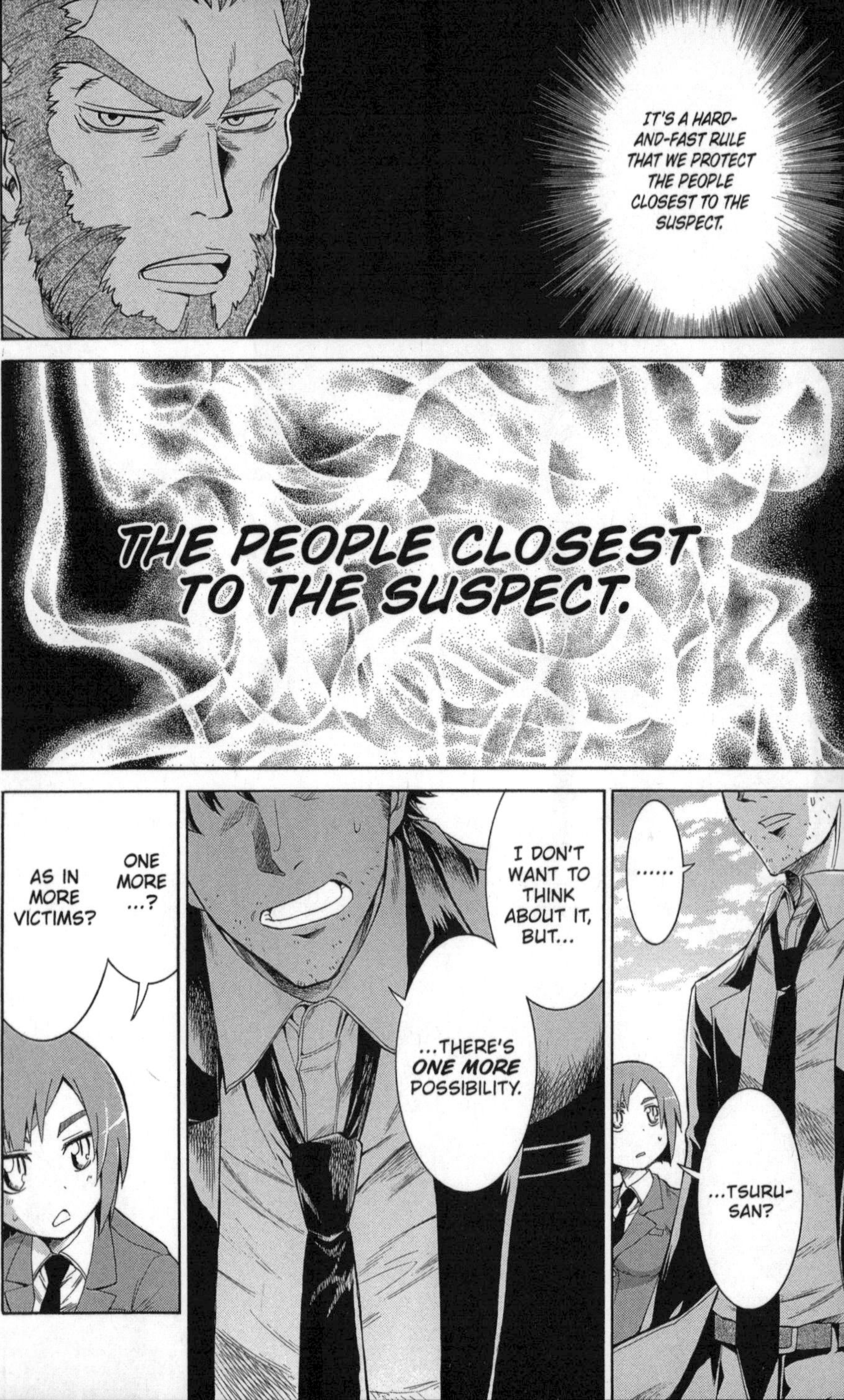
IT'S A HARD-AND-FAST RULE THAT WE PROTECT THE PEOPLE CLOSEST TO THE SUSPECT.
THE PEOPLE CLOSEST TO THE SUSPECT.
......
...TSURU-SAN?
I DON'T WANT TO THINK ABOUT IT, BUT...
...THERE'S ONE MORE POSSIBILITY.
ONE MORE ...?
AS IN MORE VICTIMS?

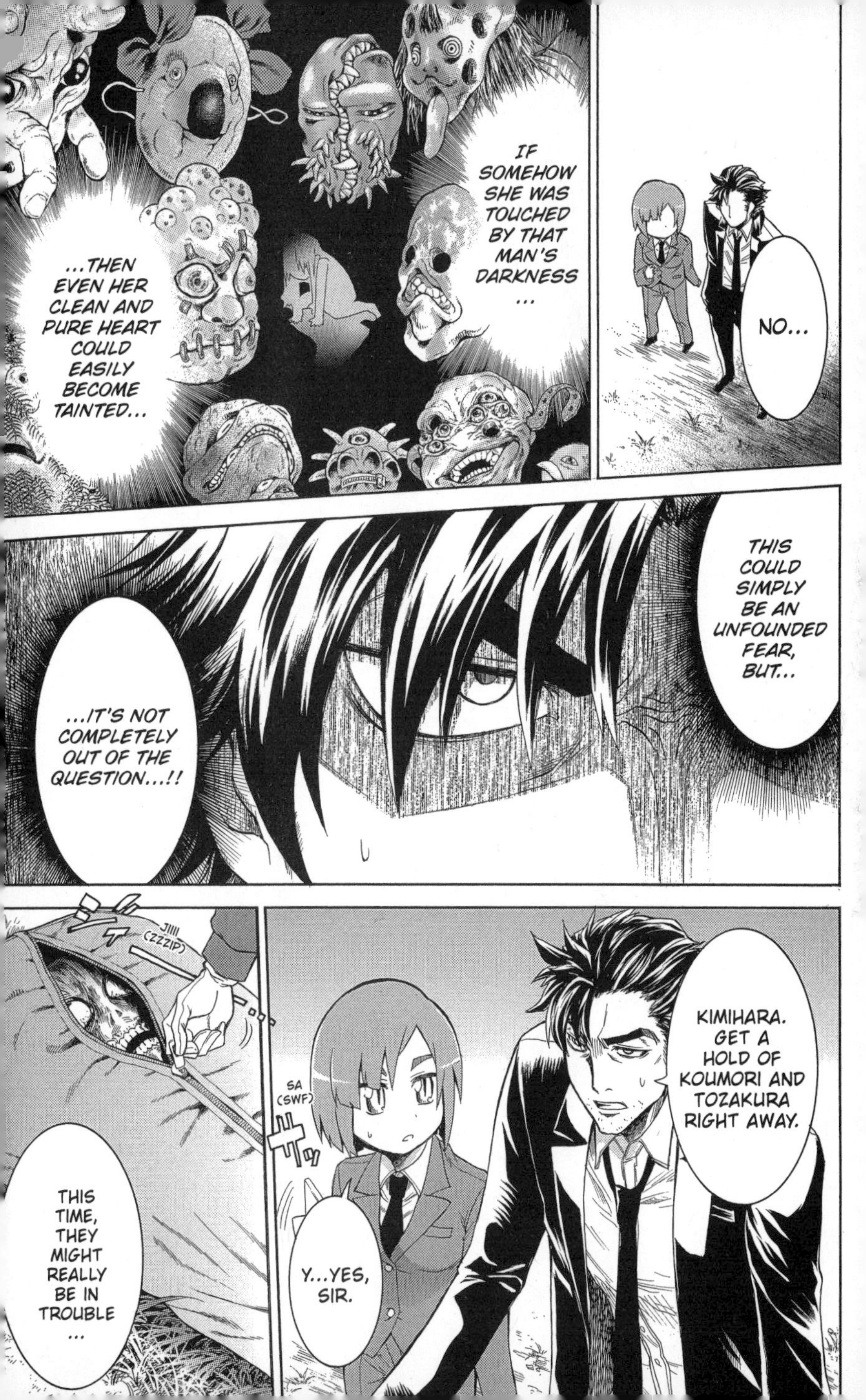
NO...
IF SOMEHOW SHE WAS TOUCHED BY THAT MAN'S DARKNESS...
...THEN EVEN HER CLEAN AND PURE HEART COULD EASILY BECOME TAINTED...
THIS COULD SIMPLY BE AN UNFOUNDED FEAR, BUT...
...IT'S NOT COMPLETELY OUT OF THE QUESTION...!!
KIMIHARA. GET A HOLD OF KOUMORI AND TOZAKURA RIGHT AWAY.
SA (SWF)
Y...YES, SIR.
JIIII (ZZZIP)
THIS TIME, THEY MIGHT REALLY BE IN TROUBLE...

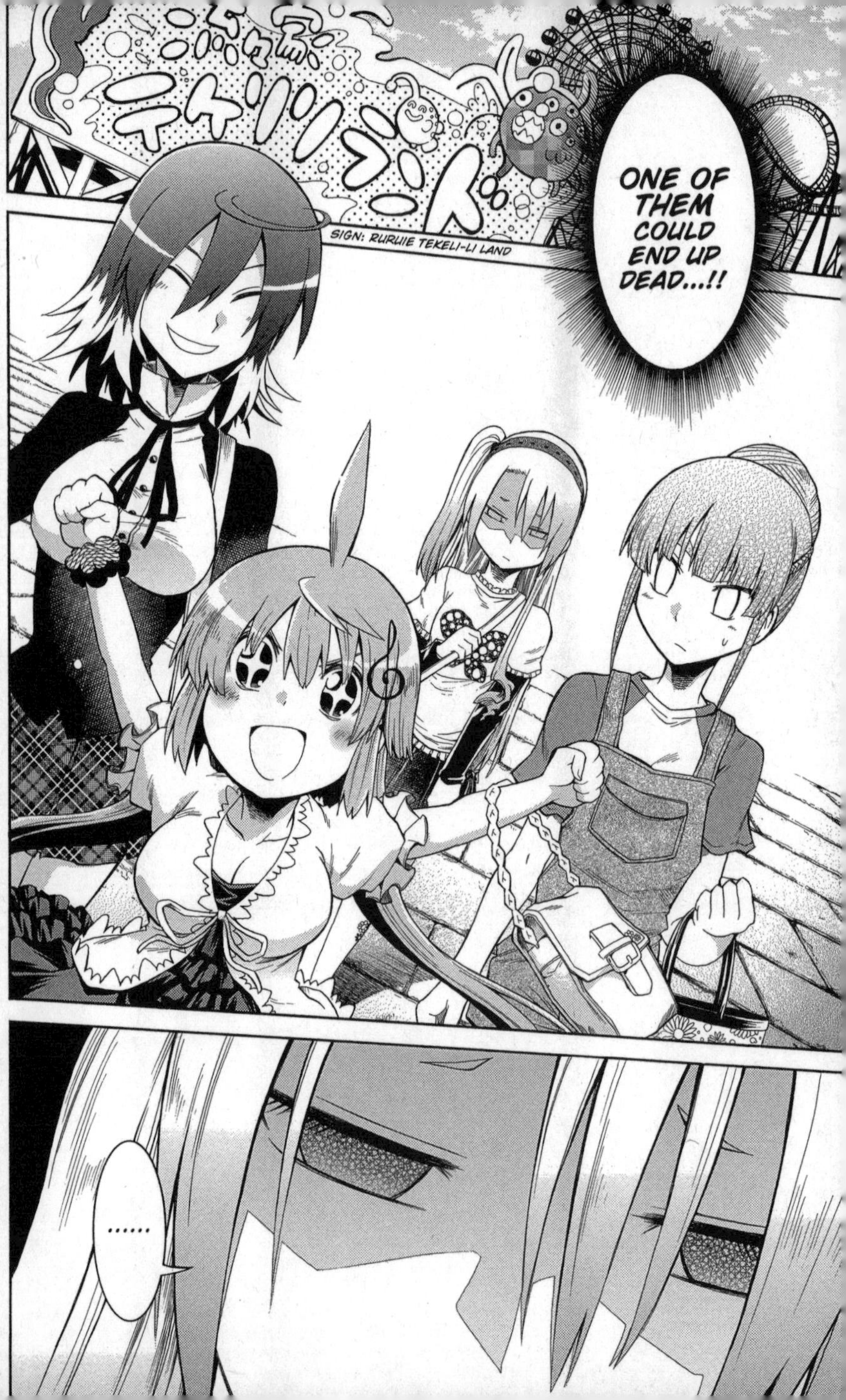
SIGN: RURUIE TEKELI-LI LAND
ONE OF THEM COULD END UP DEAD...!!
......

MURCIÉLAGO

MURCIÉLAGO

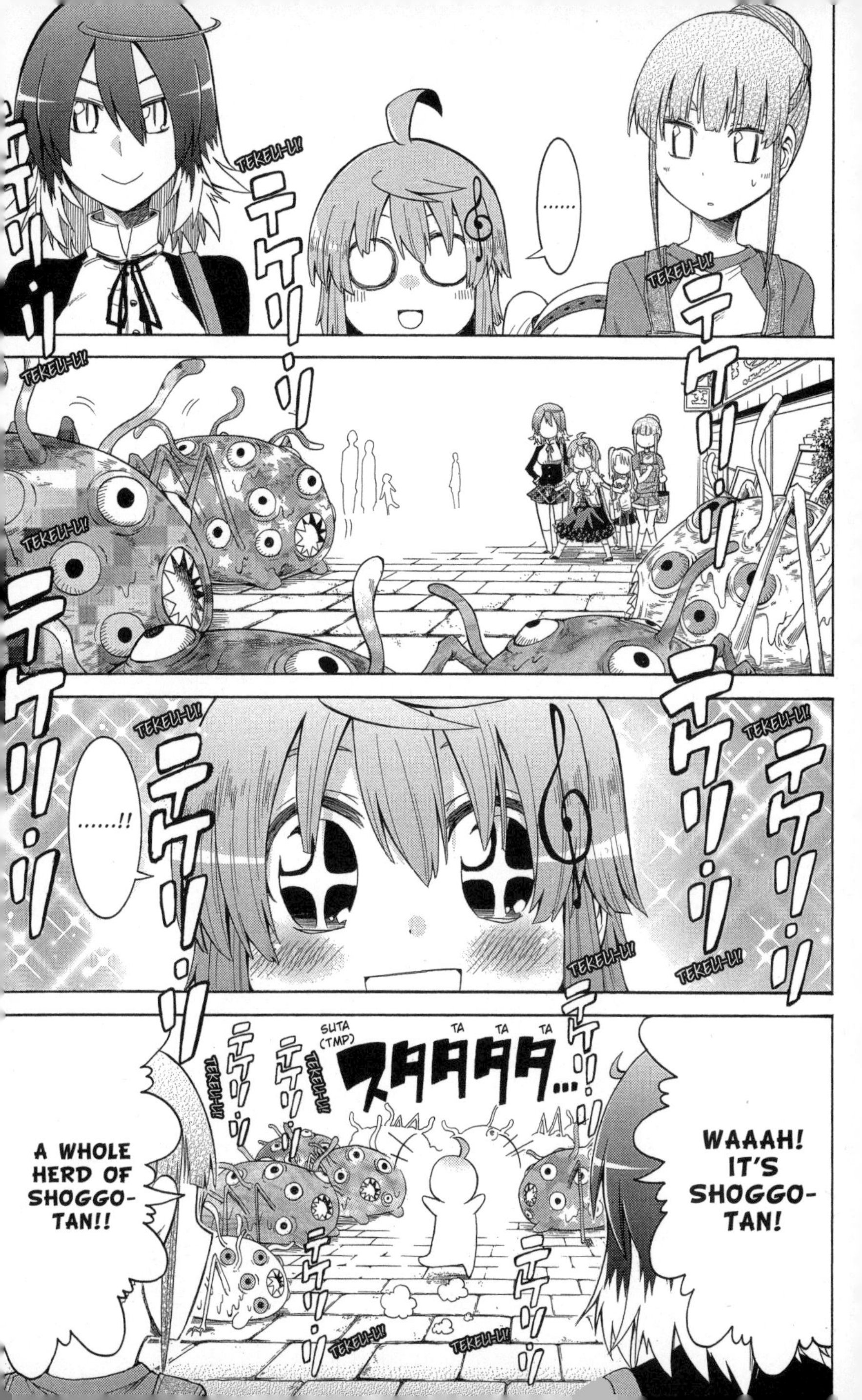
TEKELI-LI!
......
TEKELI-LI!
TEKELI-LI!
TEKELI-LI!
TEKELI-LI!
TEKELI-LI!
TEKELI-LI!
TEKELI-LI!
......!!
TEKELI-LI!
WAAAH! IT'S SHOGGO-TAN!
TA TA TA
SUTA (TMP)
スタタタタ…
TEKELI-LI!
TEKELI-LI!
TEKELI-LI!
TEKELI-LI!
A WHOLE HERD OF SHOGGO-TAN!!

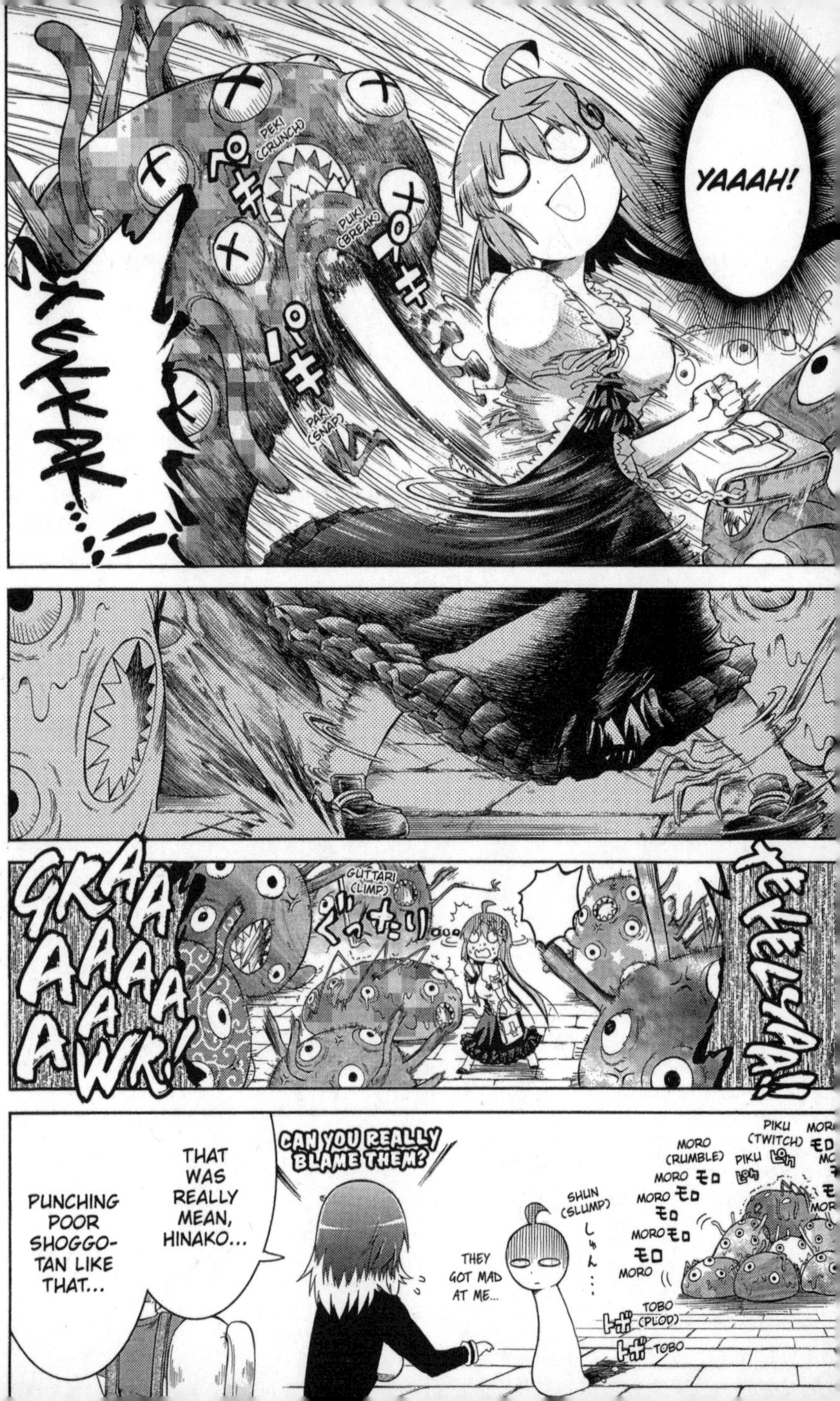
YAAAH!
PEKI (CRUNCH)
PUKI (BREAK)
PAKI (SNAP)
SKWKKRK...!!
TEKELYPA!!
GUTTARI (LIMP)
GRAAAAAAAAWR!
PIKU (TWITCH)
PIKU
MORO (RUMBLE)
MORO
MORO
MORO
MORO
SHUN (SLUMP)
THEY GOT MAD AT ME...
CAN YOU REALLY BLAME THEM?
THAT WAS REALLY MEAN, HINAKO...
PUNCHING POOR SHOGGO-TAN LIKE THAT...
TOBO (PLOD)
TOBO

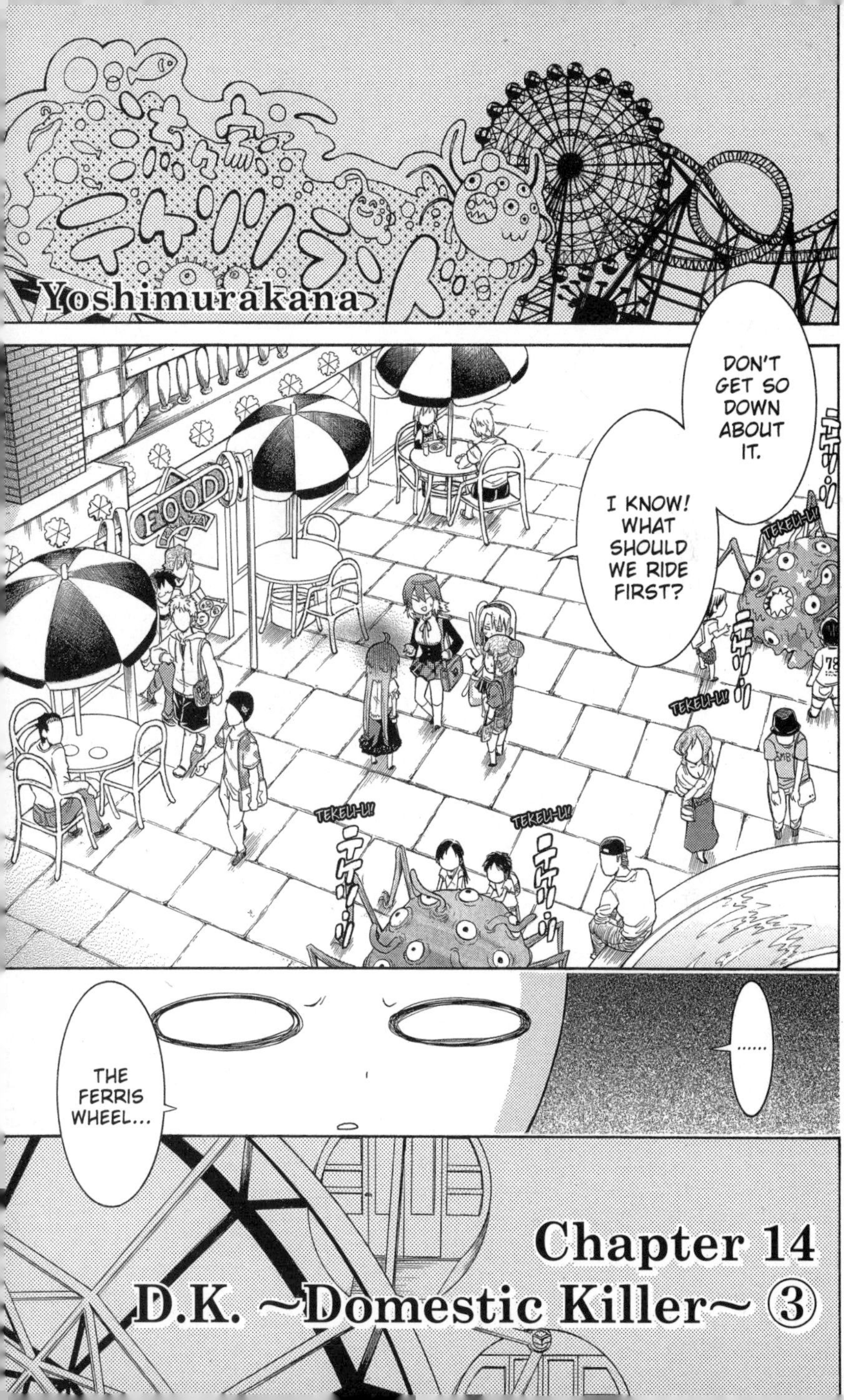
Yoshimurakana
DON'T GET SO DOWN ABOUT IT.
I KNOW! WHAT SHOULD WE RIDE FIRST?
TEKELI-LI!
TEKELI-LI!
TEKELI-LI!
TEKELI-LI!
......
THE FERRIS WHEEL...
Chapter 14
D.K. ~Domestic Killer~ ③

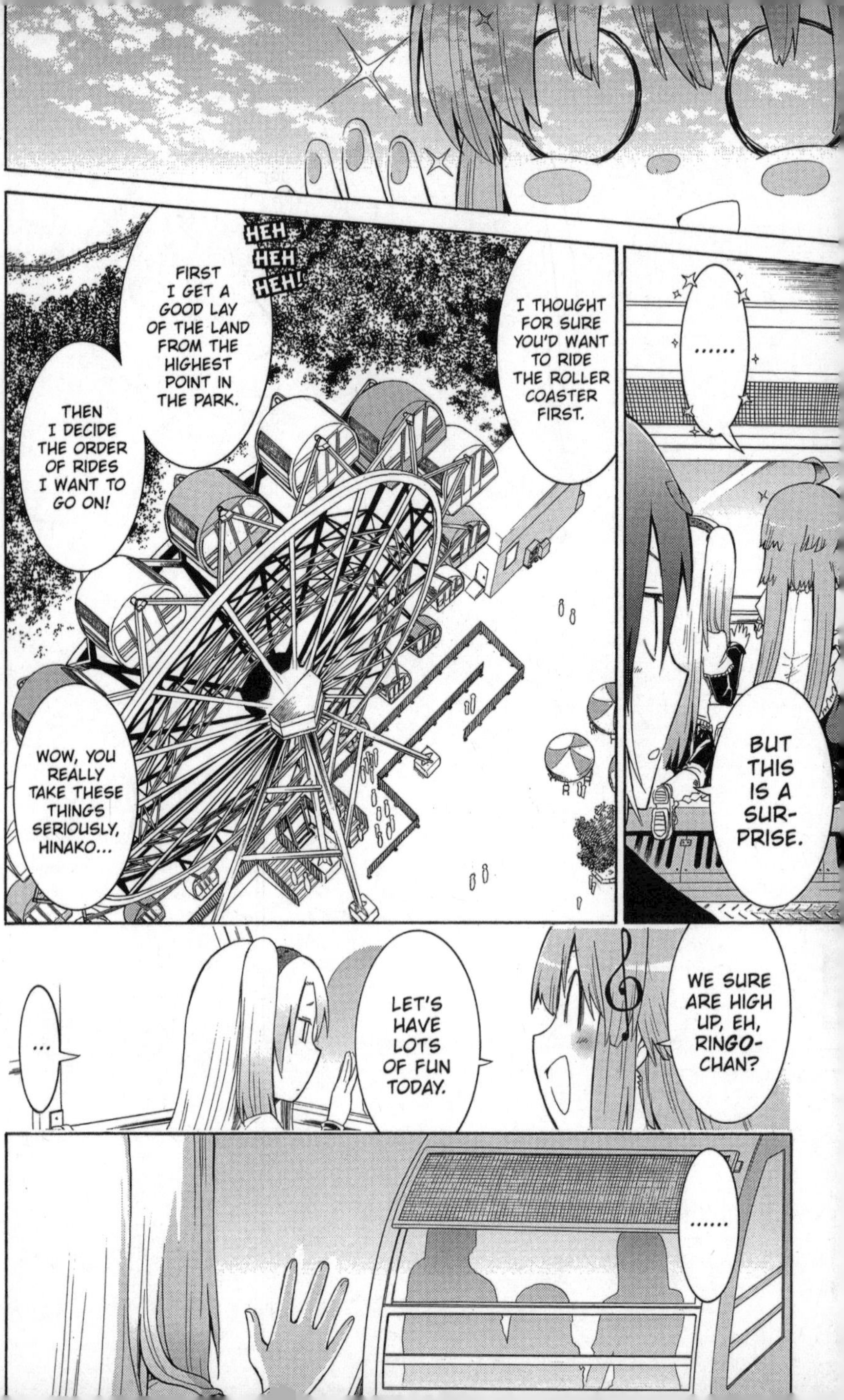
......
BUT THIS IS A SURPRISE.
I THOUGHT FOR SURE YOU'D WANT TO RIDE THE ROLLER COASTER FIRST.
HEH HEH HEH!
FIRST I GET A GOOD LAY OF THE LAND FROM THE HIGHEST POINT IN THE PARK.
THEN I DECIDE THE ORDER OF RIDES I WANT TO GO ON!
WOW, YOU REALLY TAKE THESE THINGS SERIOUSLY, HINAKO...
WE SURE ARE HIGH UP, EH, RINGO-CHAN?
LET'S HAVE LOTS OF FUN TODAY.
...
......

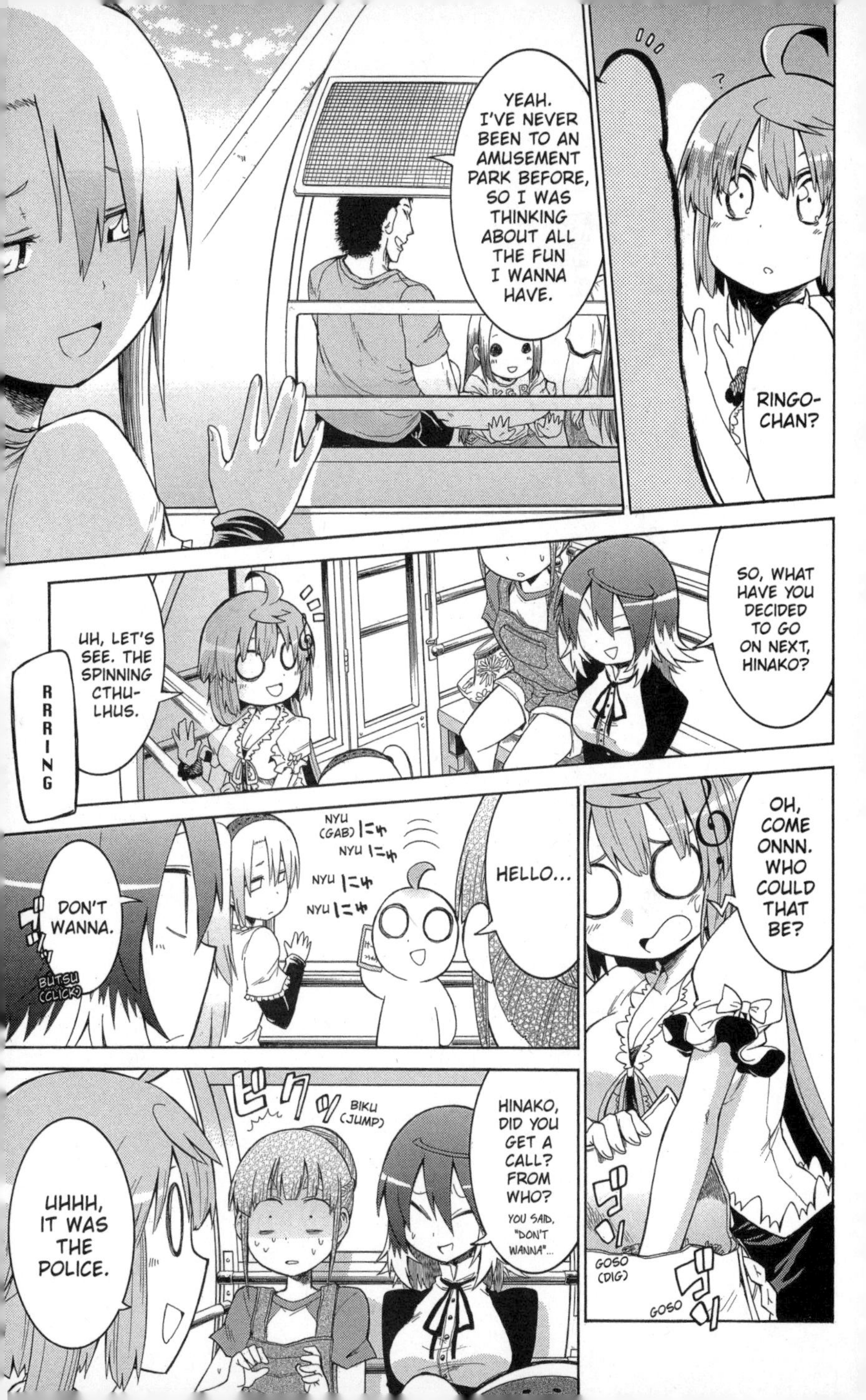
RINGO-CHAN?
YEAH. I'VE NEVER BEEN TO AN AMUSEMENT PARK BEFORE, SO I WAS THINKING ABOUT ALL THE FUN I WANNA HAVE.
SO, WHAT HAVE YOU DECIDED TO GO ON NEXT, HINAKO?
UH, LET'S SEE. THE SPINNING CTHULHUS.
RRRRING
OH, COME ONNN. WHO COULD THAT BE?
GOSO (DIG)
GOSO
HELLO...
NYU (GAB) にゅ
NYU にゅ
NYU にゅ
NYU にゅ
DON'T WANNA.
BUTSU (CLICK)
ビクッ
BIKU (JUMP)
HINAKO, DID YOU GET A CALL? FROM WHO?
YOU SAID, "DON'T WANNA"...
UHHH, IT WAS THE POLICE.

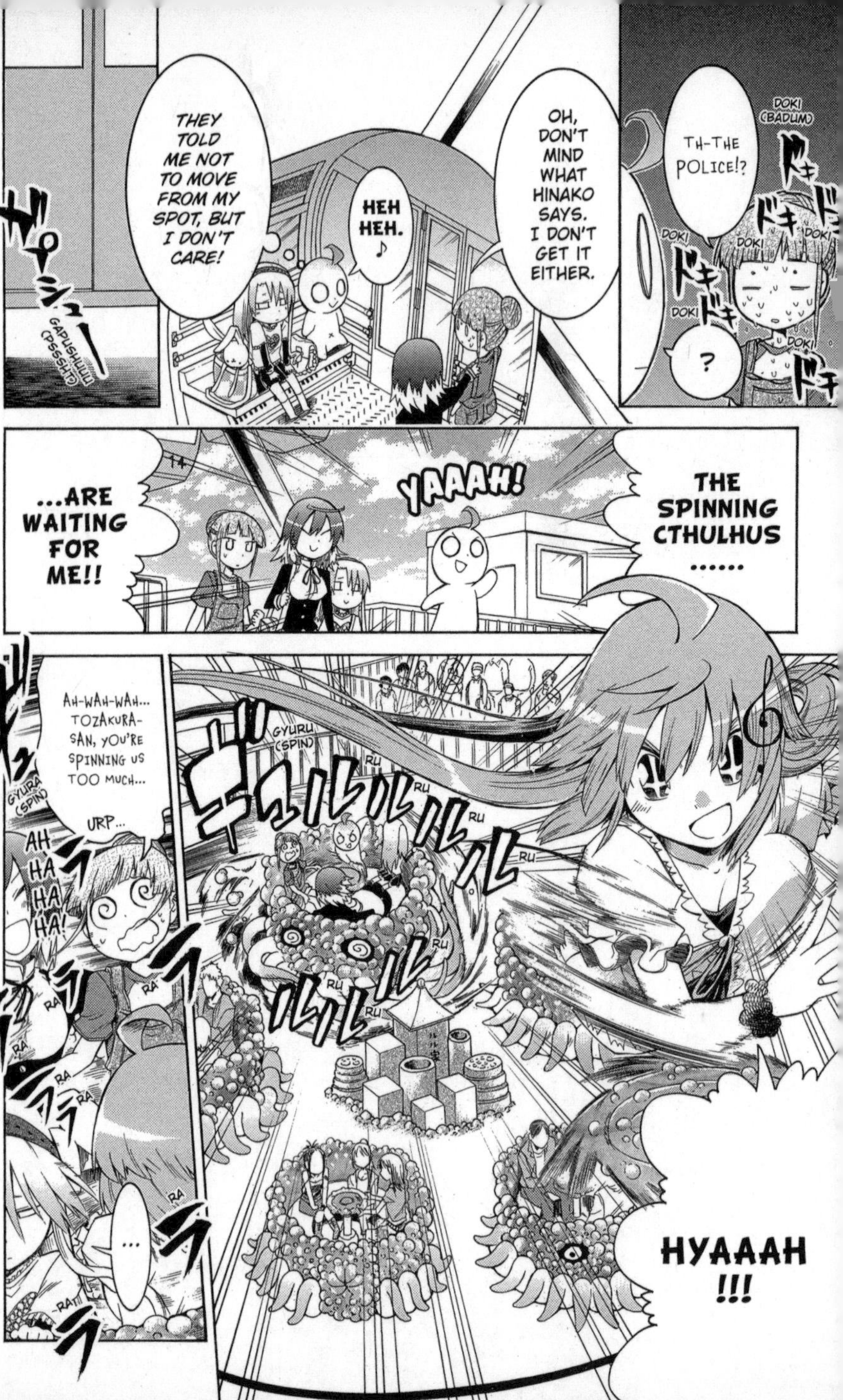
DOKI (BADUM)
TH-THE POLICE!?
DOKI DOKI DOKI DOKI DOKI DOKI
?
OH, DON'T MIND WHAT HINAKO SAYS. I DON'T GET IT EITHER.
HEH HEH. ♪
THEY TOLD ME NOT TO MOVE FROM MY SPOT, BUT I DON'T CARE!
GAPUSHUUU (PSSSHT)
THE SPINNING CTHULHUS ......
YAAAH!
...ARE WAITING FOR ME!!
HYAAAH !!!
GYURU (SPIN)
RU RU RU RU RU RU RU
AH-WAH-WAH... TOZAKURA-SAN, YOU'RE SPINNING US TOO MUCH...
URP...
GYURA (SPIN)
AH HA HA HA!
RA RA RA RA RA RA RA
...

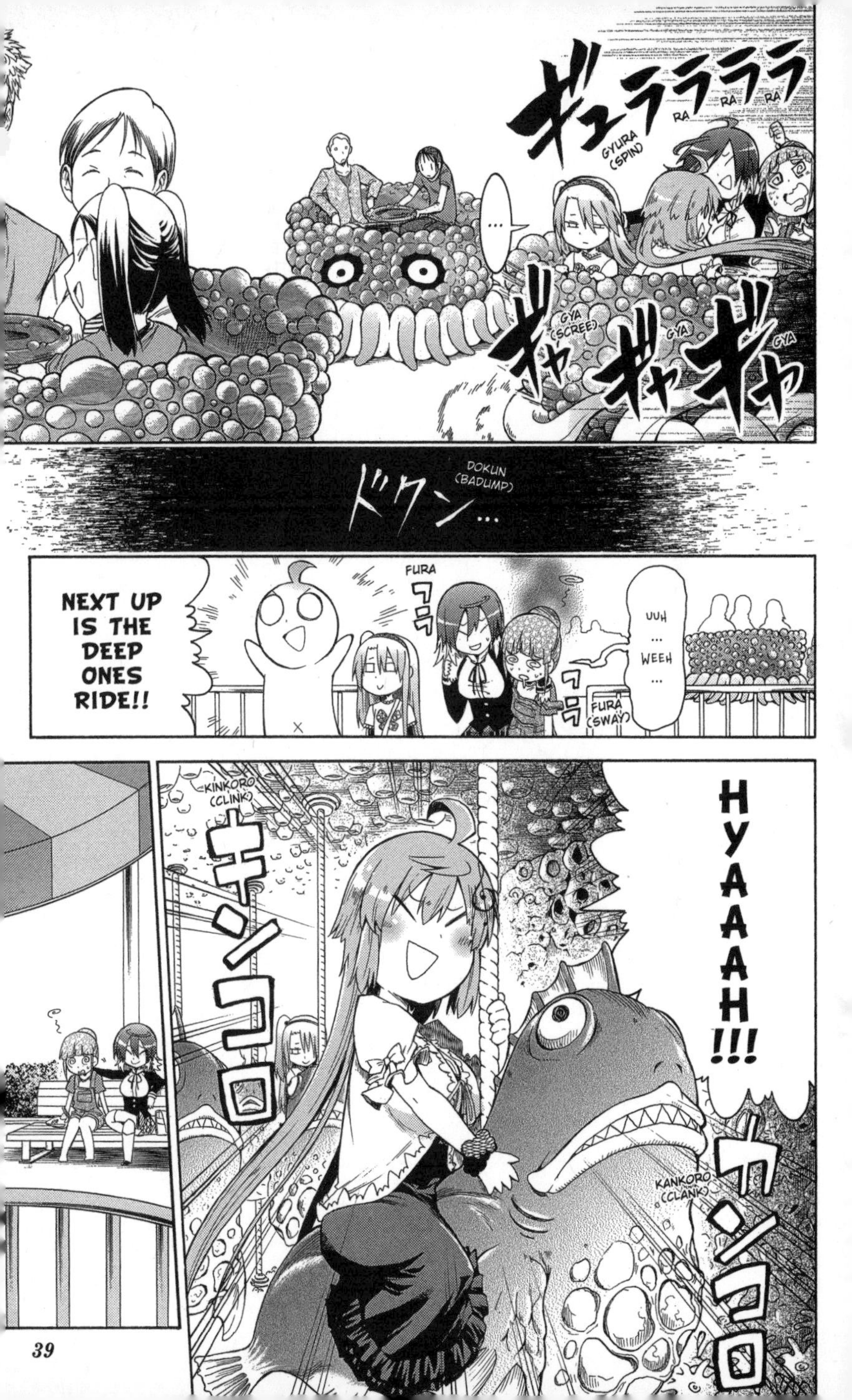
ギュラララララ
GYURA (SPIN)
RA
RA
RA
...
ギャギャギャ
GYA (SCREE)
GYA
GYA
ドクン...
DOKUN (BADUMP)
UUH ... WEEH ...
フラ
FURA (SWAY)
フラ
FURA
NEXT UP IS THE DEEP ONES RIDE!!
HYAAAAH!!!
カンコロ
KANKORO (CLANK)
キンコロ
KINKORO (CLINK)

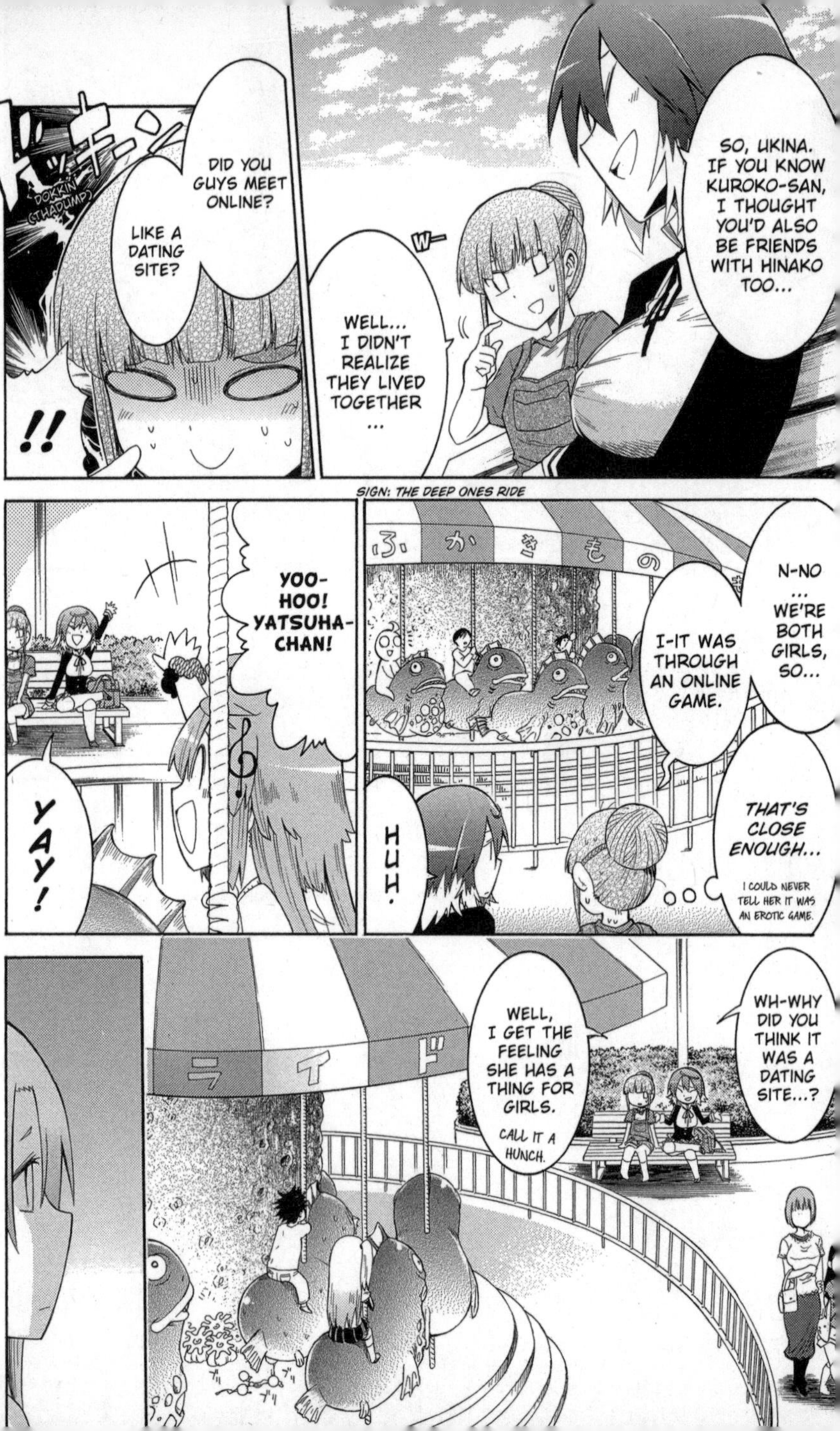
SO, UKINA. IF YOU KNOW KUROKO-SAN, I THOUGHT YOU'D ALSO BE FRIENDS WITH HINAKO TOO...
W—
WELL... I DIDN'T REALIZE THEY LIVED TOGETHER...
ドッキーン
DOKKIN (THADUMP)
DID YOU GUYS MEET ONLINE?
LIKE A DATING SITE?
!!
SIGN: THE DEEP ONES RIDE
ふかきもの
N-NO... WE'RE BOTH GIRLS, SO...
I-IT WAS THROUGH AN ONLINE GAME.
HUH.
THAT'S CLOSE ENOUGH...
I COULD NEVER TELL HER IT WAS AN EROTIC GAME.
YOO-HOO! YATSUHA-CHAN!
YAY!
WH-WHY DID YOU THINK IT WAS A DATING SITE...?
WELL, I GET THE FEELING SHE HAS A THING FOR GIRLS.
CALL IT A HUNCH.
ライド

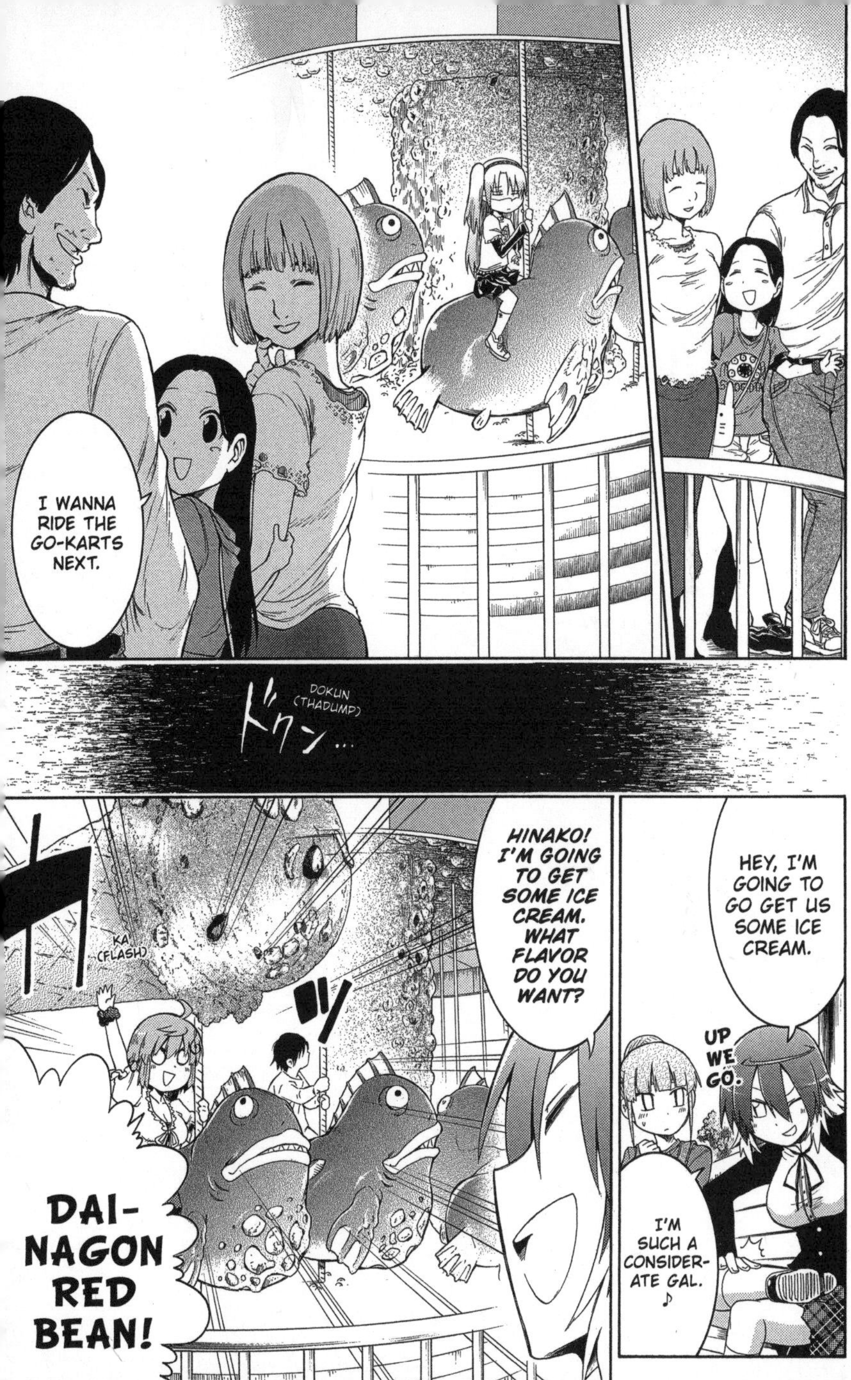

I WANNA RIDE THE GO-KARTS NEXT.
ドクン…
DOKUN (THADUMP)
HEY, I'M GOING TO GO GET US SOME ICE CREAM.
UP WE GO.
I'M SUCH A CONSIDER-ATE GAL. ♪
HINAKO! I'M GOING TO GET SOME ICE CREAM. WHAT FLAVOR DO YOU WANT?
KA (FLASH)
DAI-NAGON RED BEAN!

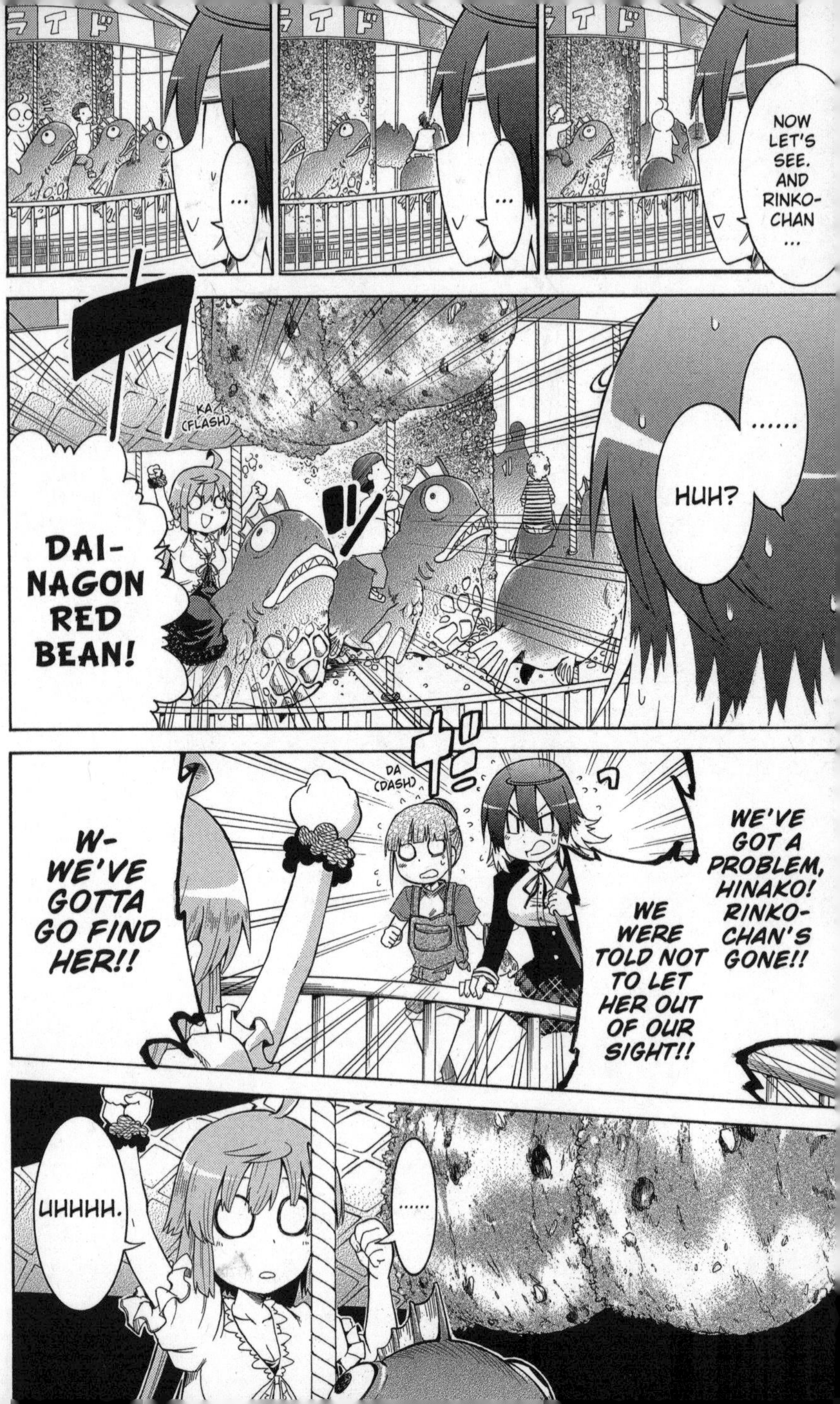
NOW LET'S SEE. AND RINKO-CHAN ...
...
...
......
HUH?
KA (FLASH)
DAI-NAGON RED BEAN!
WE'VE GOT A PROBLEM, HINAKO! RINKO-CHAN'S GONE!!
WE WERE TOLD NOT TO LET HER OUT OF OUR SIGHT!!
DA (DASH)
W-WE'VE GOTTA GO FIND HER!!
......
UHHHH.

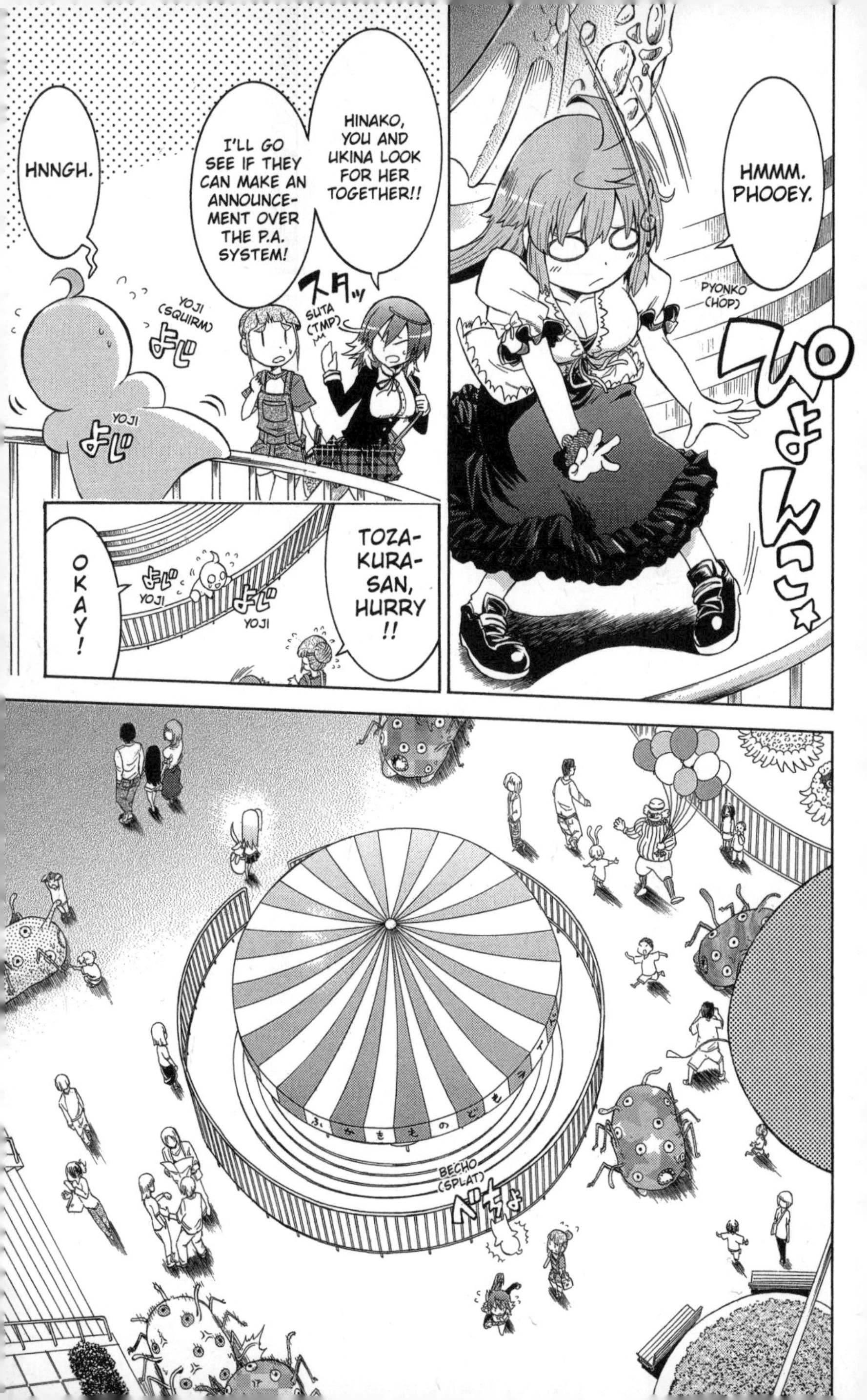

HMMM. PHOOEY.
PYONKO (HOP)
ぴょんこ★
HINAKO, YOU AND UKINA LOOK FOR HER TOGETHER!!
I'LL GO SEE IF THEY CAN MAKE AN ANNOUNCE-MENT OVER THE P.A. SYSTEM!
スタッ
SUTA (TMP)
HNNGH.
YOJI (SQUIRM)
よじ
YOJI
よじ
TOZA-KURA-SAN, HURRY!!
OKAY!
よじ
YOJI
よじ
YOJI
BECHO (SPLAT)
べちょ

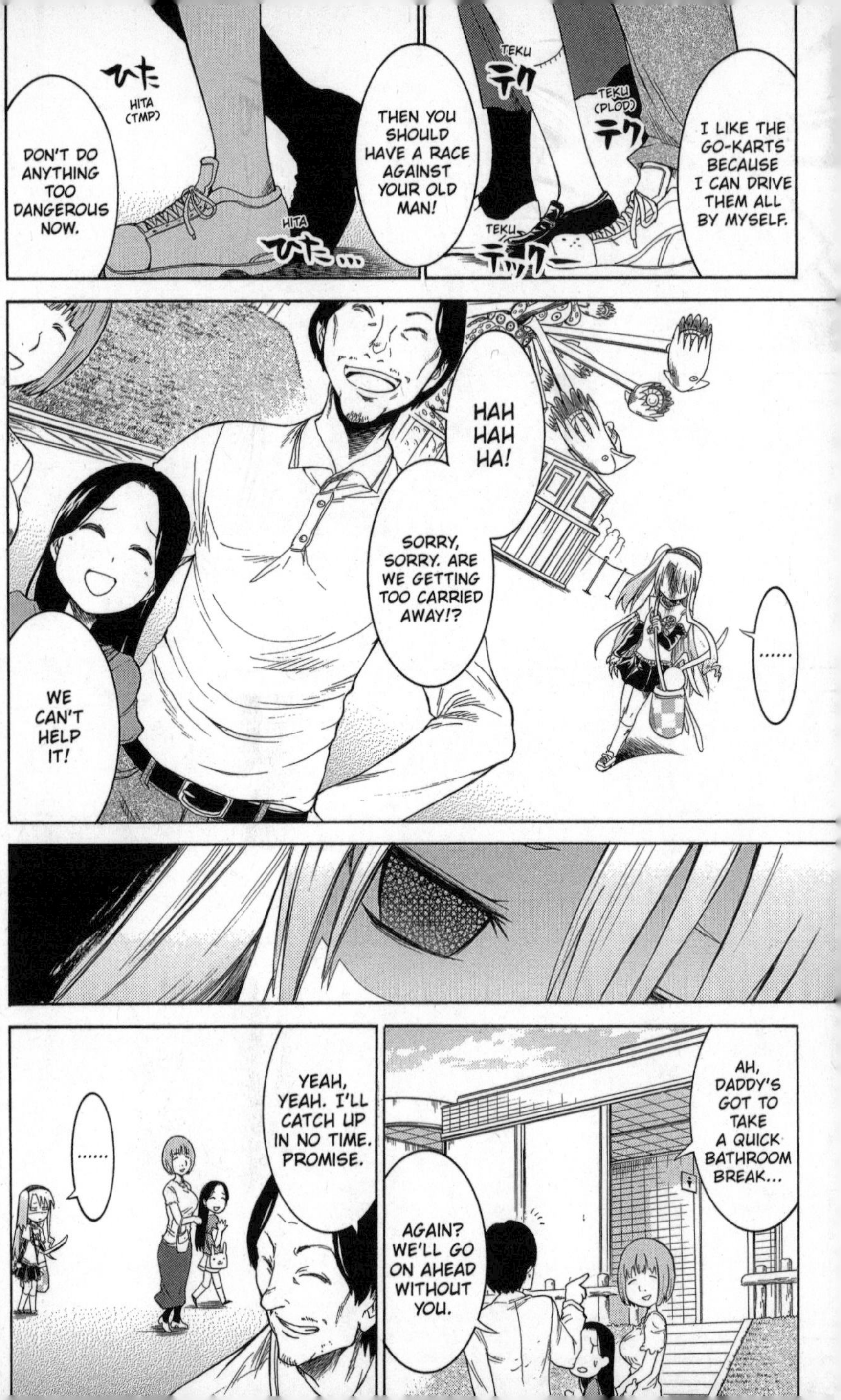
TEKU
テク
TEKU (PLOD)
テク
TEKU
テック
I LIKE THE GO-KARTS BECAUSE I CAN DRIVE THEM ALL BY MYSELF.
THEN YOU SHOULD HAVE A RACE AGAINST YOUR OLD MAN!
ひた
HITA (TMP)
DON'T DO ANYTHING TOO DANGEROUS NOW.
HITA
ひた…
......
HAH HAH HA!
SORRY, SORRY. ARE WE GETTING TOO CARRIED AWAY!?
WE CAN'T HELP IT!
AH, DADDY'S GOT TO TAKE A QUICK BATHROOM BREAK...
AGAIN? WE'LL GO ON AHEAD WITHOUT YOU.
YEAH, YEAH. I'LL CATCH UP IN NO TIME. PROMISE.
......

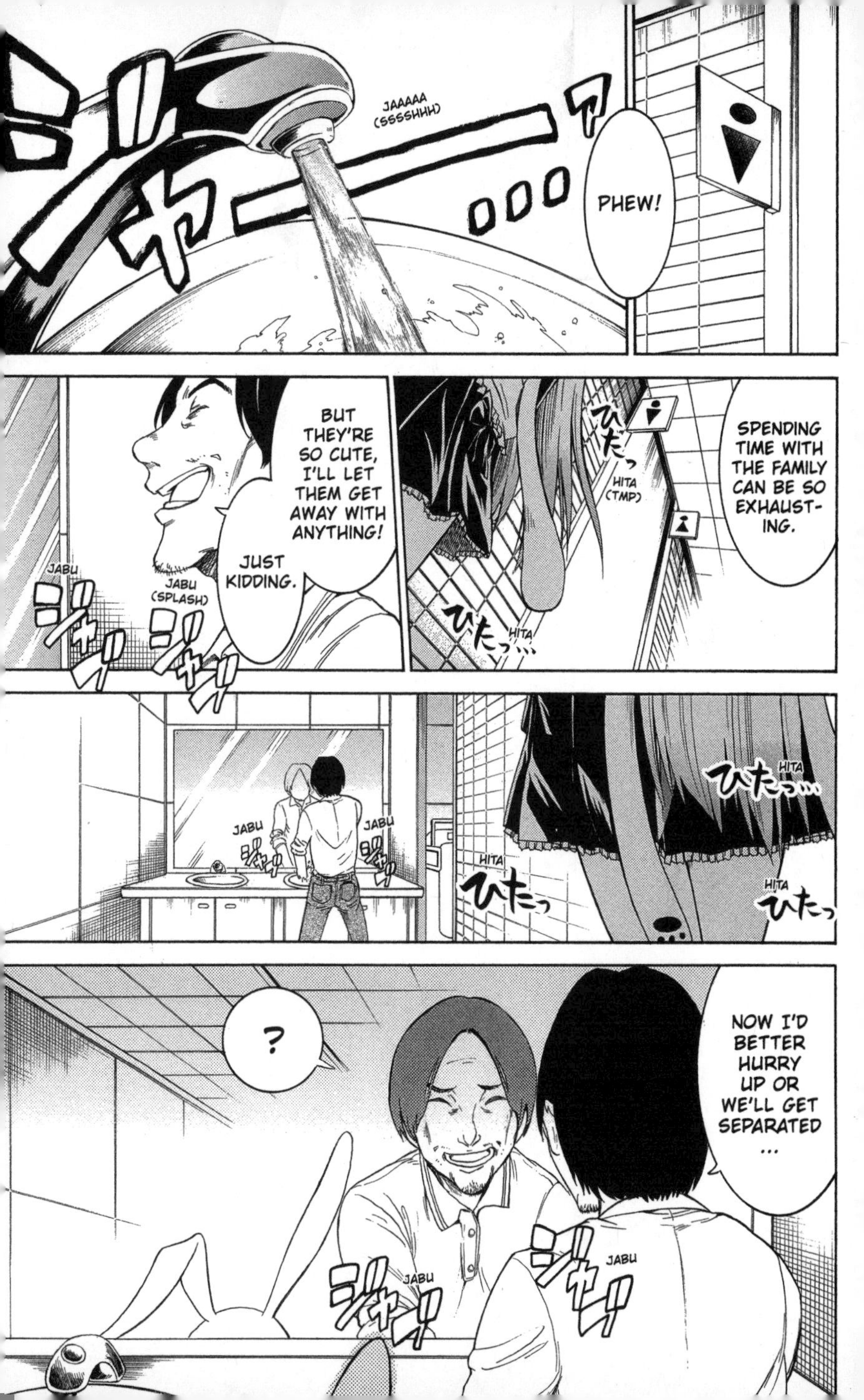
PHEW!
JAAAAA (SSSSHHH)
SPENDING TIME WITH THE FAMILY CAN BE SO EXHAUSTING.
HITA (TMP)
HITA
BUT THEY'RE SO CUTE, I'LL LET THEM GET AWAY WITH ANYTHING!
JUST KIDDING.
JABU (SPLASH)
JABU
HITA
HITA
HITA
JABU
JABU
NOW I'D BETTER HURRY UP OR WE'LL GET SEPARATED...
?
JABU
JABU

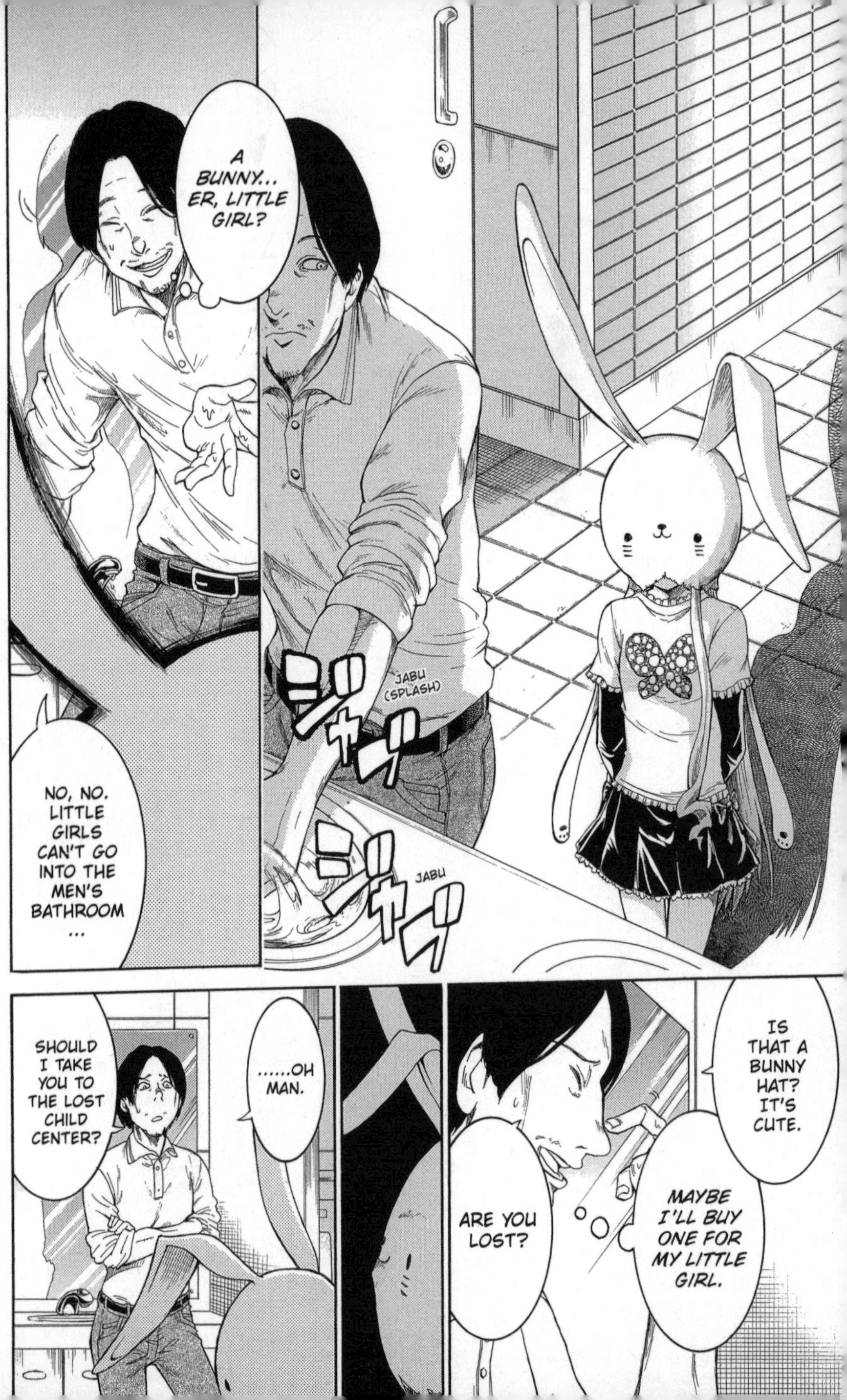
JABU (SPLASH)
JABU
A BUNNY... ER, LITTLE GIRL?
NO, NO. LITTLE GIRLS CAN'T GO INTO THE MEN'S BATHROOM ...
IS THAT A BUNNY HAT? IT'S CUTE.
MAYBE I'LL BUY ONE FOR MY LITTLE GIRL.
ARE YOU LOST?
......OH MAN.
SHOULD I TAKE YOU TO THE LOST CHILD CENTER?

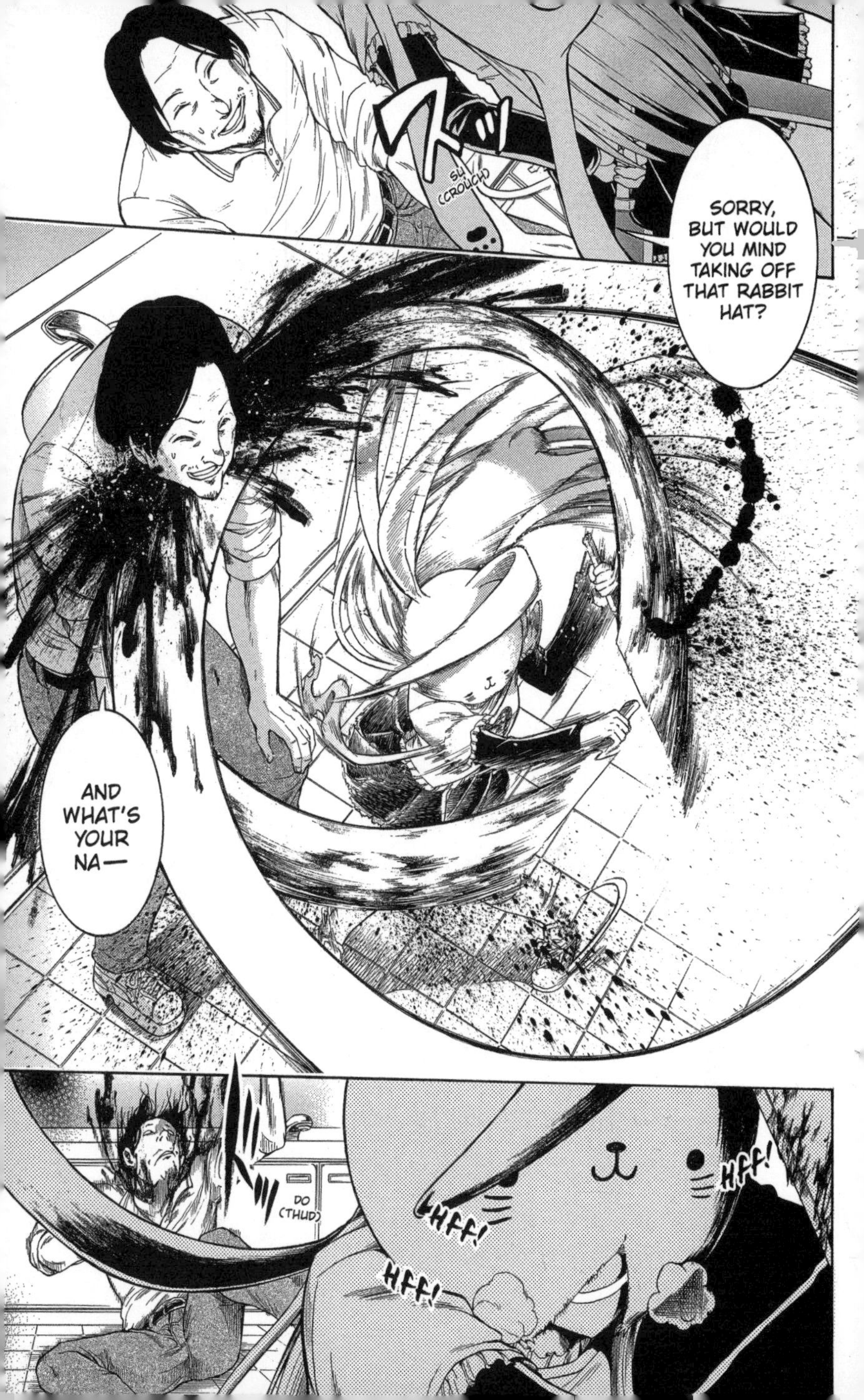

SU (CROUCH)
SORRY, BUT WOULD YOU MIND TAKING OFF THAT RABBIT HAT?
AND WHAT'S YOUR NA—
HFF!
HFF!
HFF!
DO (THUD)

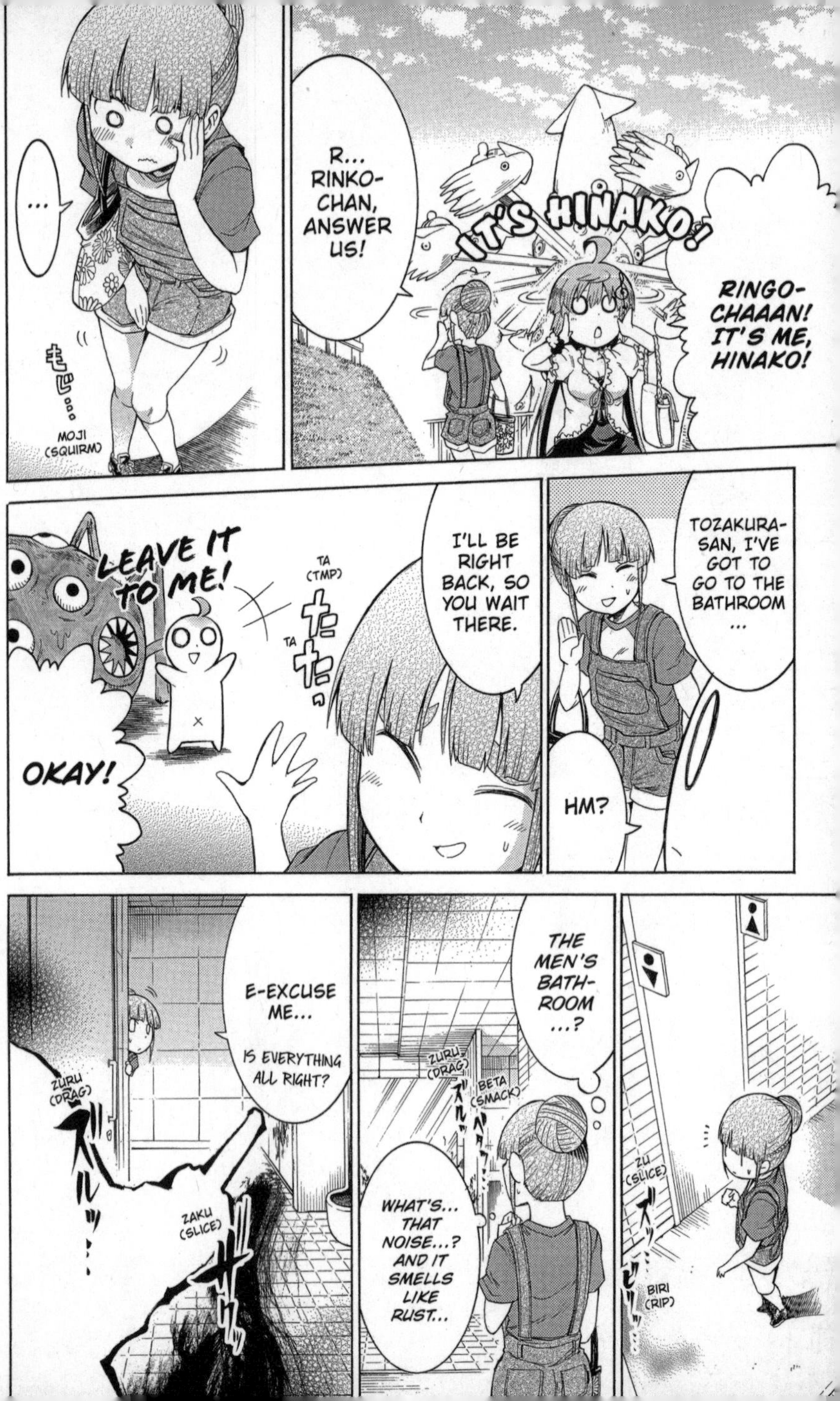
RINGO-CHAAAN! IT'S ME, HINAKO!
IT'S HINAKO!
R... RINKO-CHAN, ANSWER US!
...
MOJI (SQUIRM)
TOZAKURA-SAN, I'VE GOT TO GO TO THE BATHROOM ...
HM?
I'LL BE RIGHT BACK, SO YOU WAIT THERE.
TA (TMP) TA
LEAVE IT TO ME!
OKAY!
ZU (SLICE)
BIRI (RIP)
THE MEN'S BATH-ROOM ...?
ZURU (DRAG)
BETA (SMACK)
WHAT'S... THAT NOISE...? AND IT SMELLS LIKE RUST...
E-EXCUSE ME...
IS EVERYTHING ALL RIGHT?
ZURU (DRAG)
ZAKU (SLICE)

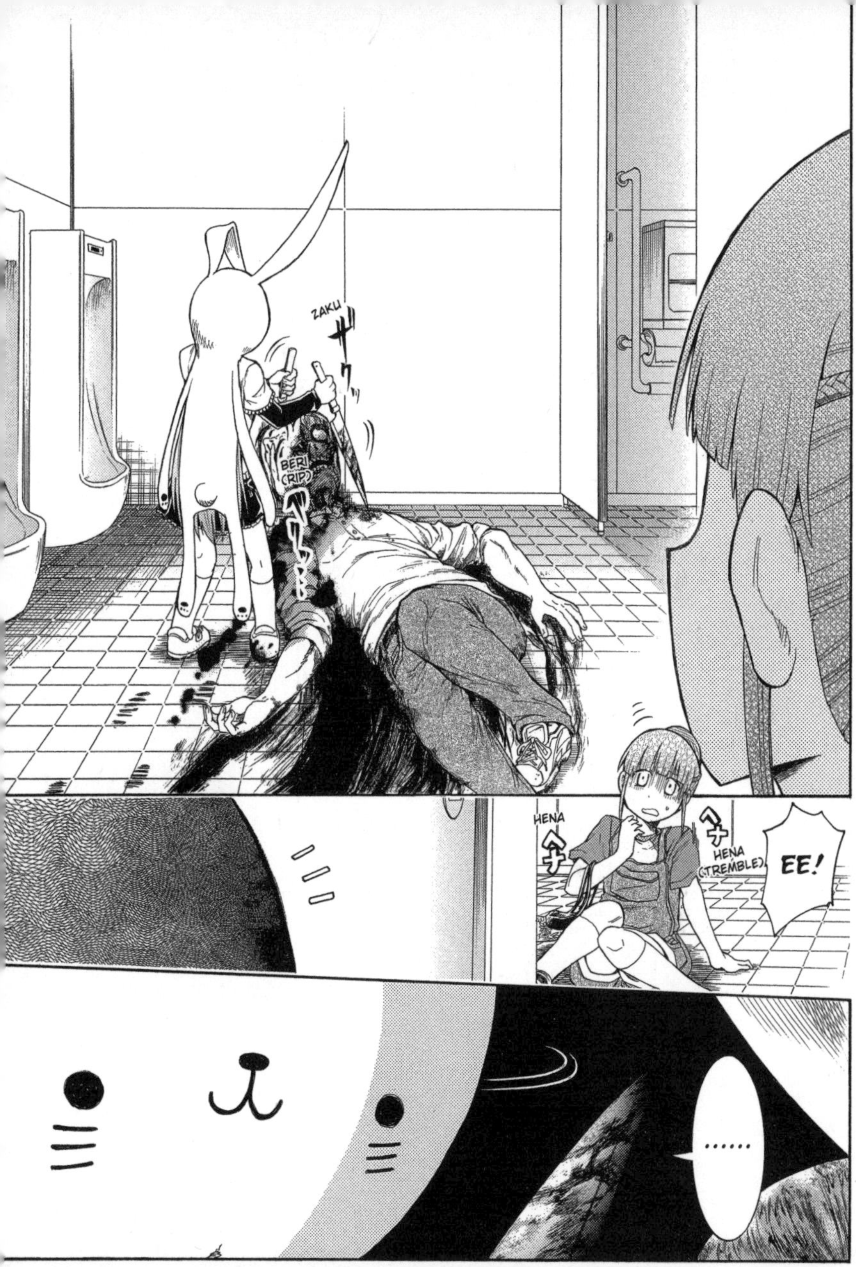
ZAKU
BERI (RIP)
EE!
HENA HENA (TREMBLE)
......

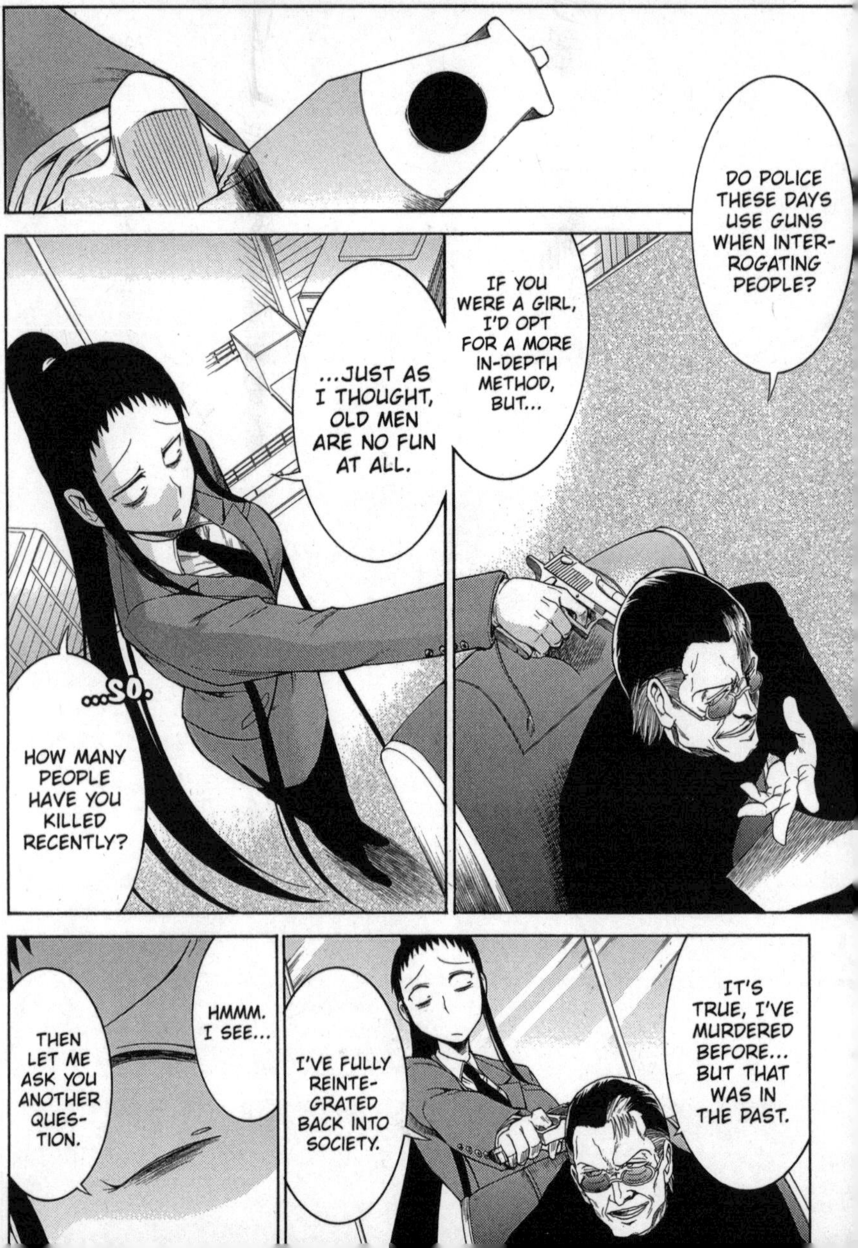
DO POLICE THESE DAYS USE GUNS WHEN INTER-ROGATING PEOPLE?
IF YOU WERE A GIRL, I'D OPT FOR A MORE IN-DEPTH METHOD, BUT...
...JUST AS I THOUGHT, OLD MEN ARE NO FUN AT ALL.
...SO.
HOW MANY PEOPLE HAVE YOU KILLED RECENTLY?
IT'S TRUE, I'VE MURDERED BEFORE... BUT THAT WAS IN THE PAST.
I'VE FULLY REINTE-GRATED BACK INTO SOCIETY.
HMMM. I SEE...
THEN LET ME ASK YOU ANOTHER QUES-TION.

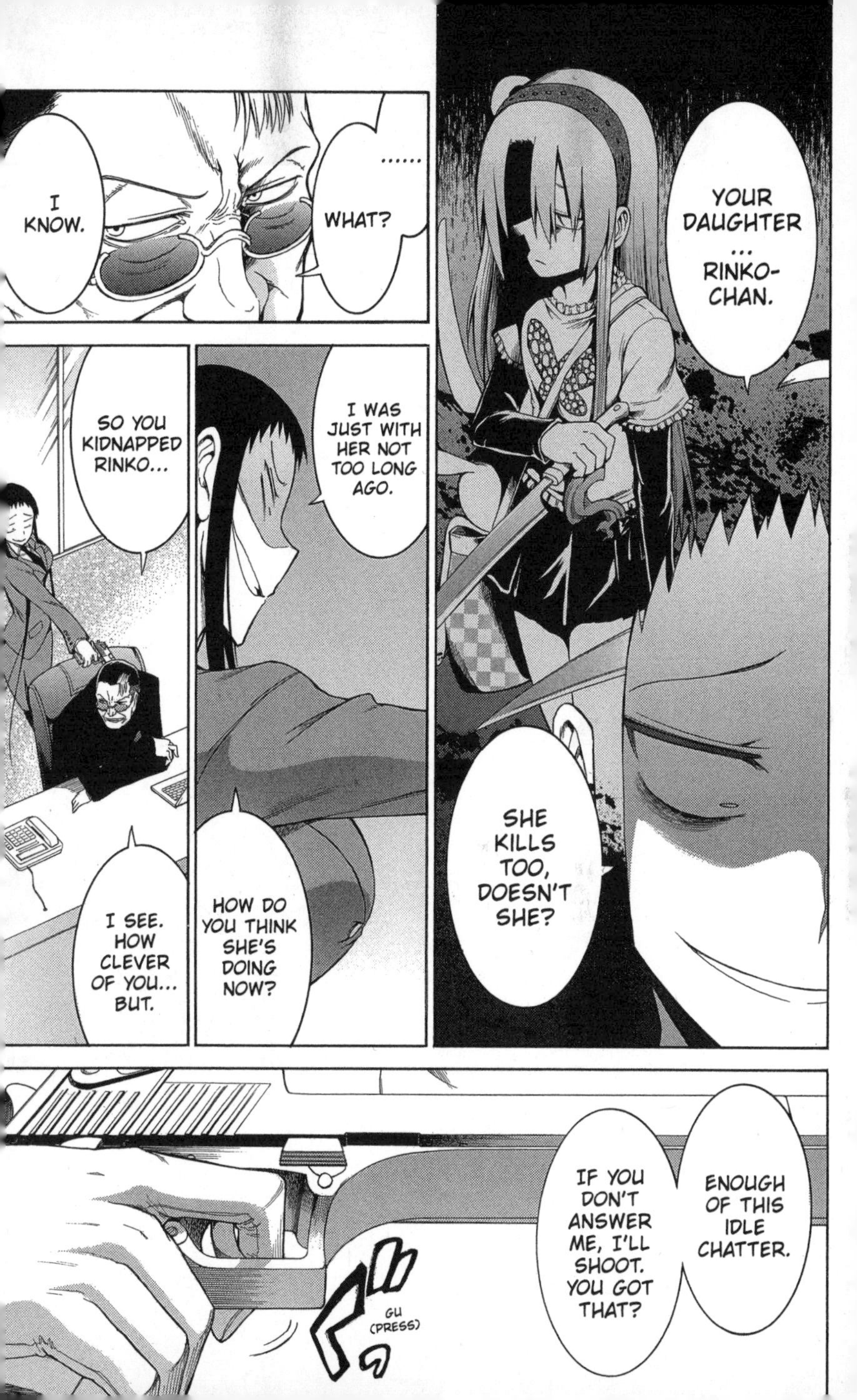
YOUR DAUGHTER ... RINKO-CHAN.
SHE KILLS TOO, DOESN'T SHE?
......
WHAT?
I KNOW.
I WAS JUST WITH HER NOT TOO LONG AGO.
HOW DO YOU THINK SHE'S DOING NOW?
SO YOU KIDNAPPED RINKO...
I SEE. HOW CLEVER OF YOU... BUT.
ENOUGH OF THIS IDLE CHATTER.
IF YOU DON'T ANSWER ME, I'LL SHOOT. YOU GOT THAT?
GU (PRESS)

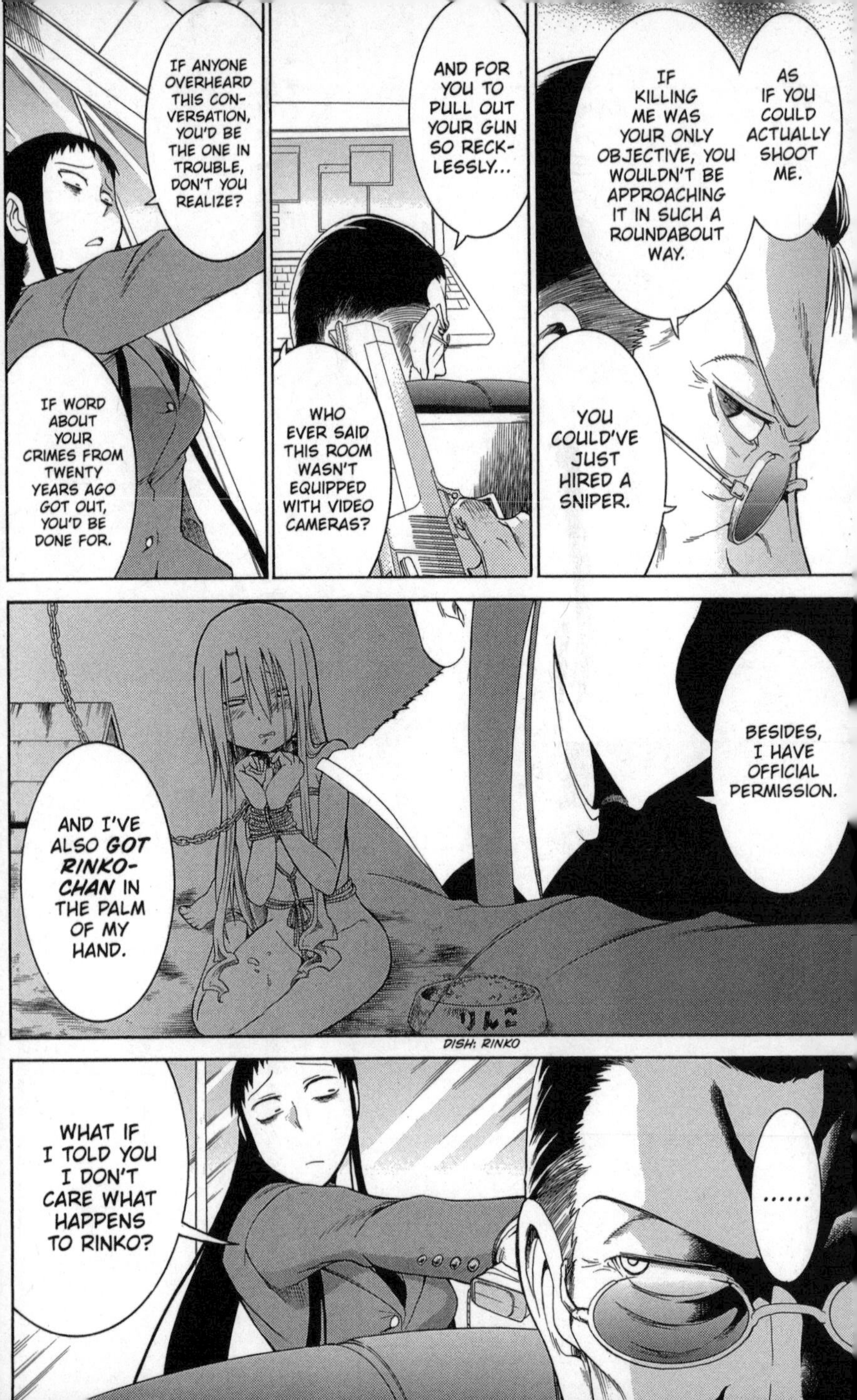
AS IF YOU COULD ACTUALLY SHOOT ME.
IF KILLING ME WAS YOUR ONLY OBJECTIVE, YOU WOULDN'T BE APPROACHING IT IN SUCH A ROUNDABOUT WAY.
YOU COULD'VE JUST HIRED A SNIPER.
AND FOR YOU TO PULL OUT YOUR GUN SO RECKLESSLY...
WHO EVER SAID THIS ROOM WASN'T EQUIPPED WITH VIDEO CAMERAS?
IF ANYONE OVERHEARD THIS CONVERSATION, YOU'D BE THE ONE IN TROUBLE, DON'T YOU REALIZE?
IF WORD ABOUT YOUR CRIMES FROM TWENTY YEARS AGO GOT OUT, YOU'D BE DONE FOR.
BESIDES, I HAVE OFFICIAL PERMISSION.
AND I'VE ALSO ***GOT RINKO-CHAN*** IN THE PALM OF MY HAND.
DISH: RINKO
......
WHAT IF I TOLD YOU I DON'T CARE WHAT HAPPENS TO RINKO?

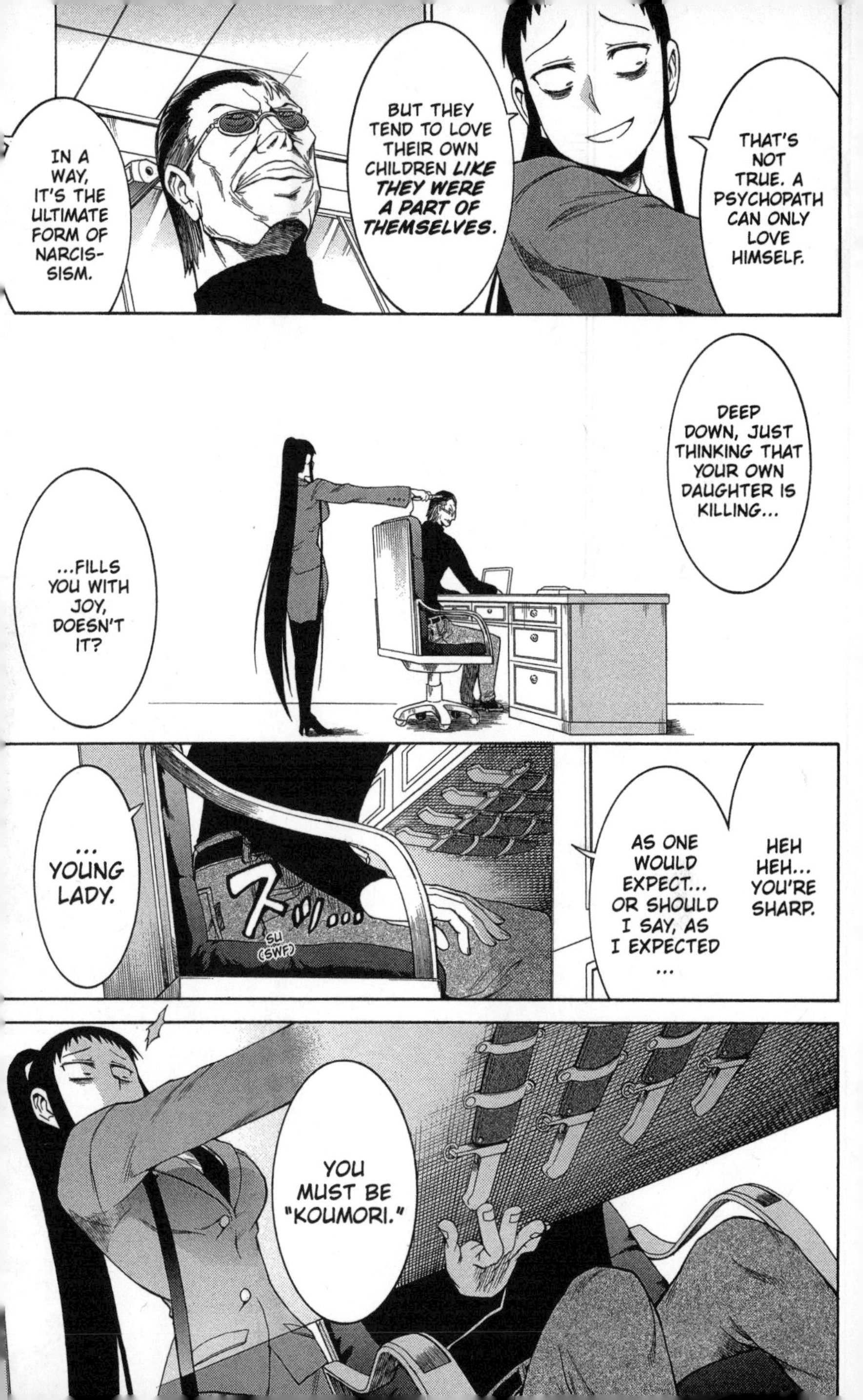
THAT'S NOT TRUE. A PSYCHOPATH CAN ONLY LOVE HIMSELF.
BUT THEY TEND TO LOVE THEIR OWN CHILDREN ***LIKE THEY WERE A PART OF THEMSELVES.***
IN A WAY, IT'S THE ULTIMATE FORM OF NARCIS-SISM.
DEEP DOWN, JUST THINKING THAT YOUR OWN DAUGHTER IS KILLING...
...FILLS YOU WITH JOY, DOESN'T IT?
HEH HEH... YOU'RE SHARP.
AS ONE WOULD EXPECT... OR SHOULD I SAY, AS I EXPECTED ...
... YOUNG LADY.
SU (SWF)
YOU MUST BE "KOUMORI."

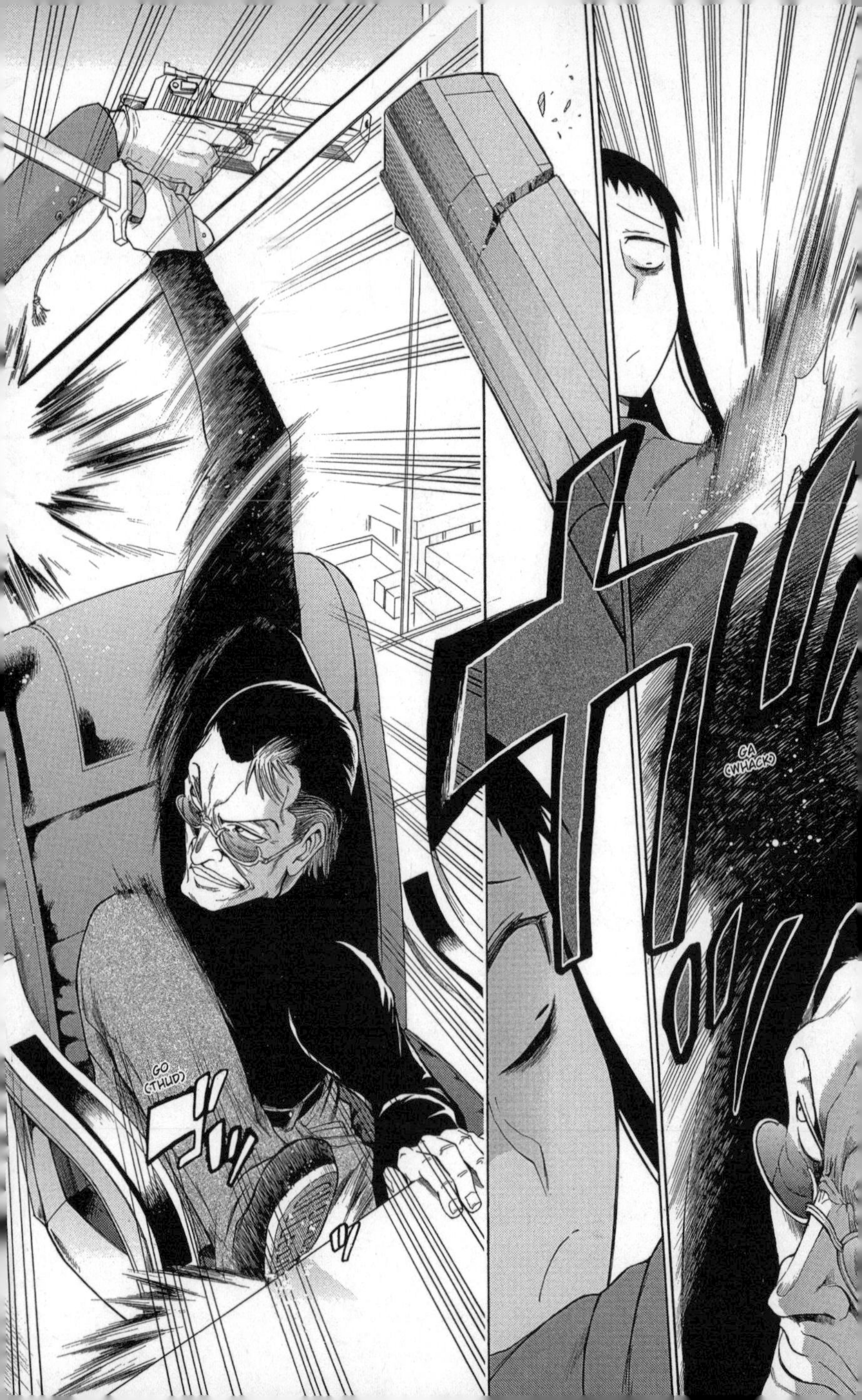
GA (WHACK)
GO (THUD)

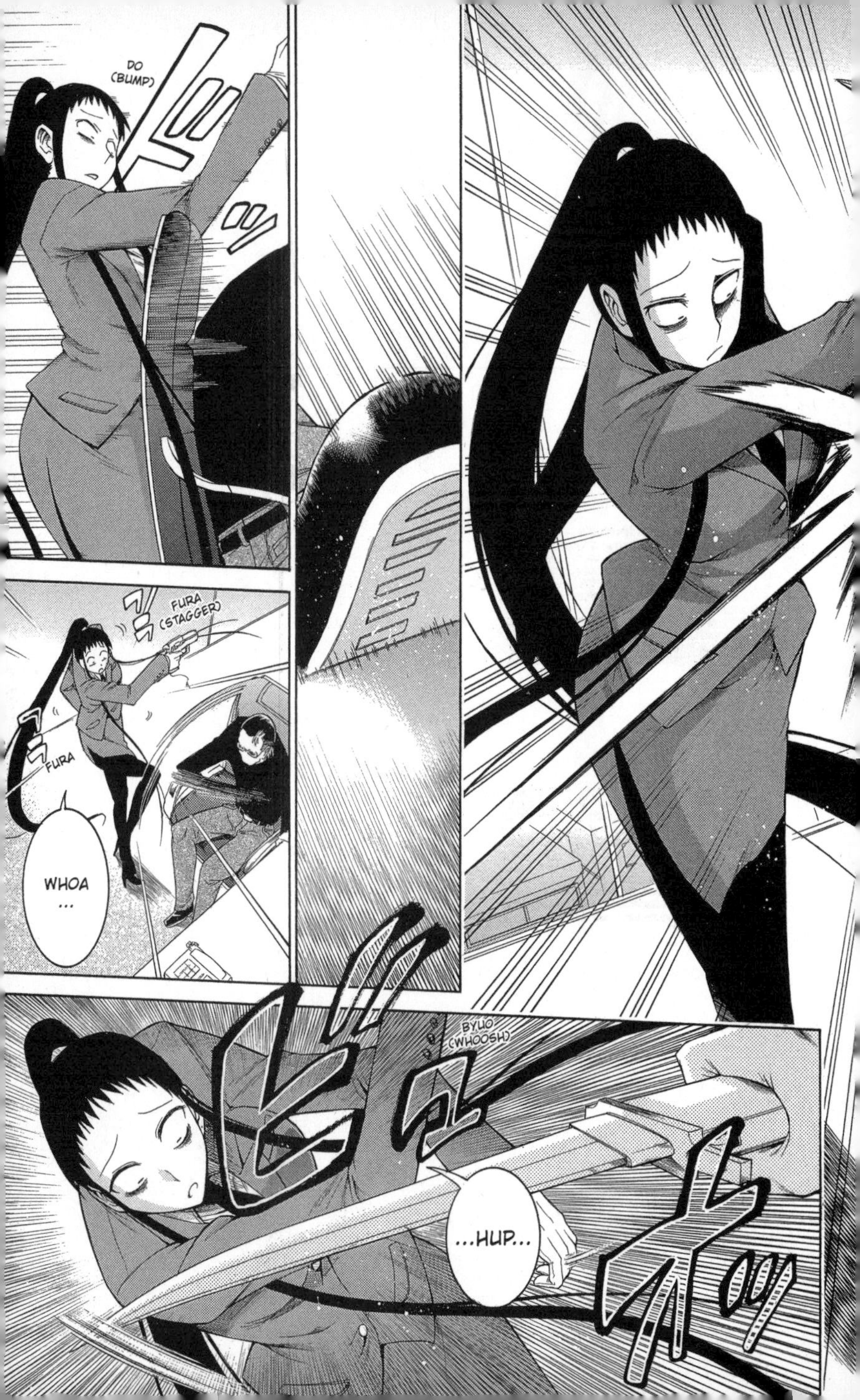
DO (BUMP)
FURA (STAGGER)
FURA
WHOA ...
BYUO (WHOOSH)
...HUP...

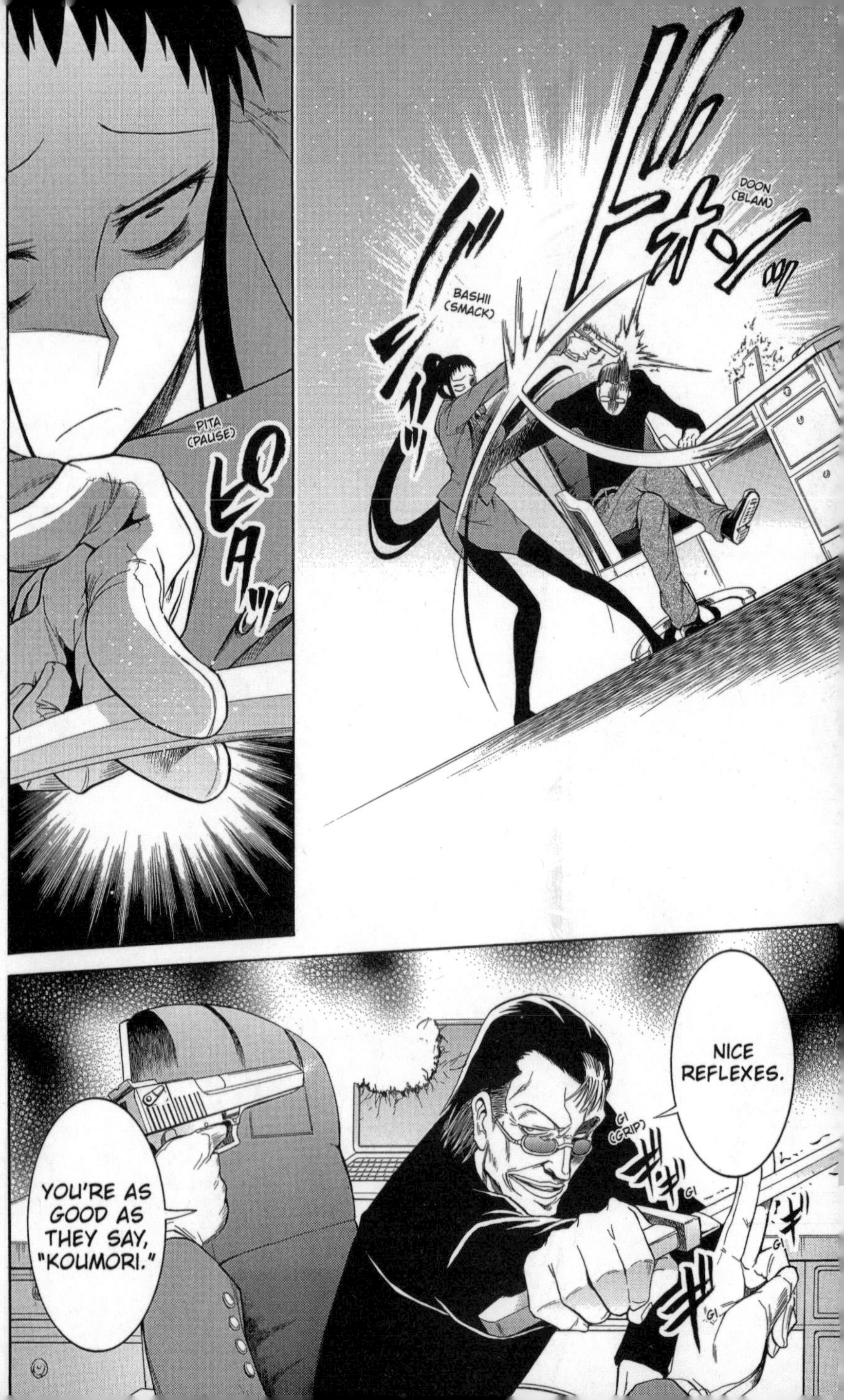
DOON (BLAM)
BASHII (SMACK)
PITA (PAUSE)
NICE REFLEXES.
GI (GRIP)
GI
GI
GI
YOU'RE AS GOOD AS THEY SAY, "KOUMORI."

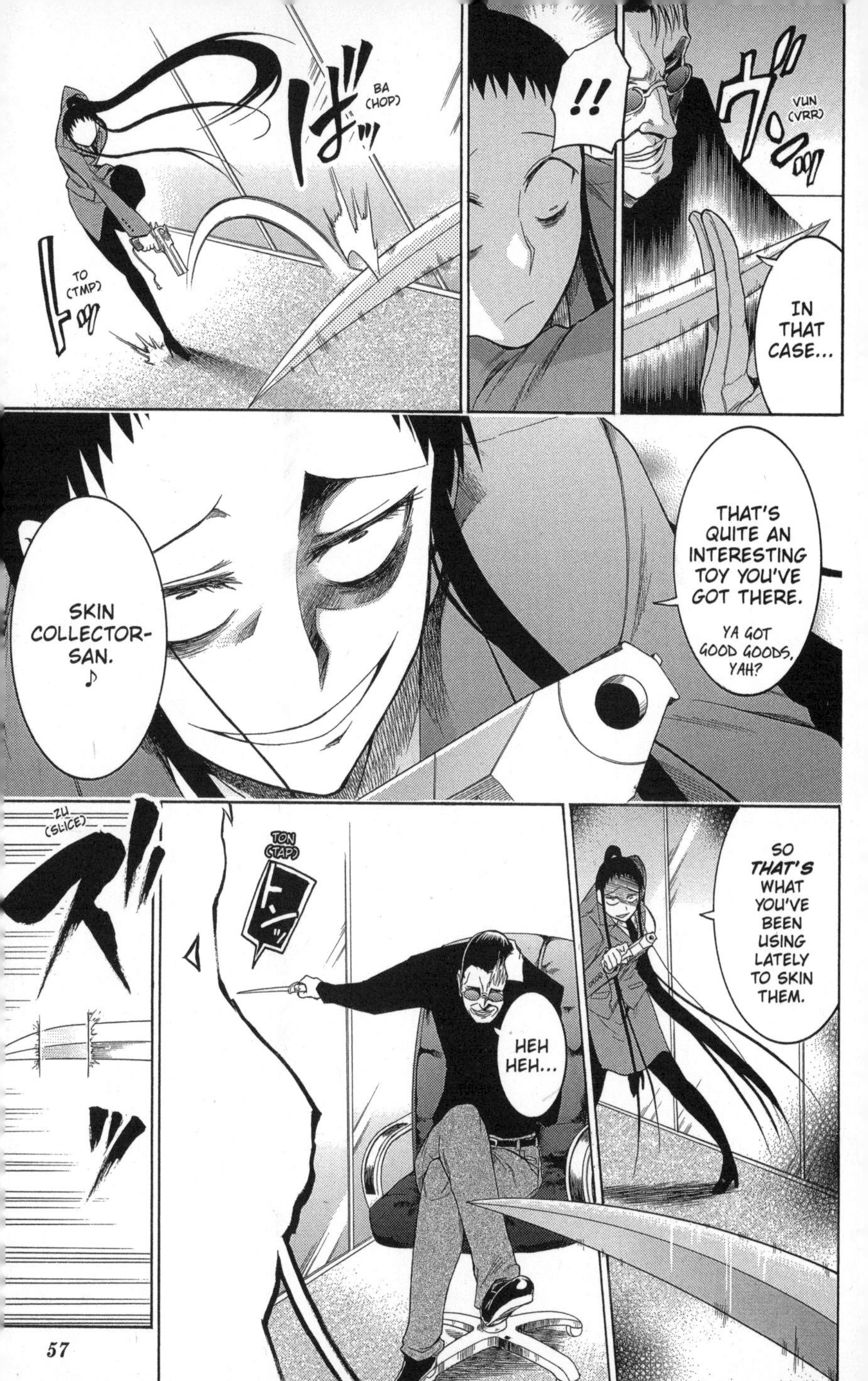
VUN (VRR)
IN THAT CASE...
!!
BA (HOP)
TO (TMP)
THAT'S QUITE AN INTERESTING TOY YOU'VE GOT THERE.
YA GOT GOOD GOODS, YAH?
SKIN COLLECTOR-SAN. ♪
SO *THAT'S* WHAT YOU'VE BEEN USING LATELY TO SKIN THEM.
HEH HEH...
TON (TAP)
ZU (SLICE)

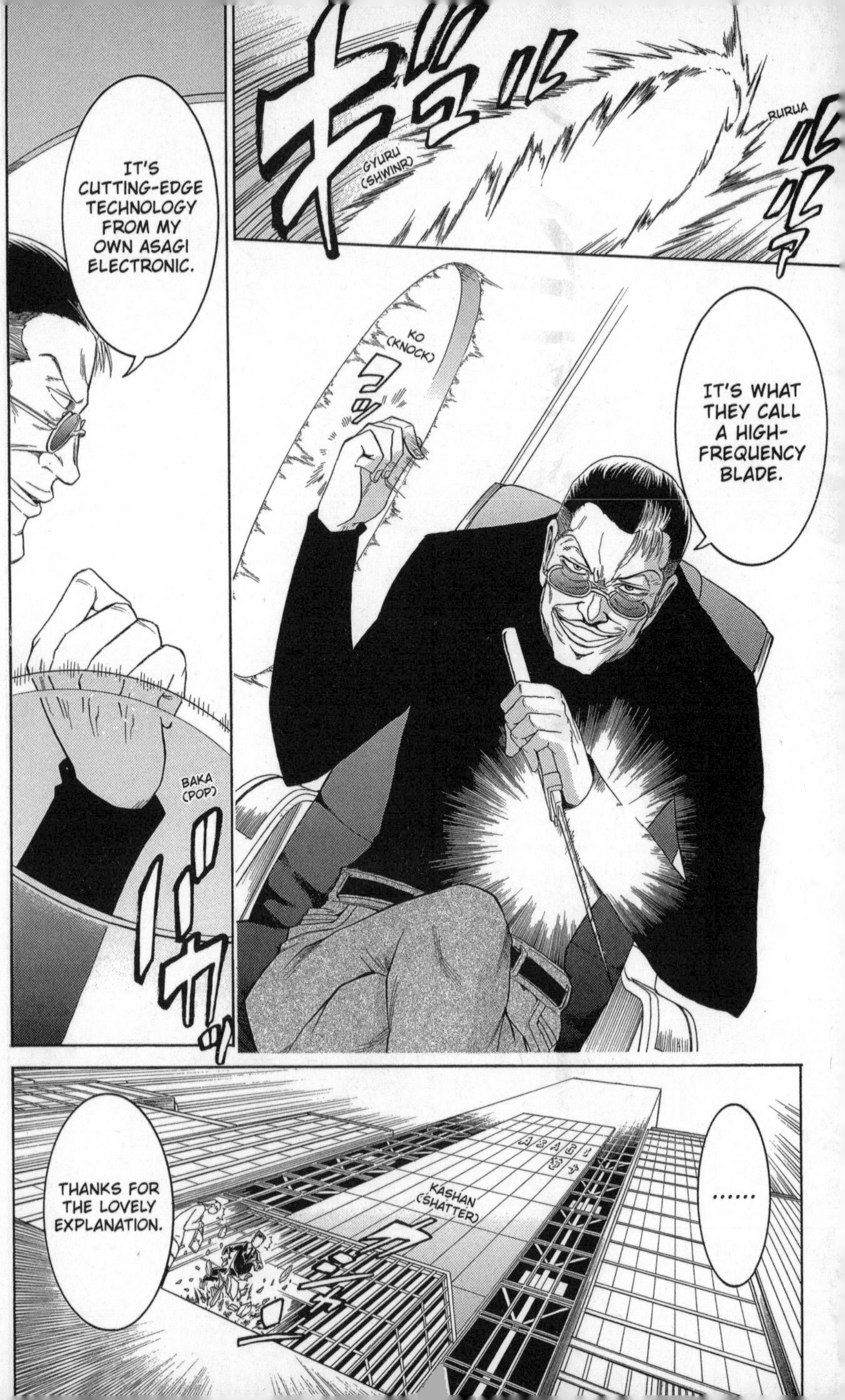
RURUA
GYURU (SHWINR)
KO (KNOCK)
IT'S WHAT THEY CALL A HIGH-FREQUENCY BLADE.
IT'S CUTTING-EDGE TECHNOLOGY FROM MY OWN ASAGI ELECTRONIC.
BAKA (POP)
......
ASAGI
KASHAN (SHATTER)
THANKS FOR THE LOVELY EXPLANATION.

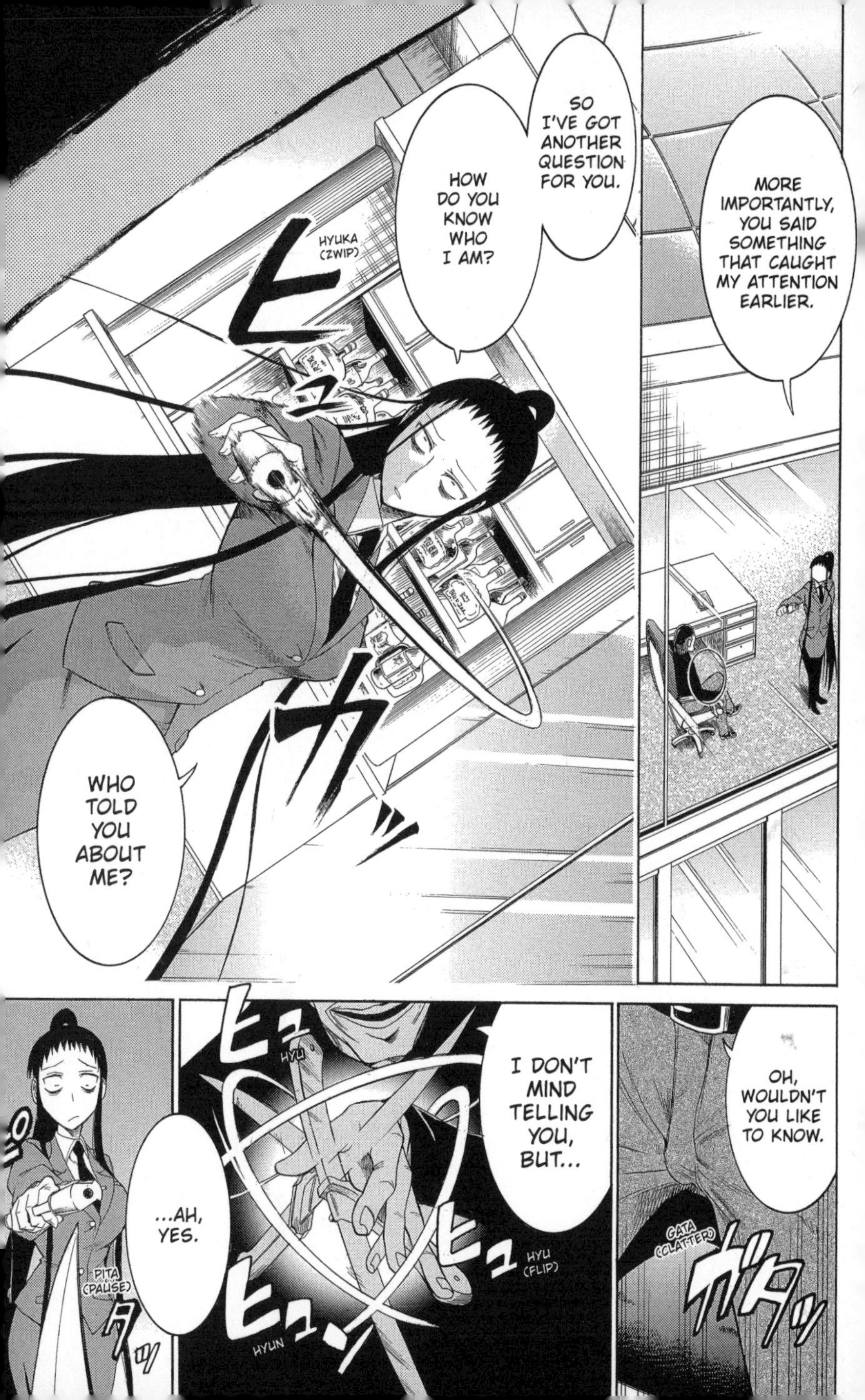
MORE IMPORTANTLY, YOU SAID SOMETHING THAT CAUGHT MY ATTENTION EARLIER.
SO I'VE GOT ANOTHER QUESTION FOR YOU.
HOW DO YOU KNOW WHO I AM?
HYUKA (ZWIP)
WHO TOLD YOU ABOUT ME?
OH, WOULDN'T YOU LIKE TO KNOW.
GATA (CLATTER)
I DON'T MIND TELLING YOU, BUT...
HYU
HYU (FLIP)
HYUN
...AH, YES.
PITA (PAUSE)

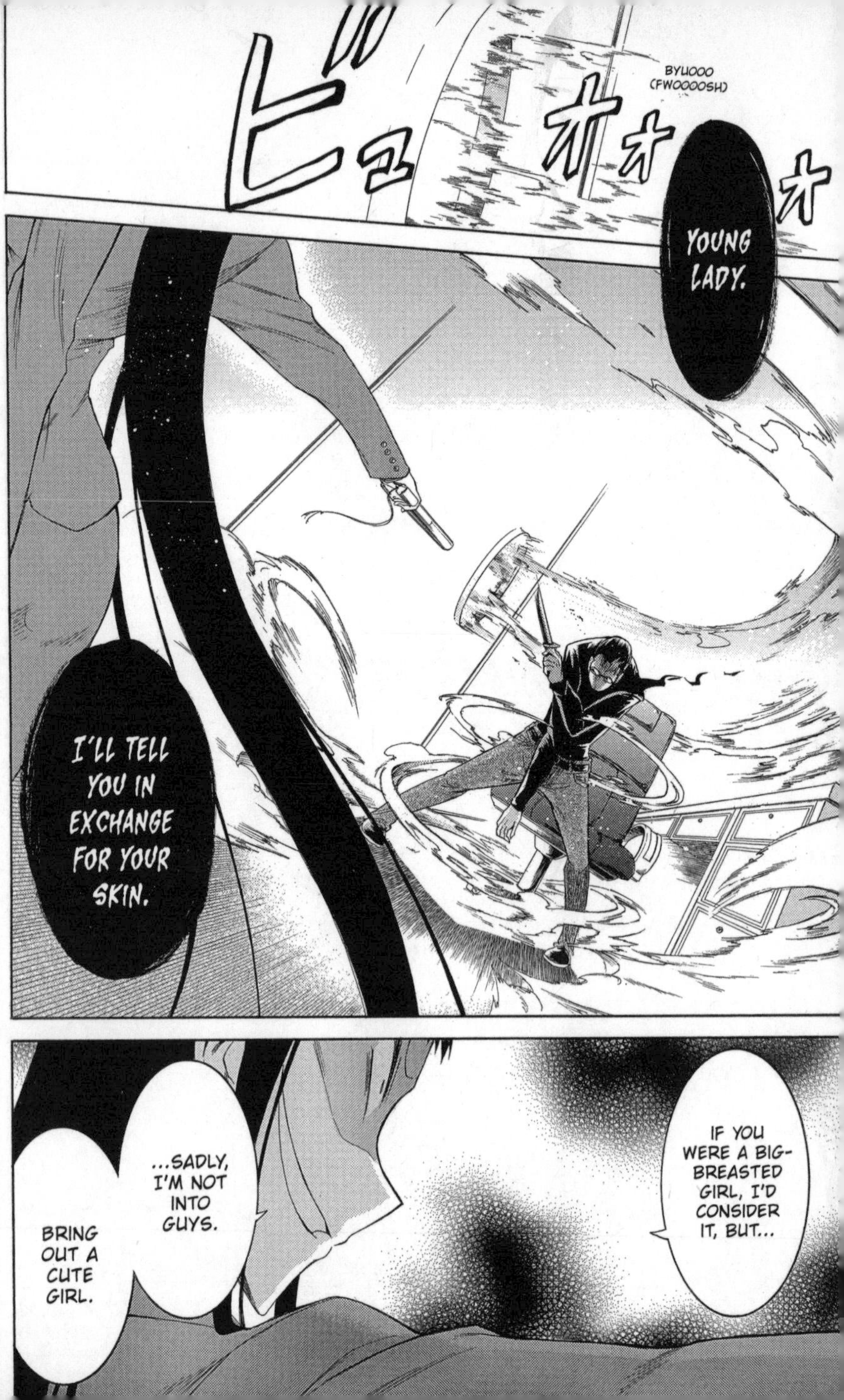
ビュオオオ
BYUOOO (FWOOOOSH)
YOUNG LADY.
I'LL TELL YOU IN EXCHANGE FOR YOUR SKIN.
IF YOU WERE A BIG-BREASTED GIRL, I'D CONSIDER IT, BUT...
...SADLY, I'M NOT INTO GUYS.
BRING OUT A CUTE GIRL.

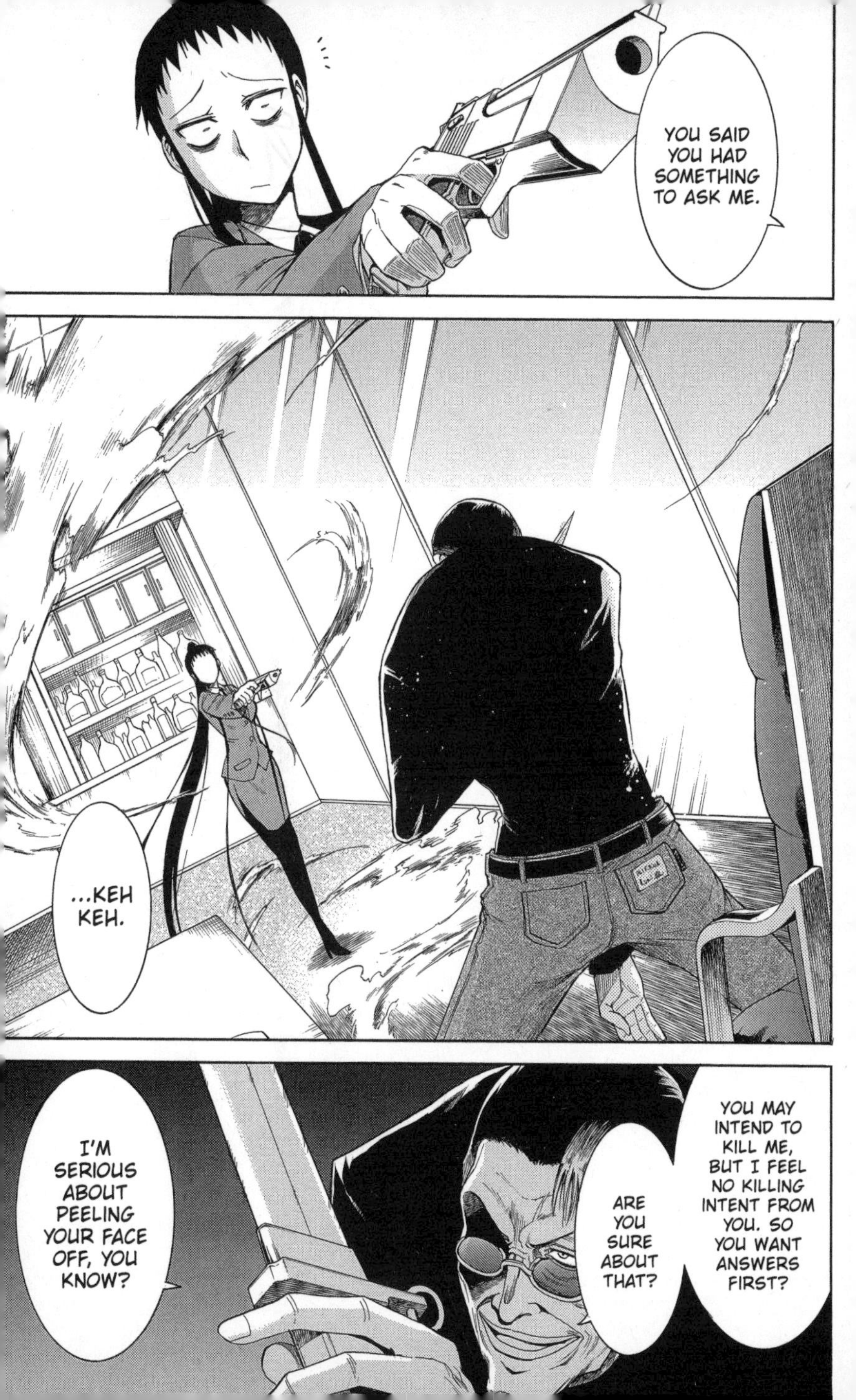
YOU SAID YOU HAD SOMETHING TO ASK ME.
...KEH KEH.
YOU MAY INTEND TO KILL ME, BUT I FEEL NO KILLING INTENT FROM YOU. SO YOU WANT ANSWERS FIRST?
ARE YOU SURE ABOUT THAT?
I'M SERIOUS ABOUT PEELING YOUR FACE OFF, YOU KNOW?

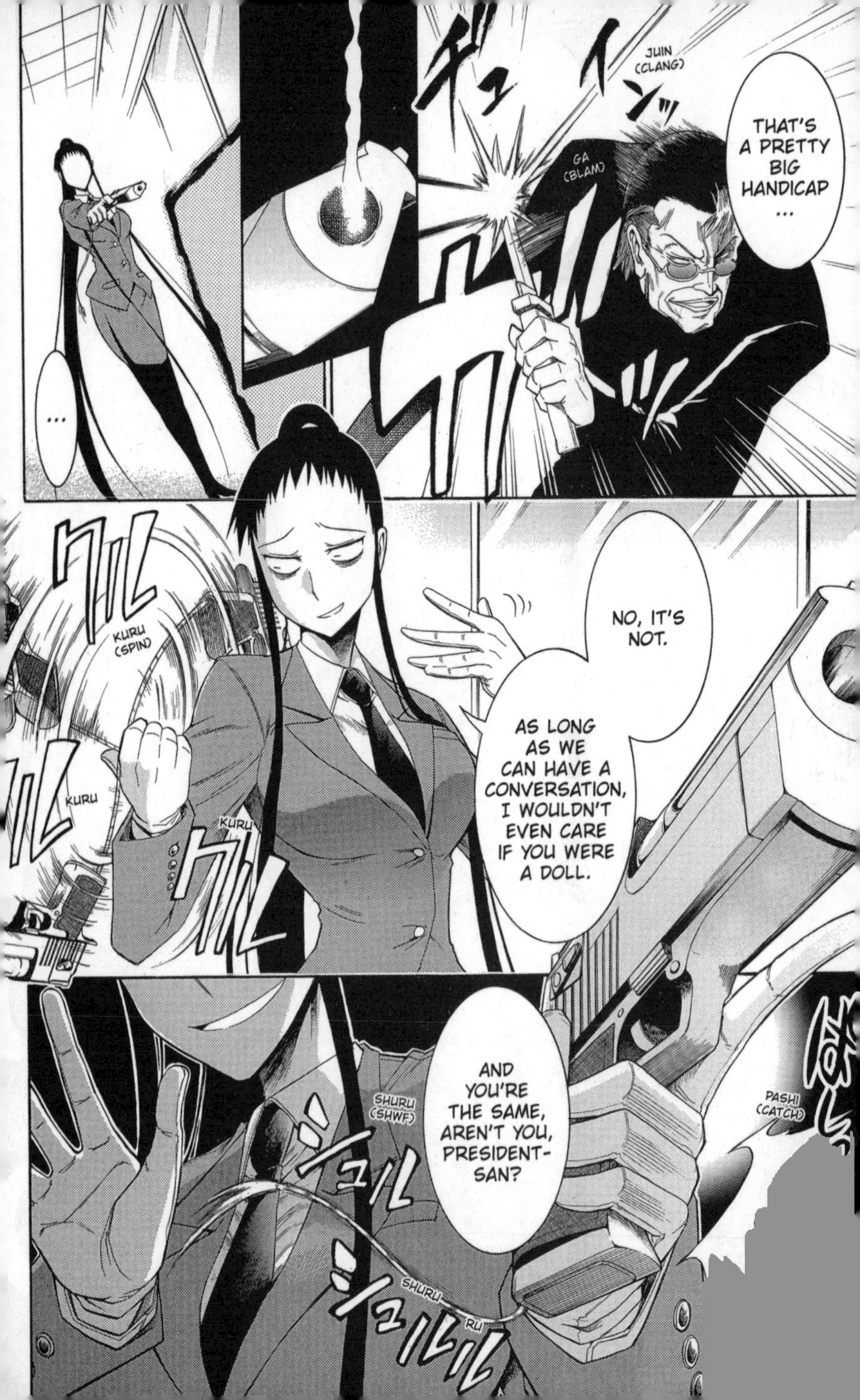
JUIN (CLANG)
THAT'S A PRETTY BIG HANDICAP ...
GA (BLAM)
...
NO, IT'S NOT.
AS LONG AS WE CAN HAVE A CONVERSATION, I WOULDN'T EVEN CARE IF YOU WERE A DOLL.
KURU (SPIN)
KURU
KURU
PASHI (CATCH)
AND YOU'RE THE SAME, AREN'T YOU, PRESIDENT-SAN?
SHURU (SHWF)
SHURU RU

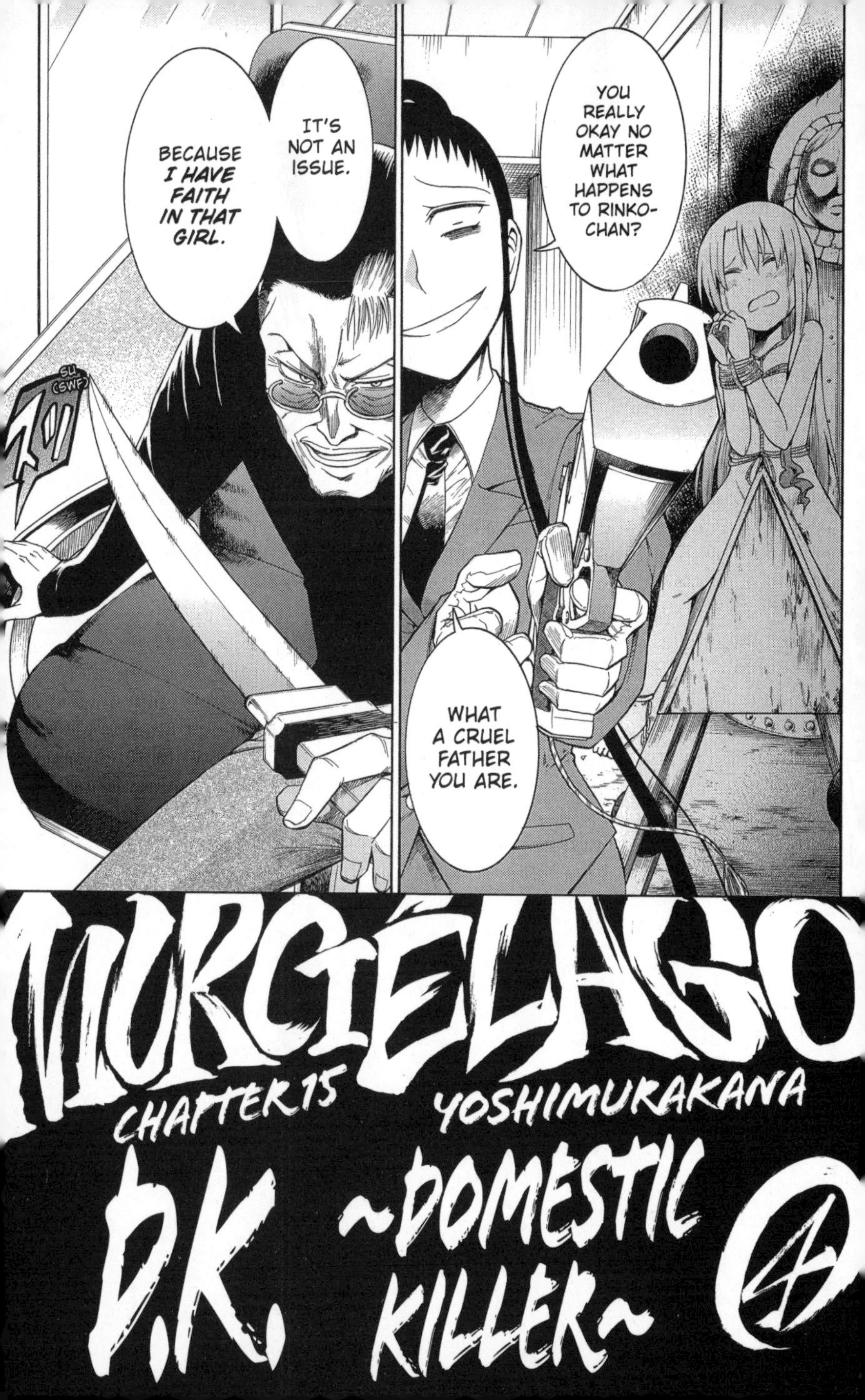
YOU REALLY OKAY NO MATTER WHAT HAPPENS TO RINKO-CHAN?
WHAT A CRUEL FATHER YOU ARE.
IT'S NOT AN ISSUE.
BECAUSE *I HAVE FAITH* IN THAT GIRL.
SU (SWF)

MURCIÉLAGO

CHAPTER 15 YOSHIMURAKANA

D.K. ~DOMESTIC KILLER~ ④

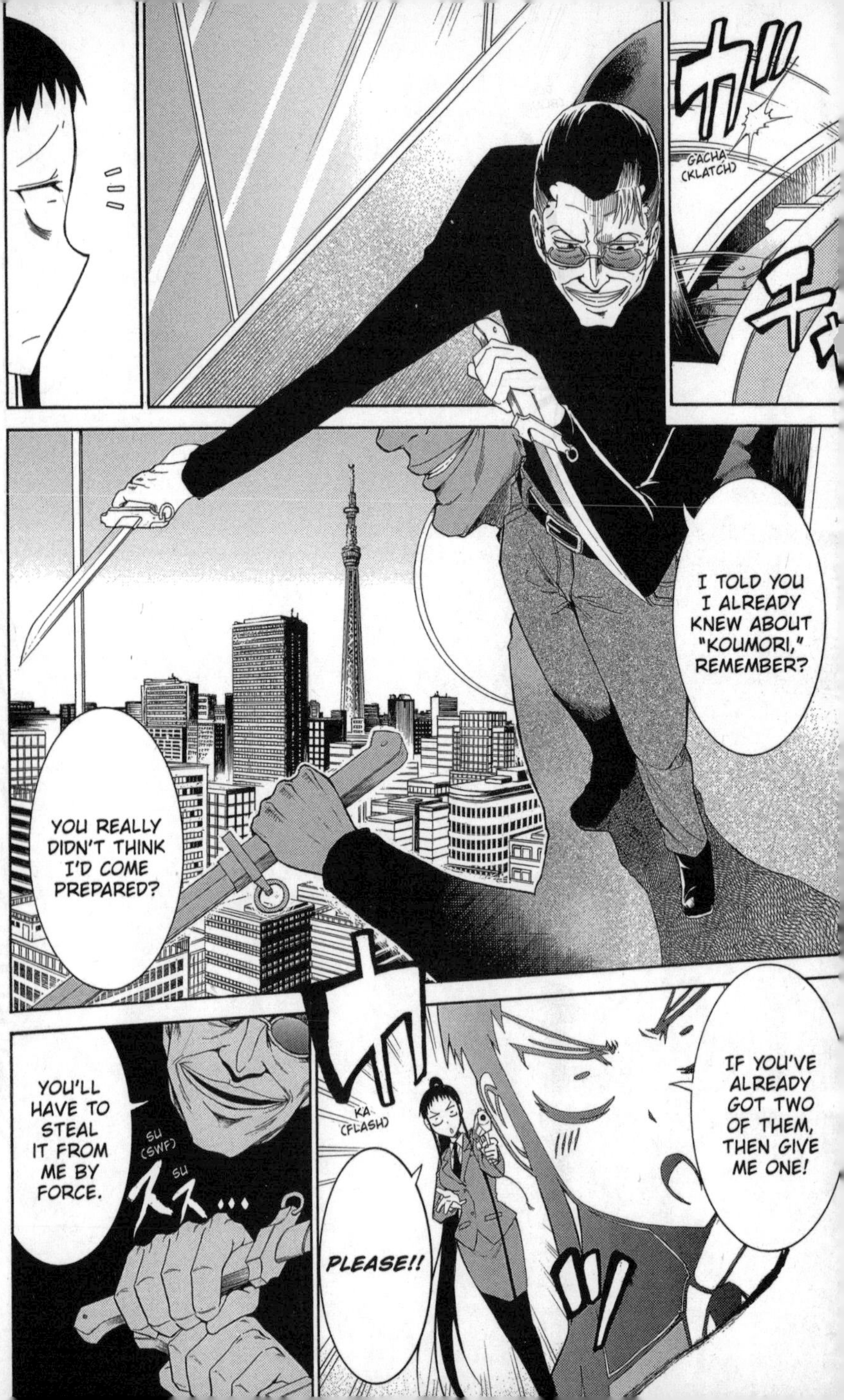
GACHA (KLATCH)
I TOLD YOU I ALREADY KNEW ABOUT "KOUMORI," REMEMBER?
YOU REALLY DIDN'T THINK I'D COME PREPARED?
IF YOU'VE ALREADY GOT TWO OF THEM, THEN GIVE ME ONE!
KA (FLASH)
PLEASE!!
YOU'LL HAVE TO STEAL IT FROM ME BY FORCE.
SU (SWF)
SU

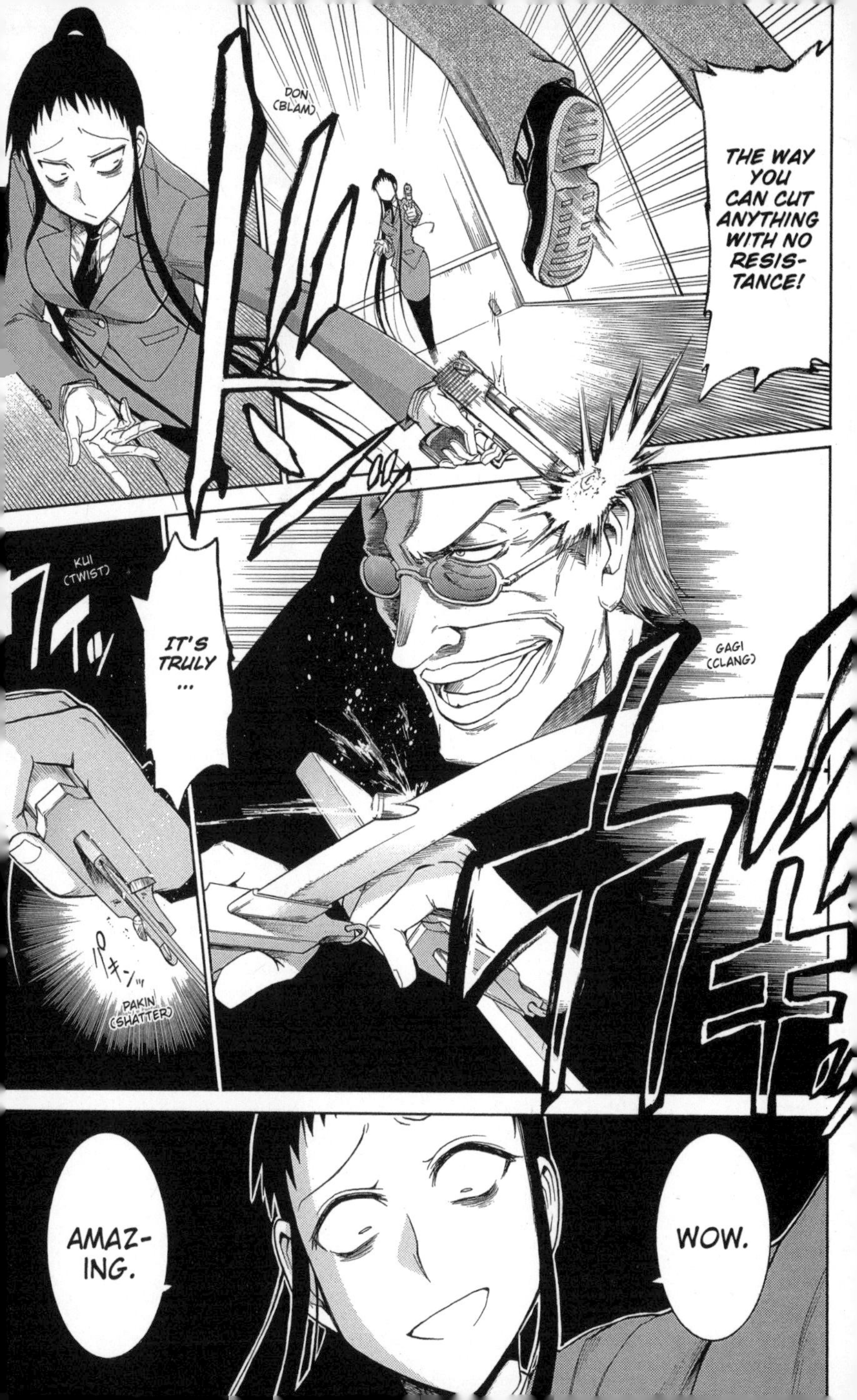
THE WAY YOU CAN CUT ANYTHING WITH NO RESISTANCE!
DON (BLAM)
GAGI (CLANG)
IT'S TRULY ...
KUI (TWIST)
PAKIN (SHATTER)
WOW.
AMAZ-ING.

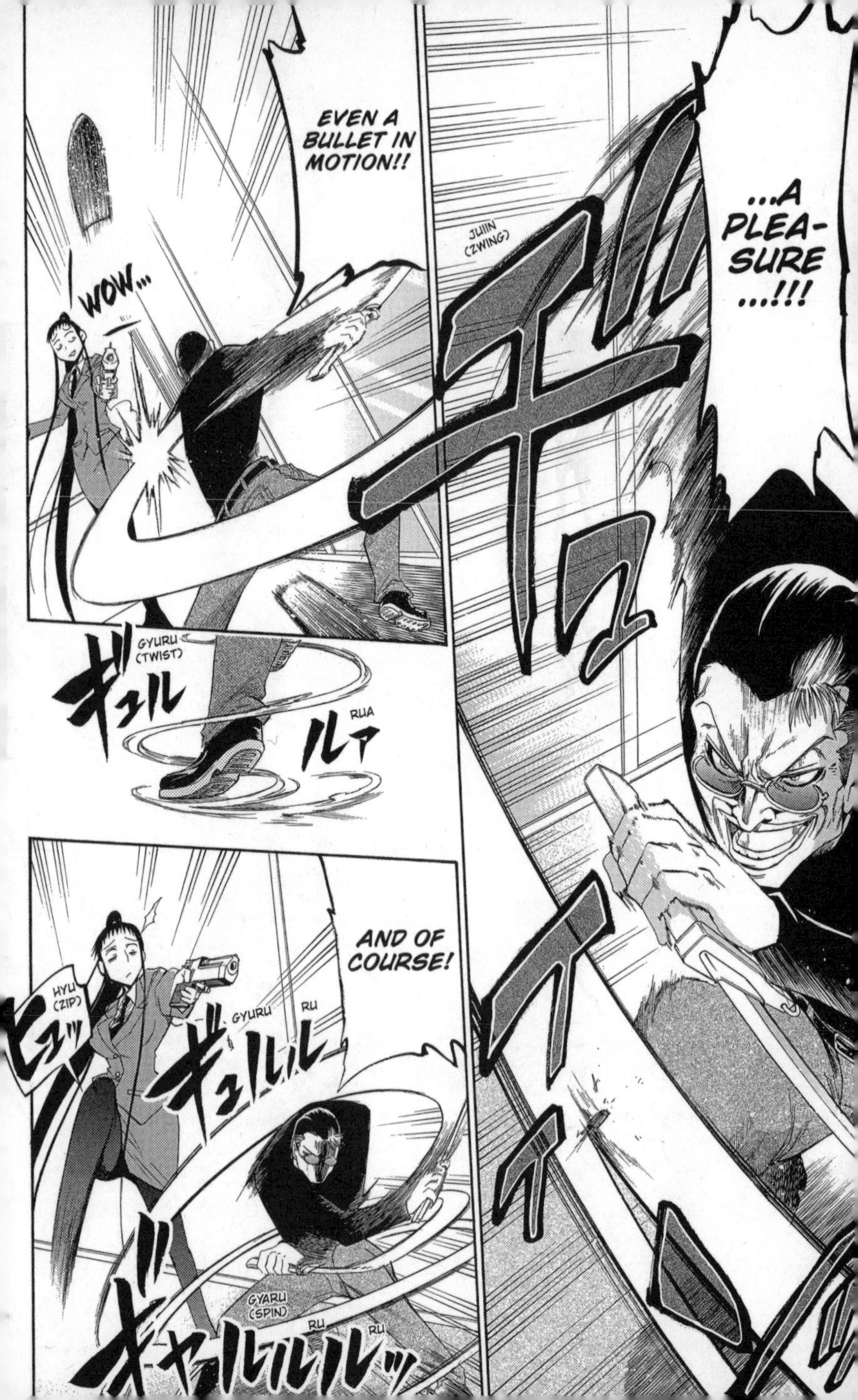

...A PLEA-SURE ...!!!
JUIIN (ZWING)
EVEN A BULLET IN MOTION!!
WOW...
GYURU (TWIST)
ギュル
RUA
ルァ
AND OF COURSE!
HYU (ZIP)
ヒュッ
GYURU RU
ギュルルル
GYARU (SPIN) RU RU
ギャルルルルッ

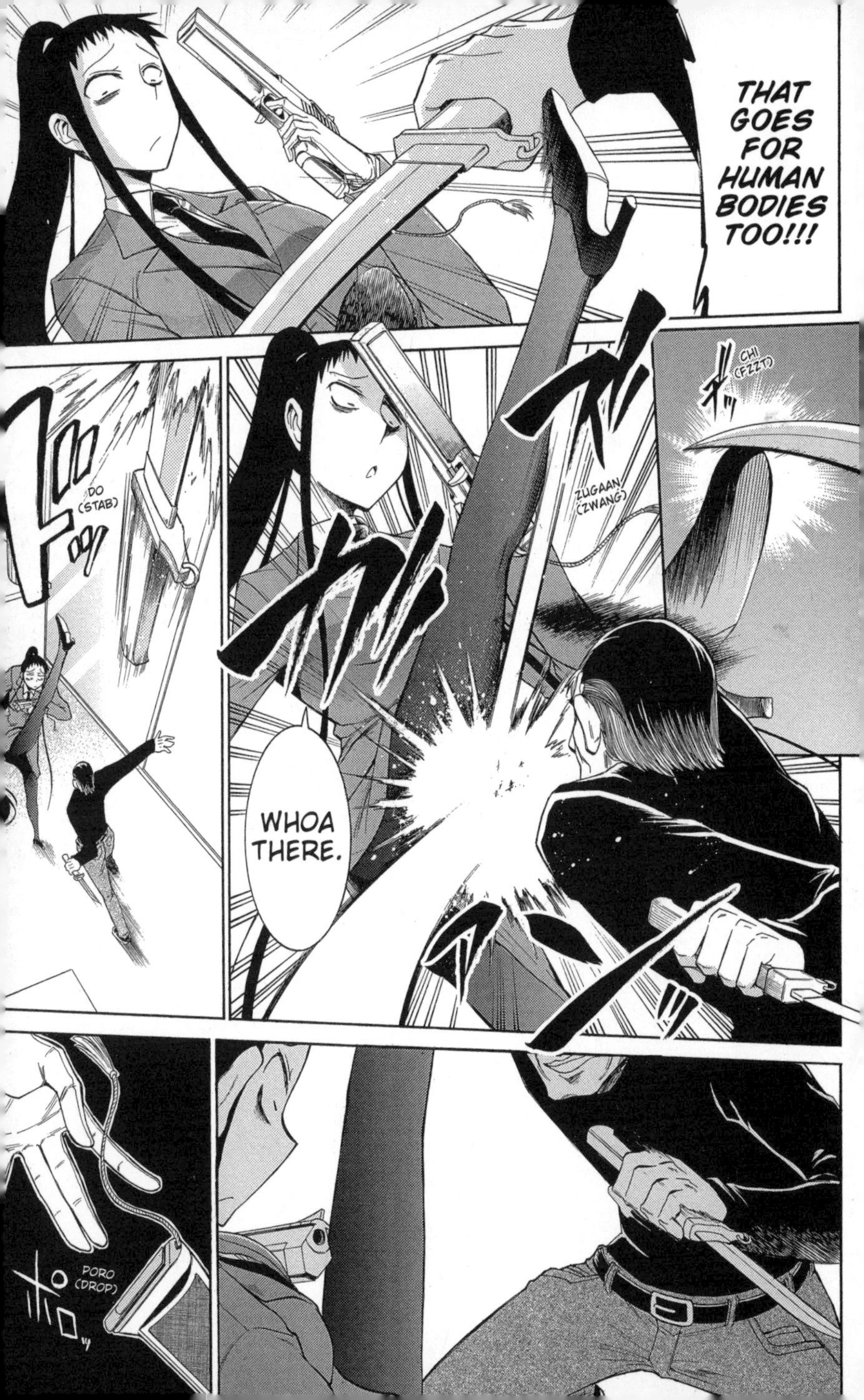
THAT GOES FOR HUMAN BODIES TOO!!!
CHI (FZZT)
ZUGAAN (ZWANG)
WHOA THERE.
DO (STAB)
PORO (DROP)

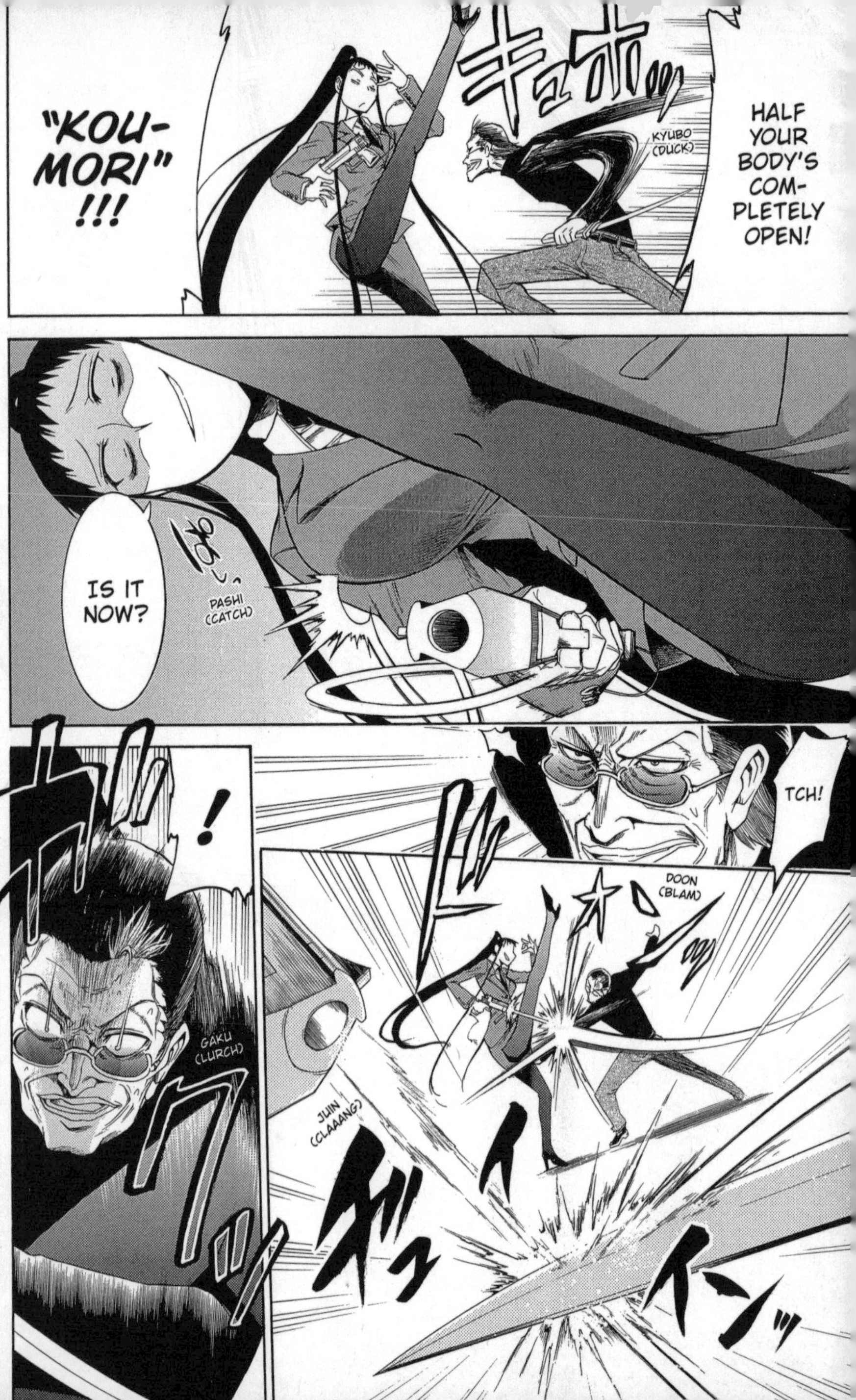
HALF YOUR BODY'S COM-PLETELY OPEN!
KYUBO (DUCK)
"KOU-MORI" !!!
PASHI (CATCH)
IS IT NOW?
TCH!
DOON (BLAM)
JUIN (CLAAANG)
!
GAKU (LURCH)

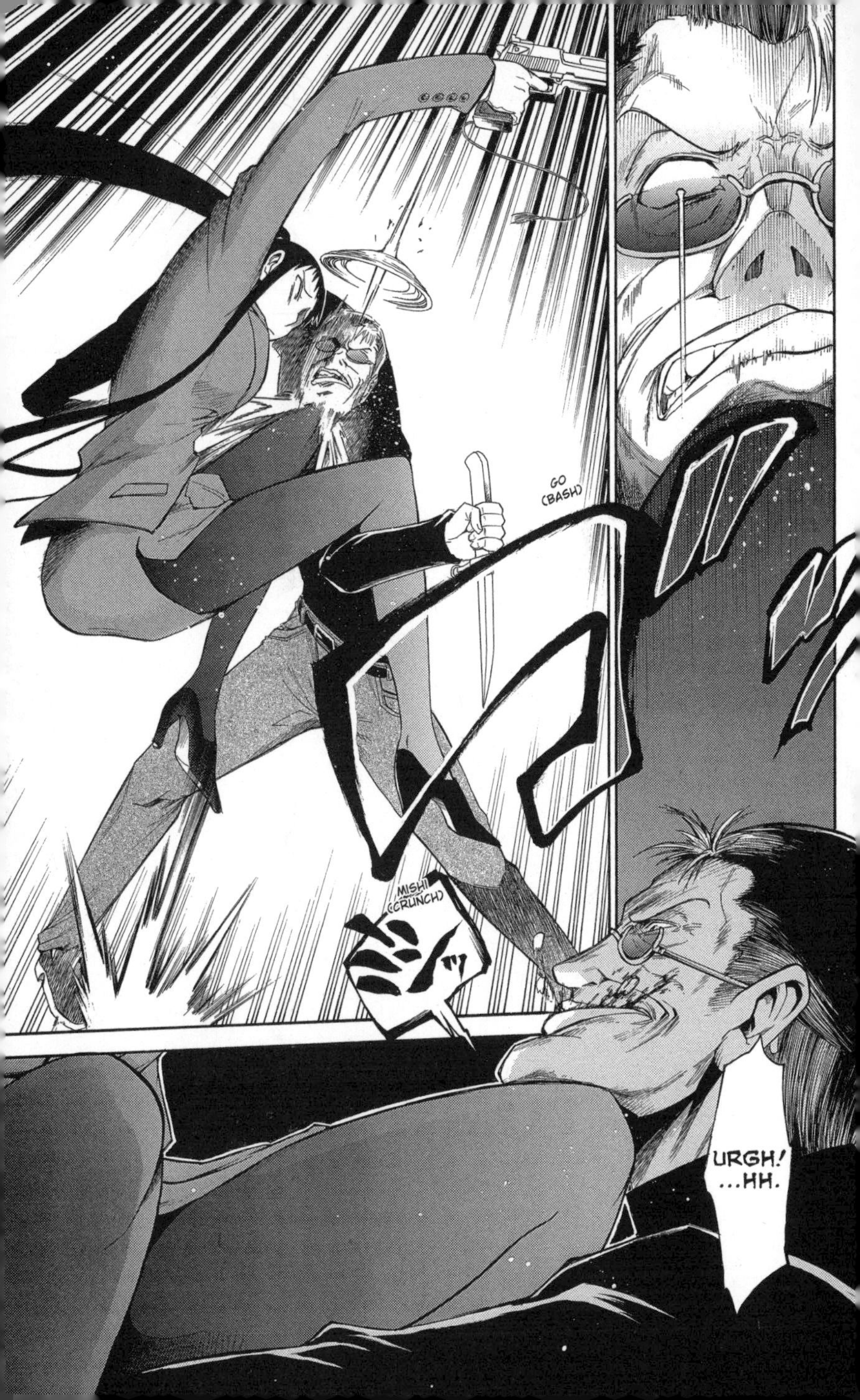
GO (BASH)
MISHI (CRUNCH)
URGH! ...HH.

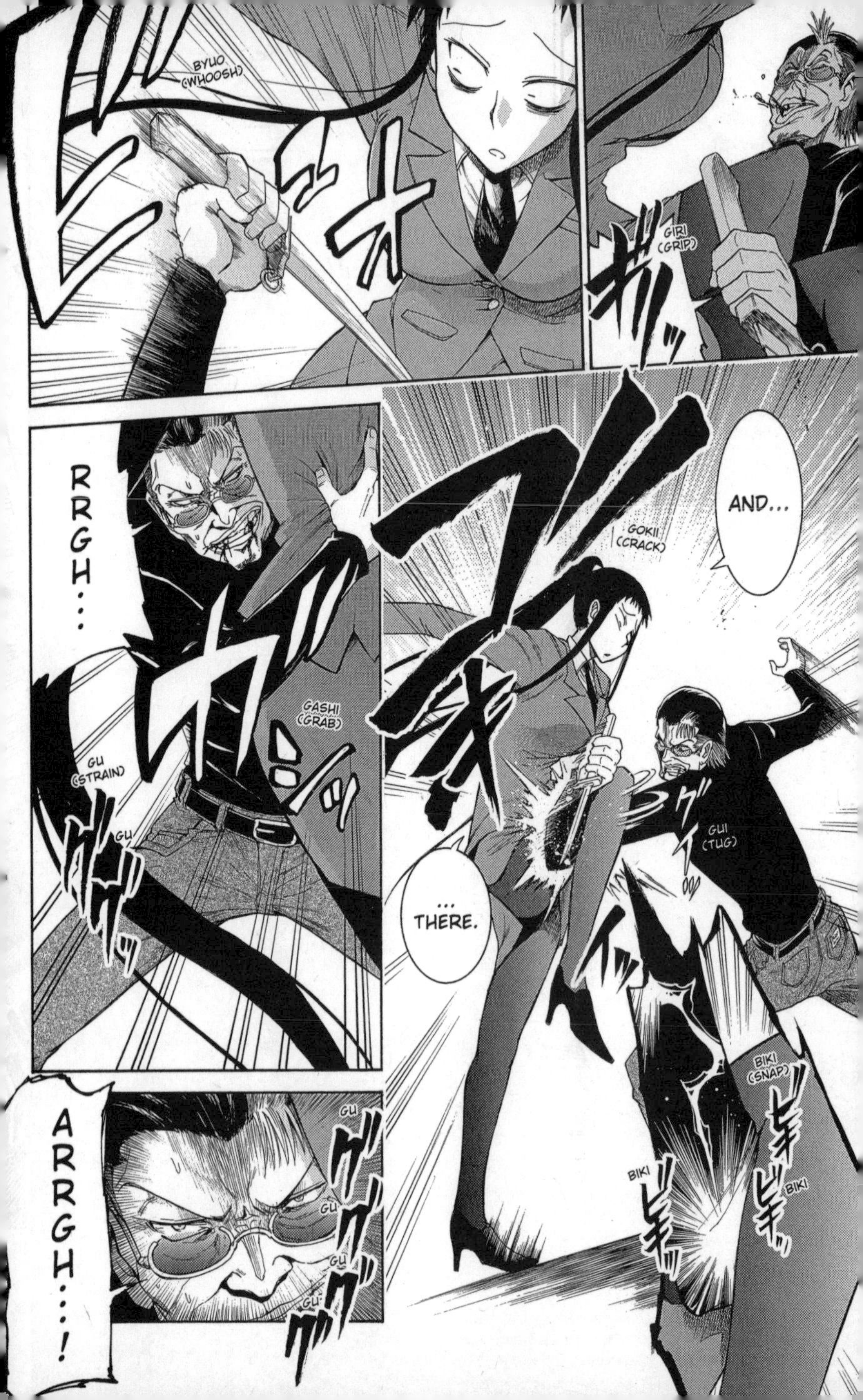
GIRI (GRIP)
BYUO (WHOOSH)
AND...
GOKI (CRACK)
GUI (TUG)
...THERE.
BIKI (SNAP)
BIKI
BIKI
RRGH...
GASHI (GRAB)
GU (STRAIN)
GU
ARRGH...!
GU
GU
GU
GU

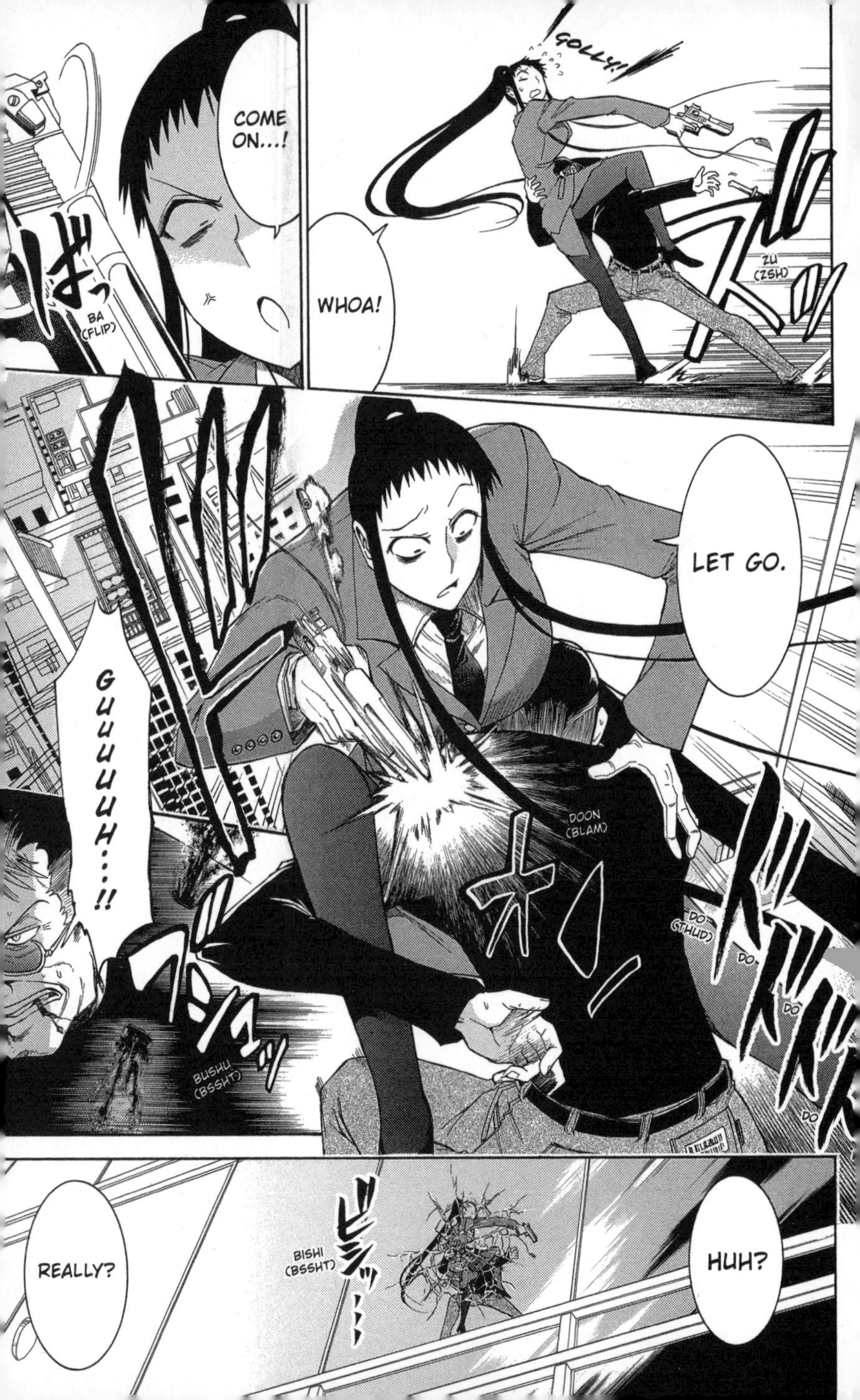
GOLLY!!
ZU (ZSH)
WHOA!
COME ON...!
BA (FLIP)
LET GO.
DOON (BLAM)
DO (THUD)
DO
DO
DO
GUUUUUH...!!
BUSHU (BSSHT)
HUH?
BISHI (BSSHT)
REALLY?

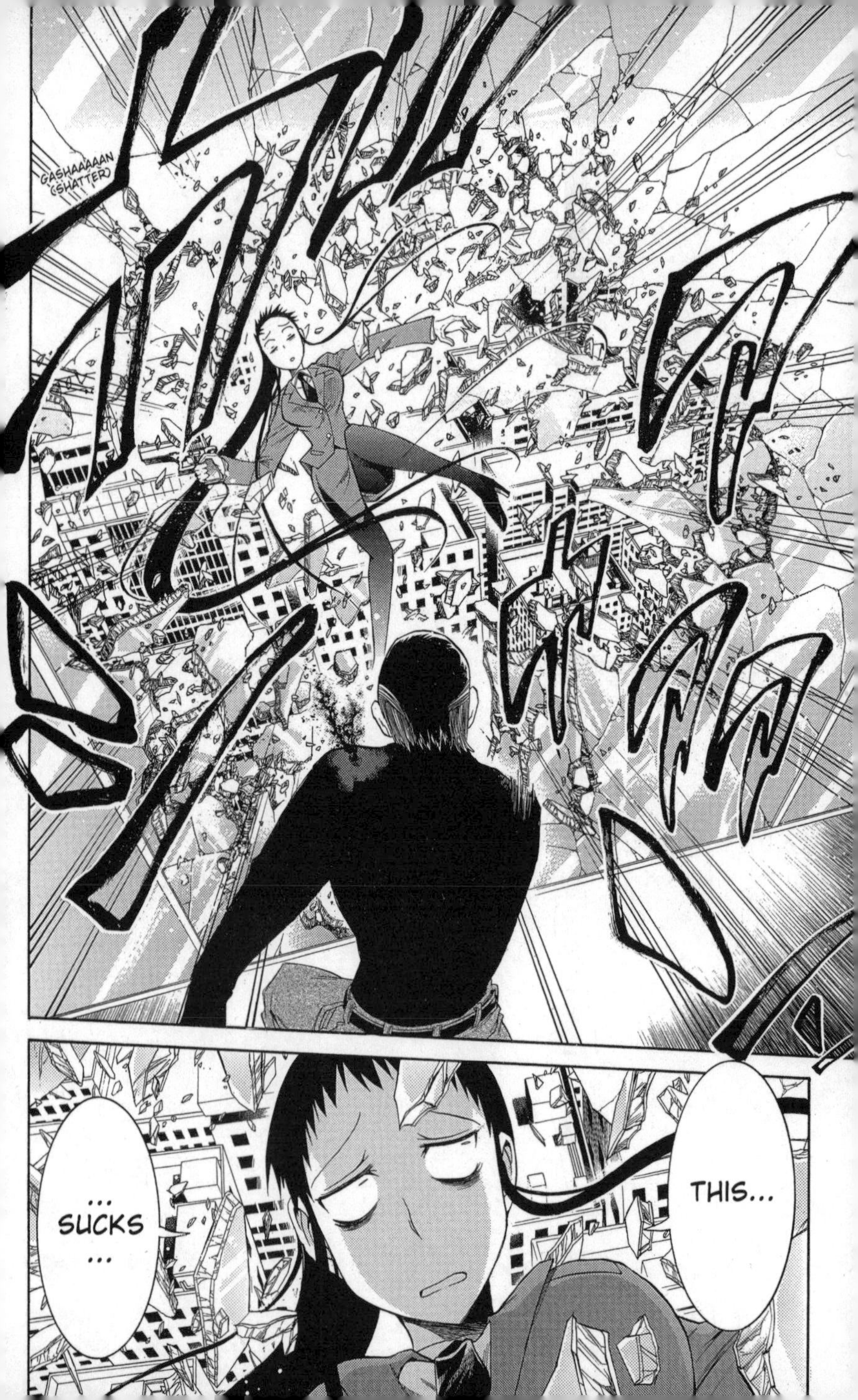
GASHAAAAAN (SHATTER)
THIS...
... SUCKS ...

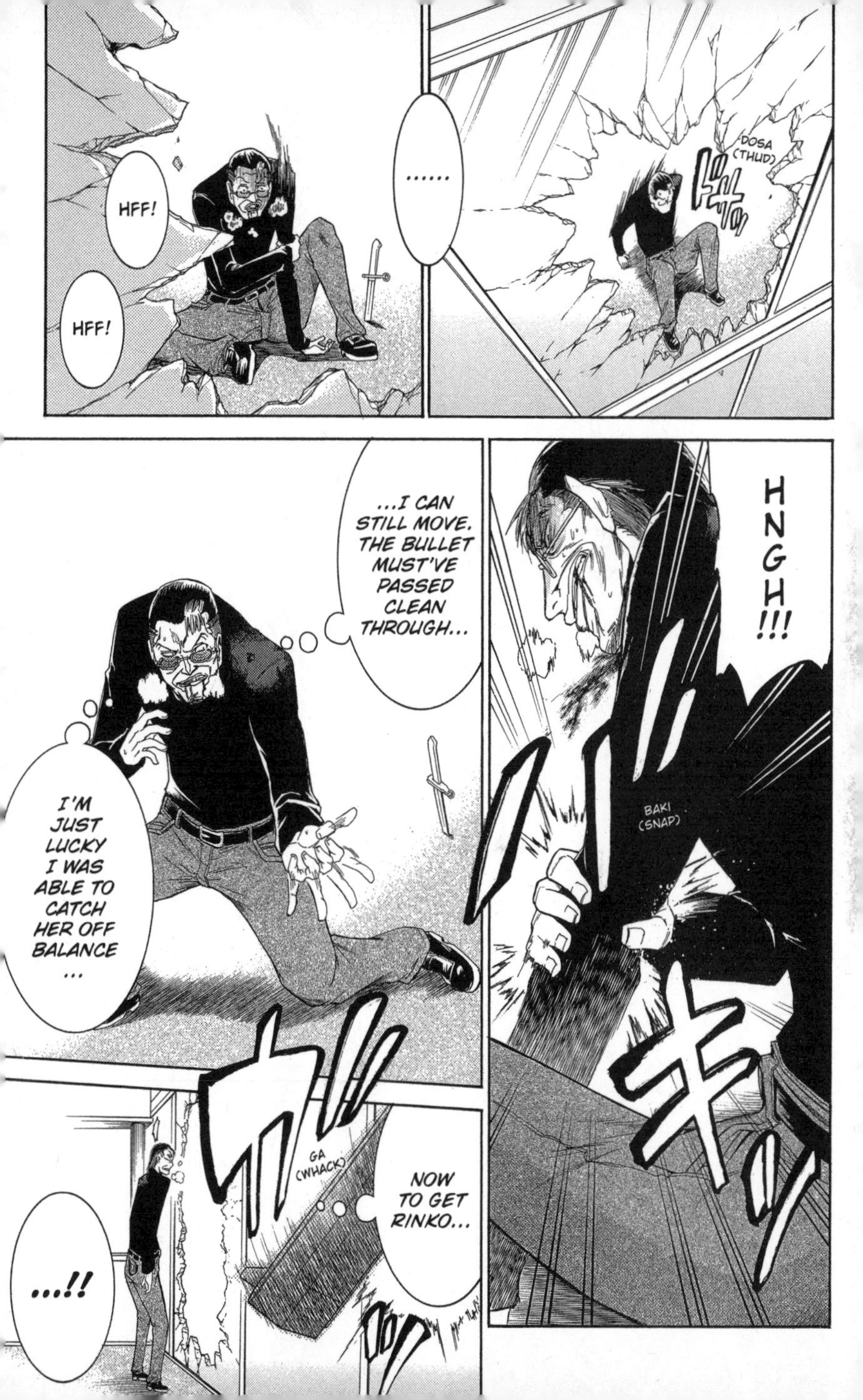
DOSA (THUD)
......
HFF!
HFF!
HNGH!!!
BAKI (SNAP)
...I CAN STILL MOVE. THE BULLET MUST'VE PASSED CLEAN THROUGH...
I'M JUST LUCKY I WAS ABLE TO CATCH HER OFF BALANCE...
GA (WHACK)
NOW TO GET RINKO...
...!!

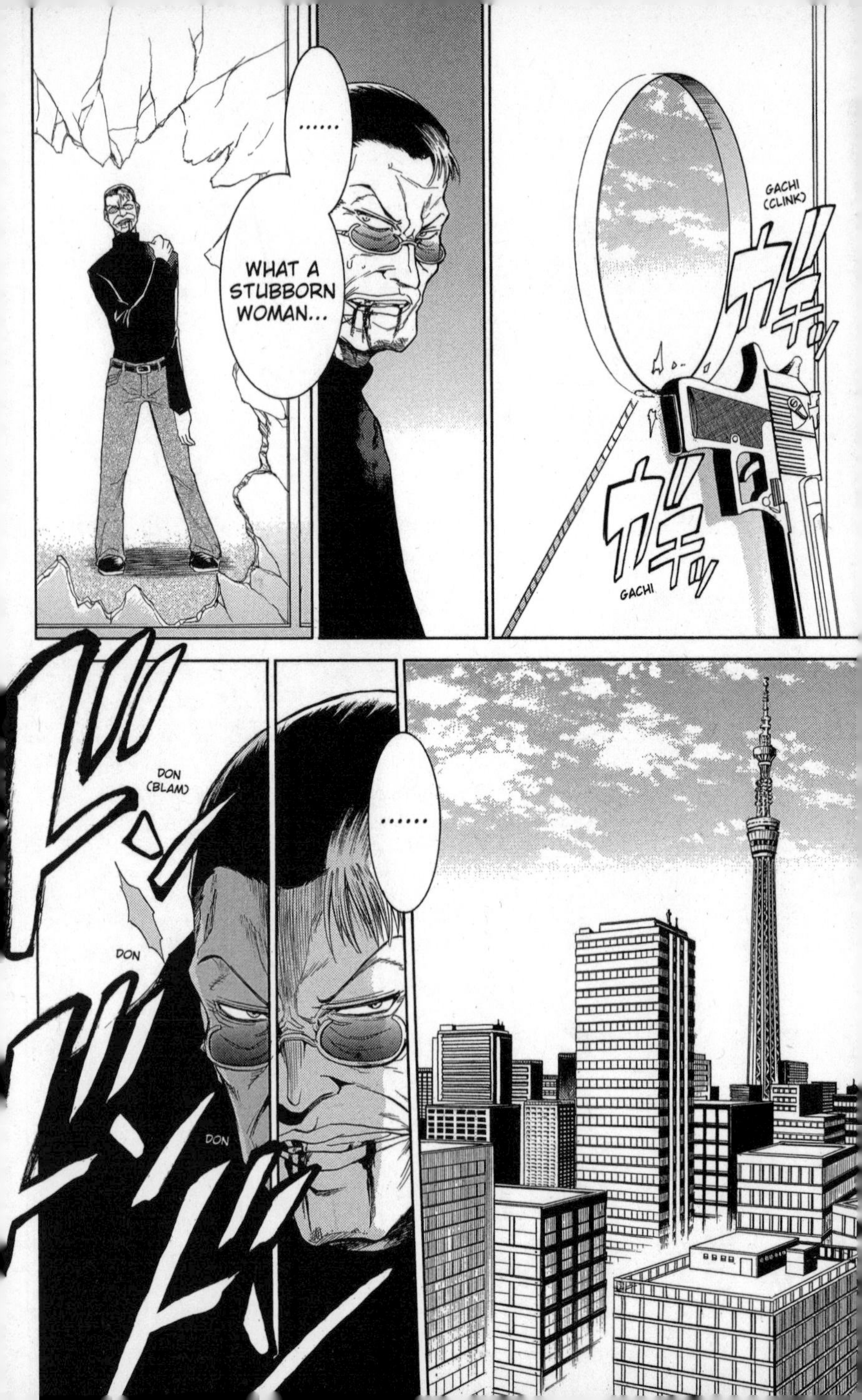
GACHI (CLINK)
GACHI
......
WHAT A STUBBORN WOMAN...
....
DON (BLAM)
DON
DON

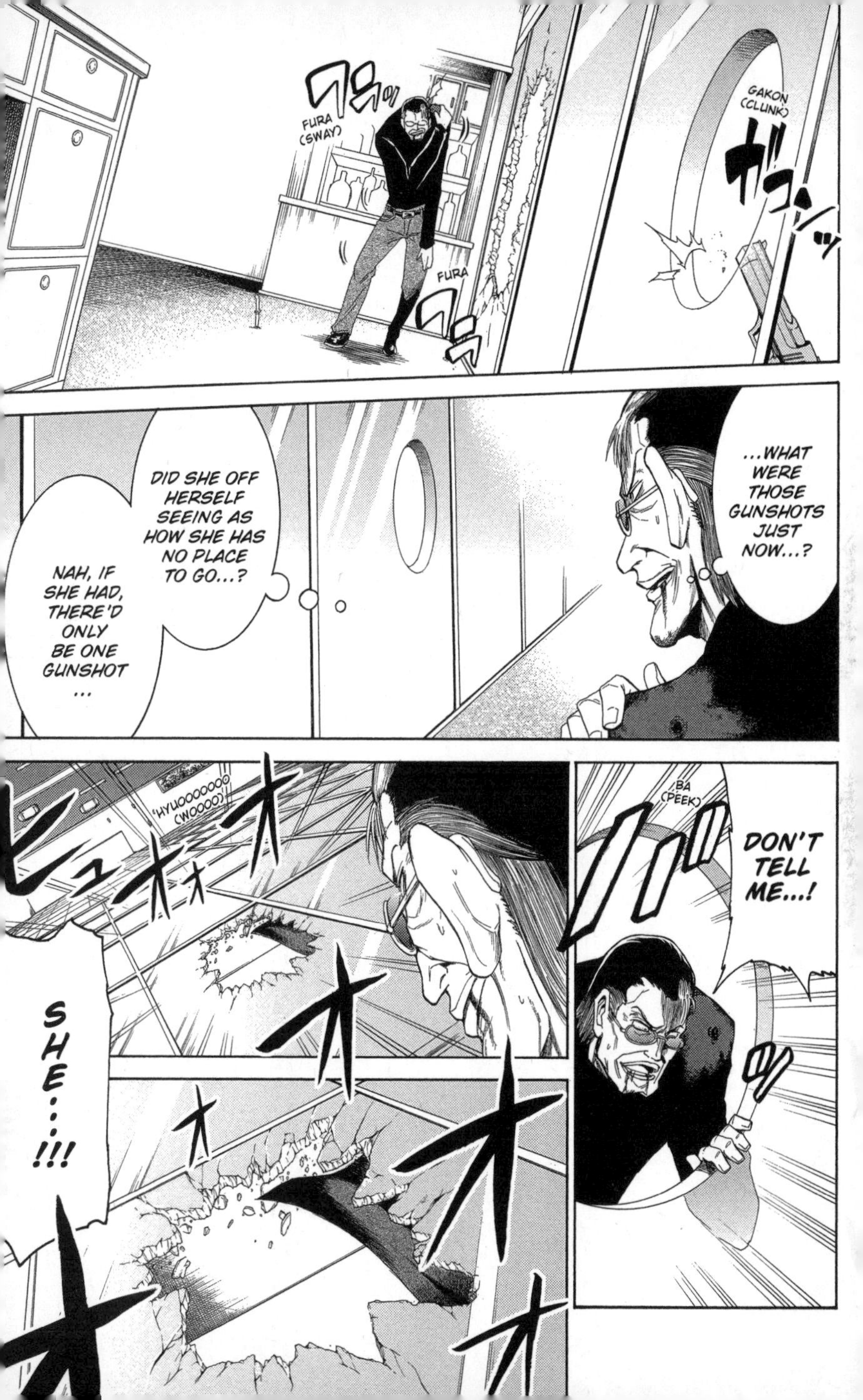
GAKON (CLUNK)
FURA (SWAY)
FURA
...WHAT WERE THOSE GUNSHOTS JUST NOW...?
DID SHE OFF HERSELF SEEING AS HOW SHE HAS NO PLACE TO GO...?
NAH, IF SHE HAD, THERE'D ONLY BE ONE GUNSHOT...
BA (PEEK)
DON'T TELL ME...!
HYUOOOOOOO (WOOOOM)
SHE...!!!

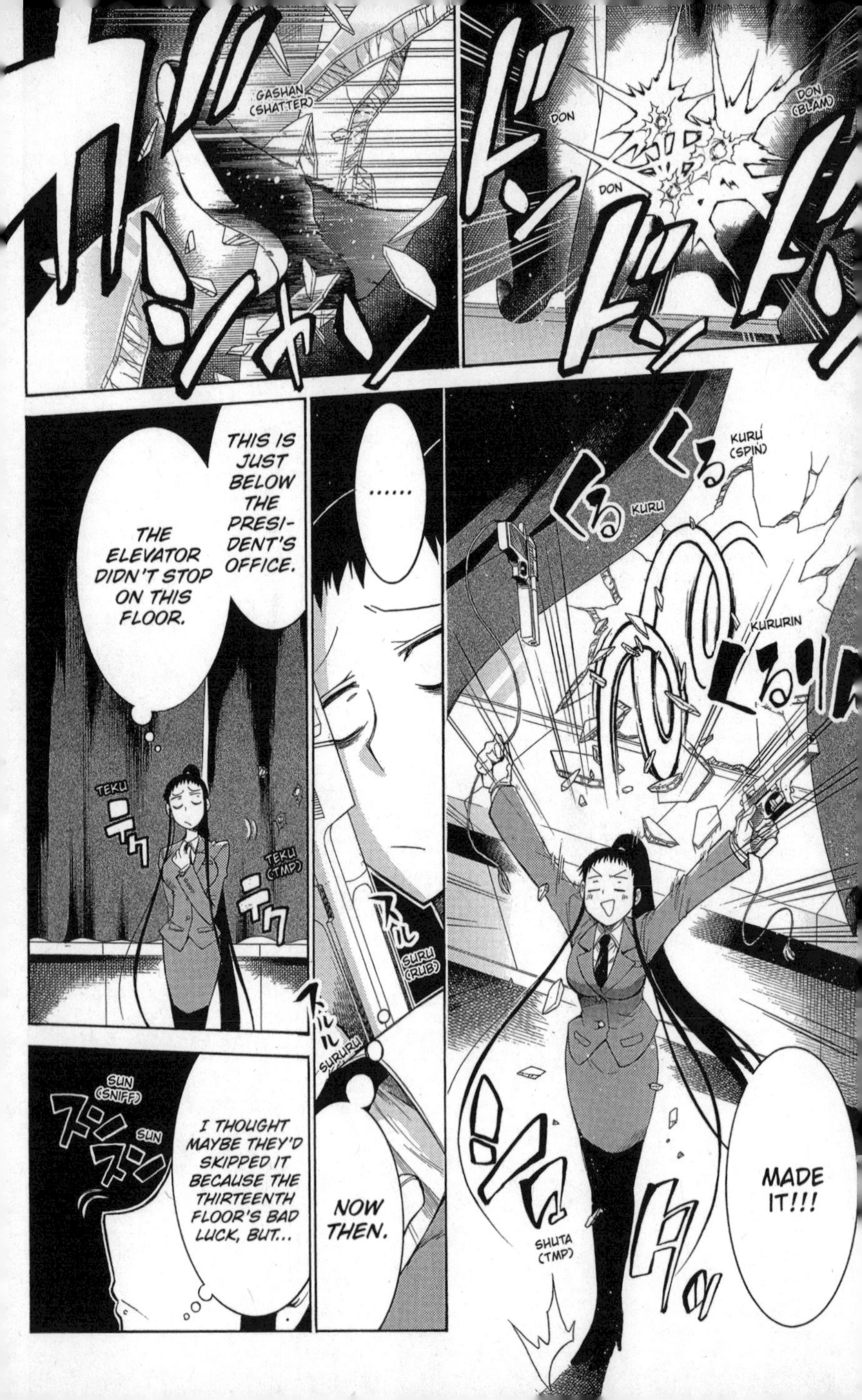
DON (BLAM)
DON
DON
GASHAN (SHATTER)
KURU (SPIN)
KURU
KURURIN
MADE IT!!!
SHUTA (TMP)
......
SURU (RUB)
SURURU
NOW THEN.
THIS IS JUST BELOW THE PRESI-DENT'S OFFICE.
THE ELEVATOR DIDN'T STOP ON THIS FLOOR.
TEKU
TEKU (TMP)
SUN (SNIFF)
SUN
I THOUGHT MAYBE THEY'D SKIPPED IT BECAUSE THE THIRTEENTH FLOOR'S BAD LUCK, BUT...

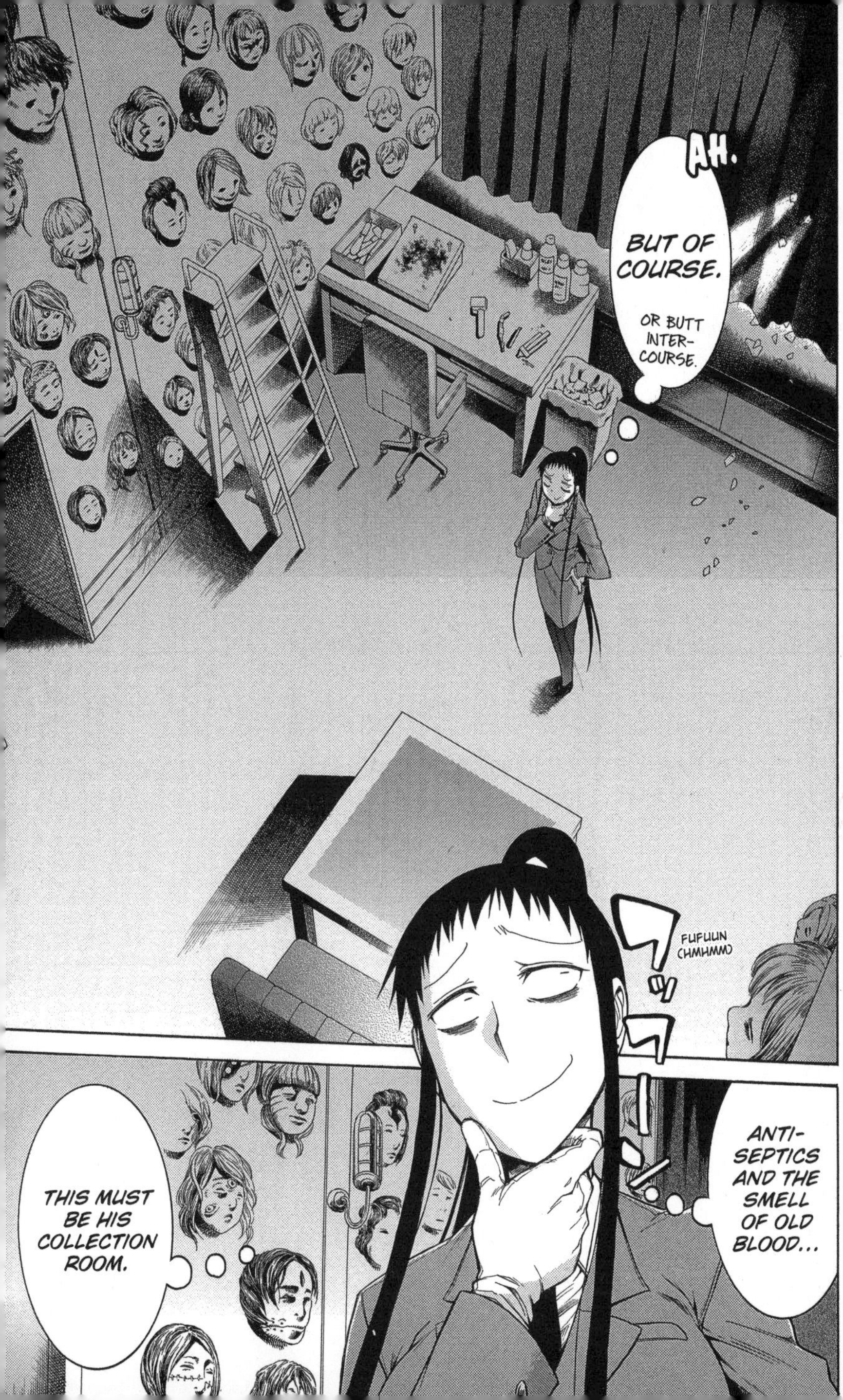
AH.
BUT OF COURSE.
OR BUTT INTER-COURSE.
FUFUUN (HMHMM)
ANTI-SEPTICS AND THE SMELL OF OLD BLOOD...
THIS MUST BE HIS COLLECTION ROOM.

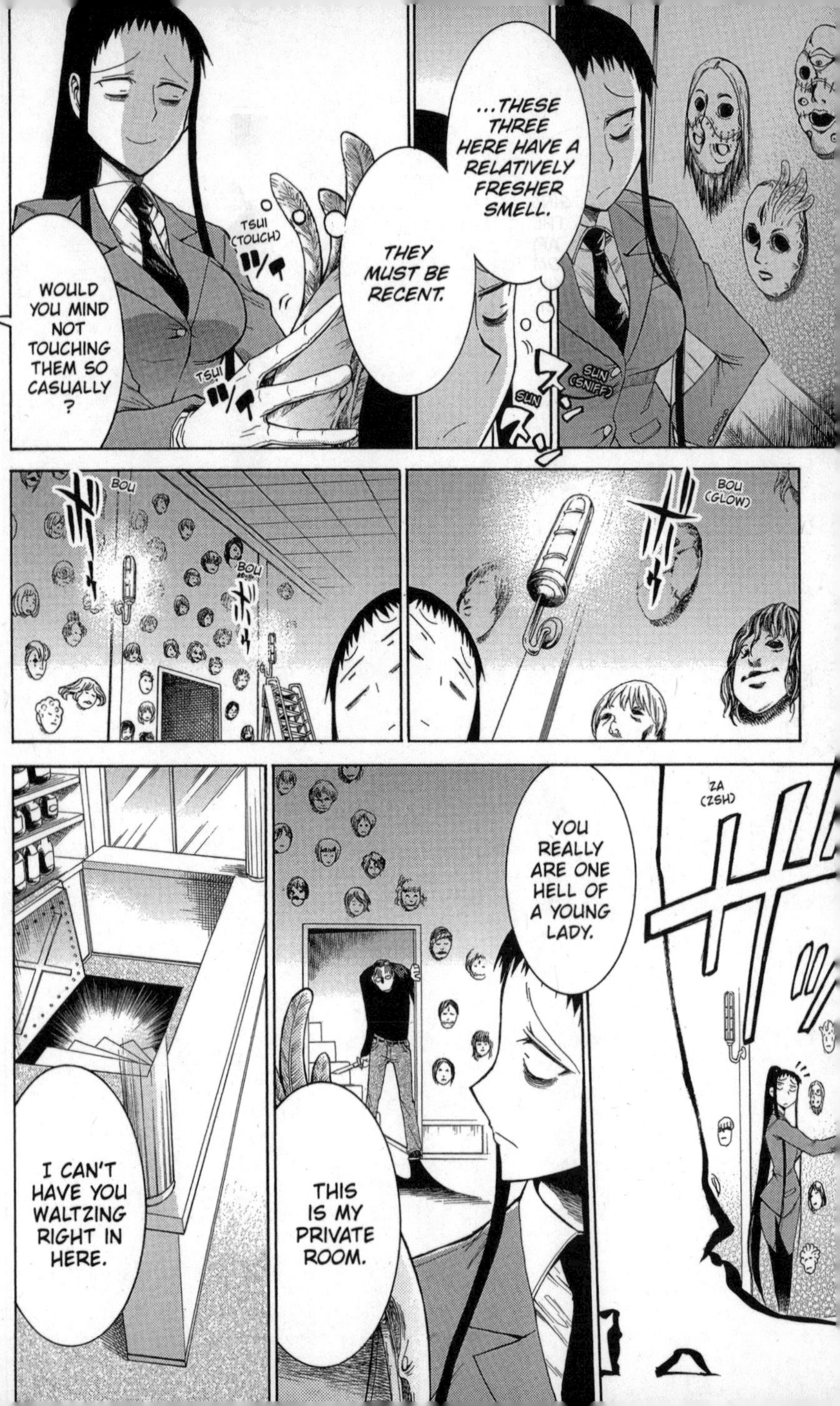
...THESE THREE HERE HAVE A RELATIVELY FRESHER SMELL.
THEY MUST BE RECENT.
SUN (SNIFF)
SUN
TSUI (TOUCH)
WOULD YOU MIND NOT TOUCHING THEM SO CASUALLY?
TSUI
BOU (GLOW)
BOU
BOU
ZA (ZSH)
YOU REALLY ARE ONE HELL OF A YOUNG LADY.
THIS IS MY PRIVATE ROOM.
I CAN'T HAVE YOU WALTZING RIGHT IN HERE.

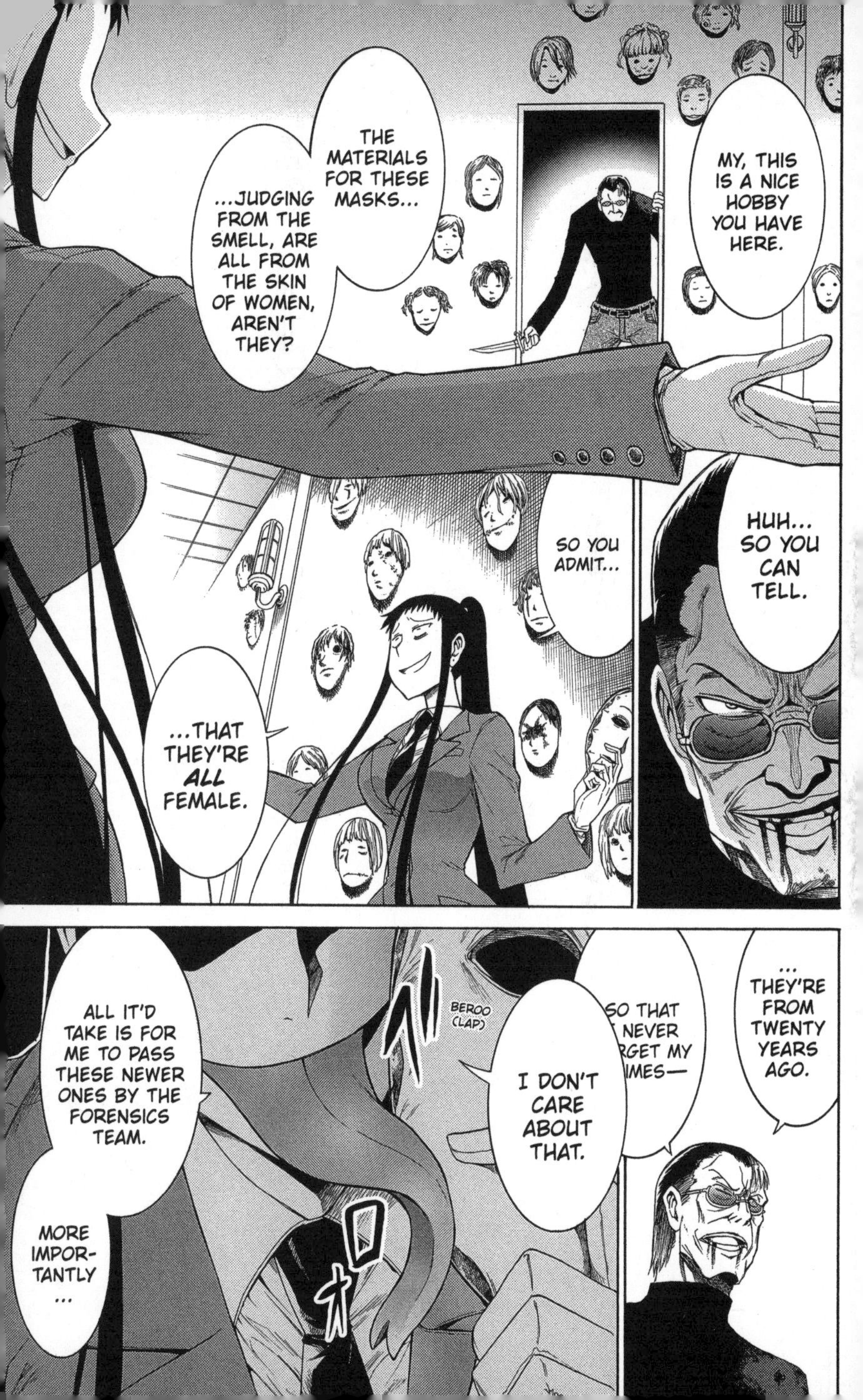
MY, THIS IS A NICE HOBBY YOU HAVE HERE.
THE MATERIALS FOR THESE MASKS...
...JUDGING FROM THE SMELL, ARE ALL FROM THE SKIN OF WOMEN, AREN'T THEY?
HUH... SO YOU CAN TELL.
SO YOU ADMIT...
...THAT THEY'RE ALL FEMALE.
... THEY'RE FROM TWENTY YEARS AGO.
SO THAT NEVER RGET MY IMES—
I DON'T CARE ABOUT THAT.
BEROO (LAP)
ALL IT'D TAKE IS FOR ME TO PASS THESE NEWER ONES BY THE FORENSICS TEAM.
MORE IMPORTANTLY ...

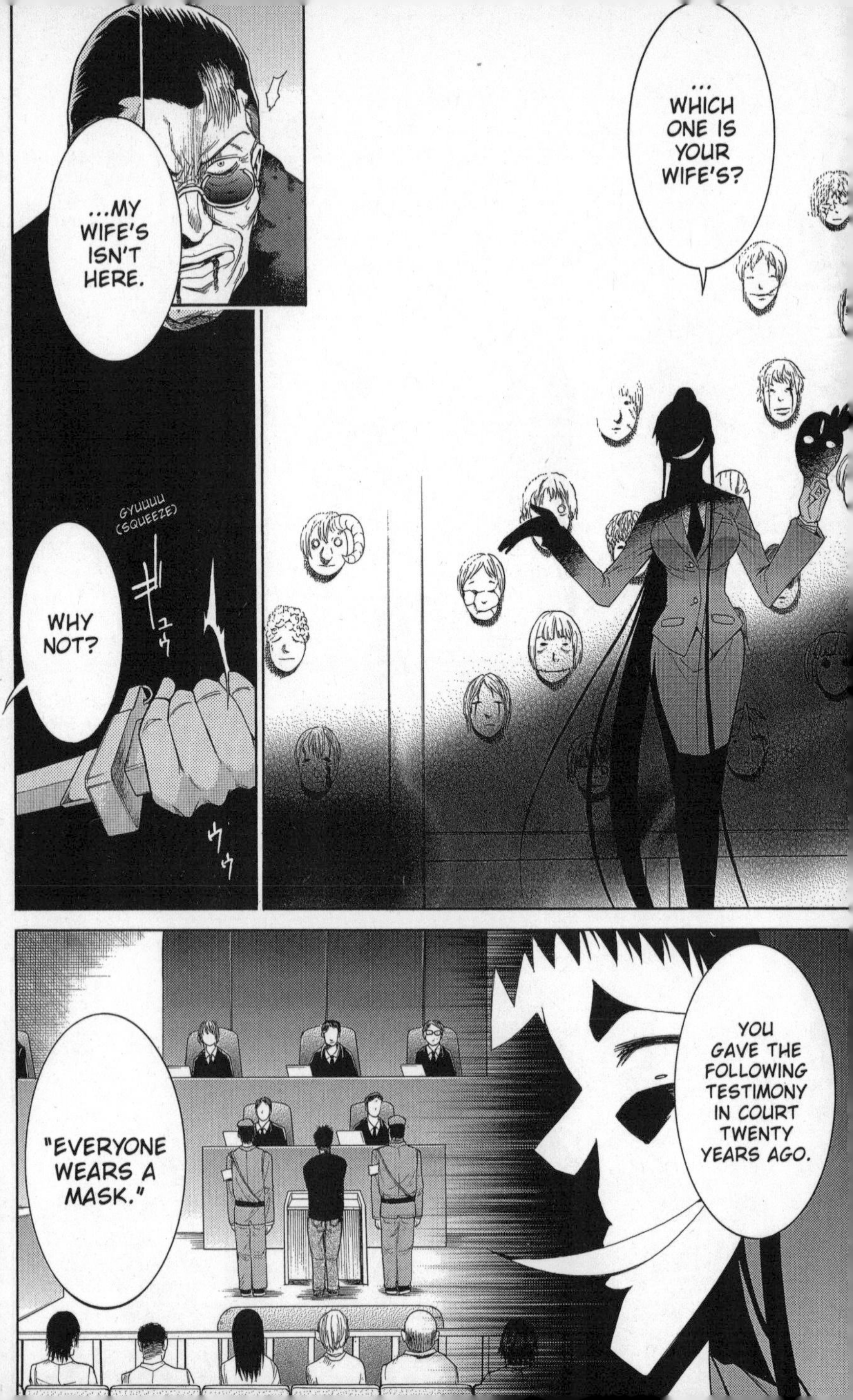
...WHICH ONE IS YOUR WIFE'S?
...MY WIFE'S ISN'T HERE.
WHY NOT?
GYUUUU (SQUEEZE)
ギュウ
ウウ
YOU GAVE THE FOLLOWING TESTIMONY IN COURT TWENTY YEARS AGO.
"EVERYONE WEARS A MASK."

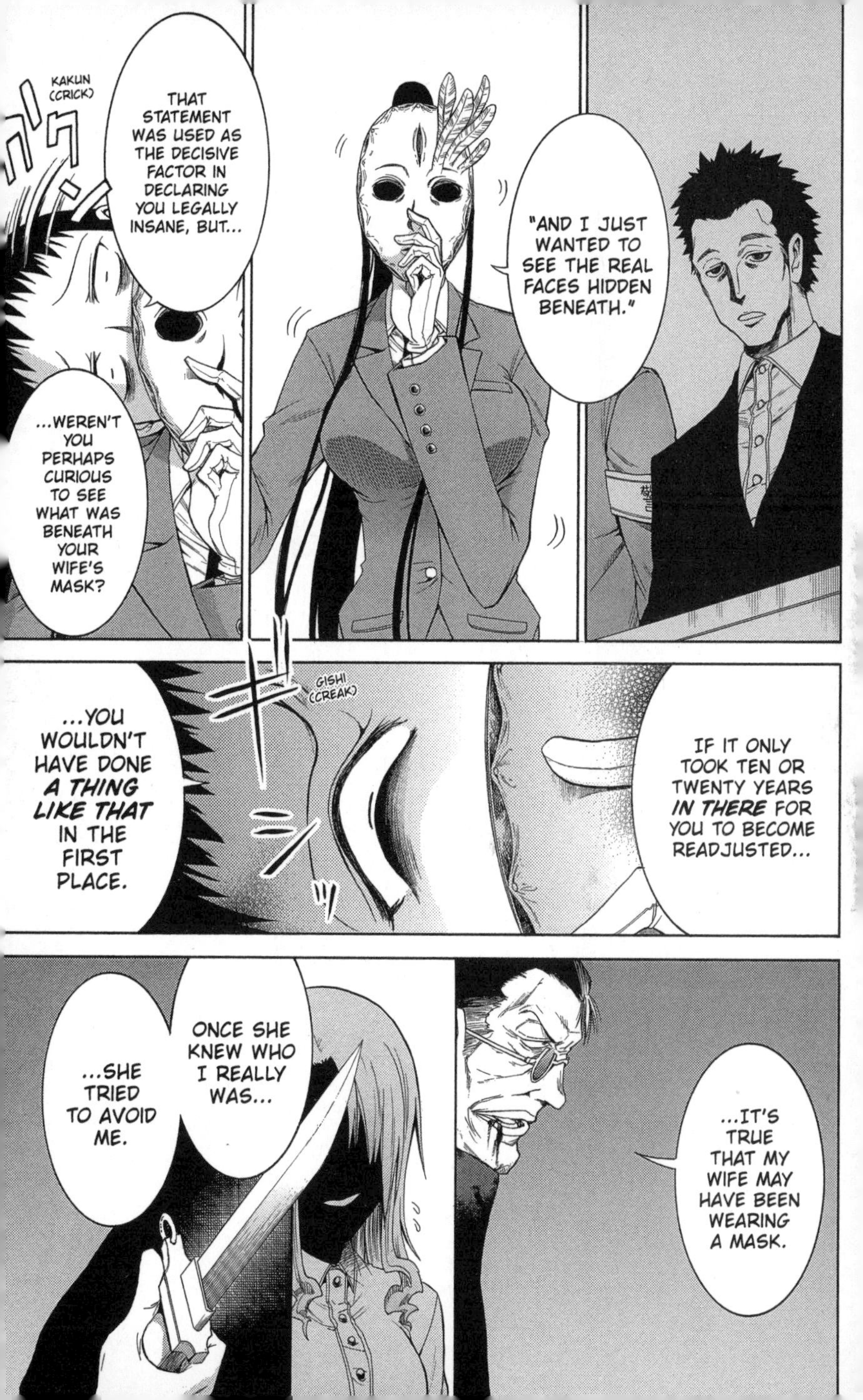
"AND I JUST WANTED TO SEE THE REAL FACES HIDDEN BENEATH."
THAT STATEMENT WAS USED AS THE DECISIVE FACTOR IN DECLARING YOU LEGALLY INSANE, BUT...
KAKUN (CRICK)
...WEREN'T YOU PERHAPS CURIOUS TO SEE WHAT WAS BENEATH YOUR WIFE'S MASK?
IF IT ONLY TOOK TEN OR TWENTY YEARS *IN THERE* FOR YOU TO BECOME READJUSTED...
GISHI (CREAK)
...YOU WOULDN'T HAVE DONE *A THING LIKE THAT* IN THE FIRST PLACE.
...IT'S TRUE THAT MY WIFE MAY HAVE BEEN WEARING A MASK.
ONCE SHE KNEW WHO I REALLY WAS...
...SHE TRIED TO AVOID ME.

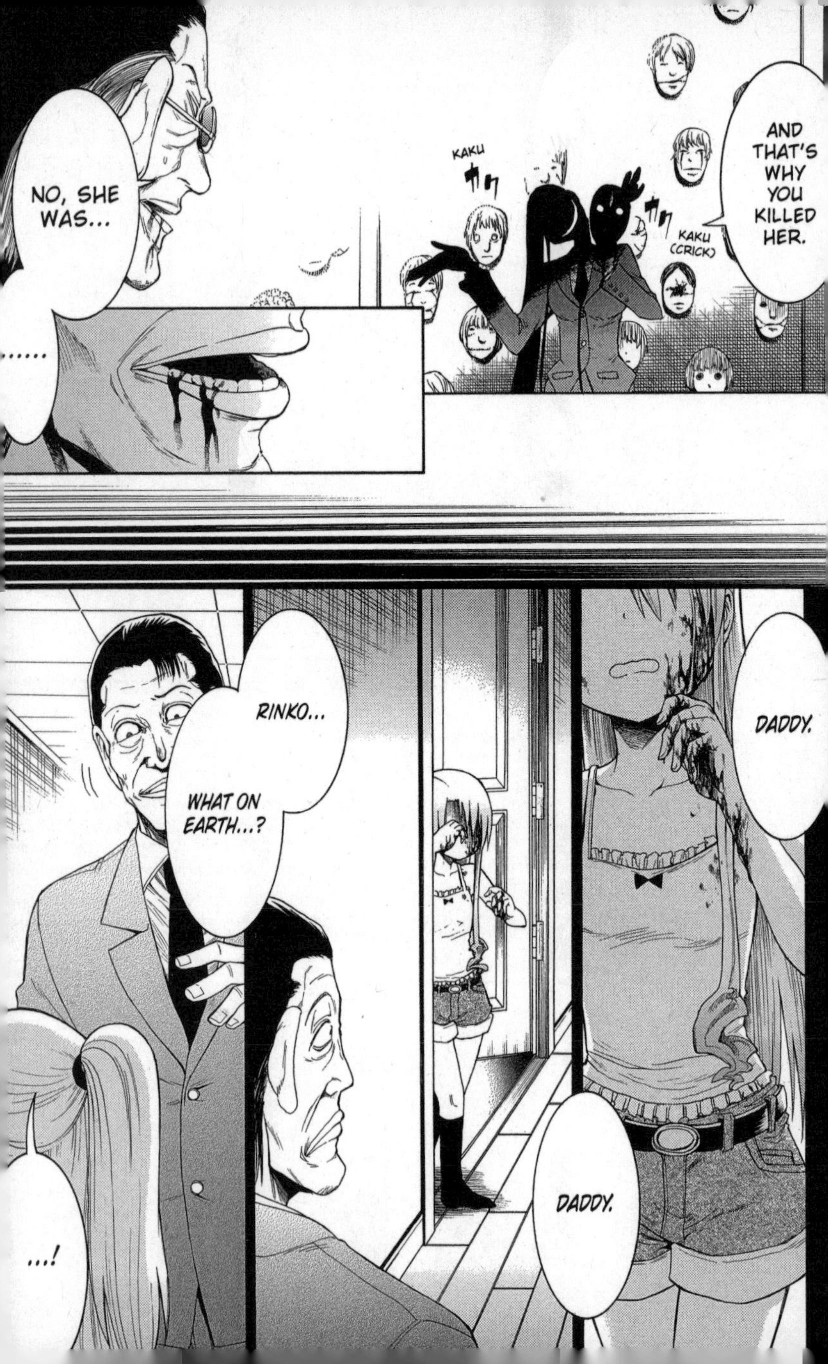
AND THAT'S WHY YOU KILLED HER.
KAKU
KAKU (CRICK)
NO, SHE WAS...
......
DADDY.
DADDY.
RINKO...
WHAT ON EARTH...?
...!

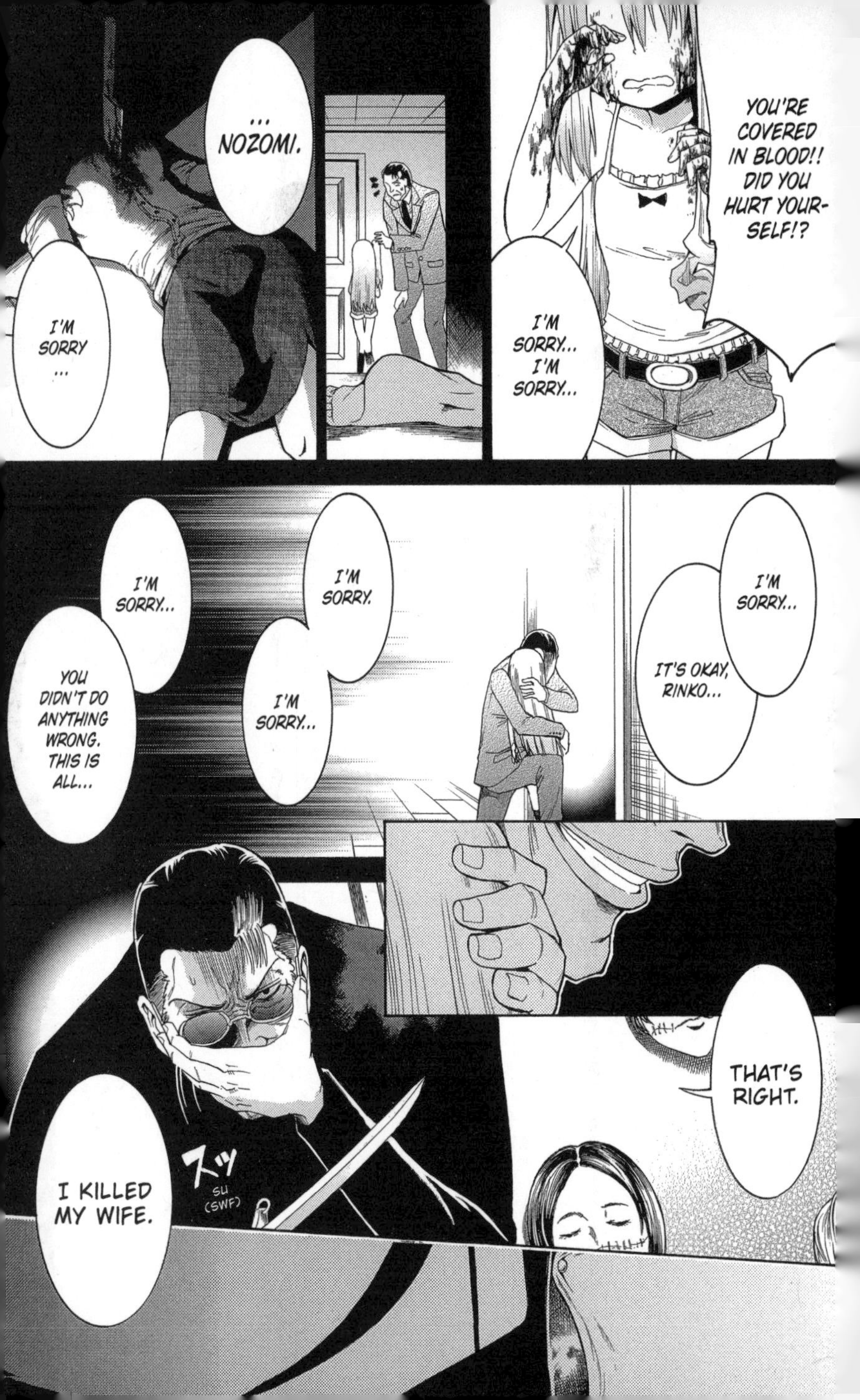
YOU'RE COVERED IN BLOOD!! DID YOU HURT YOUR-SELF!?
I'M SORRY... I'M SORRY...
... NOZOMI.
I'M SORRY ...
I'M SORRY...
IT'S OKAY, RINKO...
I'M SORRY.
I'M SORRY...
I'M SORRY...
YOU DIDN'T DO ANYTHING WRONG. THIS IS ALL...
THAT'S RIGHT.
スッ
SU (SWF)
I KILLED MY WIFE.

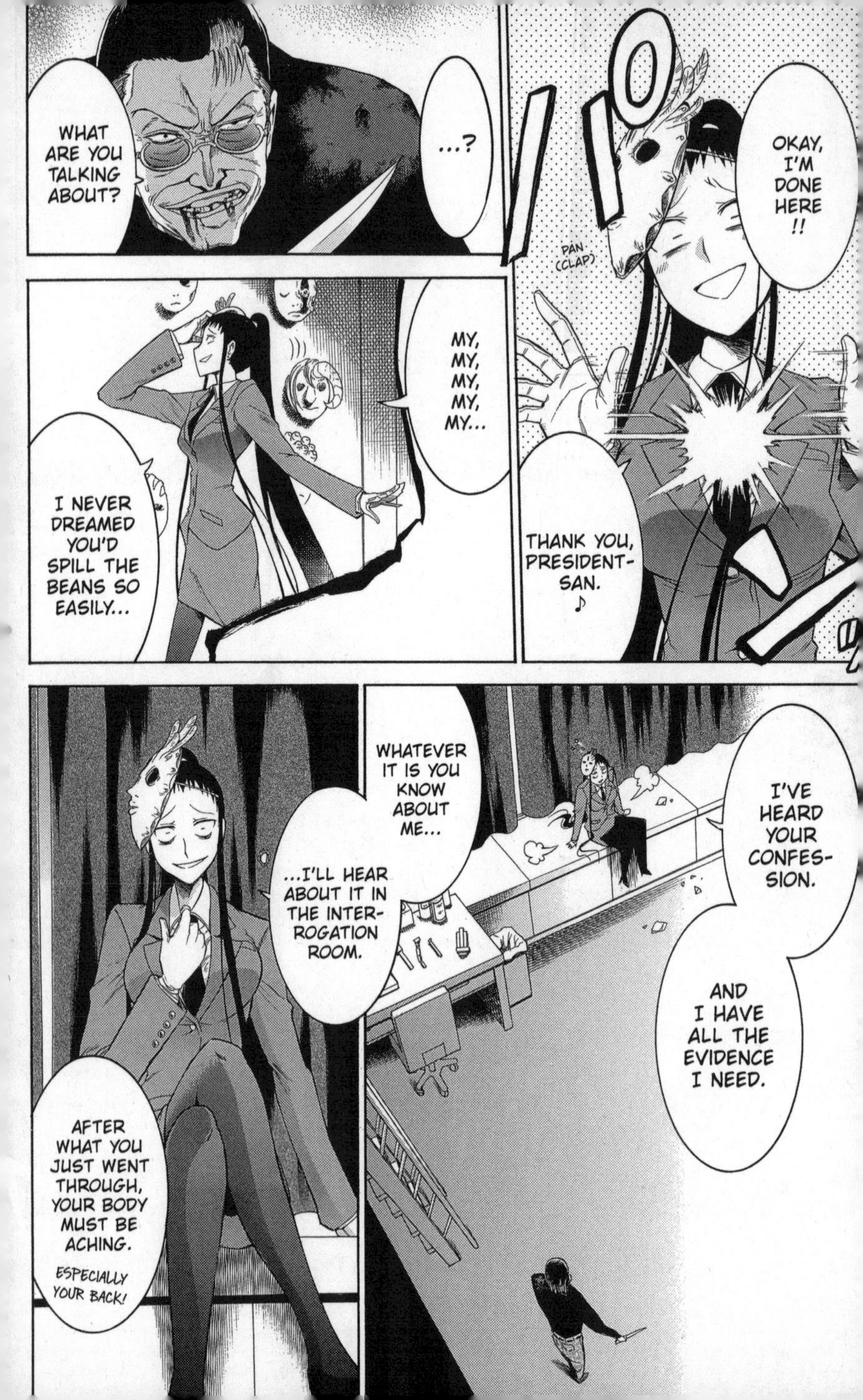
OKAY, I'M DONE HERE!!
PAN (CLAP)
THANK YOU, PRESIDENT-SAN. ♪
...?
WHAT ARE YOU TALKING ABOUT?
MY, MY, MY, MY, MY...
I NEVER DREAMED YOU'D SPILL THE BEANS SO EASILY...
I'VE HEARD YOUR CONFESSION.
AND I HAVE ALL THE EVIDENCE I NEED.
WHATEVER IT IS YOU KNOW ABOUT ME...
...I'LL HEAR ABOUT IT IN THE INTERROGATION ROOM.
AFTER WHAT YOU JUST WENT THROUGH, YOUR BODY MUST BE ACHING.
ESPECIALLY YOUR BACK!

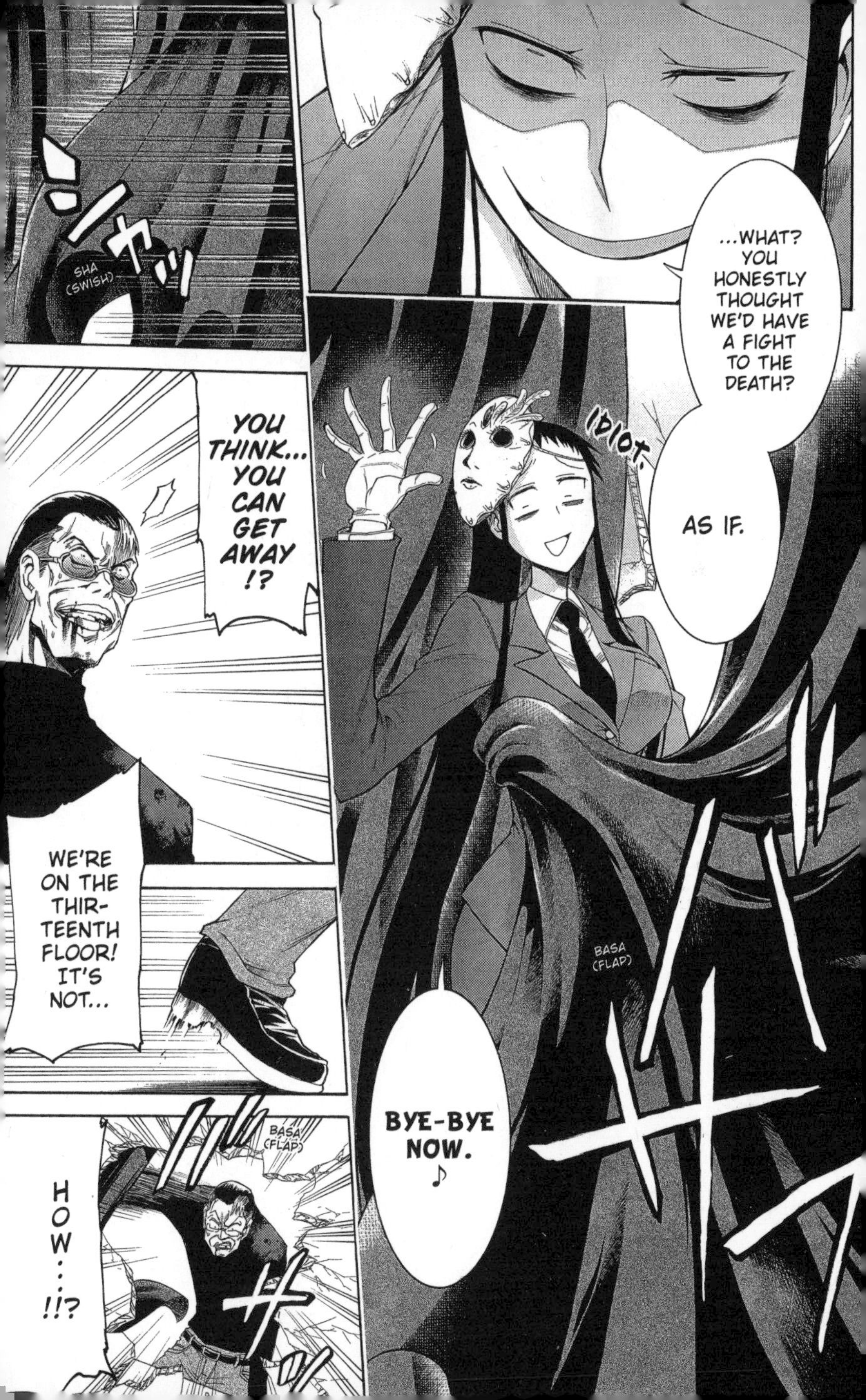
...WHAT? YOU HONESTLY THOUGHT WE'D HAVE A FIGHT TO THE DEATH?
SHA (SWISH)
IDIOT.
AS IF.
BASA (FLAP)
BYE-BYE NOW. ♪
YOU THINK... YOU CAN GET AWAY!?
WE'RE ON THE THIR-TEENTH FLOOR! IT'S NOT...
BASA (FLAP)
HOW...!!?

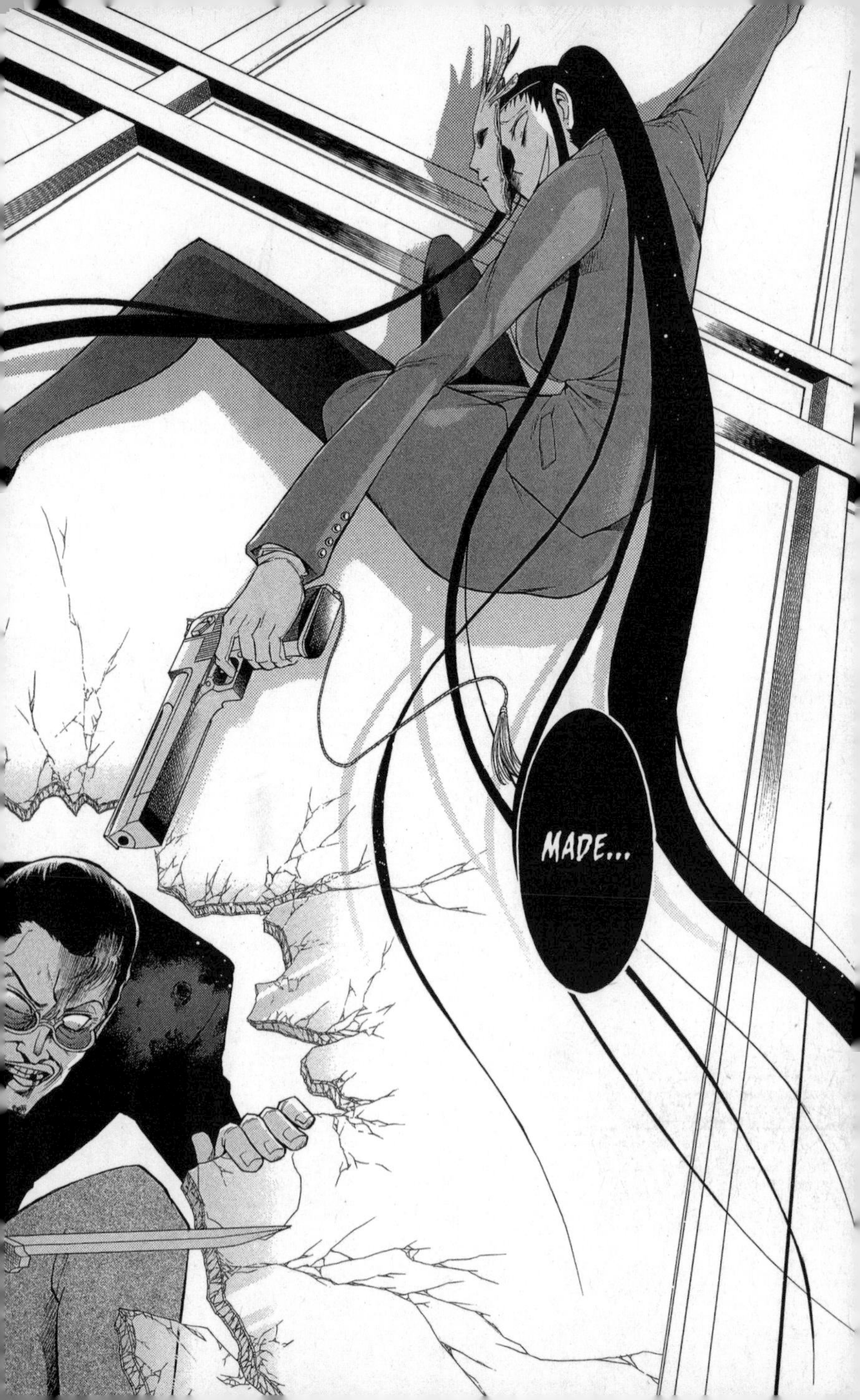
MADE...

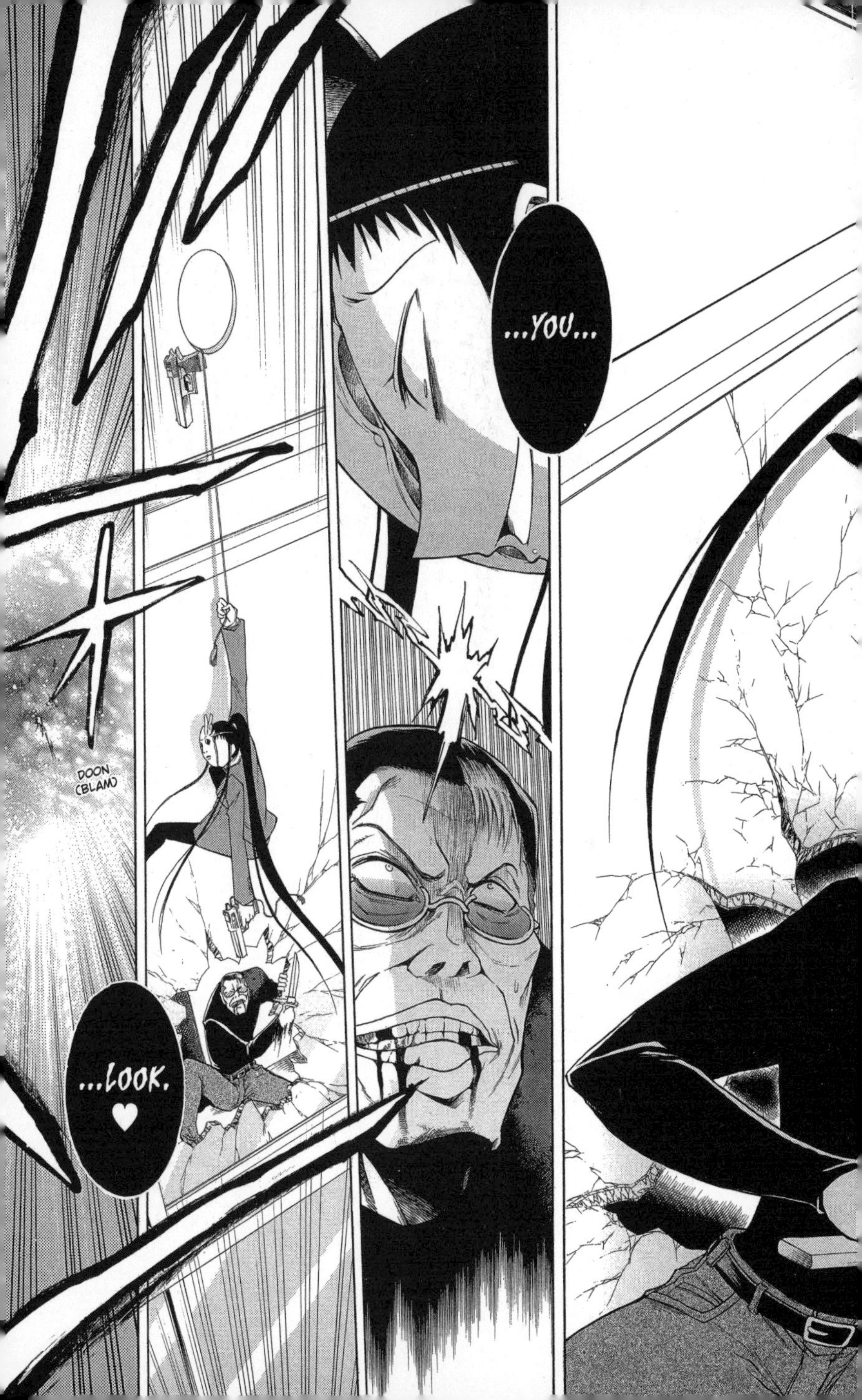
...YOU...
DOON (BLAM)
...LOOK. ♥

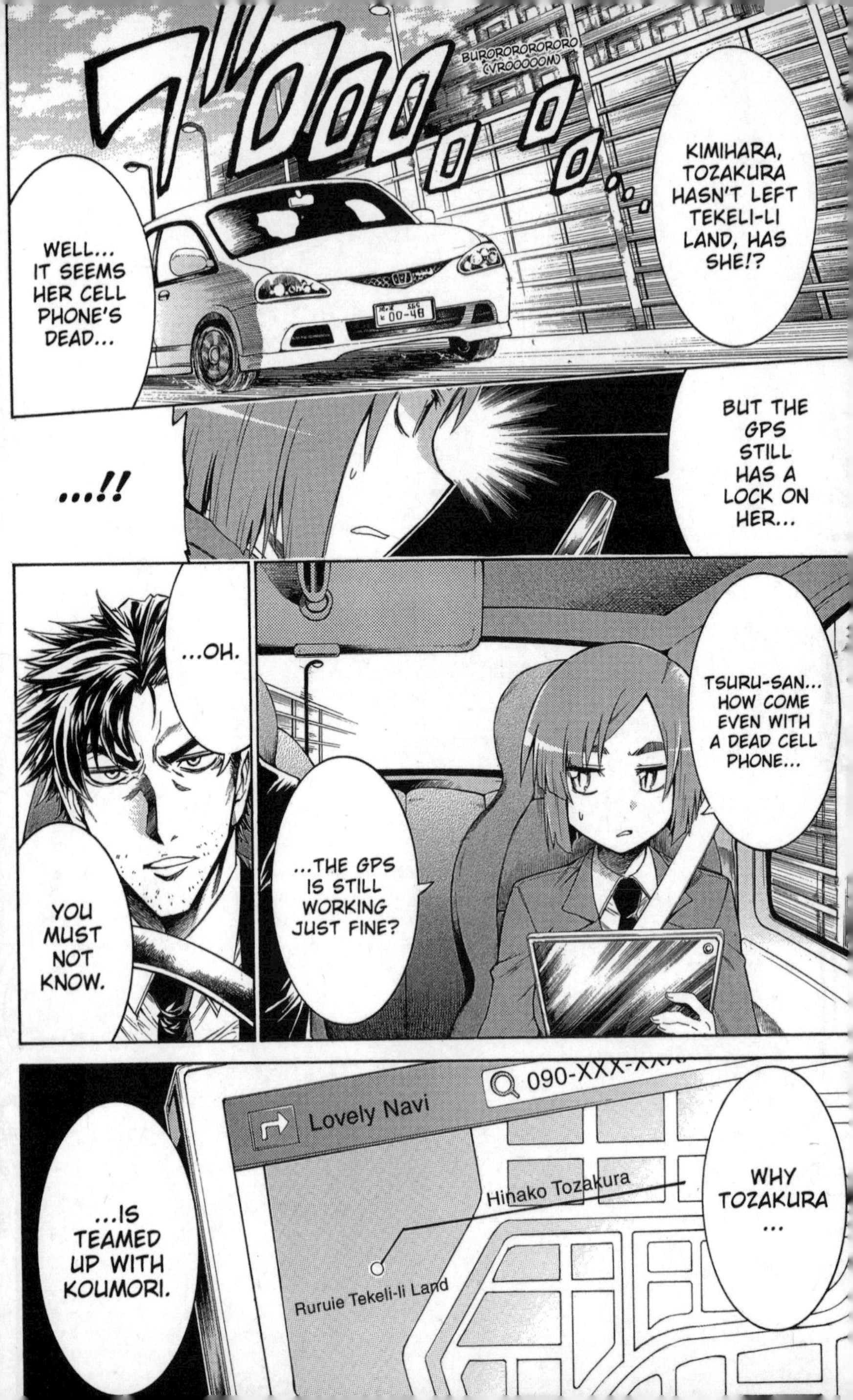
BURORORORORORO (VROOOOOM)
KIMIHARA, TOZAKURA HASN'T LEFT TEKELI-LI LAND, HAS SHE!?
WELL... IT SEEMS HER CELL PHONE'S DEAD...
BUT THE GPS STILL HAS A LOCK ON HER...
...!!
TSURU-SAN... HOW COME EVEN WITH A DEAD CELL PHONE...
...THE GPS IS STILL WORKING JUST FINE?
...OH.
YOU MUST NOT KNOW.
090-XXX-XX
Lovely Navi
Hinako Tozakura
Ruruie Tekeli-li Land
WHY TOZAKURA ...
...IS TEAMED UP WITH KOUMORI.

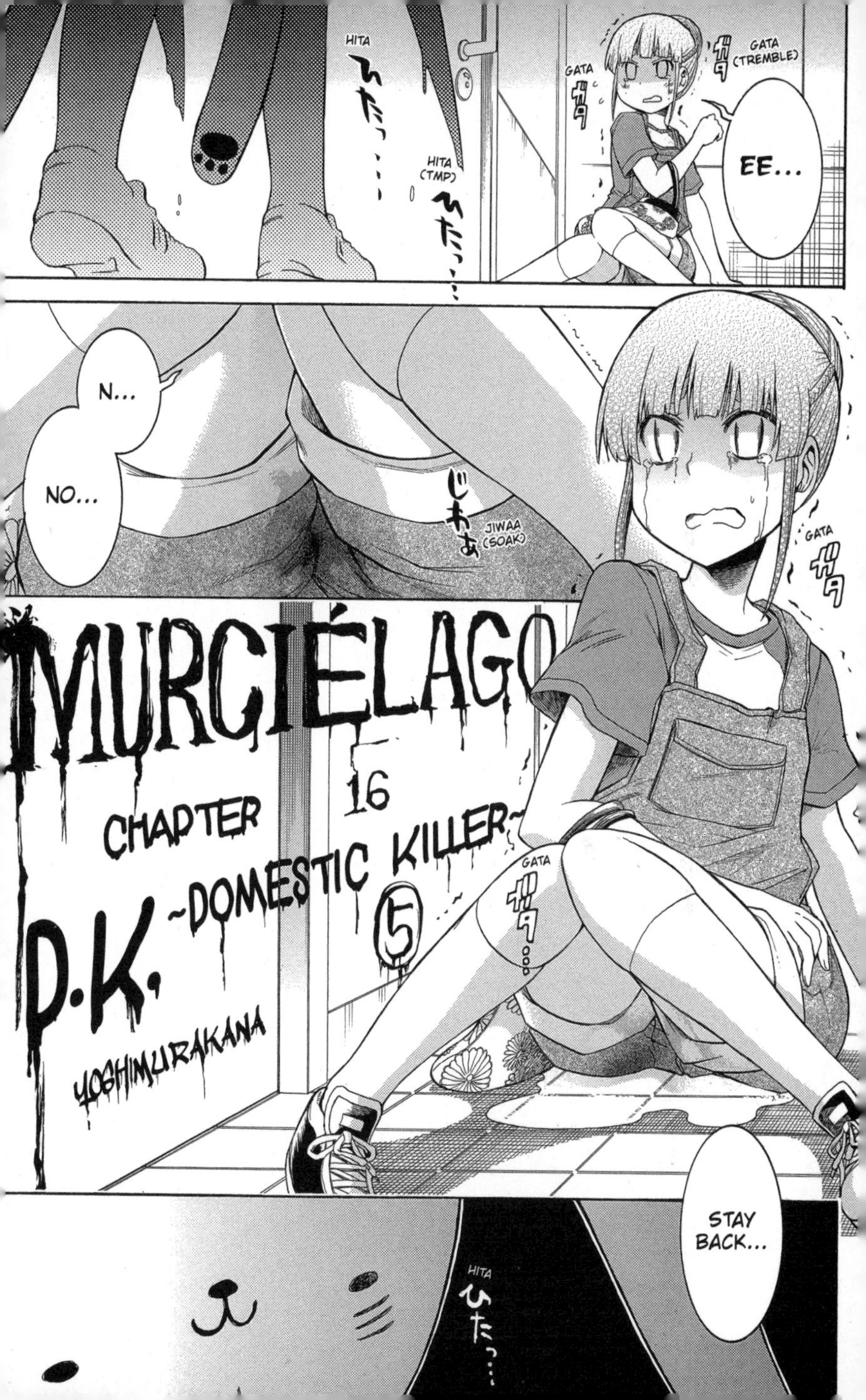
GATA (TREMBLE)
ガタ
GATA
ガタ
EE...
HITA
ひたっ...
HITA (TMP)
ひたっ...
GATA
ガタ
MURCIÉLAGO
CHAPTER 16
D.K. ~DOMESTIC KILLER~ ⑤
YOSHIMURAKANA
GATA
ガタ...
N...
NO...
じわぁ
JIWAA (SOAK)
STAY BACK...
HITA
ひたっ...

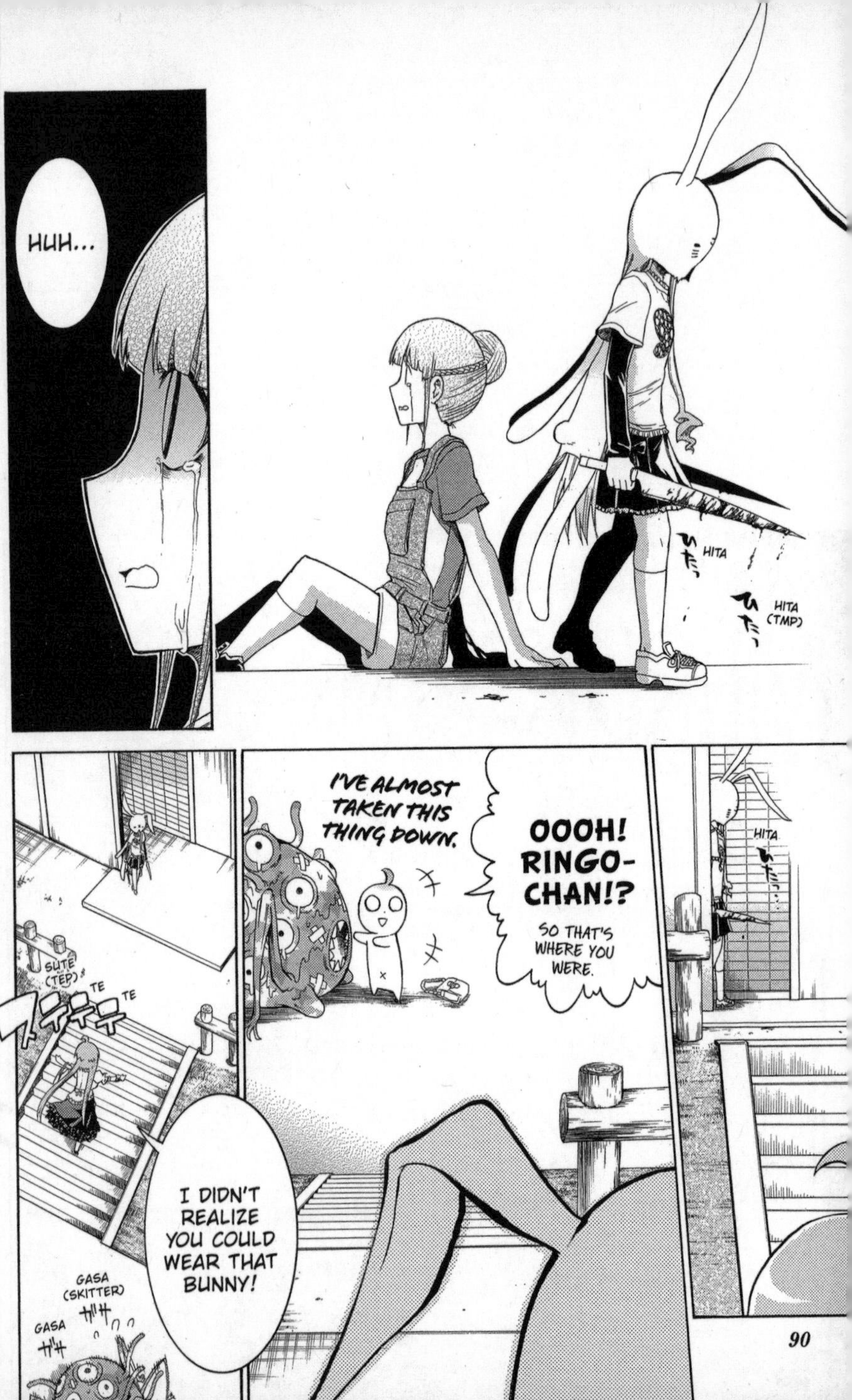
HITA
HITA (TMP)
HUH...
HITA
OOOH! RINGO-CHAN!?
SO THAT'S WHERE YOU WERE.
I'VE ALMOST TAKEN THIS THING DOWN.
SUTE (TEP)
TE
TE
I DIDN'T REALIZE YOU COULD WEAR THAT BUNNY!
GASA (SKITTER)
GASA

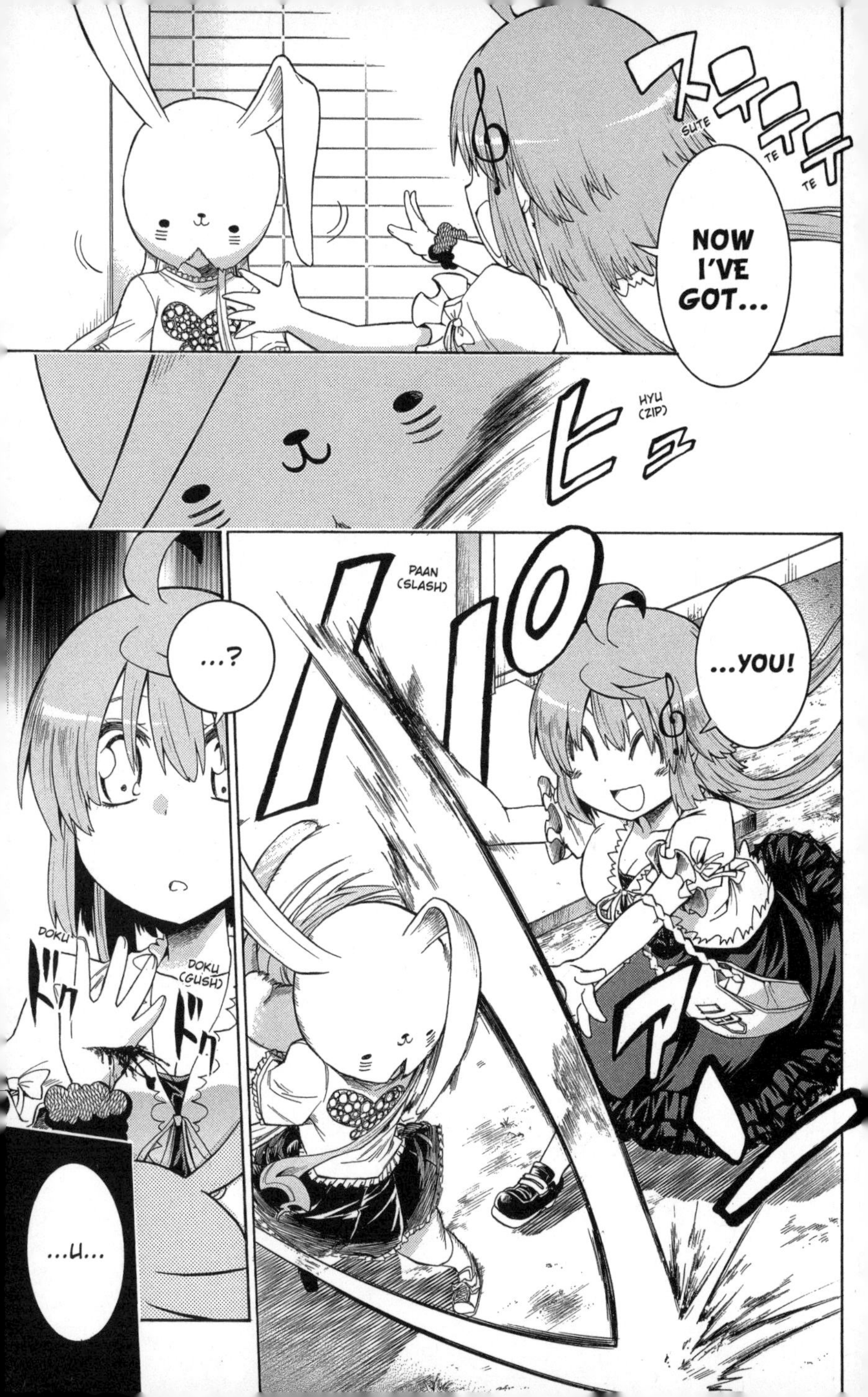
SUTE TE TE
NOW I'VE GOT...
HYU (ZIP)
PAAN (SLASH)
...YOU!
...?
DOKU DOKU (GUSH)
...U...

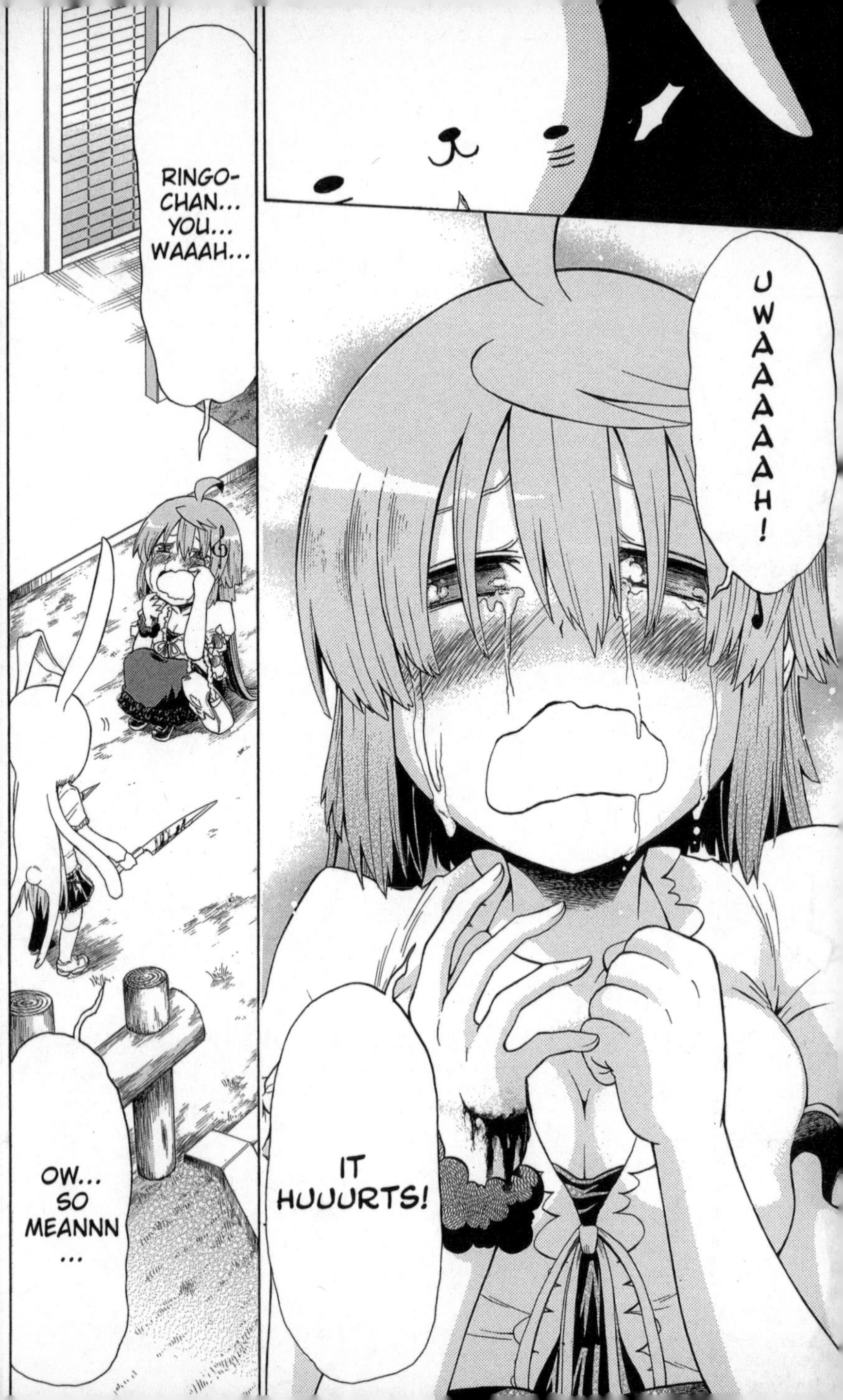
UWAAAAAAH!
IT HUUURTS!
RINGO-CHAN... YOU... WAAAH...
OW... SO MEANNN ...

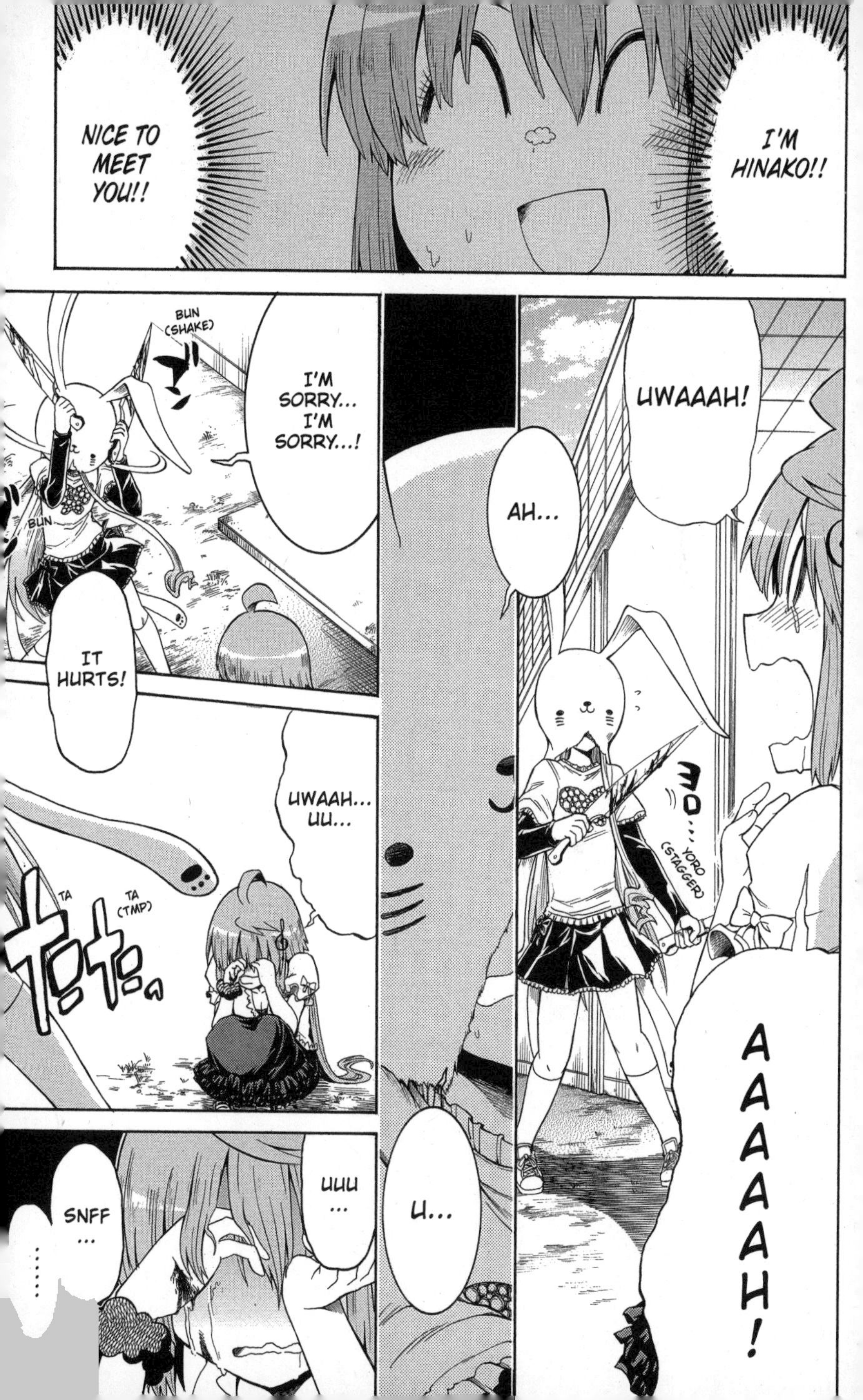
I'M HINAKO!!
NICE TO MEET YOU!!
UWAAAH!
AH...
YORO (STAGGER)
AAAAAAH!
U...
BUN (SHAKE)
I'M SORRY... I'M SORRY...!
BUN
IT HURTS!
UWAAH... UU...
TA TA (TMP)
UUU ...
SNFF ...
......

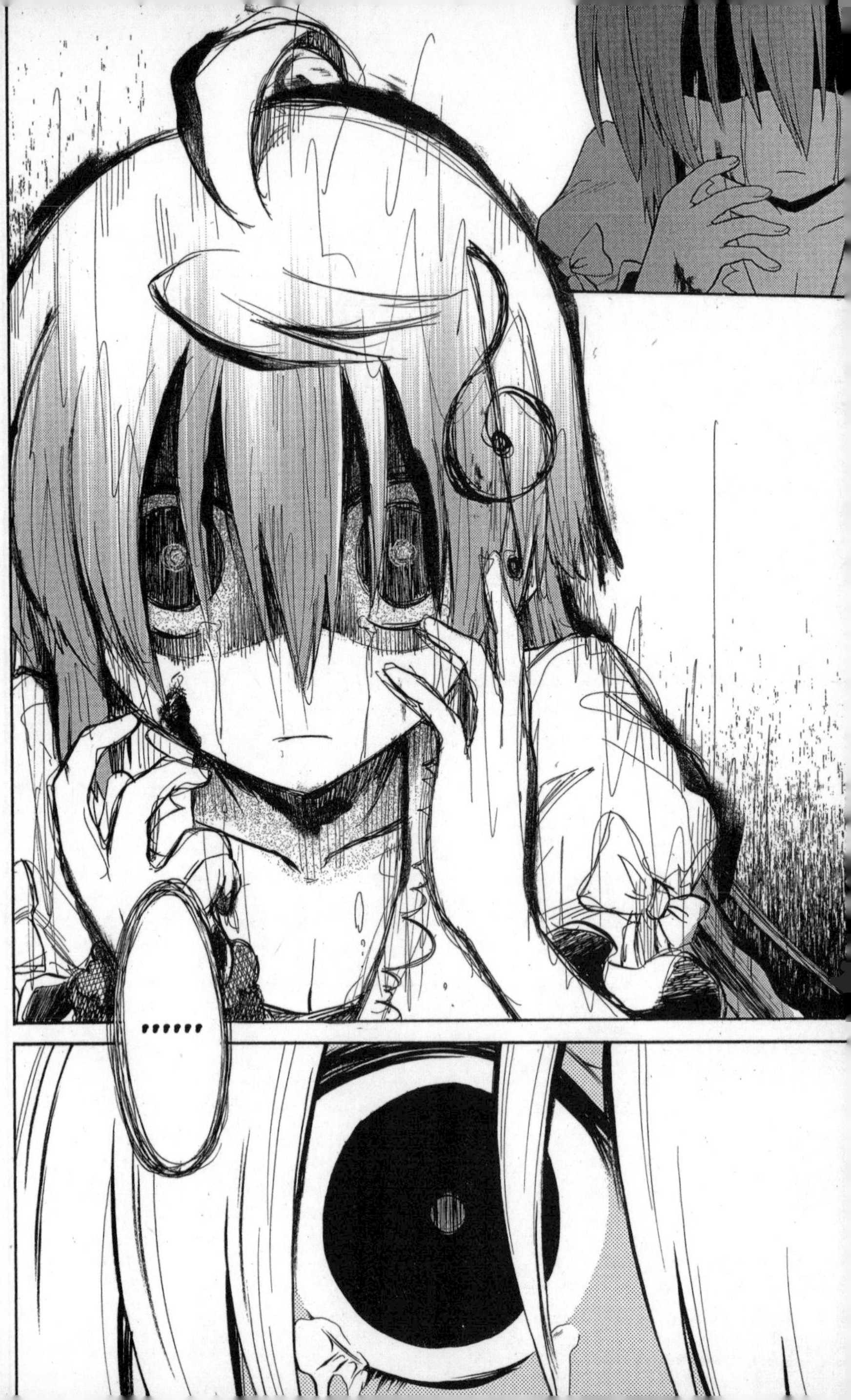
......

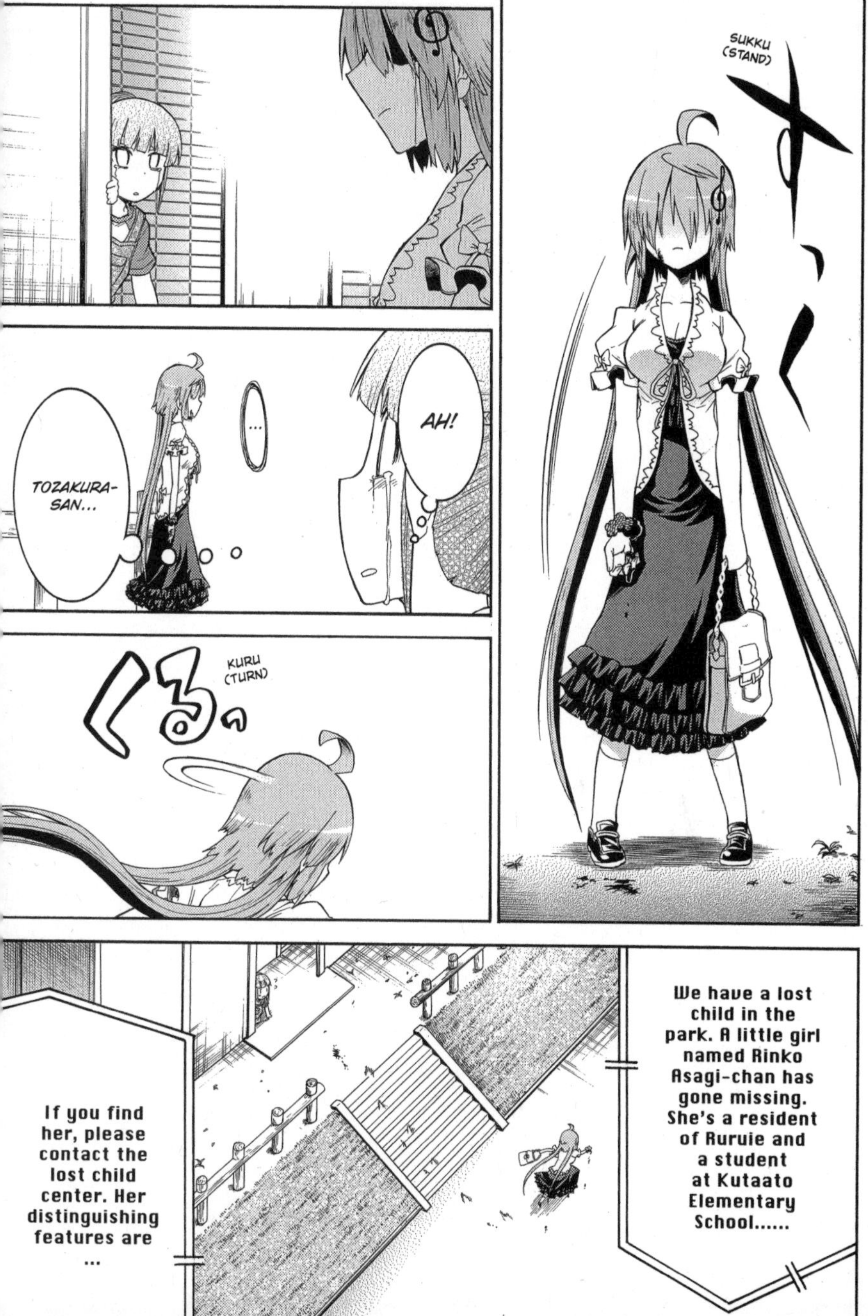
SUKKU (STAND)
AH!
...
TOZAKURA-SAN...
KURU (TURN)
We have a lost child in the park. A little girl named Rinko Asagi-chan has gone missing. She's a resident of Ruruie and a student at Kutaato Elementary School......
If you find her, please contact the lost child center. Her distinguishing features are ...

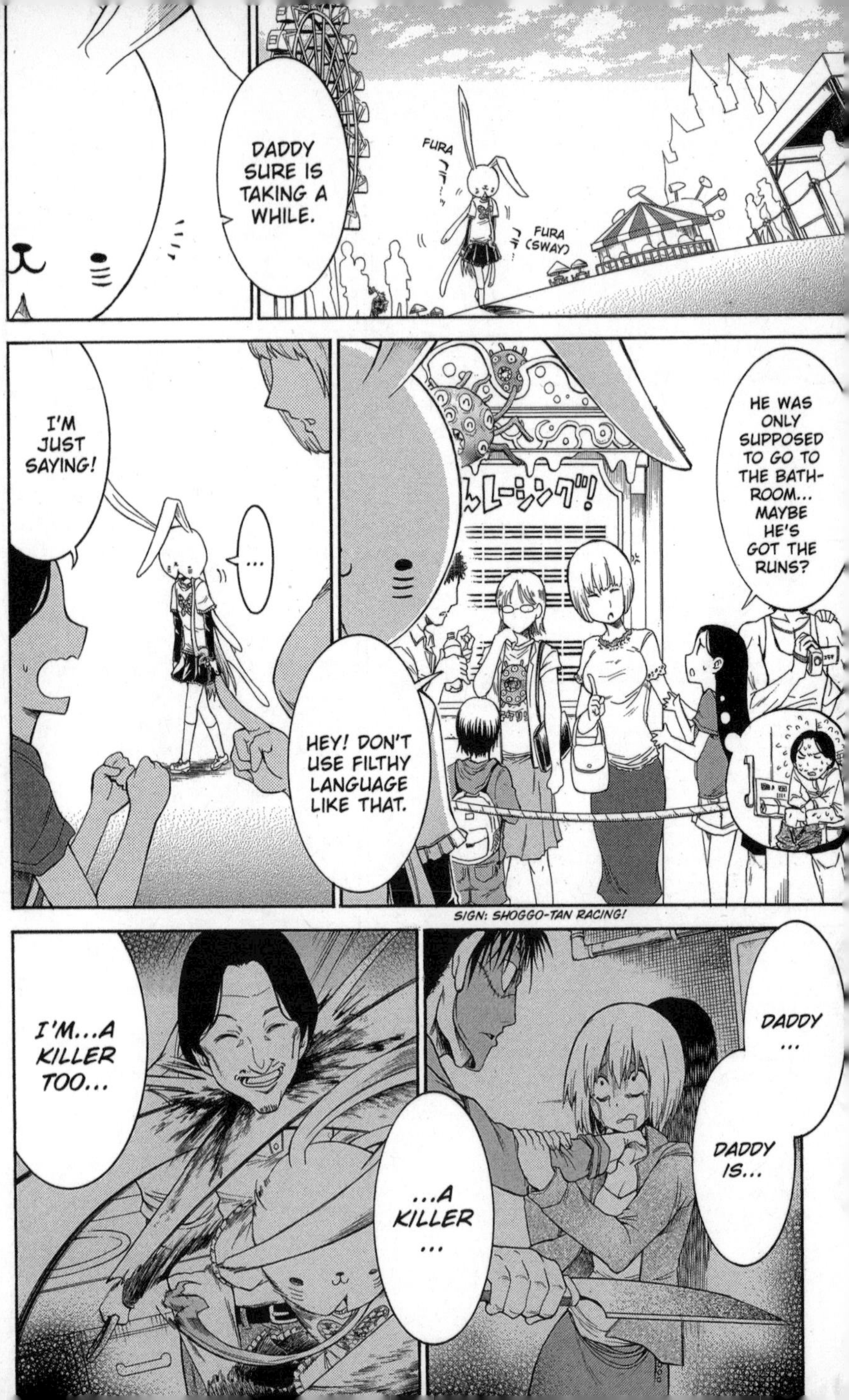
FURA
FURA (SWAY)
DADDY SURE IS TAKING A WHILE.
HE WAS ONLY SUPPOSED TO GO TO THE BATH-ROOM... MAYBE HE'S GOT THE RUNS?
HEY! DON'T USE FILTHY LANGUAGE LIKE THAT.
I'M JUST SAYING!
...
SIGN: SHOGGO-TAN RACING!
DADDY ...
DADDY IS...
...A KILLER ...
I'M...A KILLER TOO...

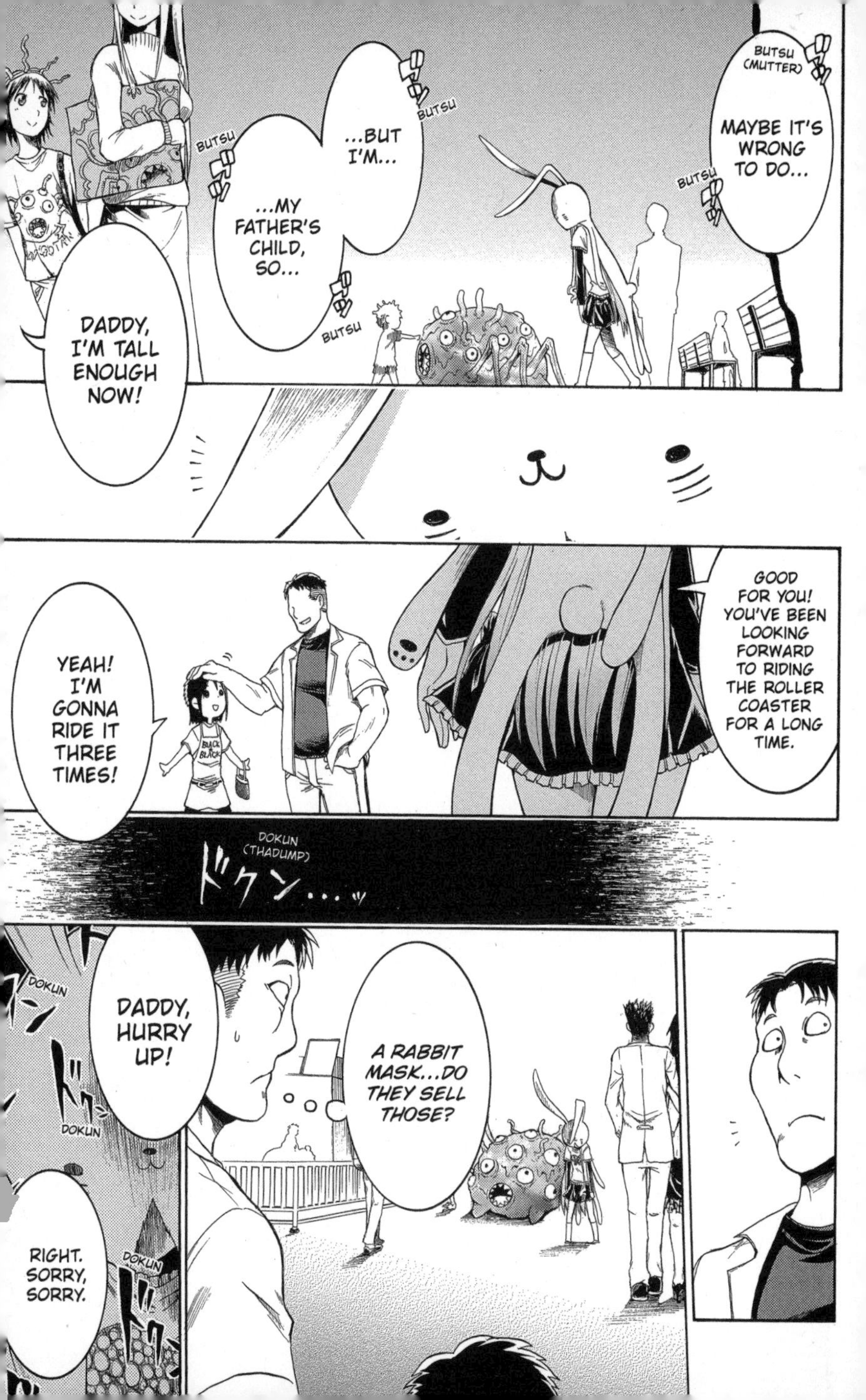
BUTSU (MUTTER)
MAYBE IT'S WRONG TO DO...
BUTSU
BUTSU
...BUT I'M...
BUTSU
...MY FATHER'S CHILD, SO...
BUTSU
DADDY, I'M TALL ENOUGH NOW!
GOOD FOR YOU! YOU'VE BEEN LOOKING FORWARD TO RIDING THE ROLLER COASTER FOR A LONG TIME.
YEAH! I'M GONNA RIDE IT THREE TIMES!
DOKUN (THADUMP)
ドクン…ッ
A RABBIT MASK...DO THEY SELL THOSE?
DADDY, HURRY UP!
DOKUN
DOKUN
RIGHT. SORRY, SORRY.
DOKUN

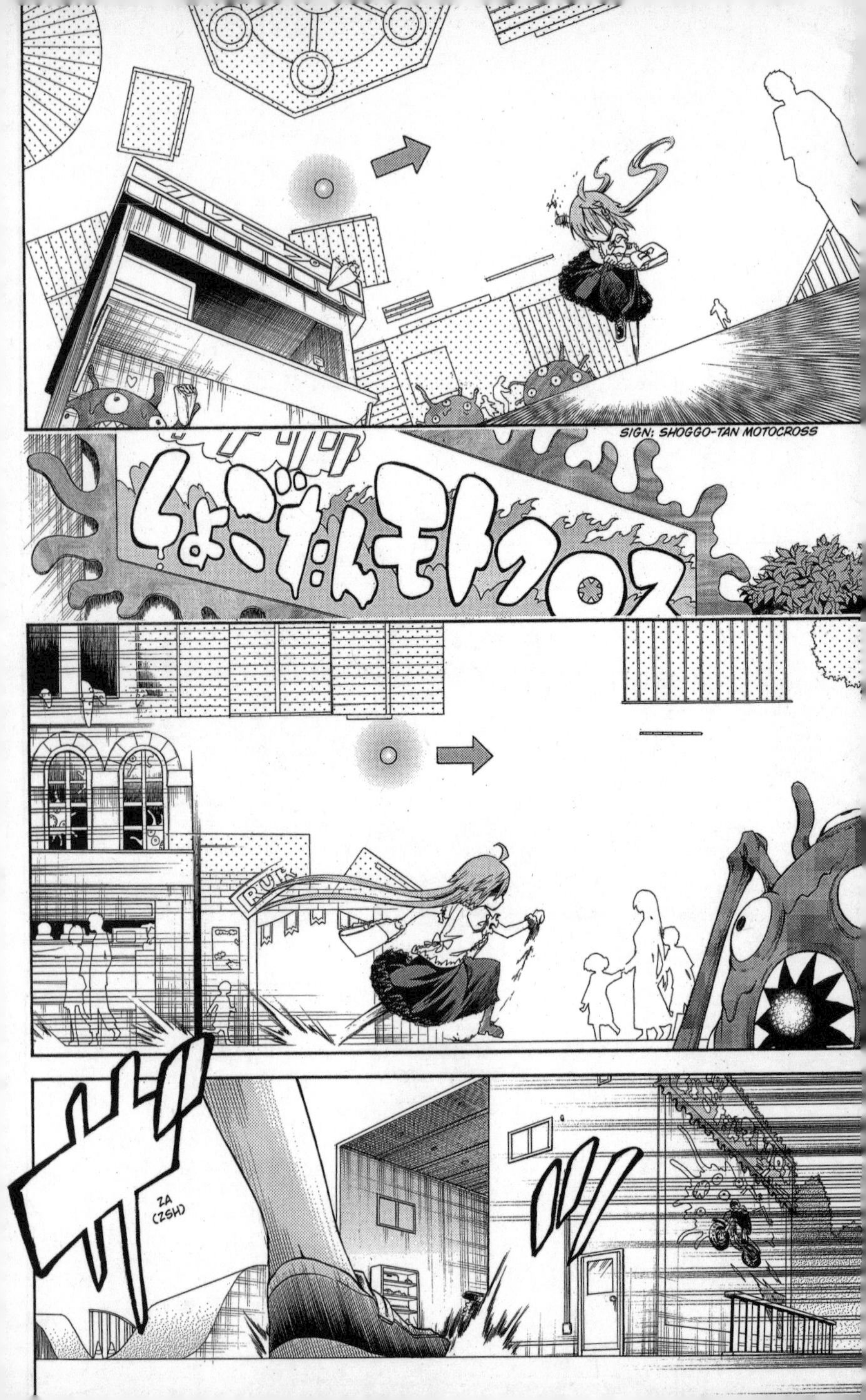
SIGN: SHOGGO-TAN MOTOCROSS
しょごたんモトクロス
ZA (ZSH)

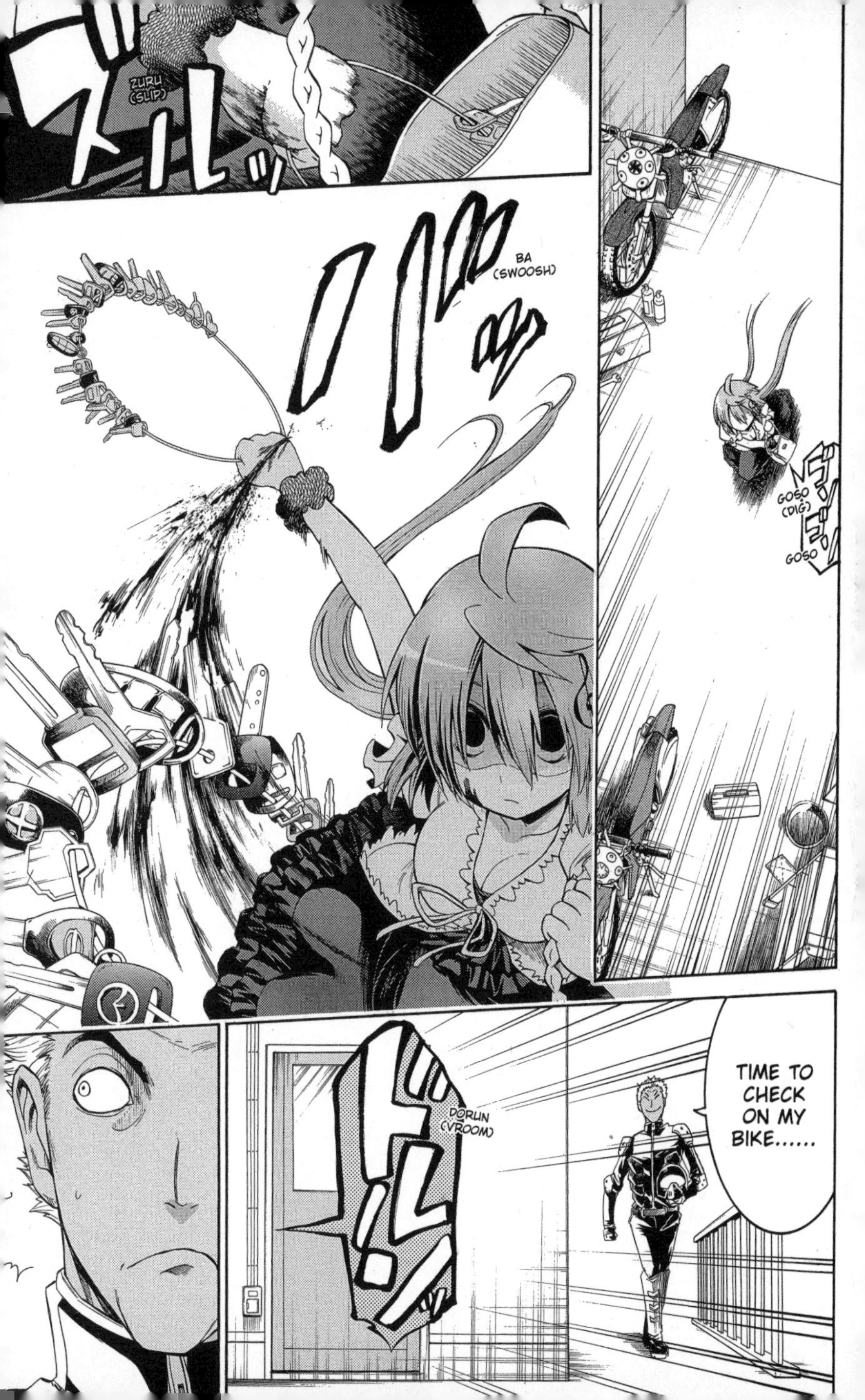
GOSO (DIG)
GOSO
ZURU (SLIP)
BA (SWOOSH)
TIME TO CHECK ON MY BIKE......
DORUN (VROOM)

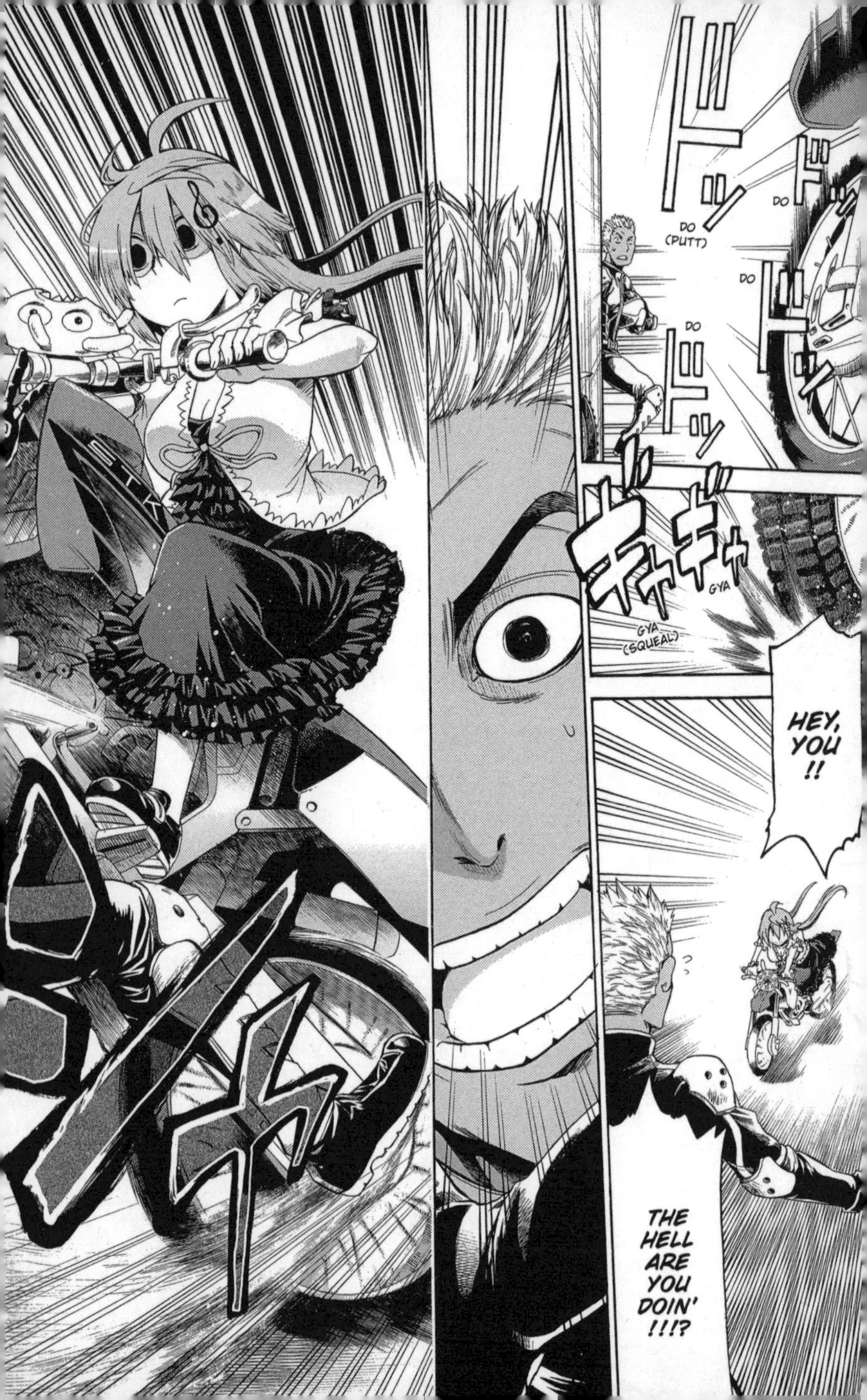
ドッドッドッドッ
DO
DO (PUTT)
DO
DO
ギャギャ
GYA
GYA (SQUEAL)
HEY, YOU!!
THE HELL ARE YOU DOIN'!!!?

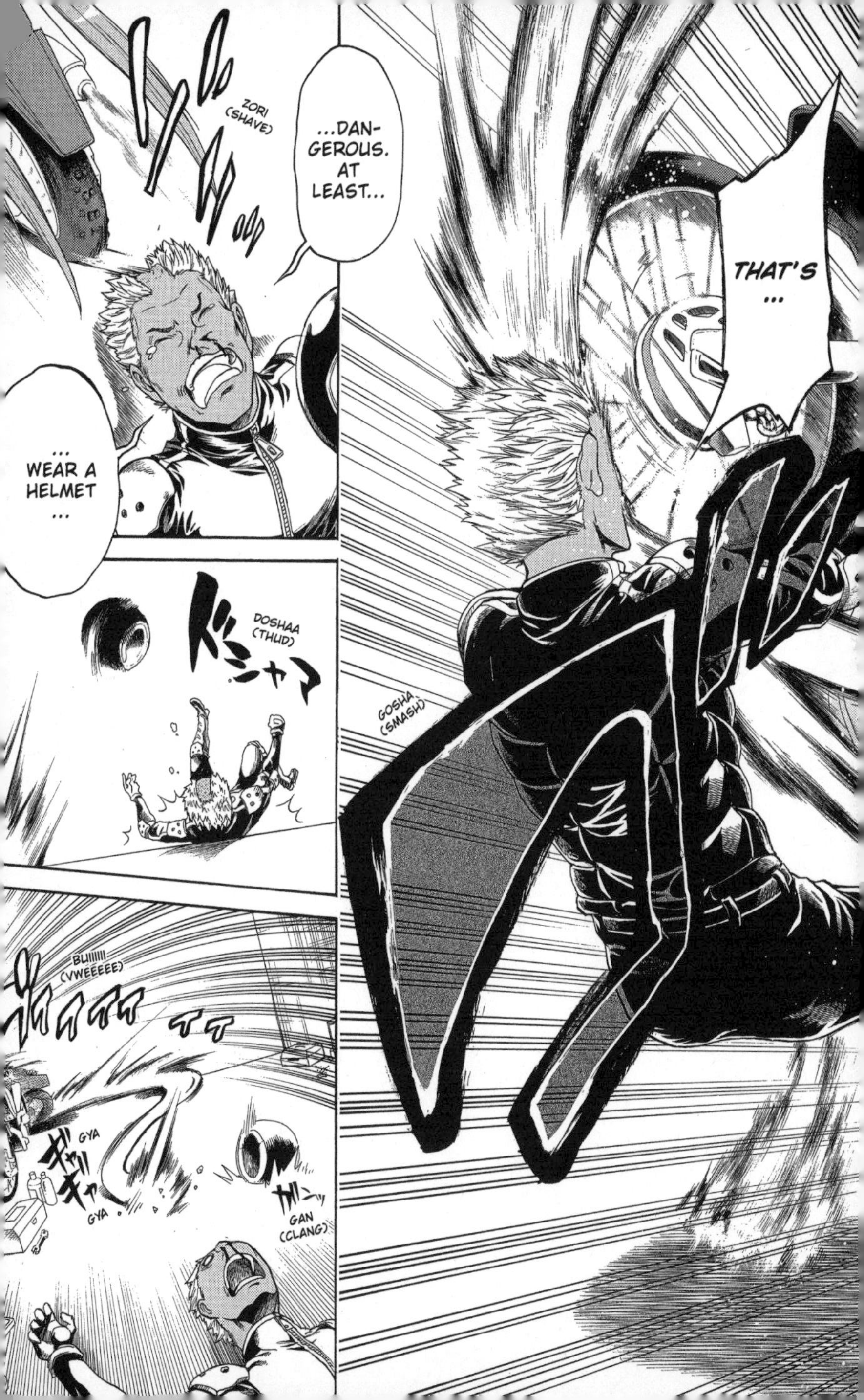
THAT'S ...
GOSHA (SMASH)
ZORI (SHAVE)
...DAN-GEROUS. AT LEAST...
... WEAR A HELMET ...
DOSHAA (THUD)
BUIIIII (VWEEEEE)
GYA
GYA
GAN (CLANG)

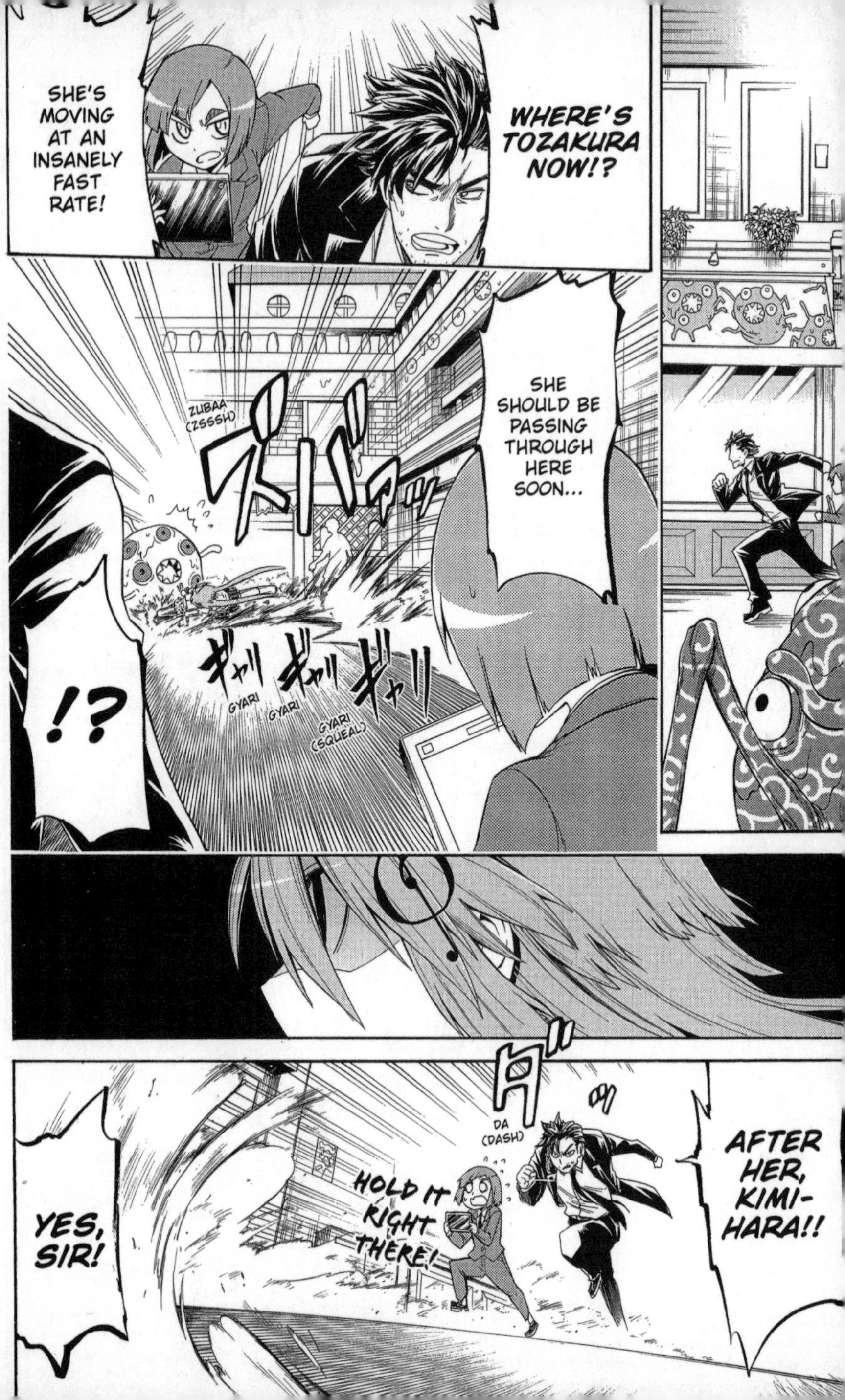
WHERE'S TOZAKURA NOW!?
SHE'S MOVING AT AN INSANELY FAST RATE!
SHE SHOULD BE PASSING THROUGH HERE SOON...
ズバァッ
ZUBAA (ZSSSH)
!?
ギャリ ギャリ ギャリ
GYARI GYARI GYARI (SQUEAL)
AFTER HER, KIMI-HARA!!
ダッ
DA (DASH)
HOLD IT RIGHT THERE!
YES, SIR!

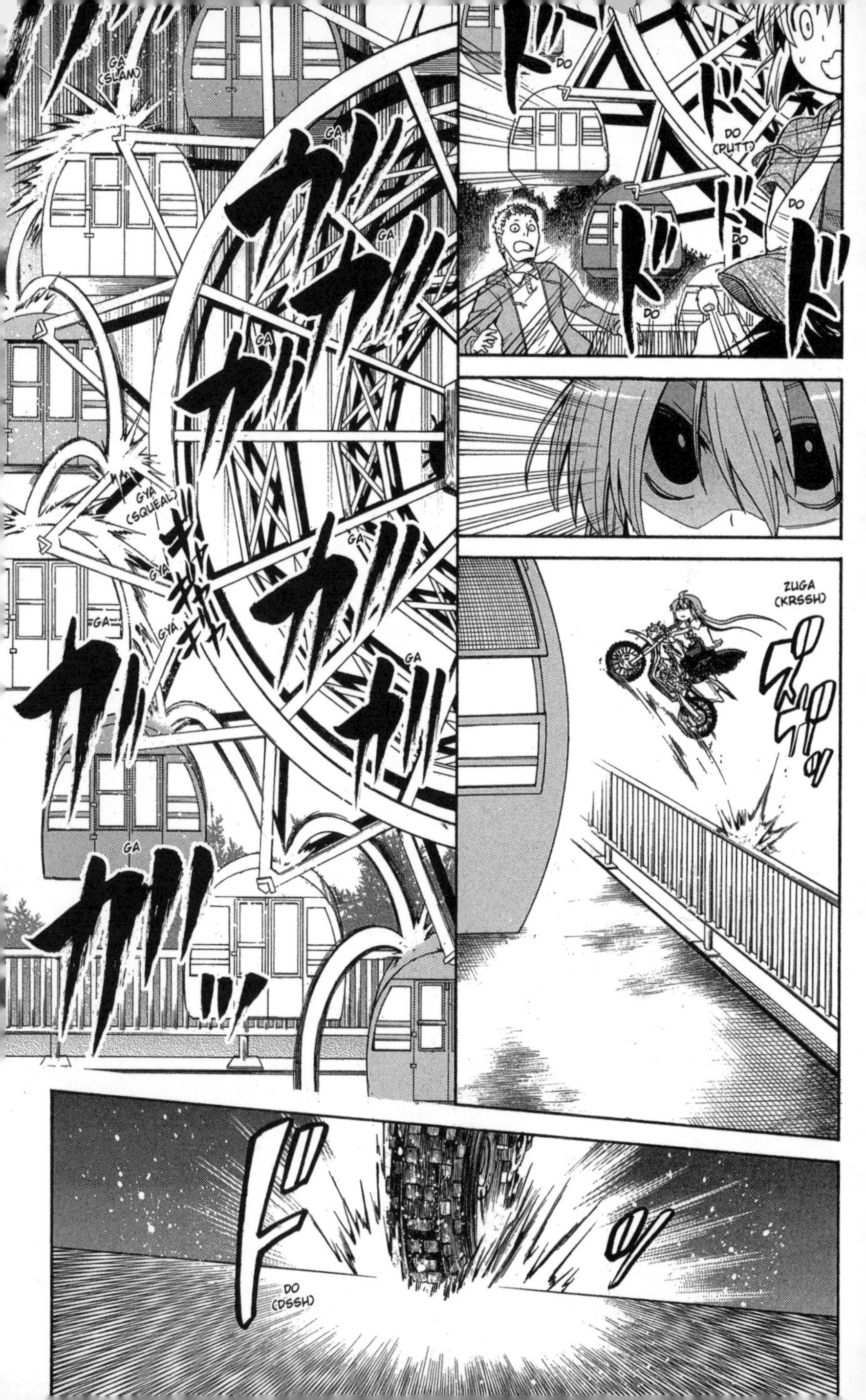
DO
DO
(PUTT)
DO
DO
DO
ZUGA
(KRSSH)
GA
(SLAM)
GA
GA
GA
GYA
(SQUEAL)
GYA
GYA
GA
GA
GA
GA
DO
(DSSH)

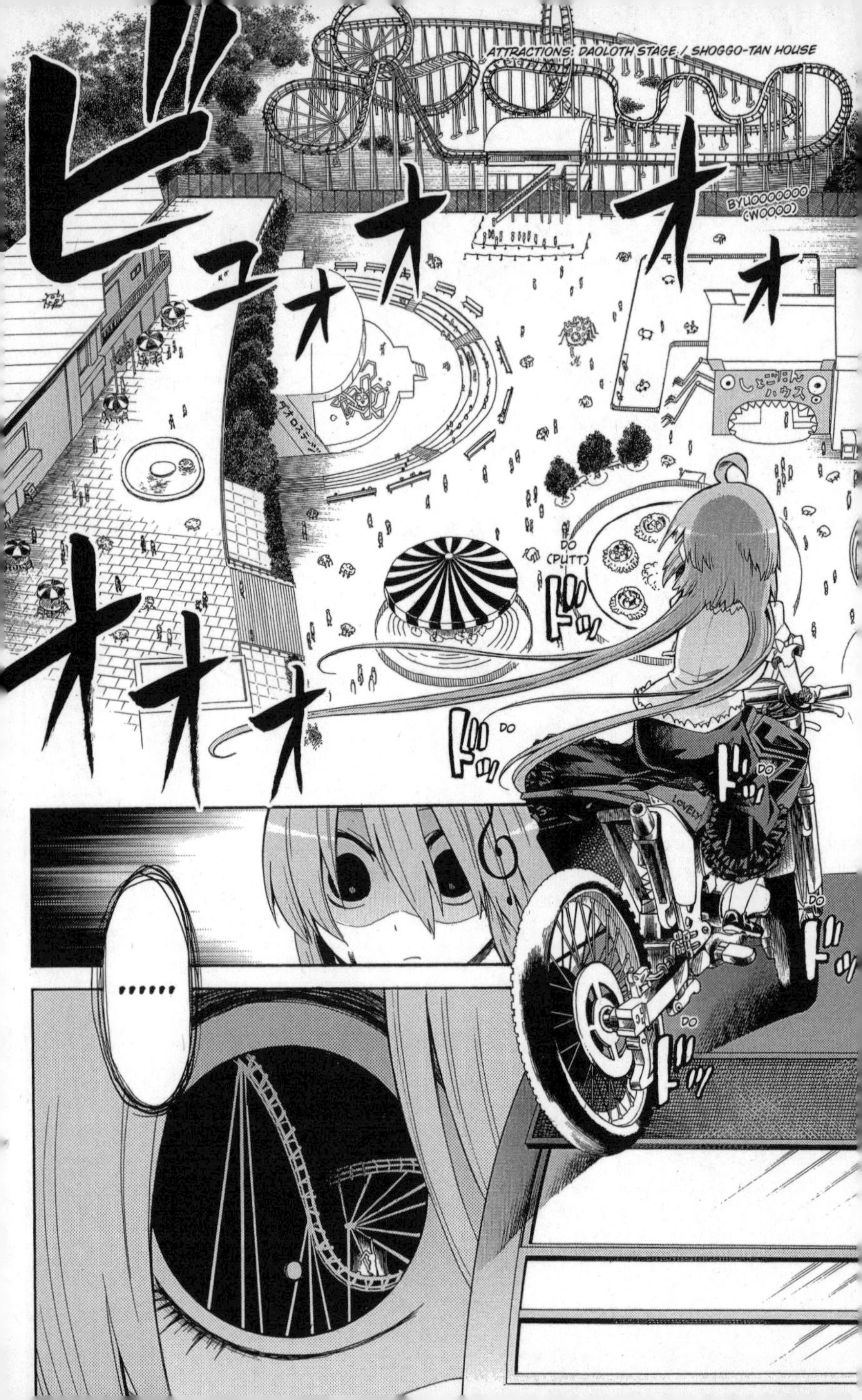
ATTRACTIONS: DAOLOTH STAGE / SHOGGO-TAN HOUSE
BYUOOOOOOO (WOOOO)
DO (PUTT)
DO
DO
LOVELY
DO
DO
......

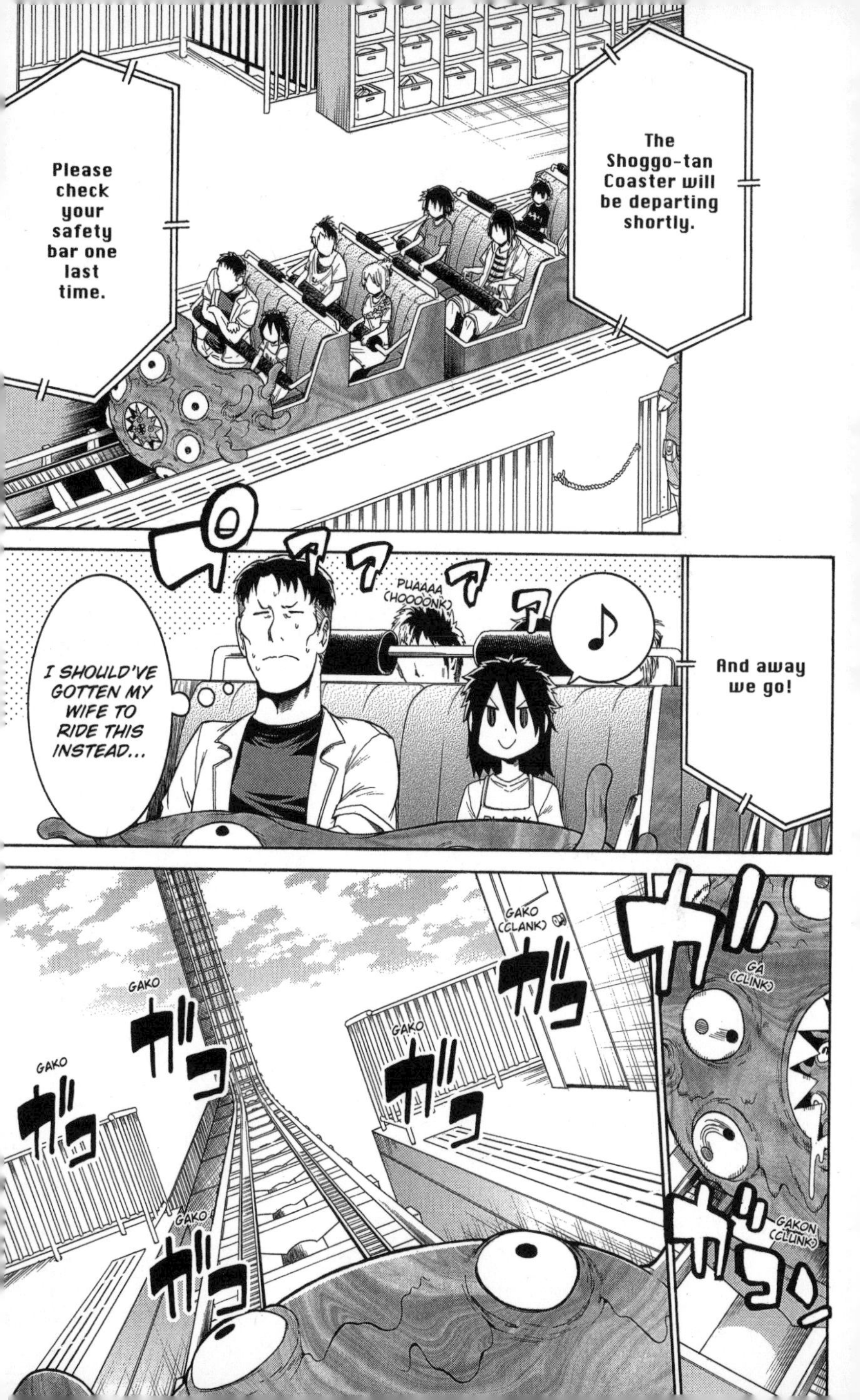
The Shoggo-tan Coaster will be departing shortly.
Please check your safety bar one last time.
And away we go!
PUAAAA (HOOOONK)
♪
I SHOULD'VE GOTTEN MY WIFE TO RIDE THIS INSTEAD...
GA (CLINK)
GAKON (CLUNK)
GAKO (CLANK)
GAKO
GAKO
GAKO
GAKO

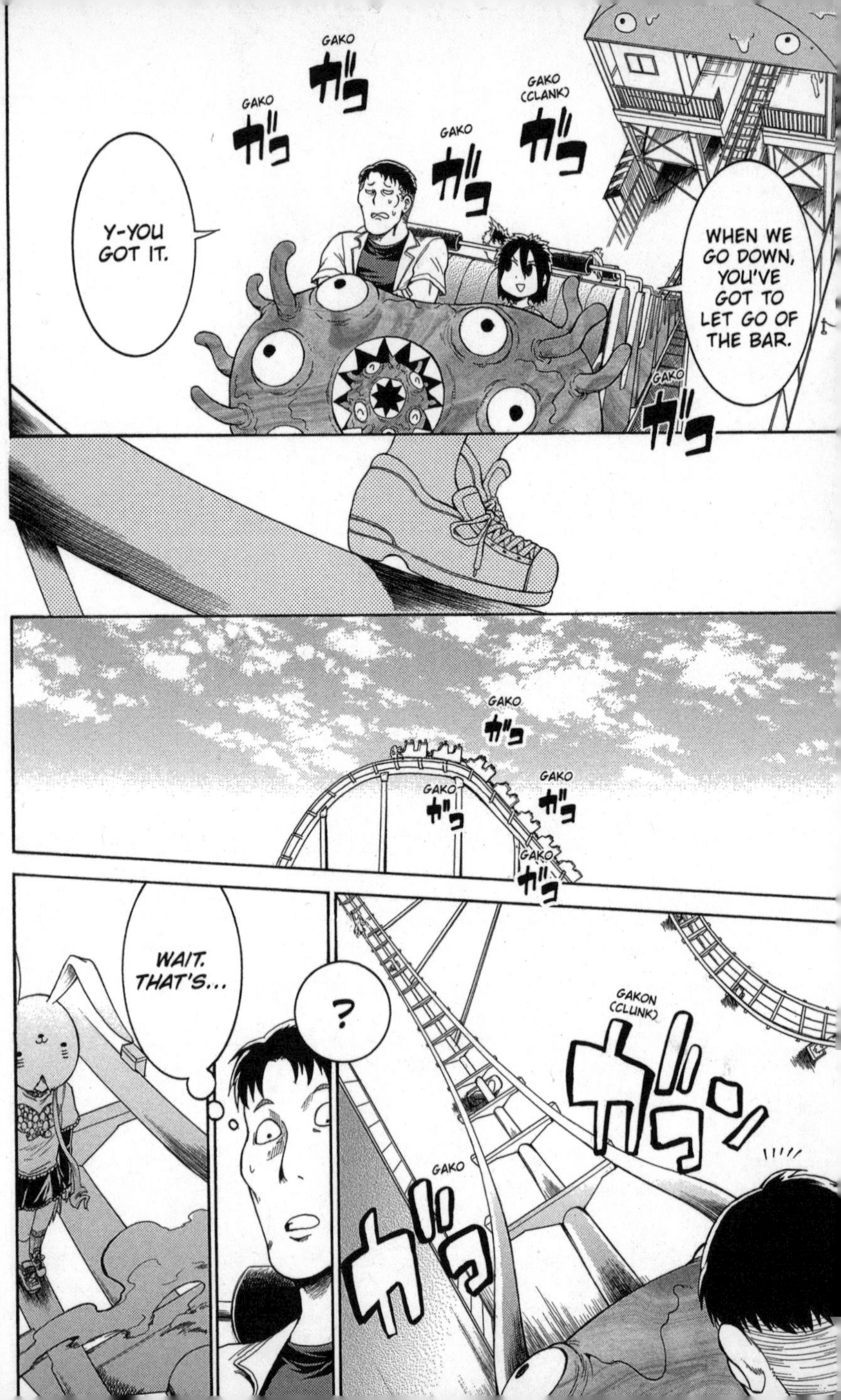
WHEN WE GO DOWN, YOU'VE GOT TO LET GO OF THE BAR.
GAKO (CLANK)
GAKO
GAKO
GAKO
GAKO
Y-YOU GOT IT.
GAKO
GAKO
GAKO
GAKO
GAKON (CLUNK)
GAKO
?
WAIT. THAT'S...

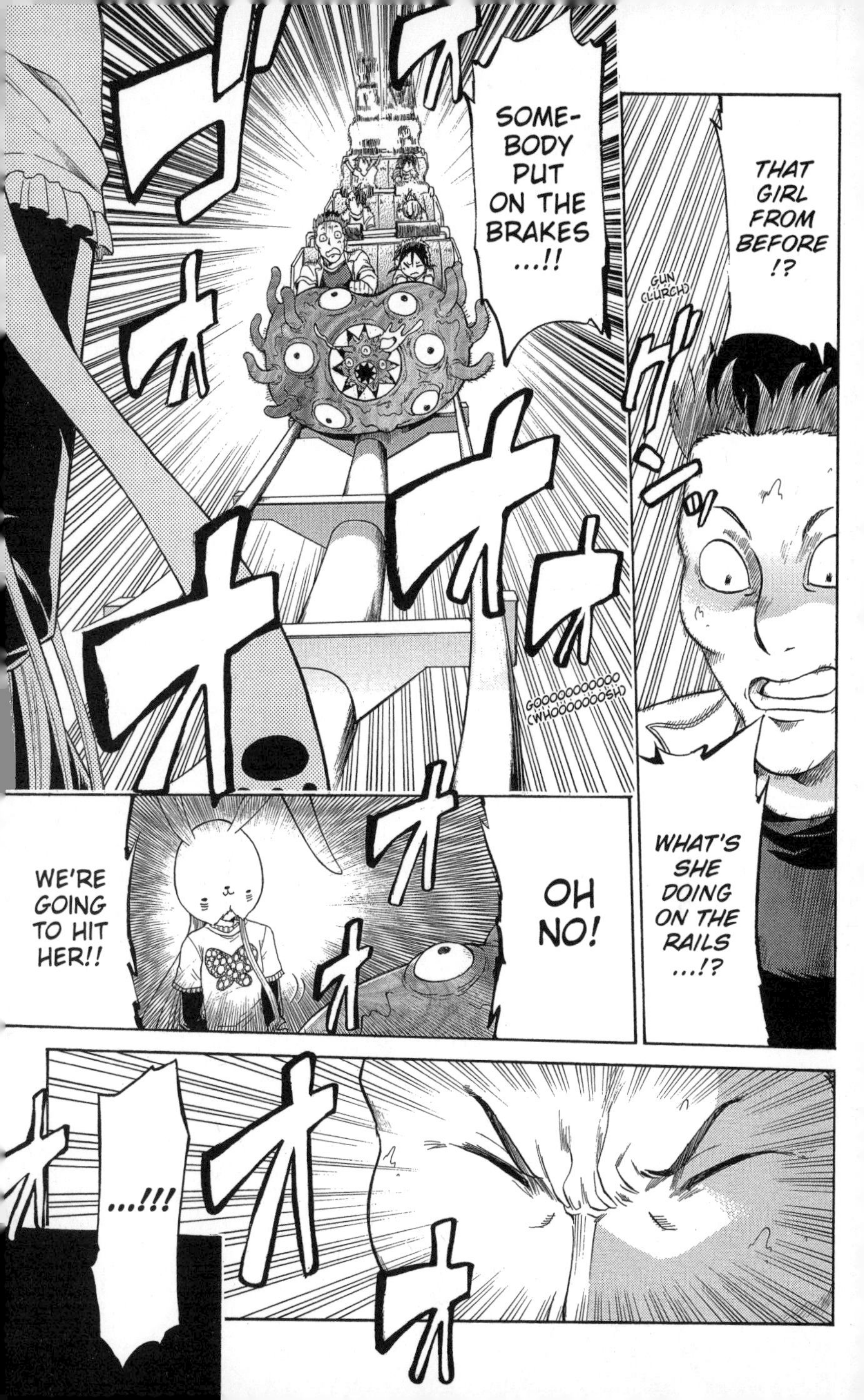
THAT GIRL FROM BEFORE!?
GUN (LURCH)
WHAT'S SHE DOING ON THE RAILS ...!?
SOME-BODY PUT ON THE BRAKES ...!!
GOOOOOOOOOOO (WHOOOOOOOOSH)
OH NO!
WE'RE GOING TO HIT HER!!
...!!!

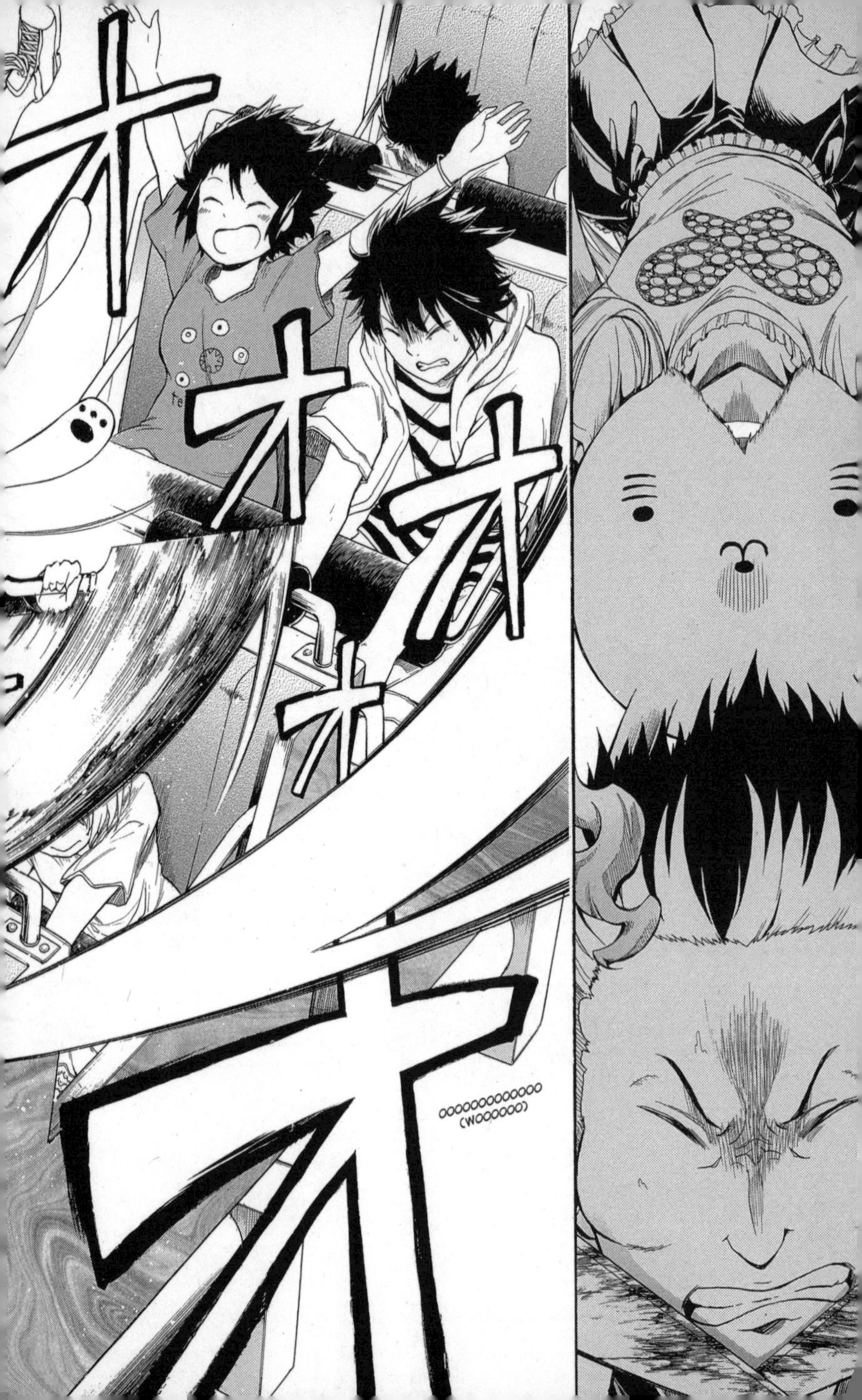
オオオオオ
OOOOOOOOOOOOO
(WOOOOOO)

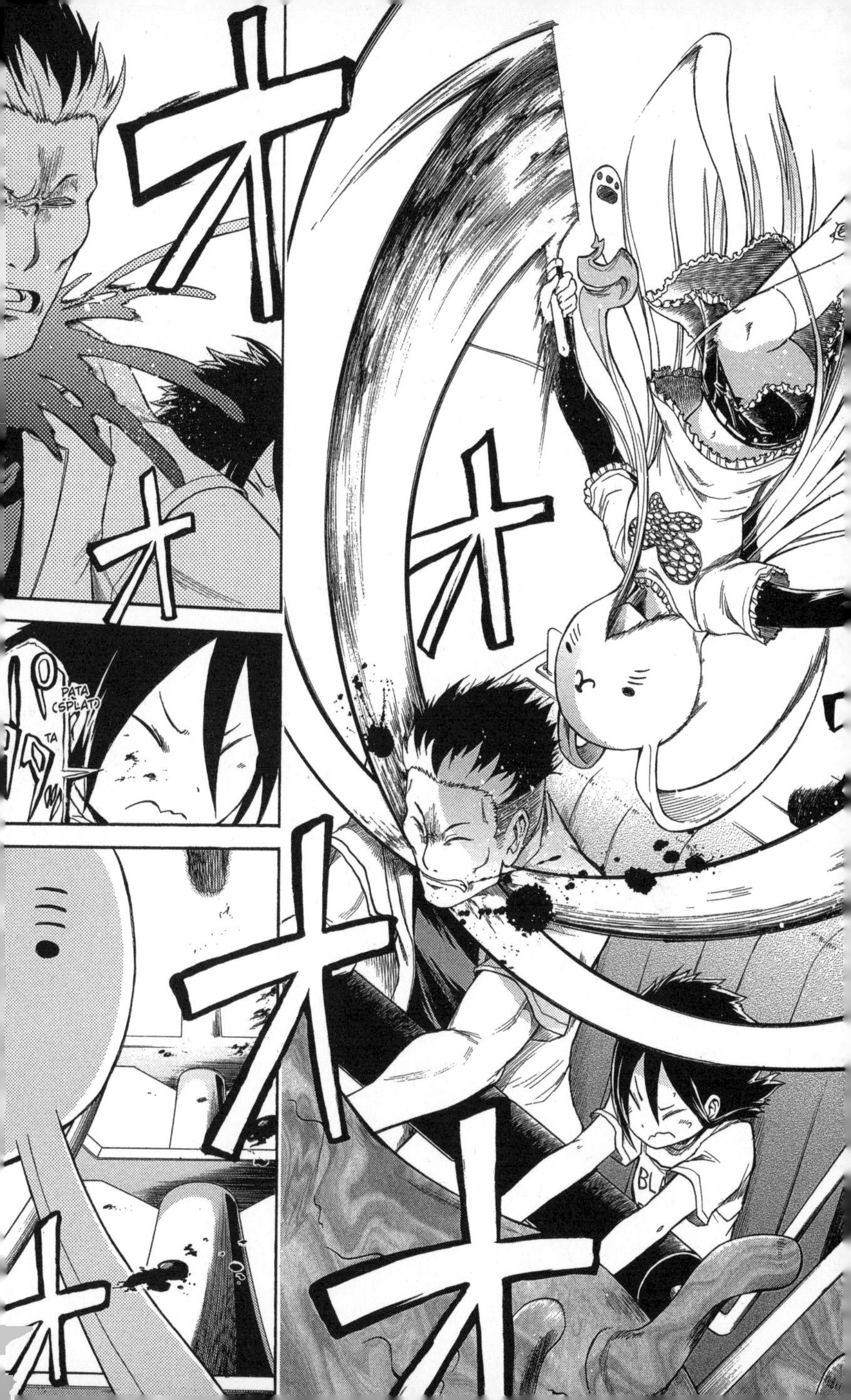
オ
オ
オ
オ
オ
PATA (SPLAT)
TA
オ

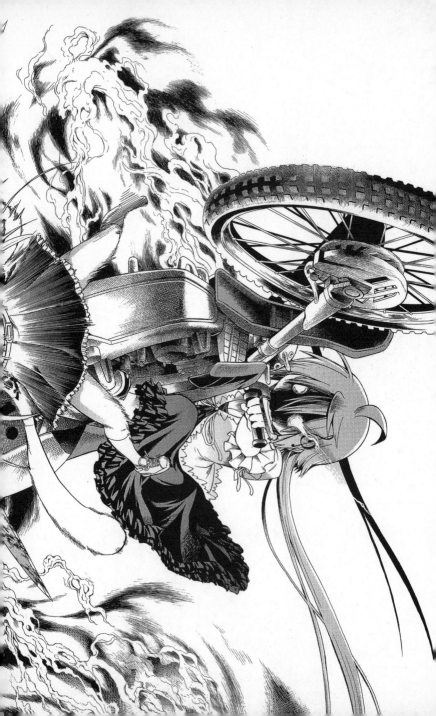

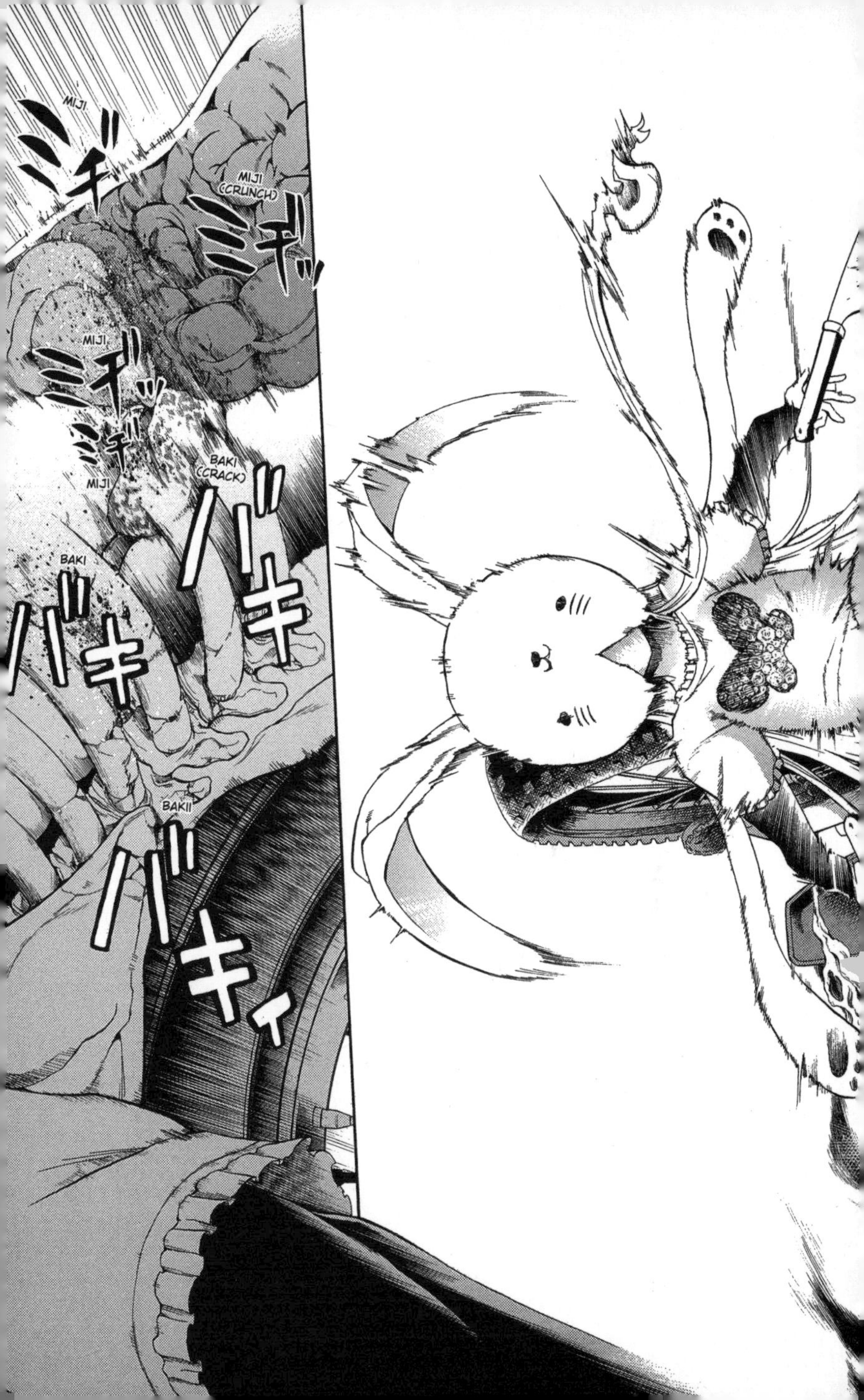
MIJI (CRUNCH)
ミヂッ
MIJI
ミヂ
MIJI
ミヂッ
MIJI
ミヂ
BAKI (CRACK)
バキ
BAKI
バキ
BAKII
バキィ

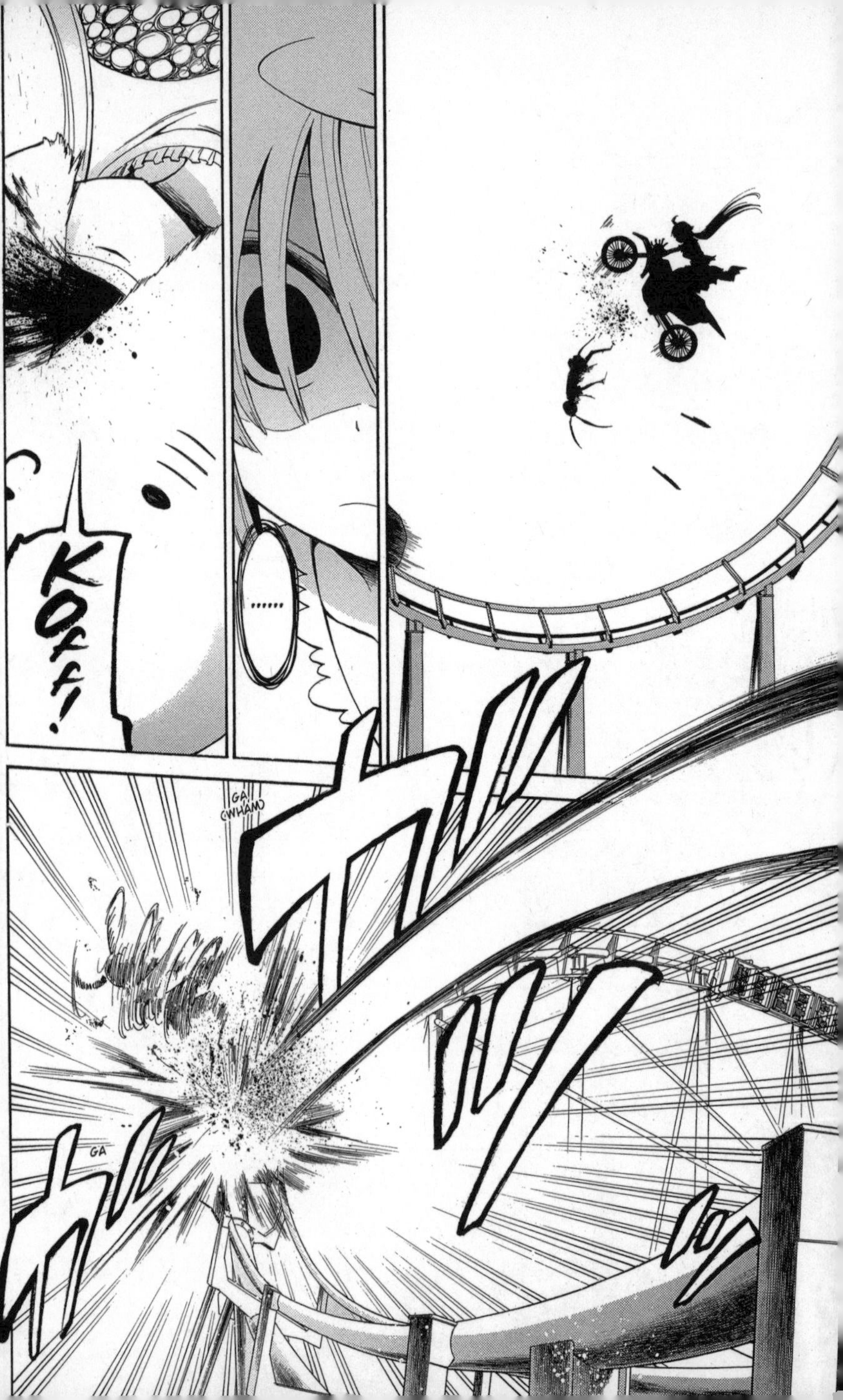
......
KOFF!
GA (WHAM)
GA

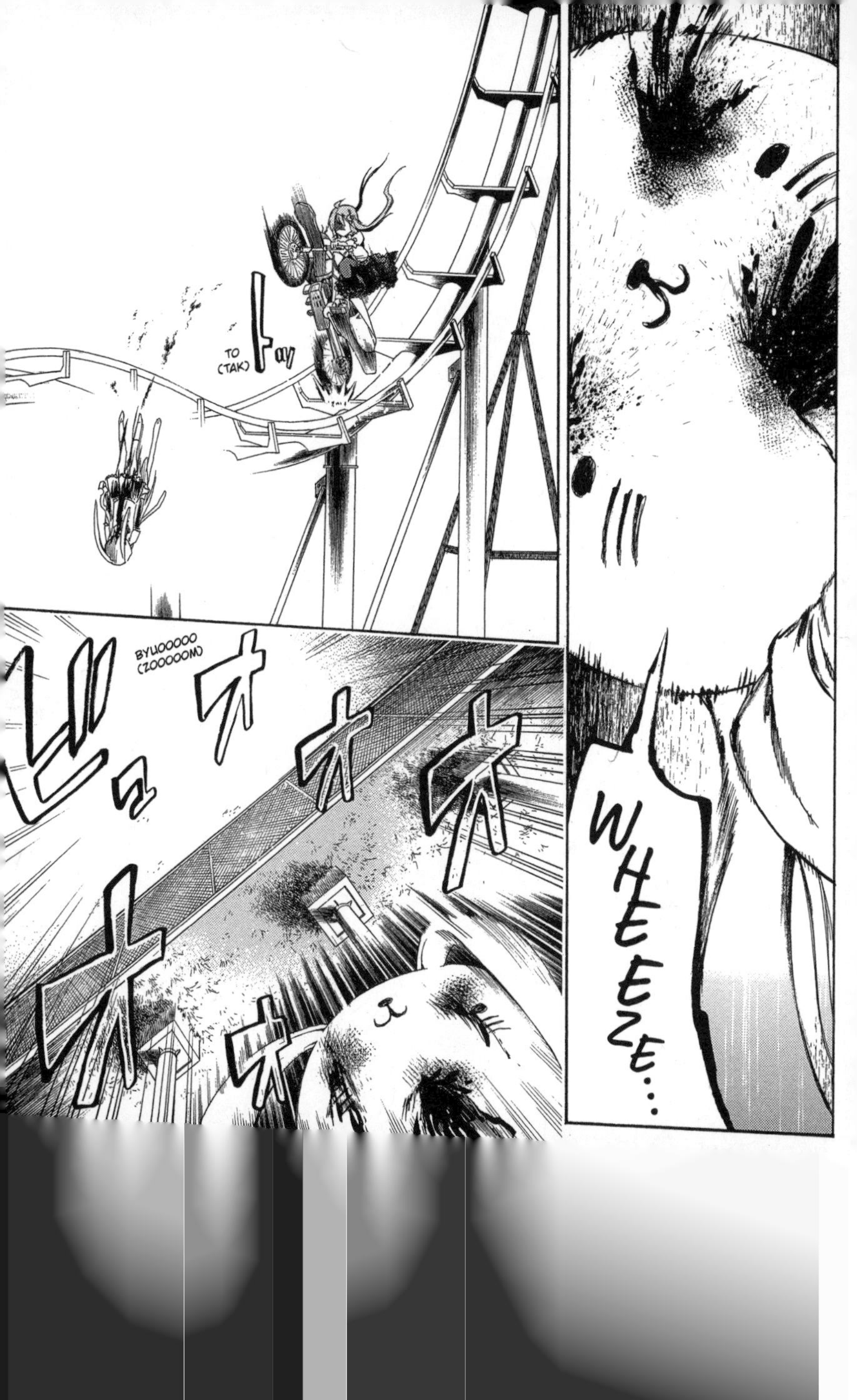
WHEEZE...
TO (TAK)
BYUOOOOO (ZOOOOOM)

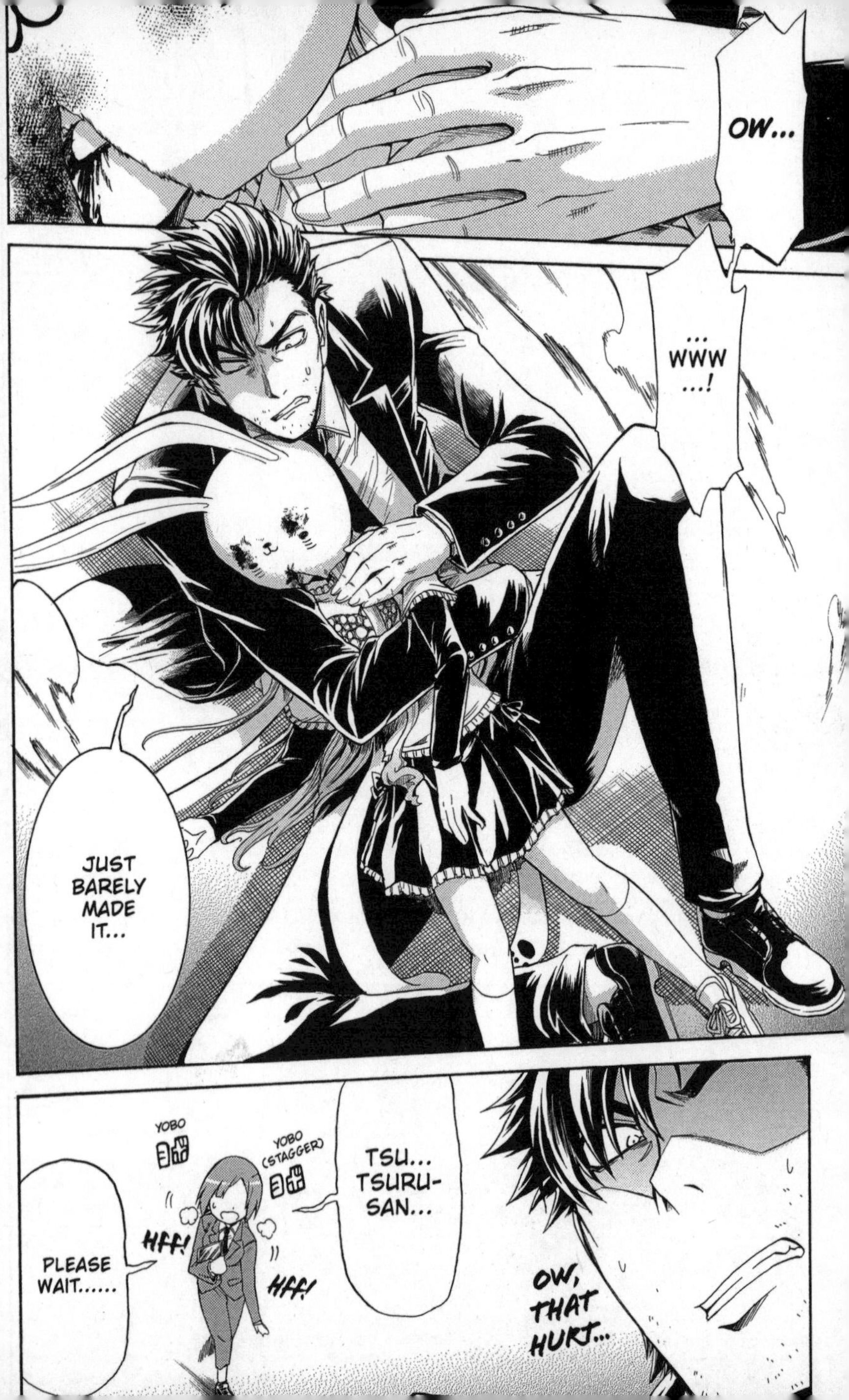
OW...
...WWW...!
JUST BARELY MADE IT...
OW, THAT HURT...
TSU... TSURU-SAN...
YOBO (STAGGER)
YOBO
HFF!
HFF!
PLEASE WAIT......

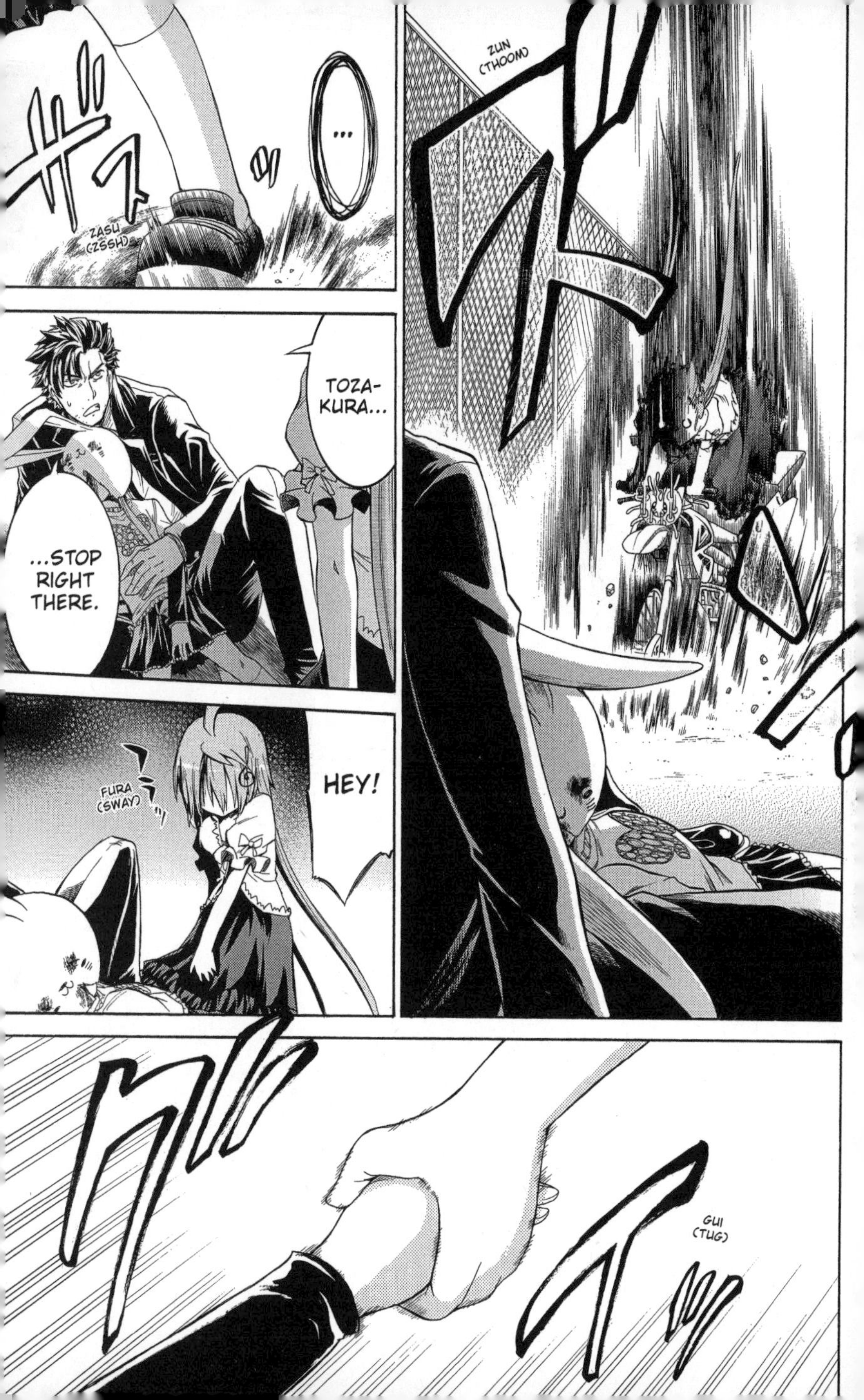
ZUN (THOOM)
...
ZASU (ZSSH)
TOZA-KURA...
...STOP RIGHT THERE.
HEY!
FURA (SWAY)
GUI (TUG)

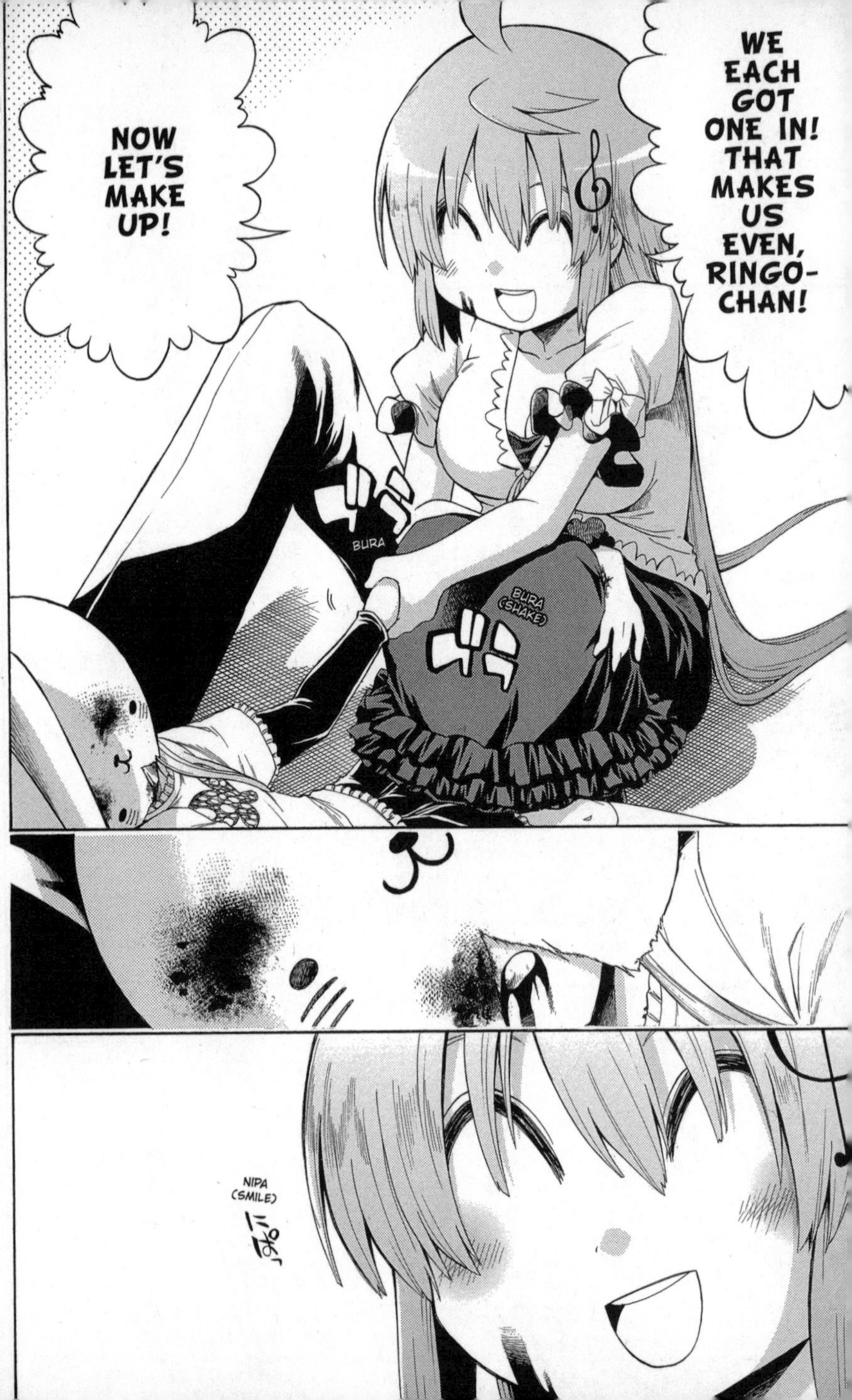
WE EACH GOT ONE IN! THAT MAKES US EVEN, RINGO-CHAN!
NOW LET'S MAKE UP!
BURA (SHAKE)
BURA
NIPA (SMILE)

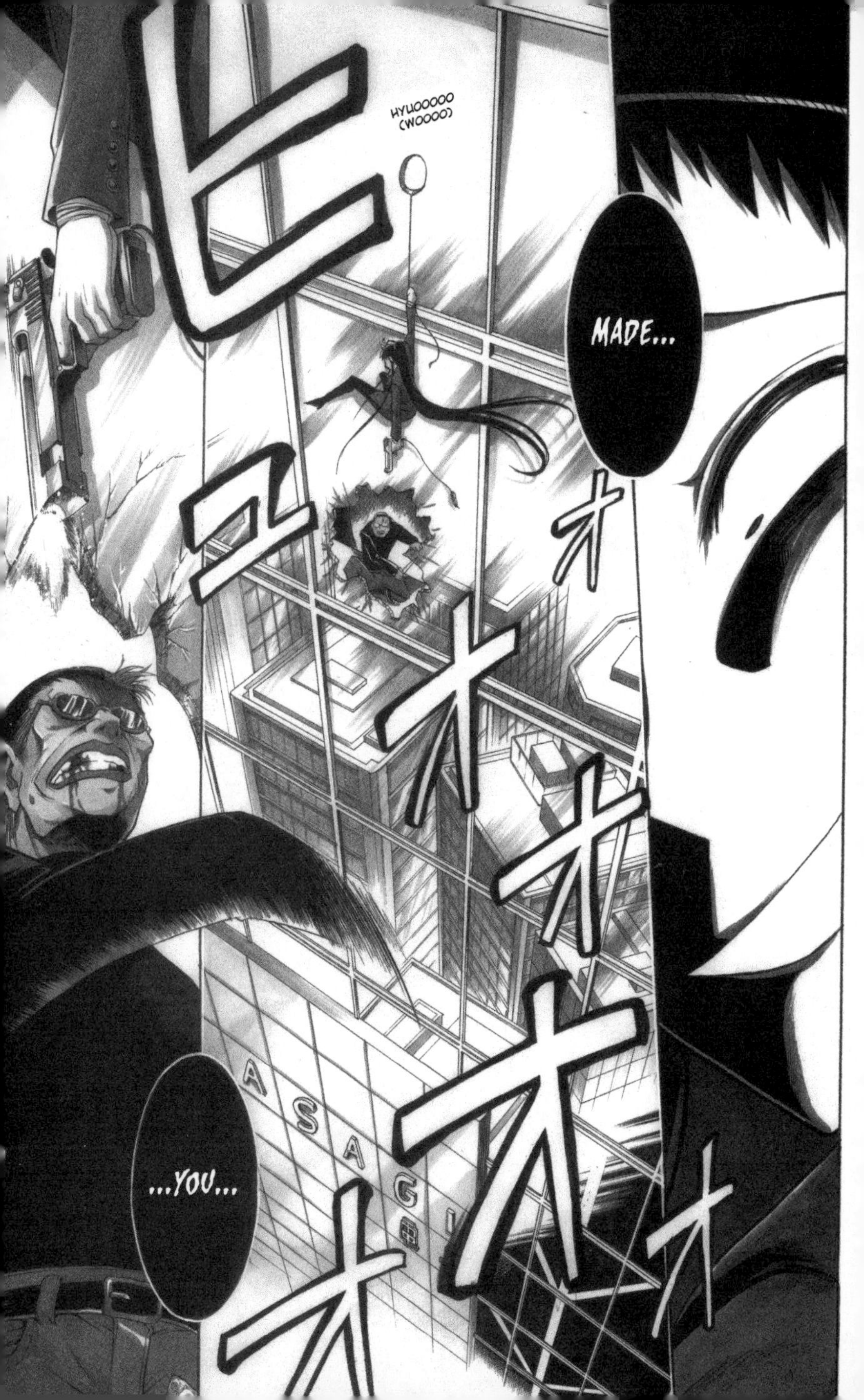
MADE...
HYUOOOOO
(WOOOO)
...YOU...

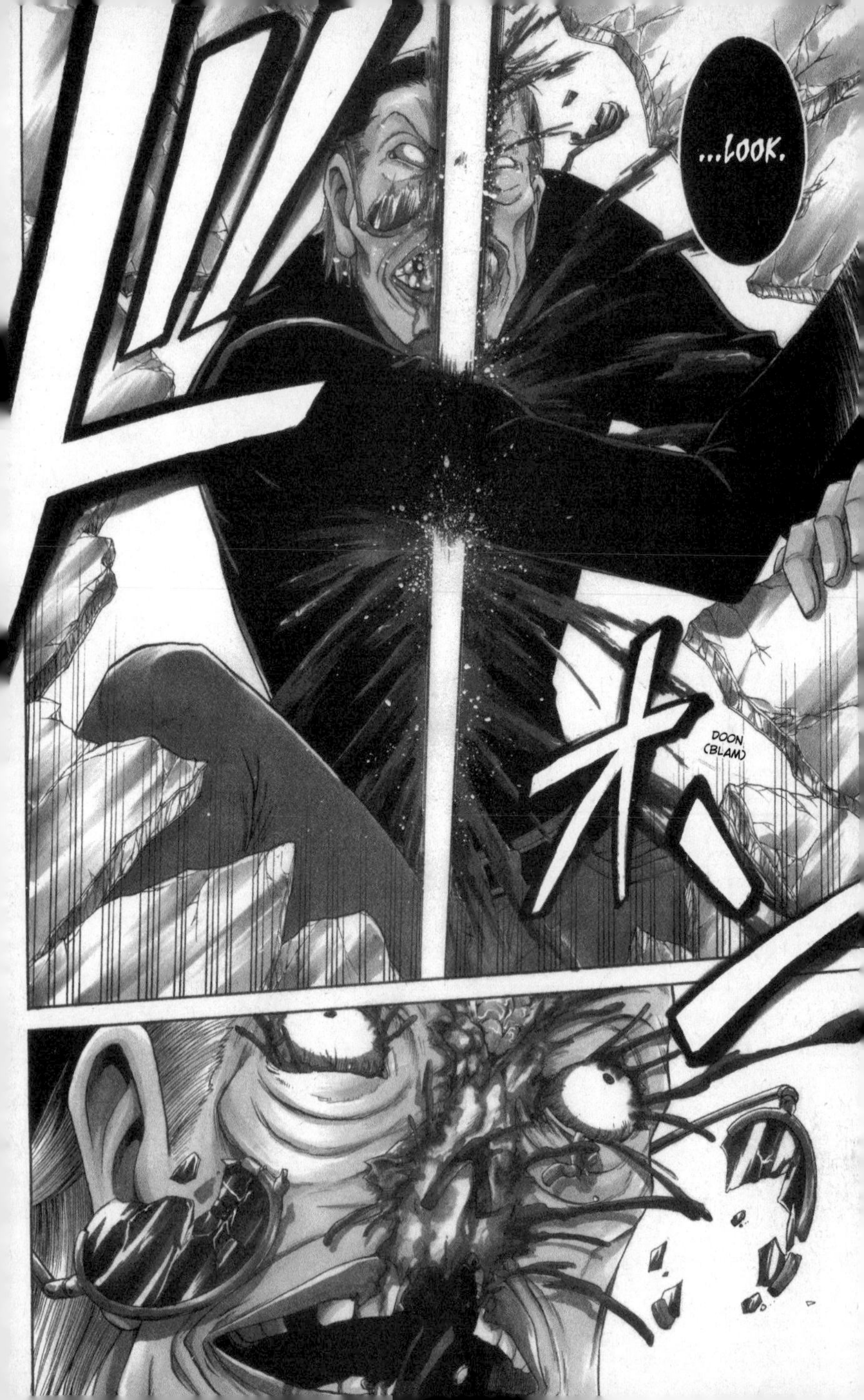
...LOOK.
DOON
(BLAM)

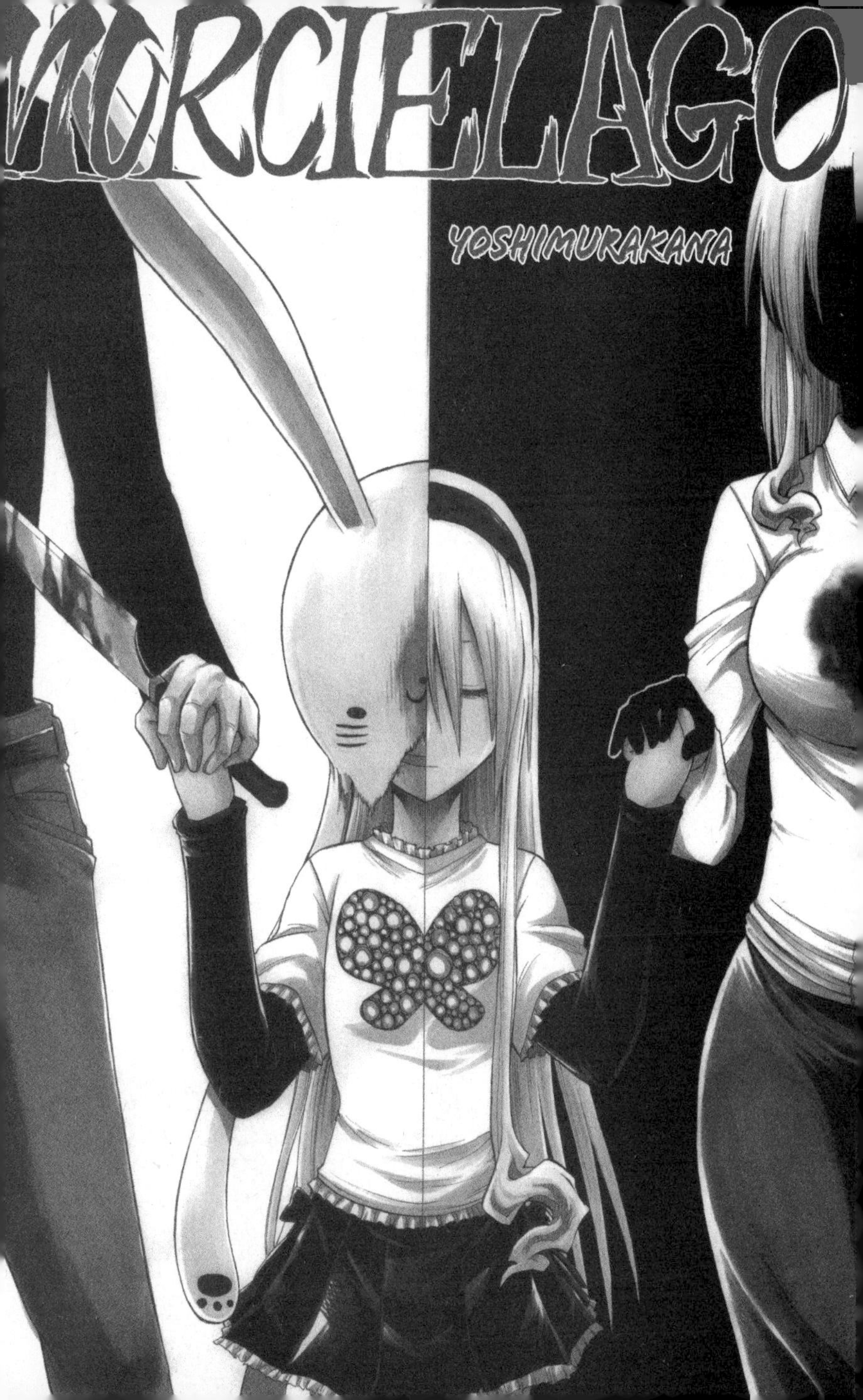
MURCIELAGO
YOSHIMURAKANA

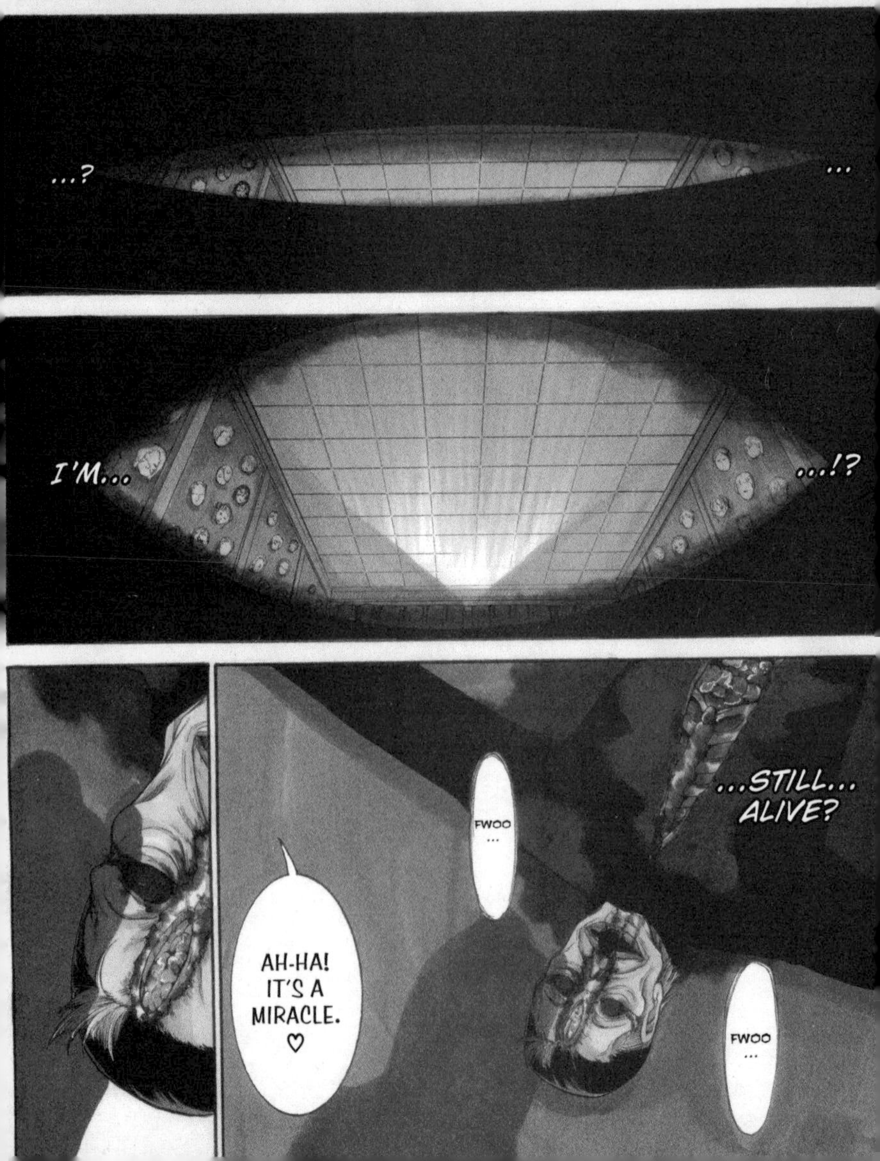
...
...?
...!?
I'M...
...STILL... ALIVE?
FWOO...
FWOO...
AH-HA! IT'S A MIRACLE. ♡

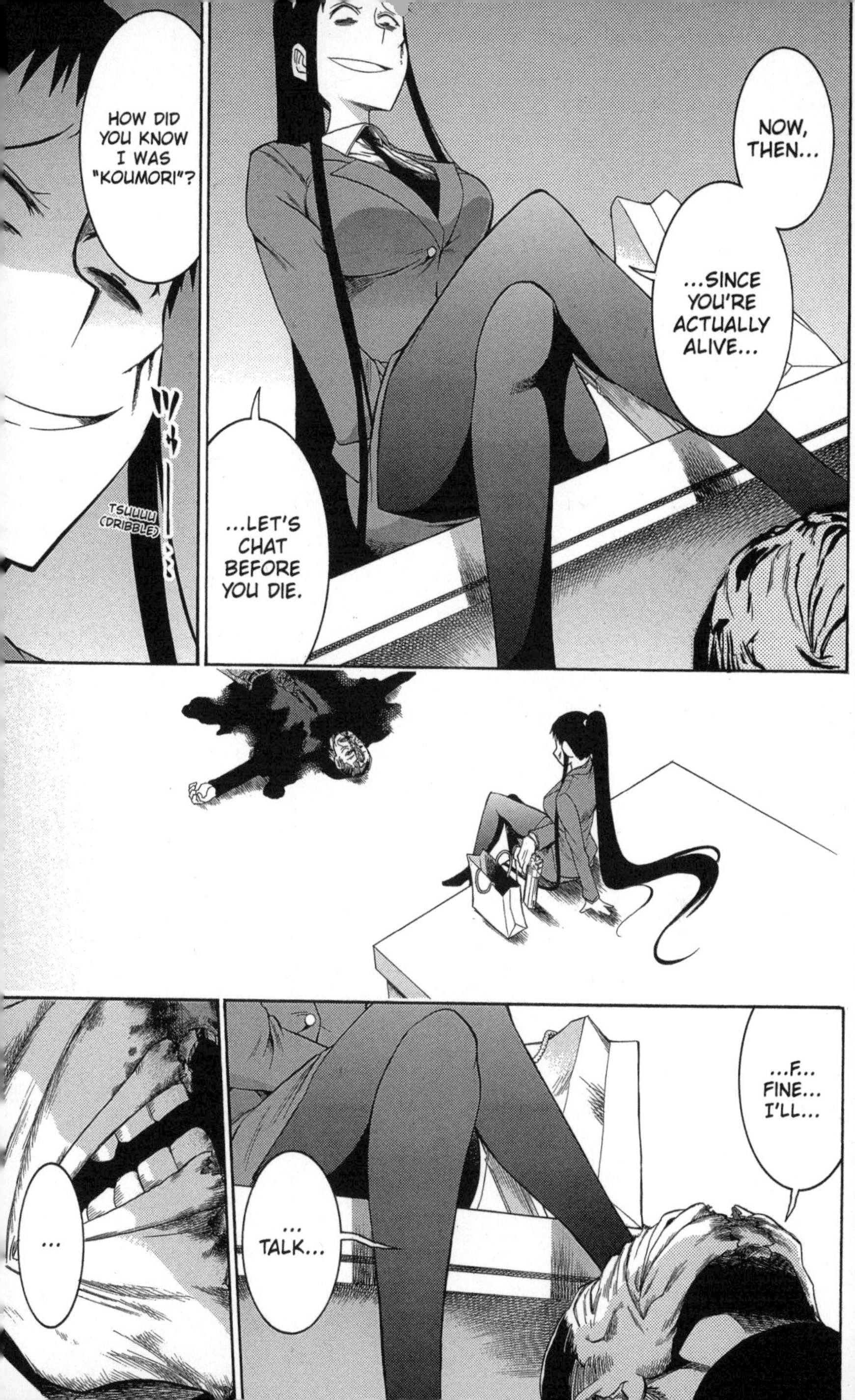
NOW, THEN...
...SINCE YOU'RE ACTUALLY ALIVE...
...LET'S CHAT BEFORE YOU DIE.
HOW DID YOU KNOW I WAS "KOUMORI"?
TSUUUU (DRIBBLE)
...F... FINE... I'LL...
... TALK...
...

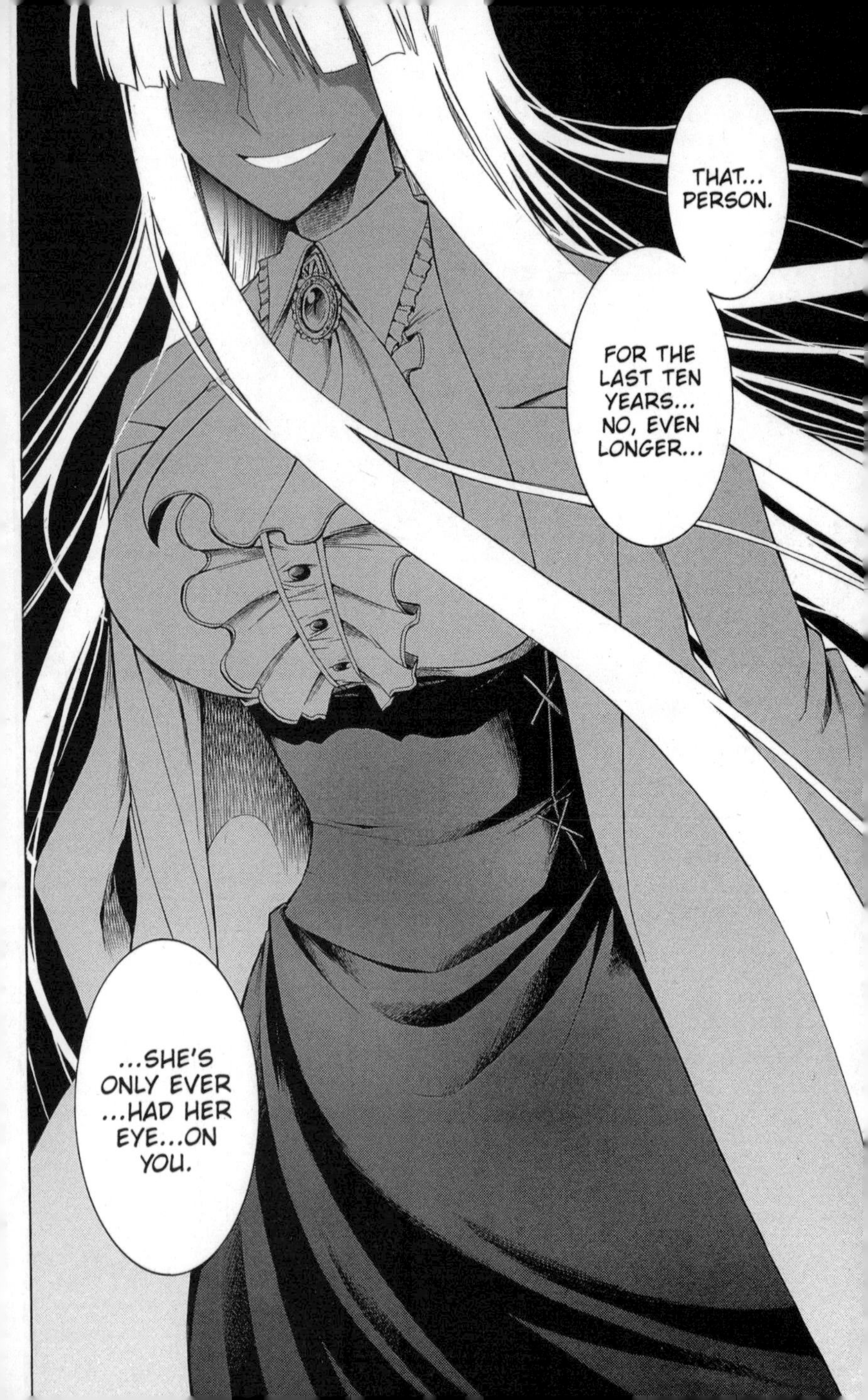
THAT... PERSON.
FOR THE LAST TEN YEARS... NO, EVEN LONGER...
...SHE'S ONLY EVER ...HAD HER EYE...ON YOU.

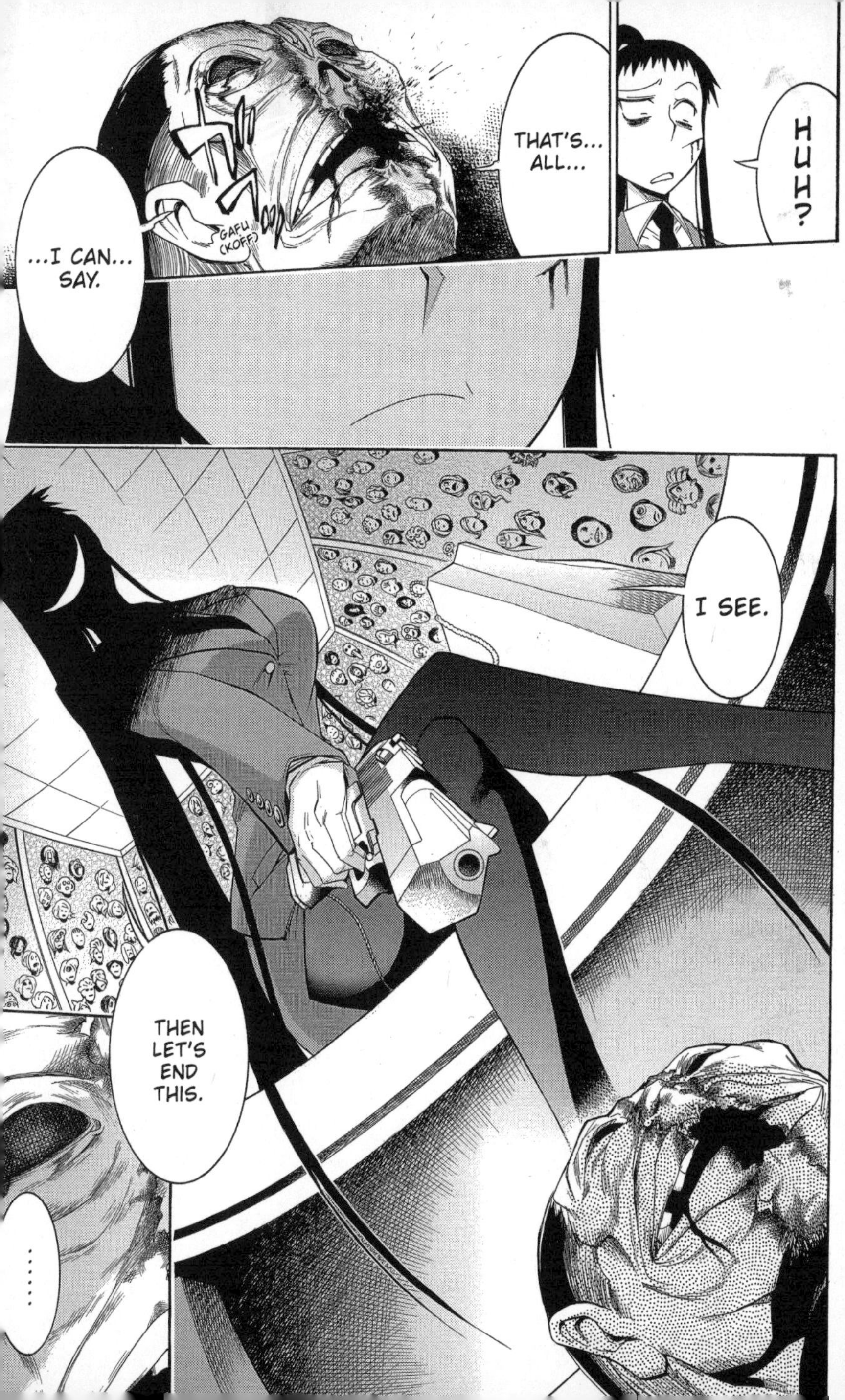
HUH?
THAT'S... ALL...
GAFU (KOFF)
...I CAN... SAY.
I SEE.
THEN LET'S END THIS.
......

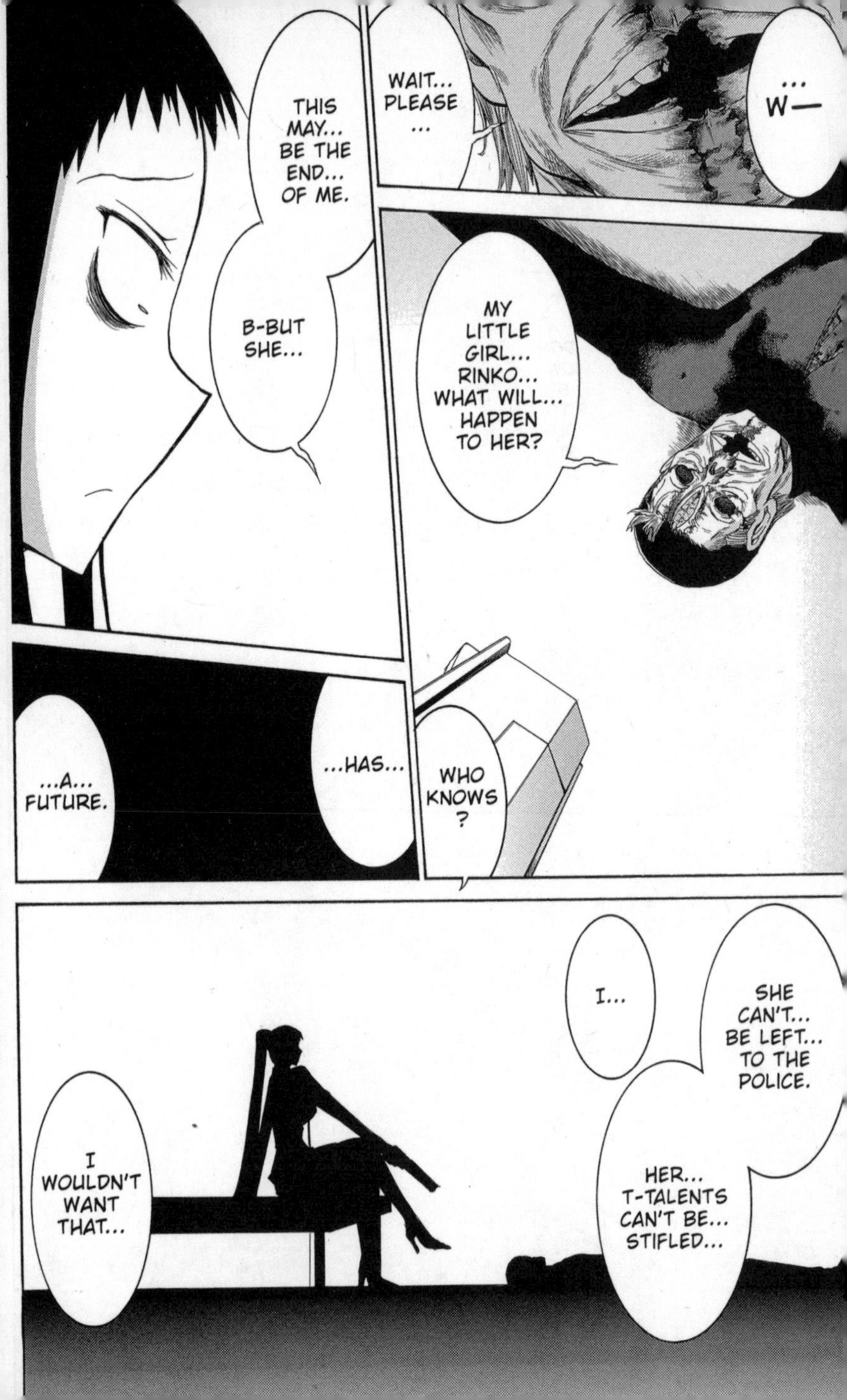
...W—
WAIT... PLEASE ...
MY LITTLE GIRL... RINKO... WHAT WILL... HAPPEN TO HER?
THIS MAY... BE THE END... OF ME.
B-BUT SHE...
WHO KNOWS?
...HAS...
...A... FUTURE.
SHE CAN'T... BE LEFT... TO THE POLICE.
I...
HER... T-TALENTS CAN'T BE... STIFLED...
I WOULDN'T WANT THAT...

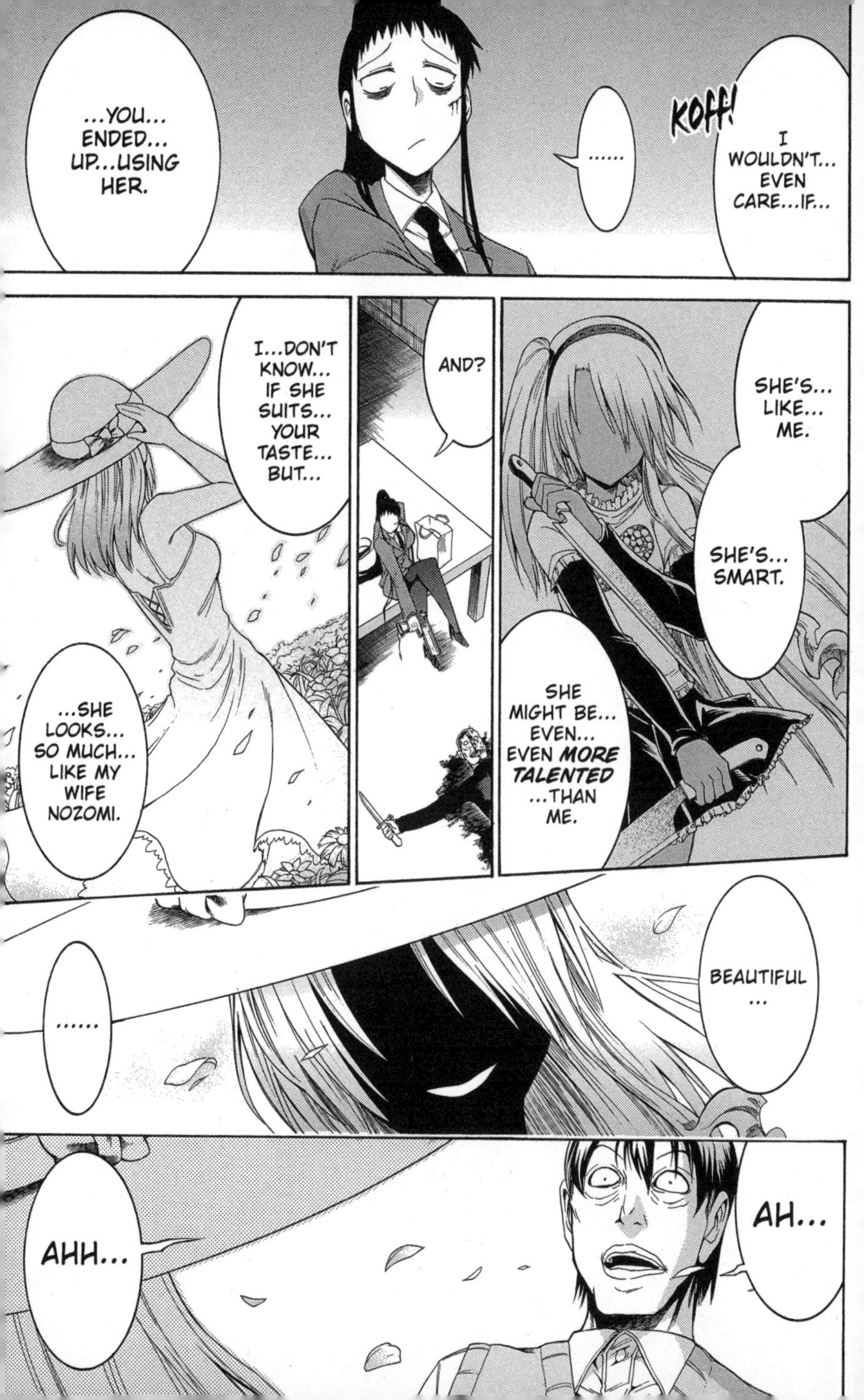
KOFF!
I WOULDN'T... EVEN CARE...IF...
......
...YOU... ENDED... UP...USING HER.
SHE'S... LIKE... ME.
SHE'S... SMART.
SHE MIGHT BE... EVEN... EVEN MORE TALENTED ...THAN ME.
AND?
I...DON'T KNOW... IF SHE SUITS... YOUR TASTE... BUT...
...SHE LOOKS... SO MUCH... LIKE MY WIFE NOZOMI.
BEAUTIFUL ...
......
AH...
AHH...

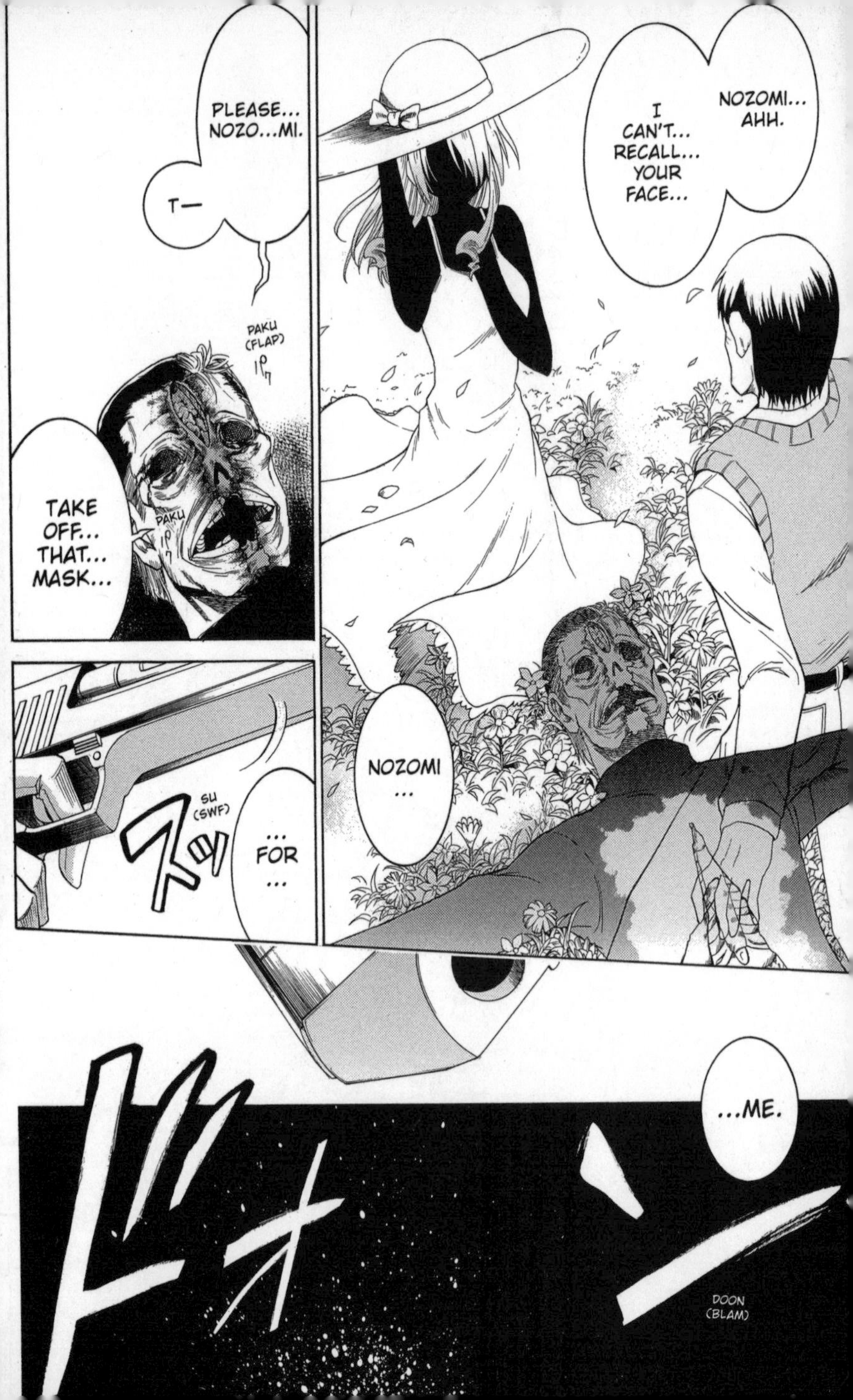
NOZOMI... AHH.
I CAN'T... RECALL... YOUR FACE...
NOZOMI ...
PLEASE... NOZO...MI.
T—
PAKU (FLAP)
PAKU
TAKE OFF... THAT... MASK...
... FOR ...
SU (SWF)
...ME.
DOON (BLAM)

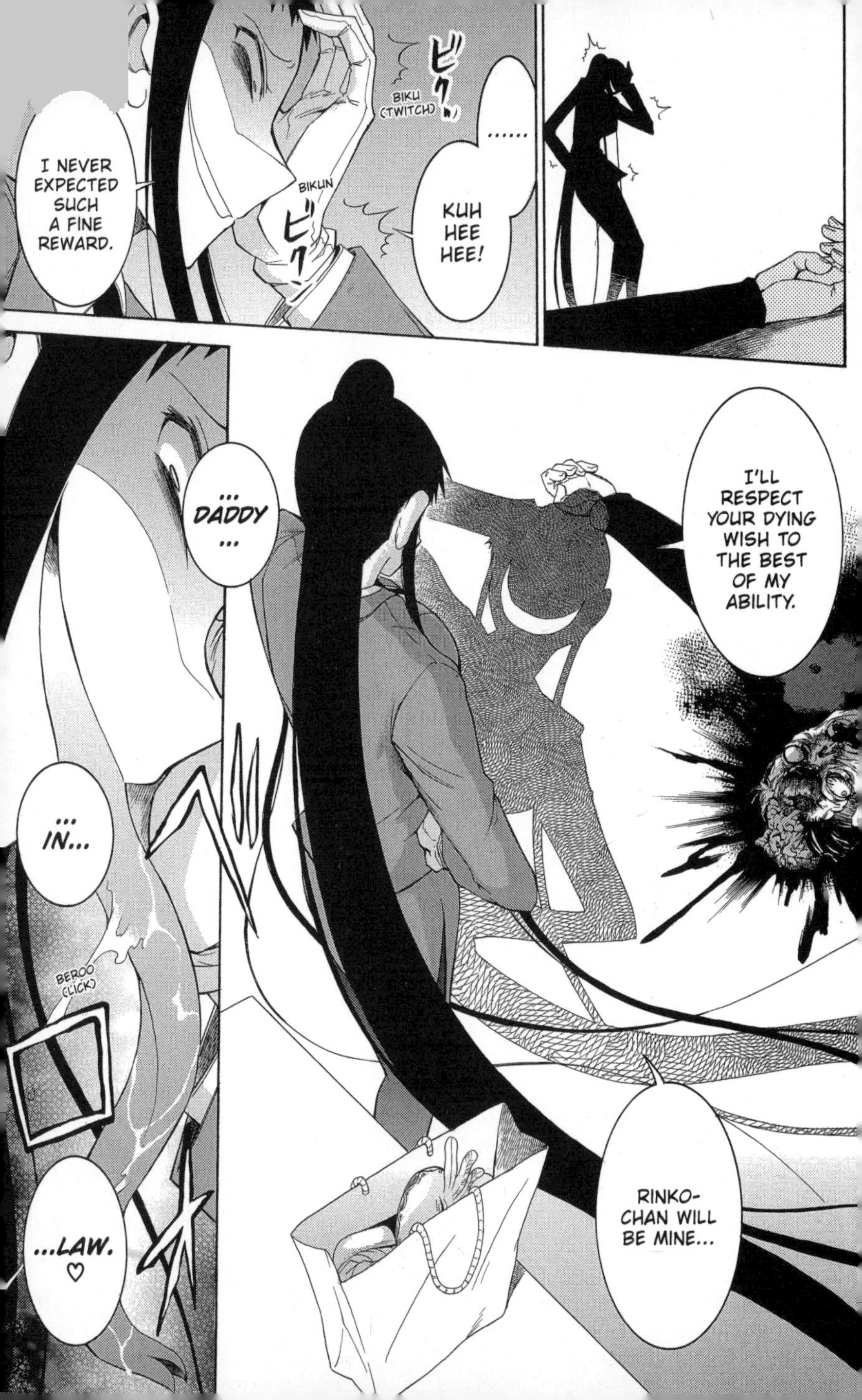

BIKU (TWITCH)
......
KUH HEE HEE!
BIKUN
I NEVER EXPECTED SUCH A FINE REWARD.
I'LL RESPECT YOUR DYING WISH TO THE BEST OF MY ABILITY.
RINKO-CHAN WILL BE MINE...
...DADDY...
...IN...
BEROO (LICK)
...LAW. ♡

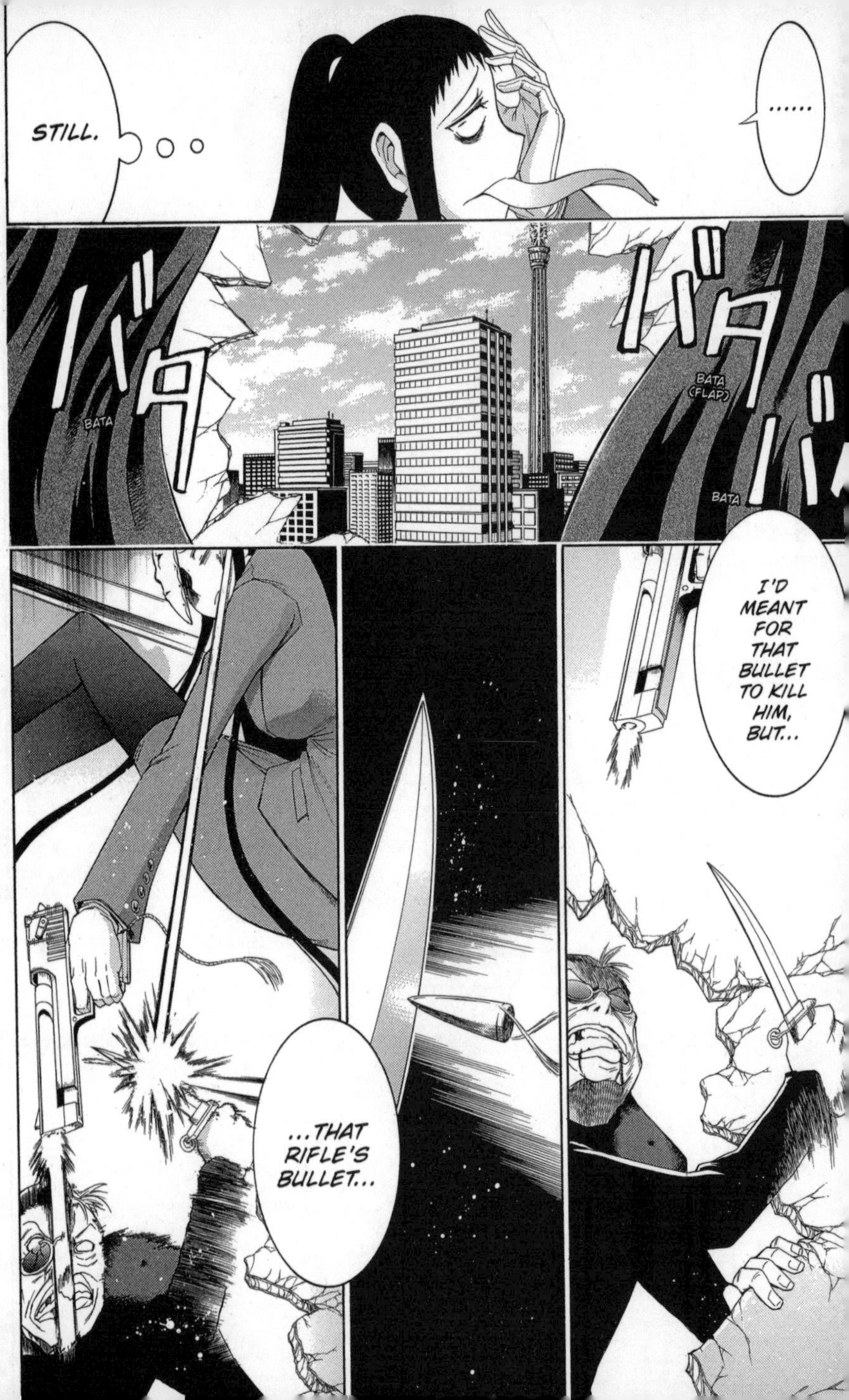
......
STILL.
バタ
BATA (FLAP)
バ
BATA
バタ
BATA
I'D MEANT FOR THAT BULLET TO KILL HIM, BUT...
...THAT RIFLE'S BULLET...

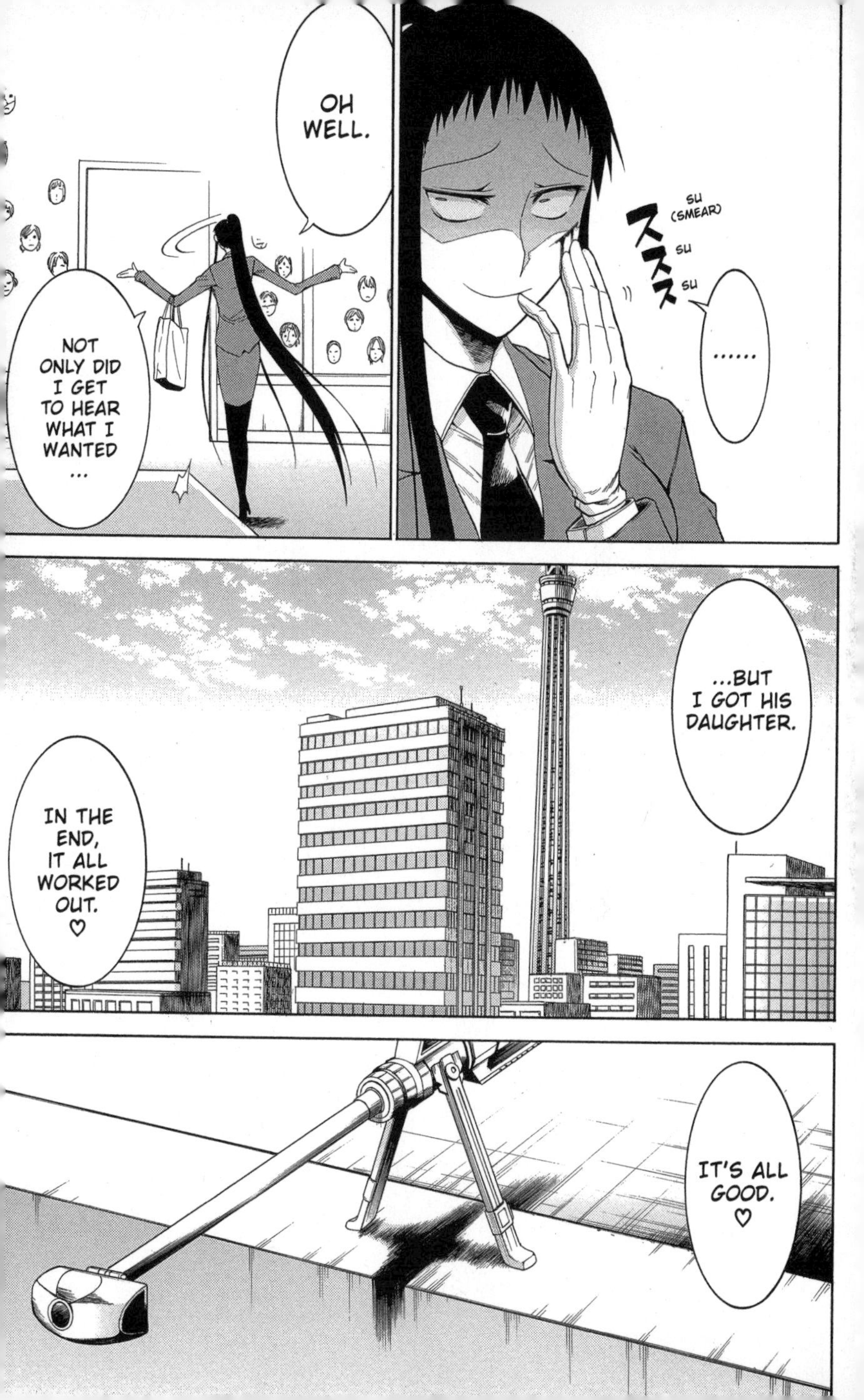
ススス
SU (SMEAR)
SU
SU
......
OH WELL.
NOT ONLY DID I GET TO HEAR WHAT I WANTED ...
...BUT I GOT HIS DAUGHTER.
IN THE END, IT ALL WORKED OUT. ♡
IT'S ALL GOOD. ♡

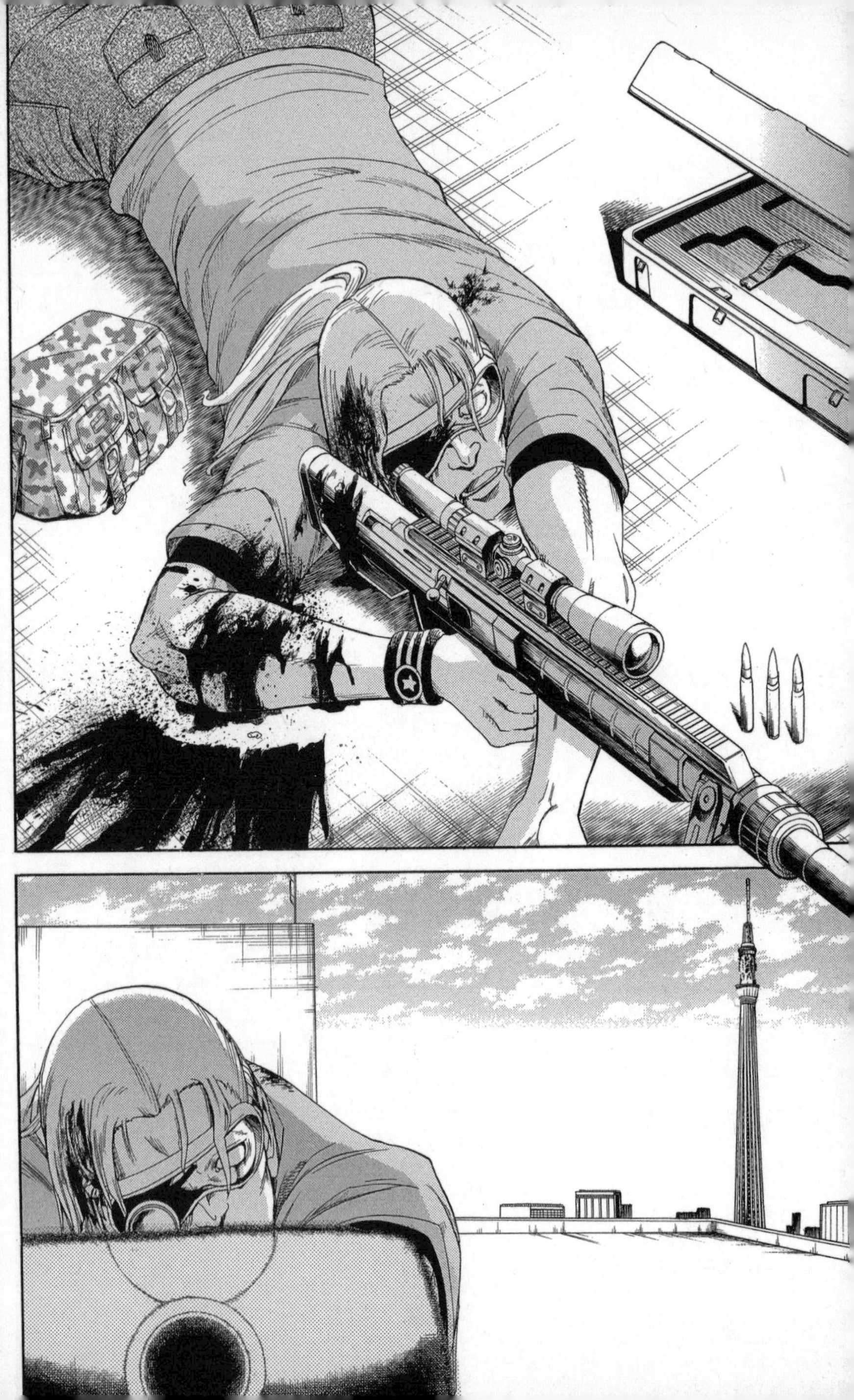

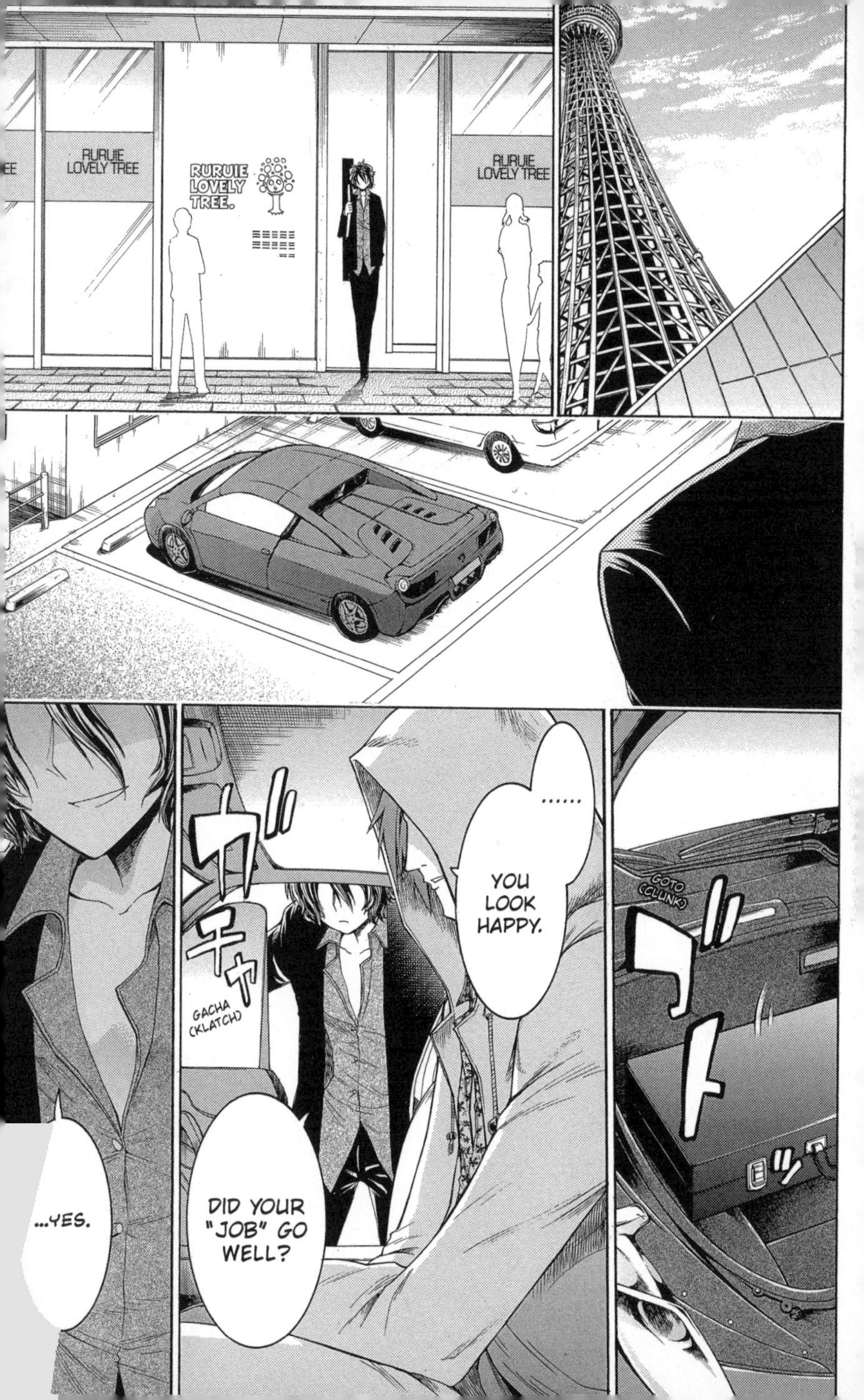
RURUIE LOVELY TREE
RURUIE LOVELY TREE.
RURUIE LOVELY TREE
EE
ゴト
GOTO (CLUNK)
......
YOU LOOK HAPPY.
ガチャ
GACHA (KLATCH)
DID YOUR "JOB" GO WELL?
...YES.

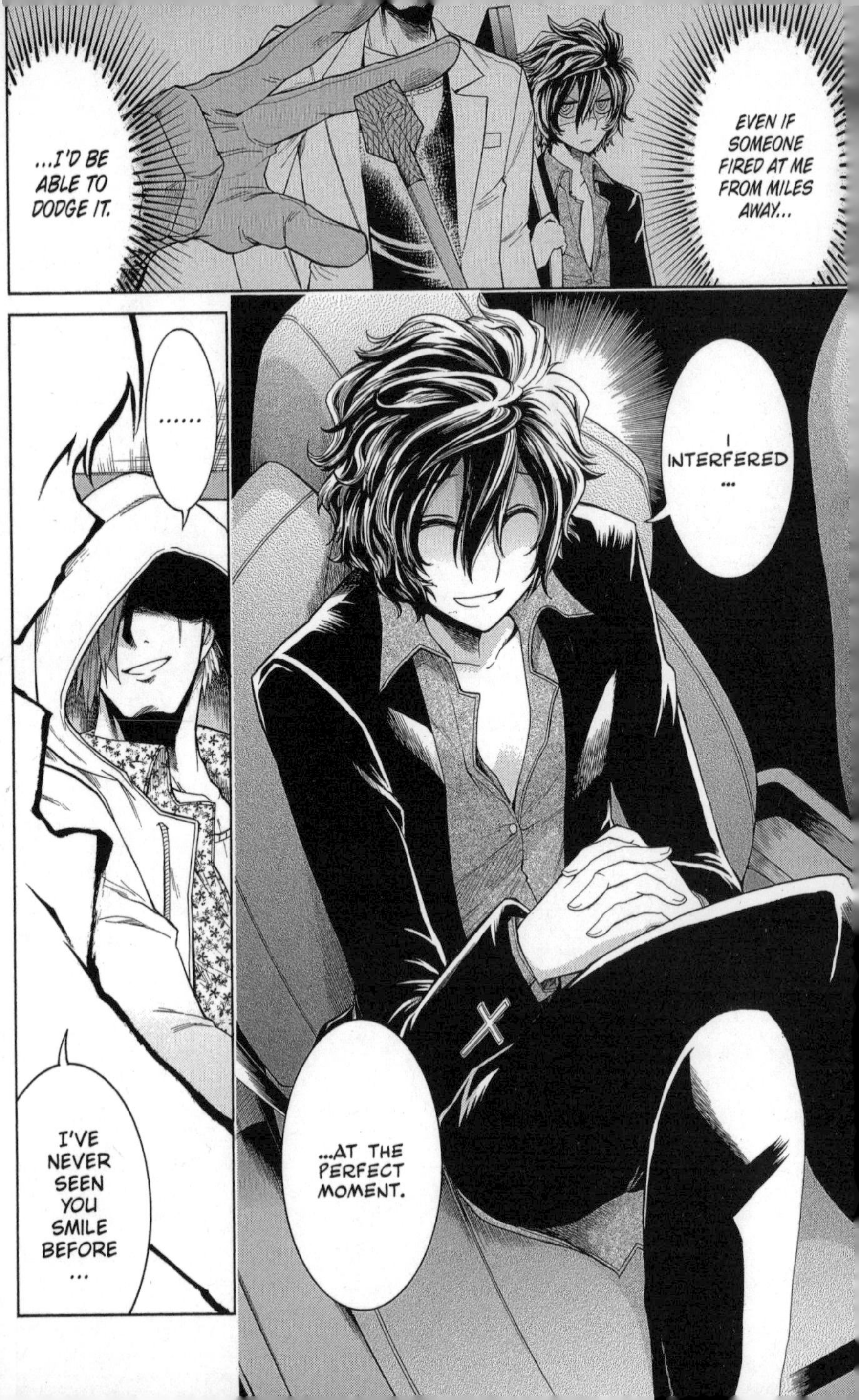
EVEN IF SOMEONE FIRED AT ME FROM MILES AWAY...
...I'D BE ABLE TO DODGE IT.
I INTERFERED...
...AT THE PERFECT MOMENT.
......
I'VE NEVER SEEN YOU SMILE BEFORE...

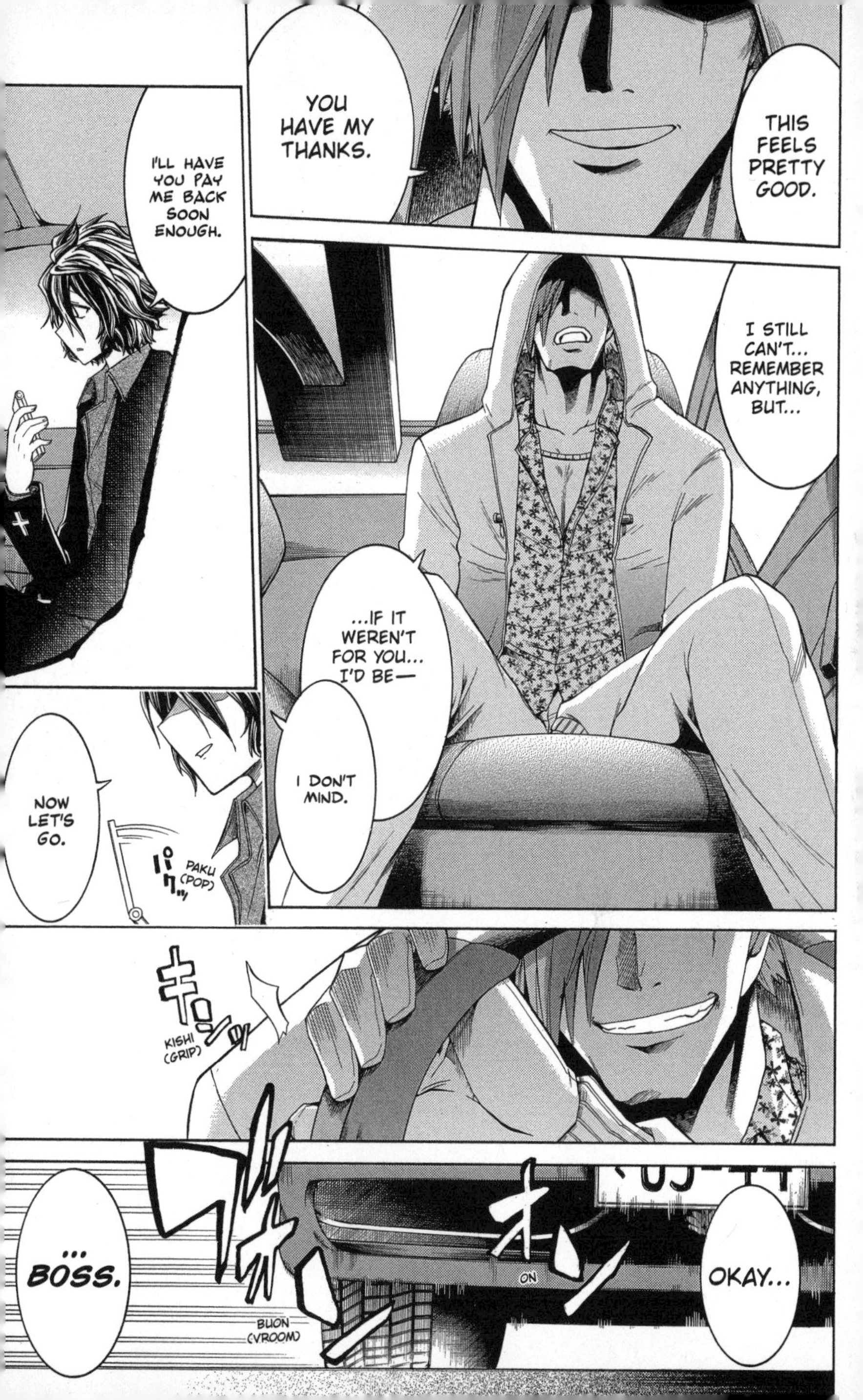
THIS FEELS PRETTY GOOD.
YOU HAVE MY THANKS.
I'LL HAVE YOU PAY ME BACK SOON ENOUGH.
I STILL CAN'T... REMEMBER ANYTHING, BUT...
...IF IT WEREN'T FOR YOU... I'D BE—
I DON'T MIND.
NOW LET'S GO.
PAKU (POP)
KISHI (GRIP)
OKAY...
ON
BUON (VROOM)
... BOSS.

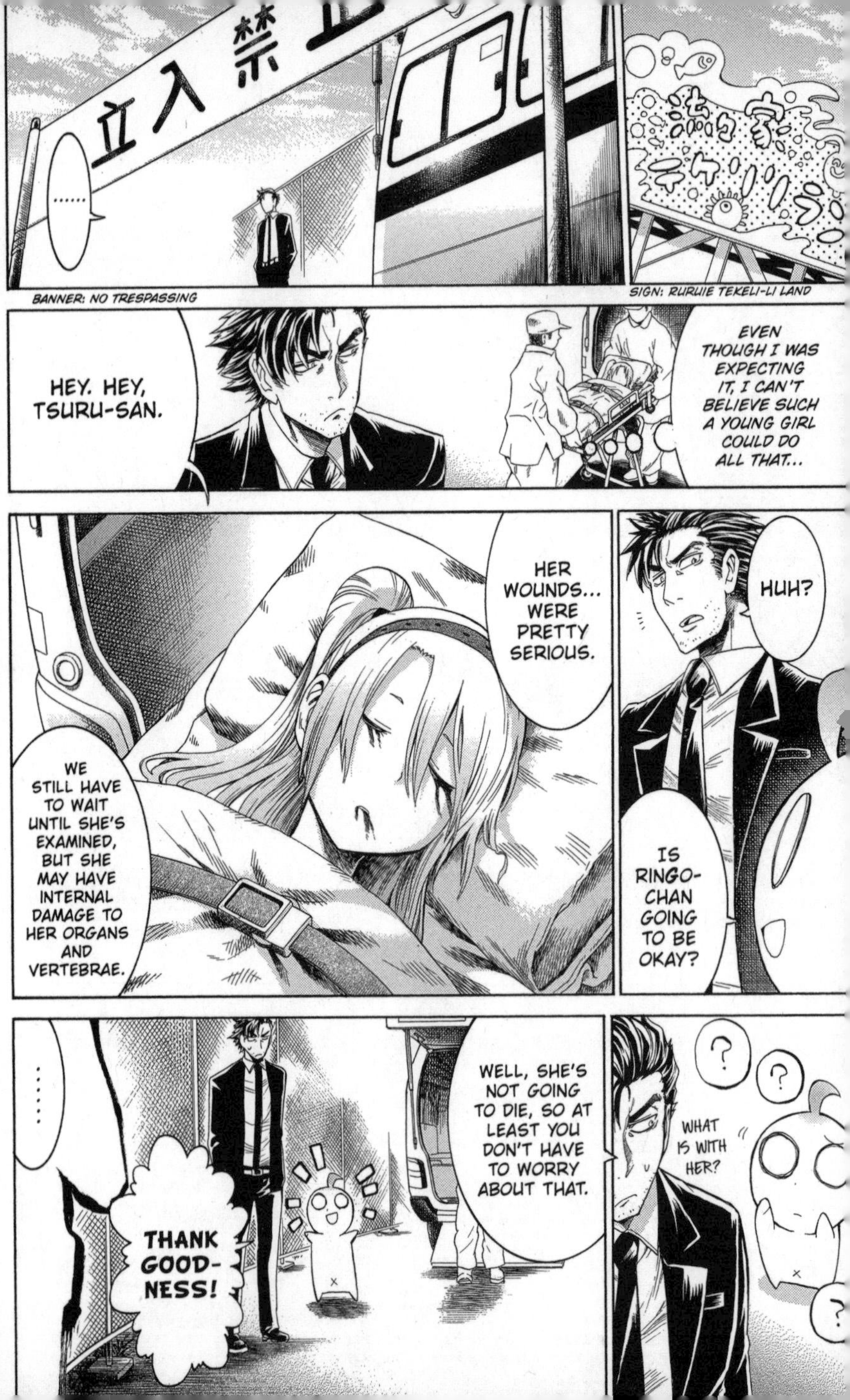
SIGN: RURUIE TEKELI-LI LAND
……
BANNER: NO TRESPASSING
EVEN THOUGH I WAS EXPECTING IT, I CAN'T BELIEVE SUCH A YOUNG GIRL COULD DO ALL THAT…
HEY. HEY, TSURU-SAN.
HUH?
IS RINGO-CHAN GOING TO BE OKAY?
HER WOUNDS… WERE PRETTY SERIOUS.
WE STILL HAVE TO WAIT UNTIL SHE'S EXAMINED, BUT SHE MAY HAVE INTERNAL DAMAGE TO HER ORGANS AND VERTEBRAE.
?
?
WHAT IS WITH HER?
?
WELL, SHE'S NOT GOING TO DIE, SO AT LEAST YOU DON'T HAVE TO WORRY ABOUT THAT.
……
THANK GOODNESS!

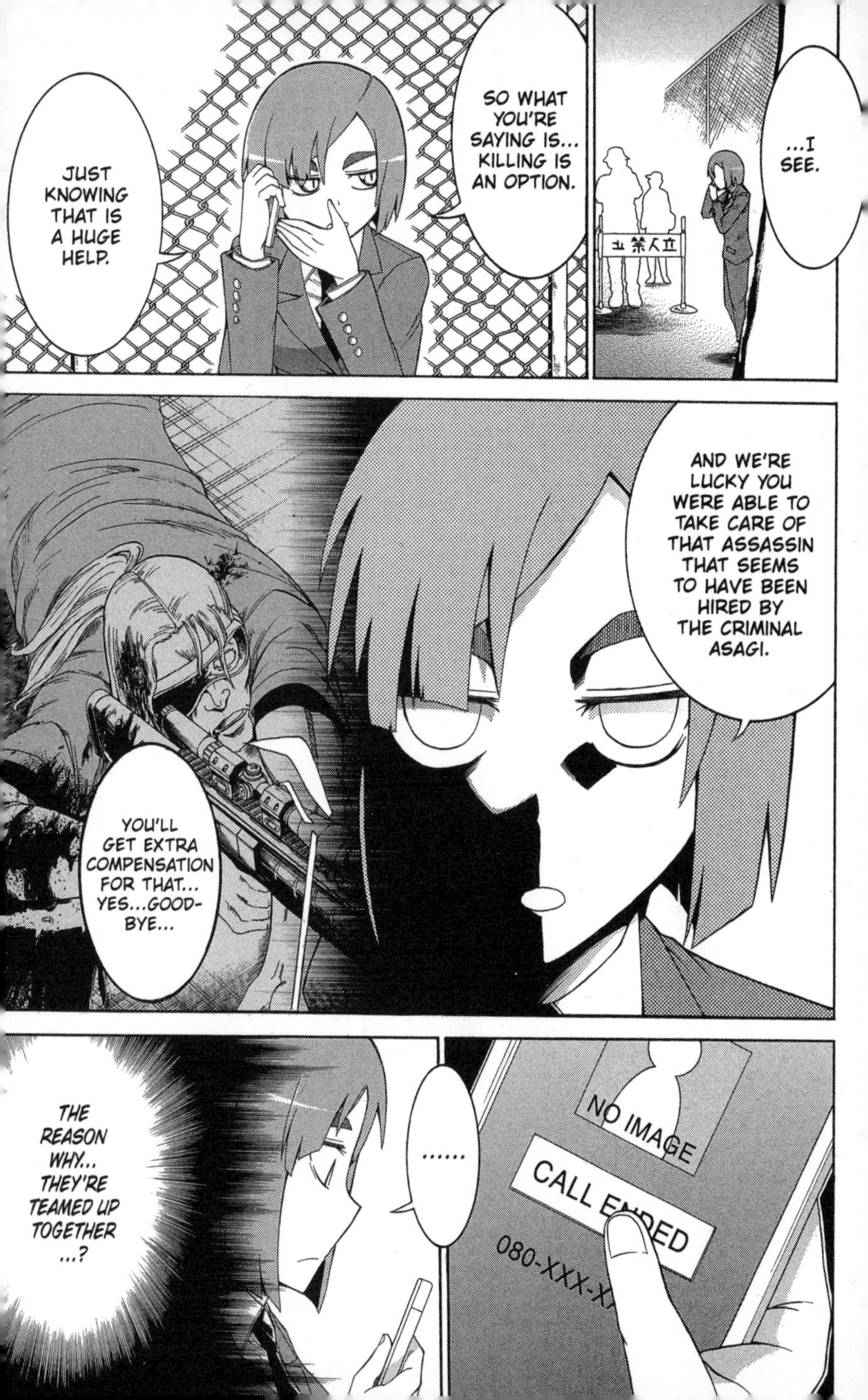
...I SEE.
SO WHAT YOU'RE SAYING IS... KILLING IS AN OPTION.
JUST KNOWING THAT IS A HUGE HELP.
AND WE'RE LUCKY YOU WERE ABLE TO TAKE CARE OF THAT ASSASSIN THAT SEEMS TO HAVE BEEN HIRED BY THE CRIMINAL ASAGI.
YOU'LL GET EXTRA COMPENSATION FOR THAT... YES...GOOD-BYE...
NO IMAGE
CALL ENDED
080-XXX-XX
......
THE REASON WHY... THEY'RE TEAMED UP TOGETHER ...?

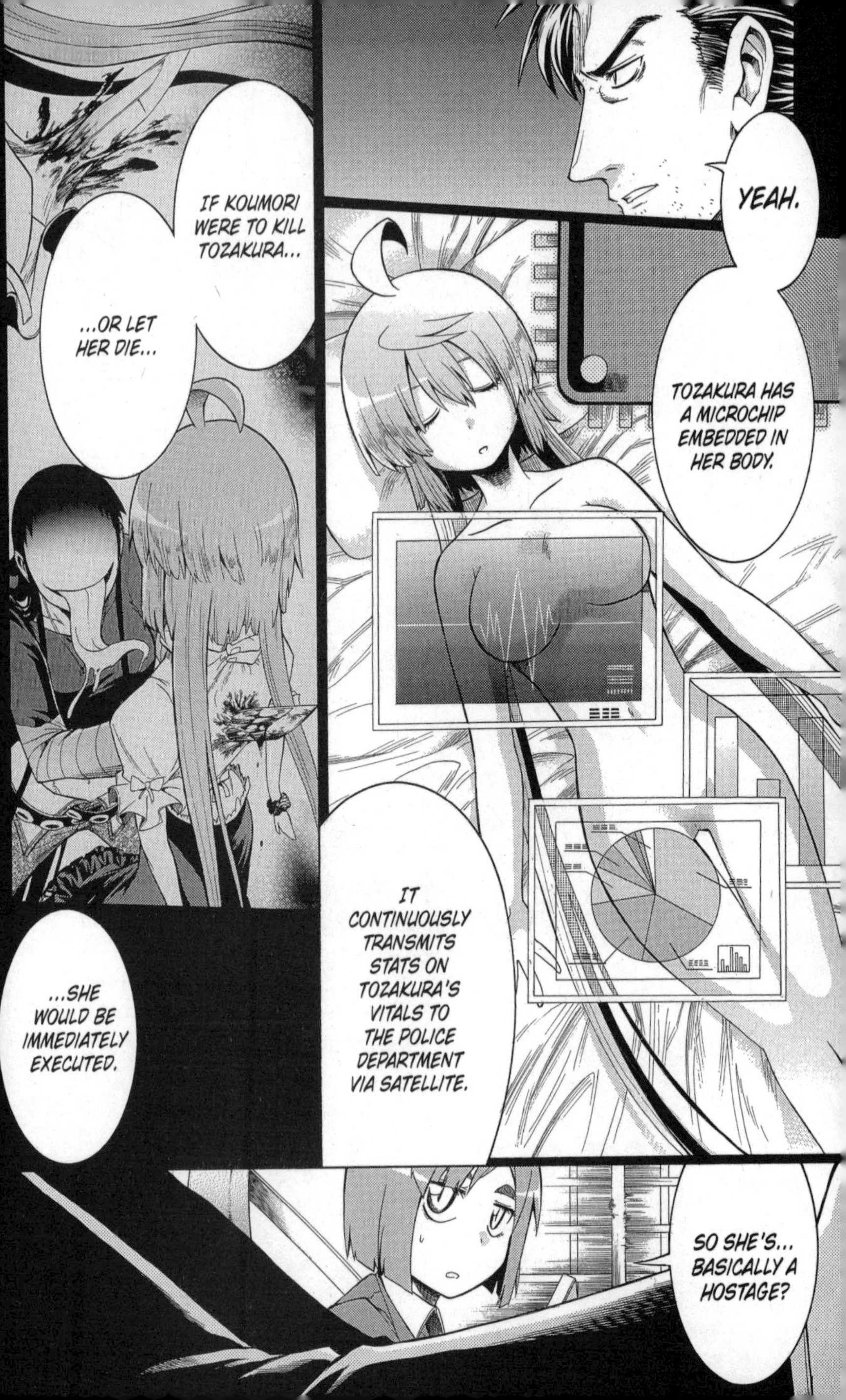
YEAH.
TOZAKURA HAS A MICROCHIP EMBEDDED IN HER BODY.
IT CONTINUOUSLY TRANSMITS STATS ON TOZAKURA'S VITALS TO THE POLICE DEPARTMENT VIA SATELLITE.
IF KOUMORI WERE TO KILL TOZAKURA...
...OR LET HER DIE...
...SHE WOULD BE IMMEDIATELY EXECUTED.
SO SHE'S... BASICALLY A HOSTAGE?

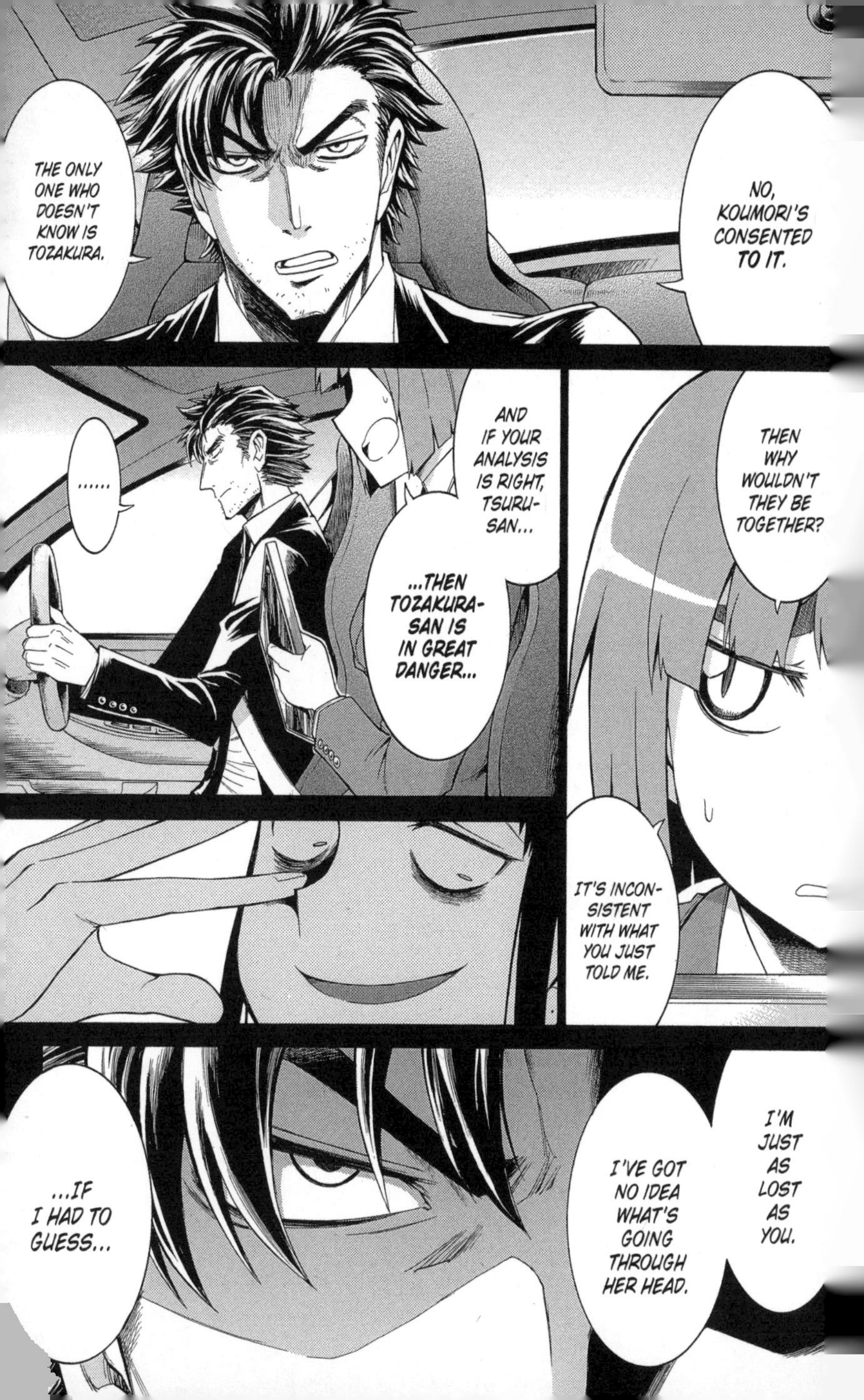
NO, KOUMORI'S CONSENTED TO IT.
THE ONLY ONE WHO DOESN'T KNOW IS TOZAKURA.
THEN WHY WOULDN'T THEY BE TOGETHER?
IT'S INCON-SISTENT WITH WHAT YOU JUST TOLD ME.
AND IF YOUR ANALYSIS IS RIGHT, TSURU-SAN...
...THEN TOZAKURA-SAN IS IN GREAT DANGER...
......
I'M JUST AS LOST AS YOU.
I'VE GOT NO IDEA WHAT'S GOING THROUGH HER HEAD.
...IF I HAD TO GUESS...

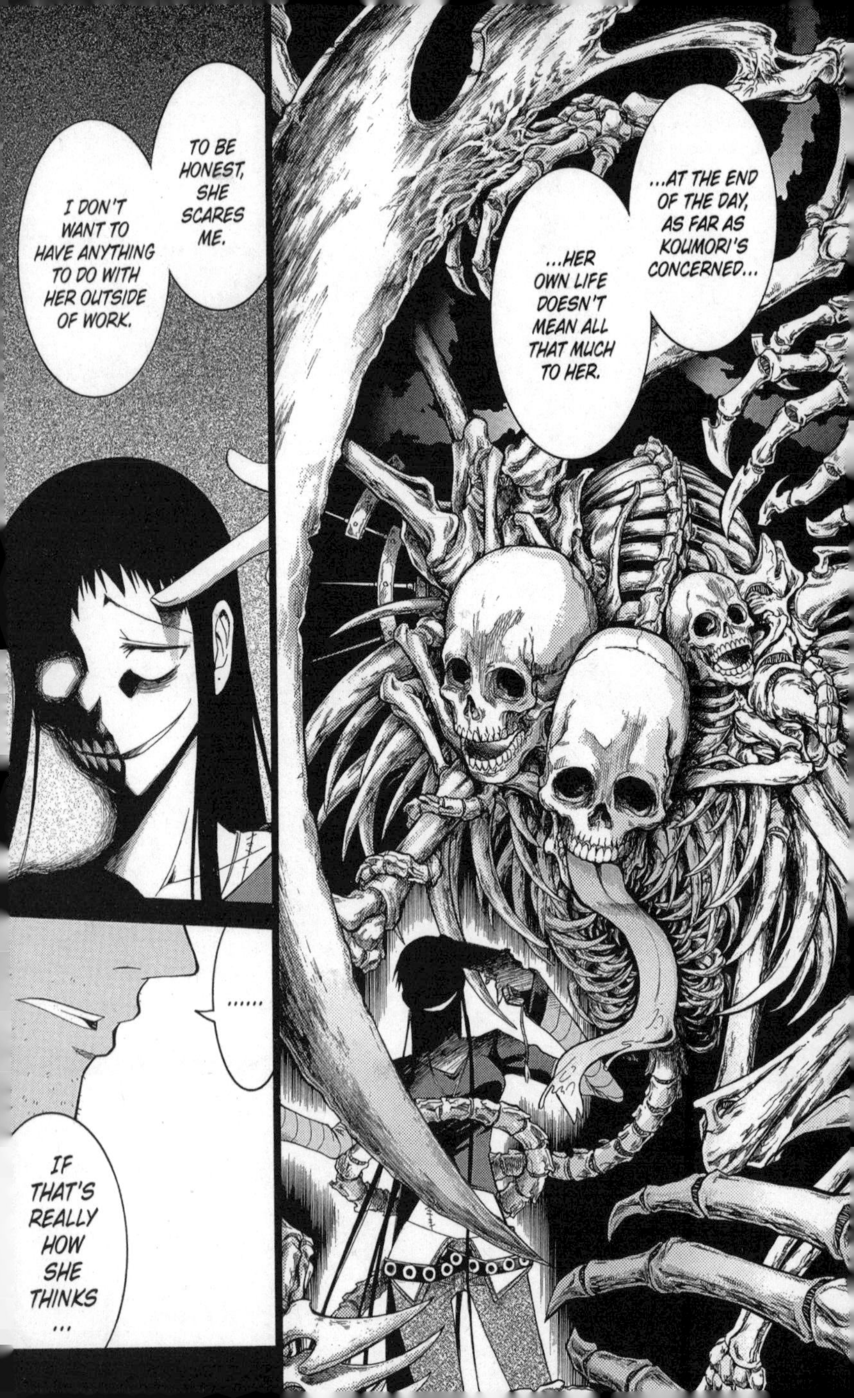
...AT THE END OF THE DAY, AS FAR AS KOUMORI'S CONCERNED...
...HER OWN LIFE DOESN'T MEAN ALL THAT MUCH TO HER.
TO BE HONEST, SHE SCARES ME.
I DON'T WANT TO HAVE ANYTHING TO DO WITH HER OUTSIDE OF WORK.
......
IF THAT'S REALLY HOW SHE THINKS...

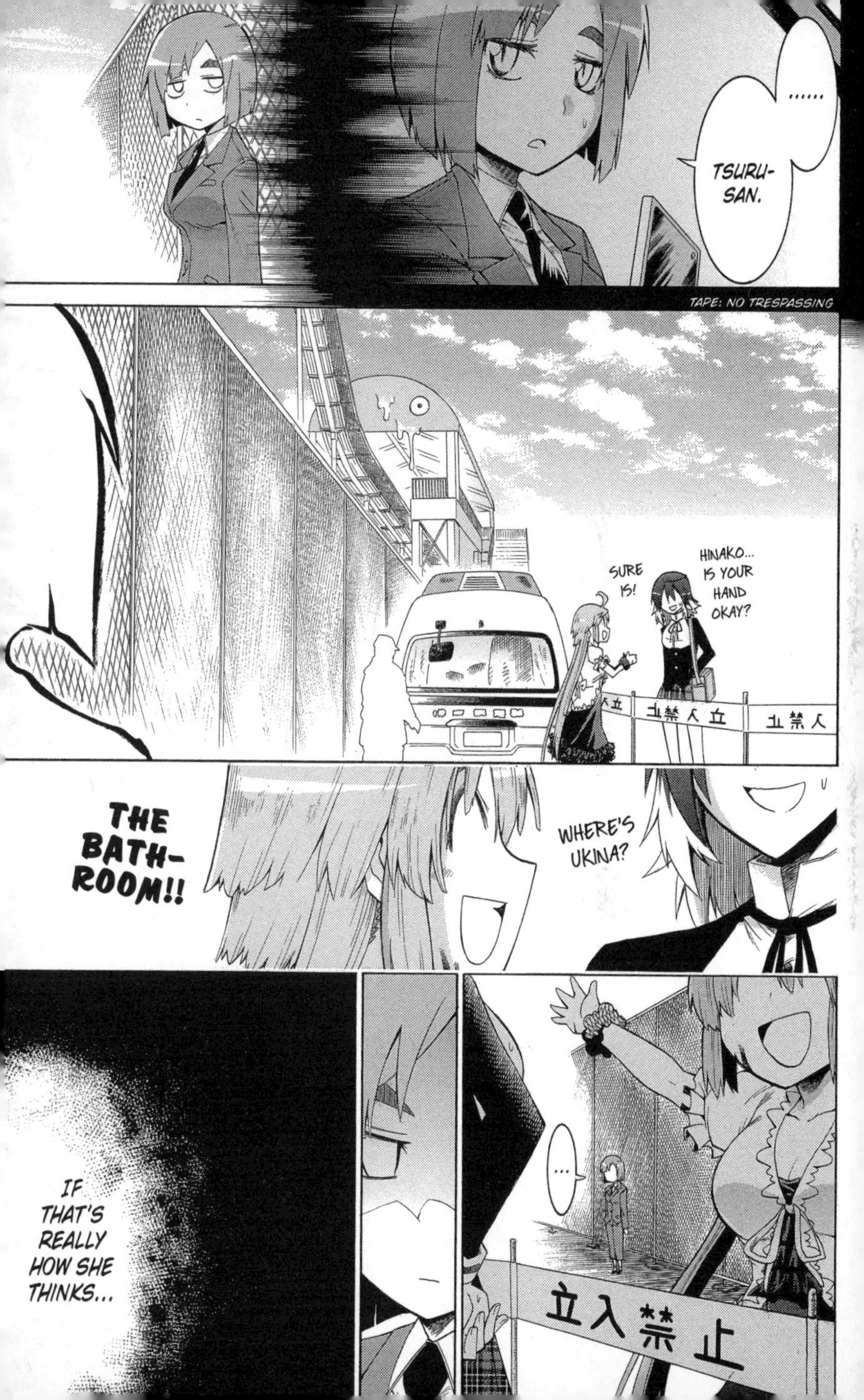
......
TSURU-SAN.
TAPE: NO TRESPASSING
HINAKO... IS YOUR HAND OKAY?
SURE IS!
WHERE'S UKINA?
THE BATHROOM!!
...
立入禁止
IF THAT'S REALLY HOW SHE THINKS...

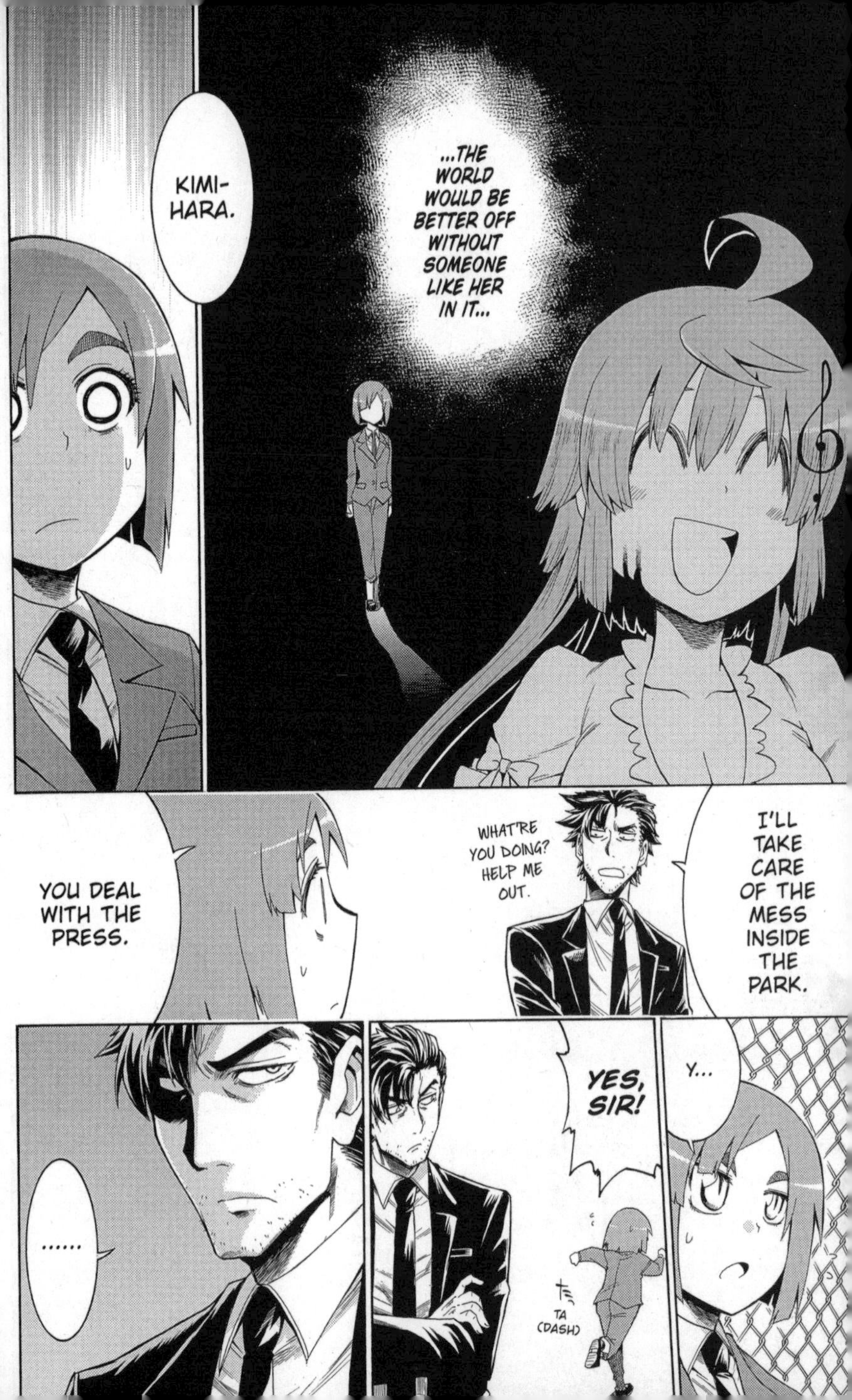
...THE WORLD WOULD BE BETTER OFF WITHOUT SOMEONE LIKE HER IN IT...
KIMI-HARA.
I'LL TAKE CARE OF THE MESS INSIDE THE PARK.
WHAT'RE YOU DOING? HELP ME OUT.
YOU DEAL WITH THE PRESS.
Y...
YES, SIR!
TA (DASH)
......

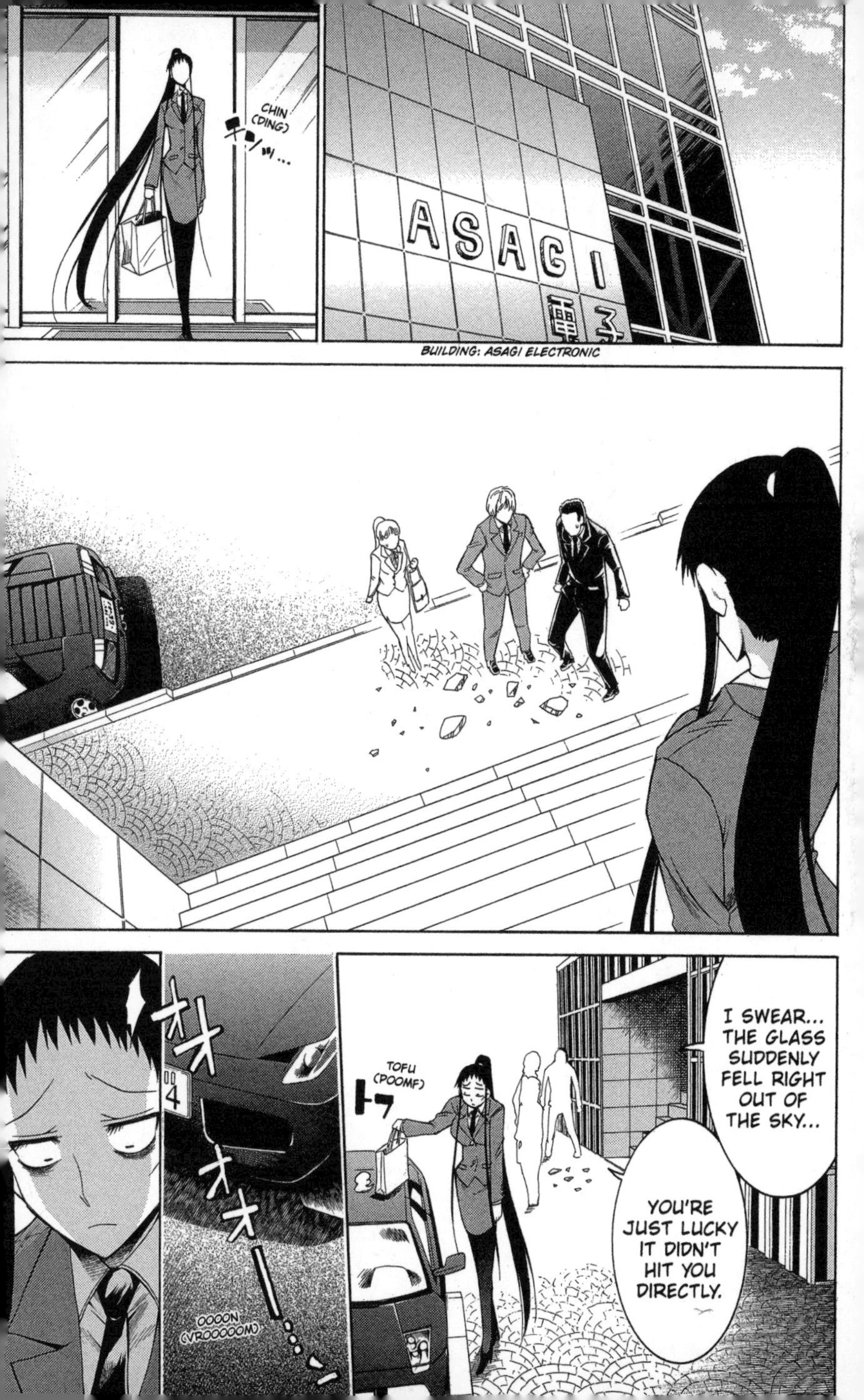
ASAGI
BUILDING: ASAGI ELECTRONIC
CHIN (DING)
I SWEAR... THE GLASS SUDDENLY FELL RIGHT OUT OF THE SKY...
YOU'RE JUST LUCKY IT DIDN'T HIT YOU DIRECTLY.
TOFU (POOMF)
OOOON (VROOOOOM)

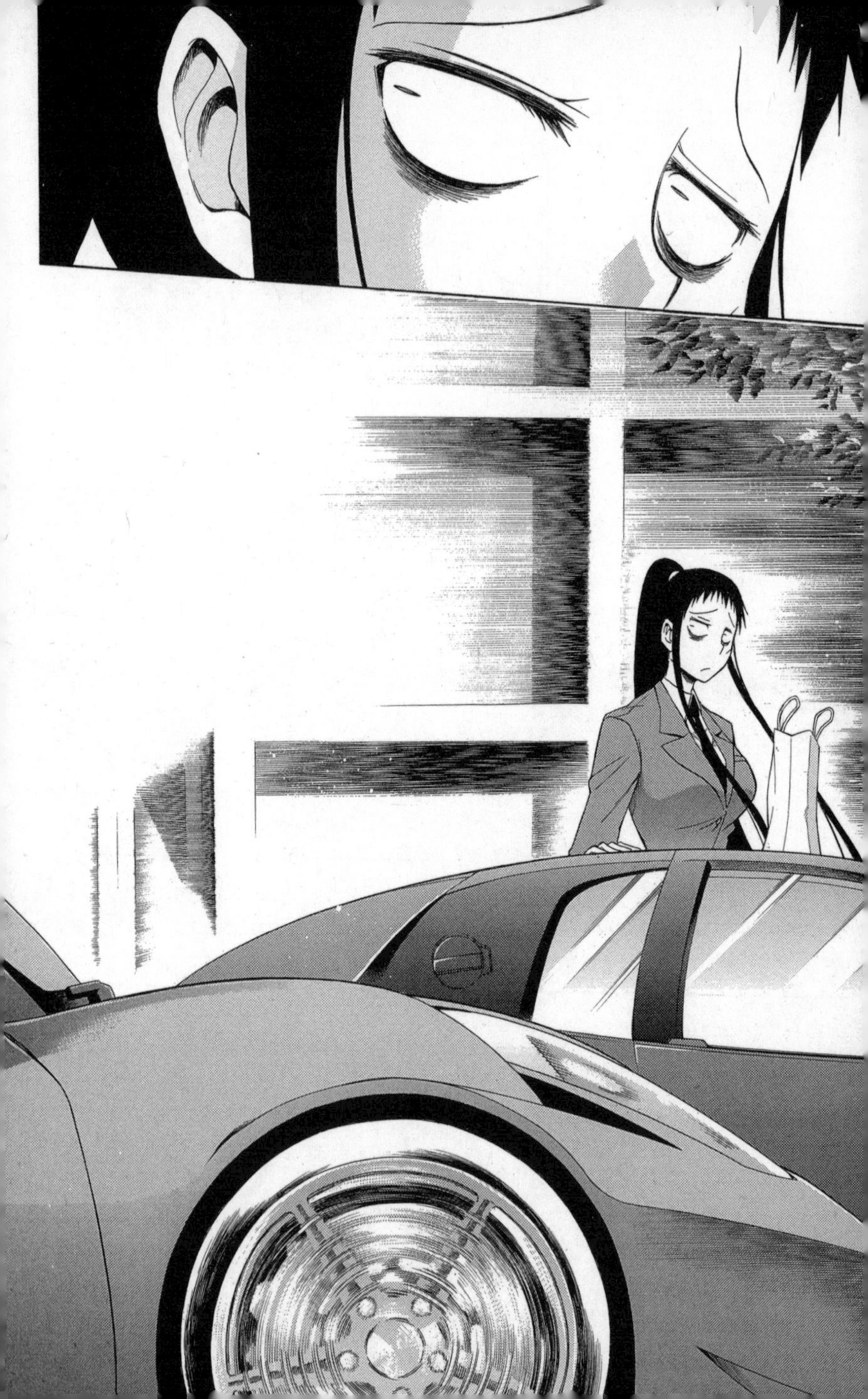

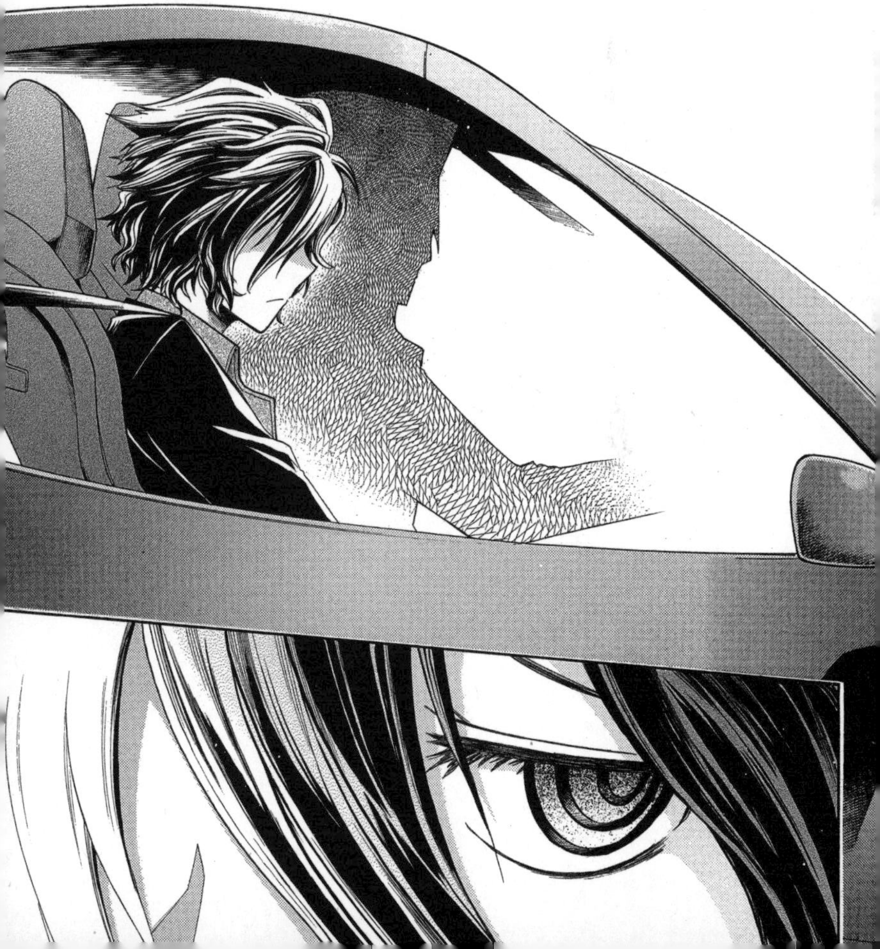

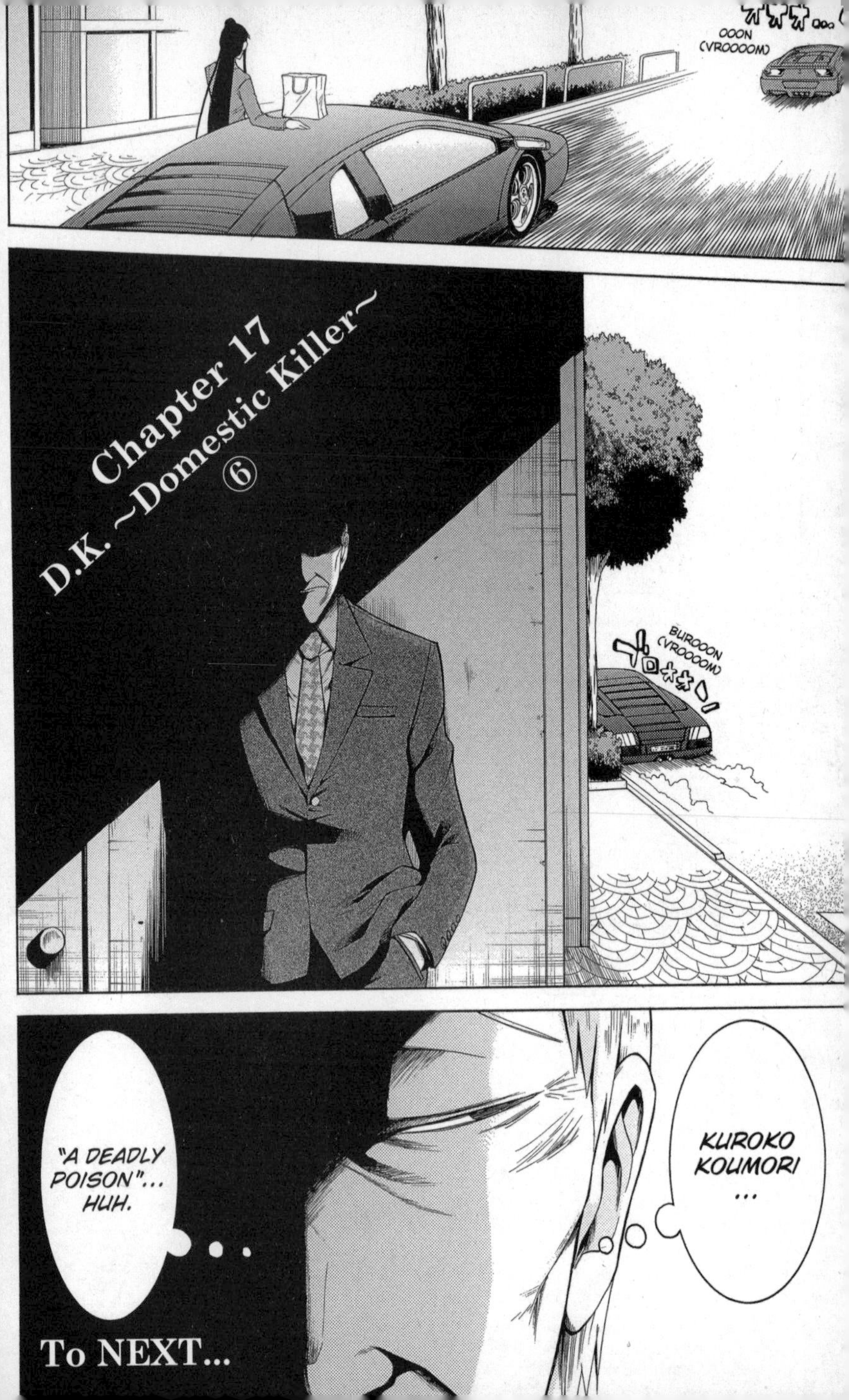
OOON (VROOOOM)
BUROOON (VROOOOM)
Chapter 17
D.K. ~Domestic Killer~
⑥
KUROKO KOUMORI ...
"A DEADLY POISON"... HUH.
To NEXT...

MURCIÉLAGO

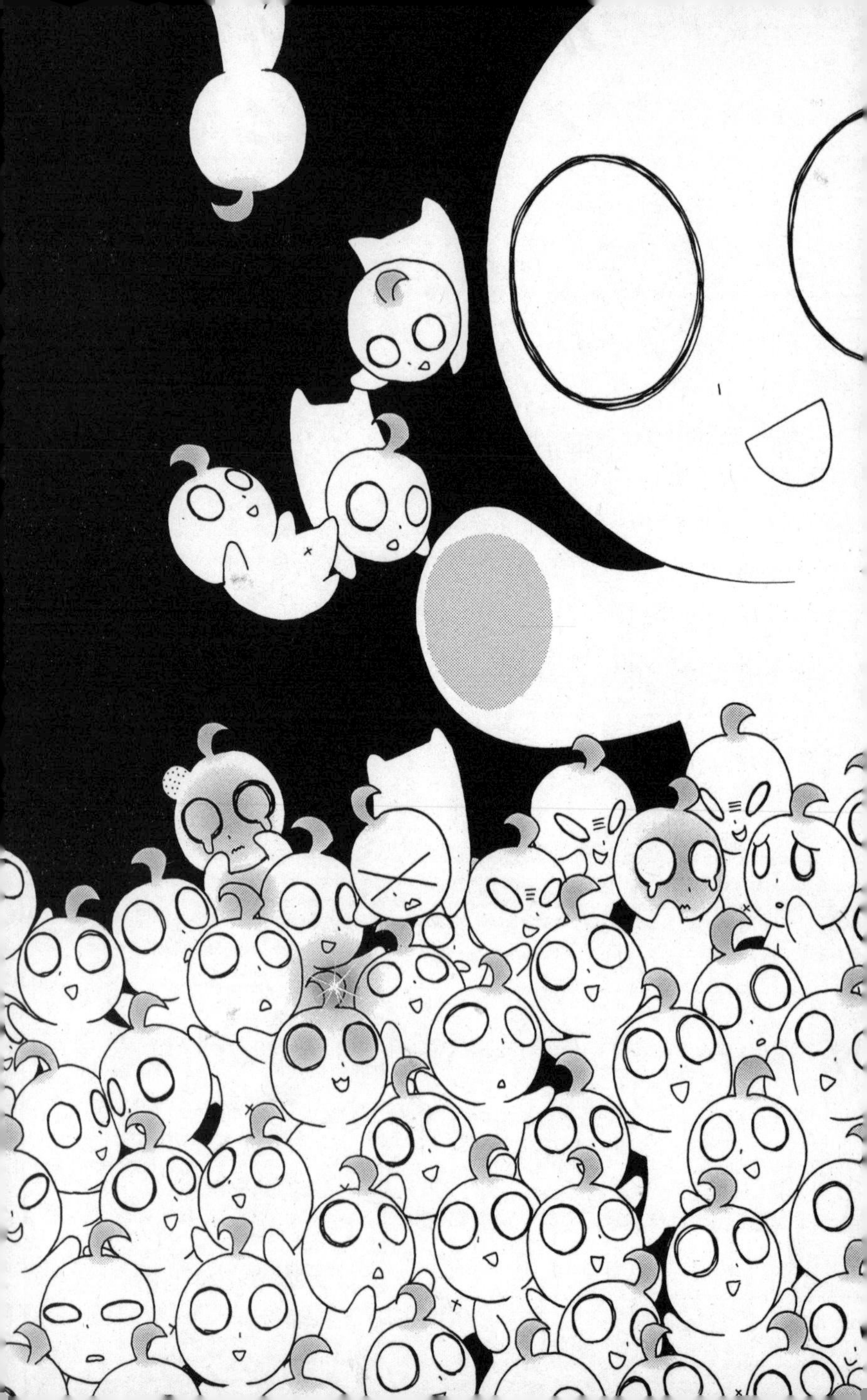

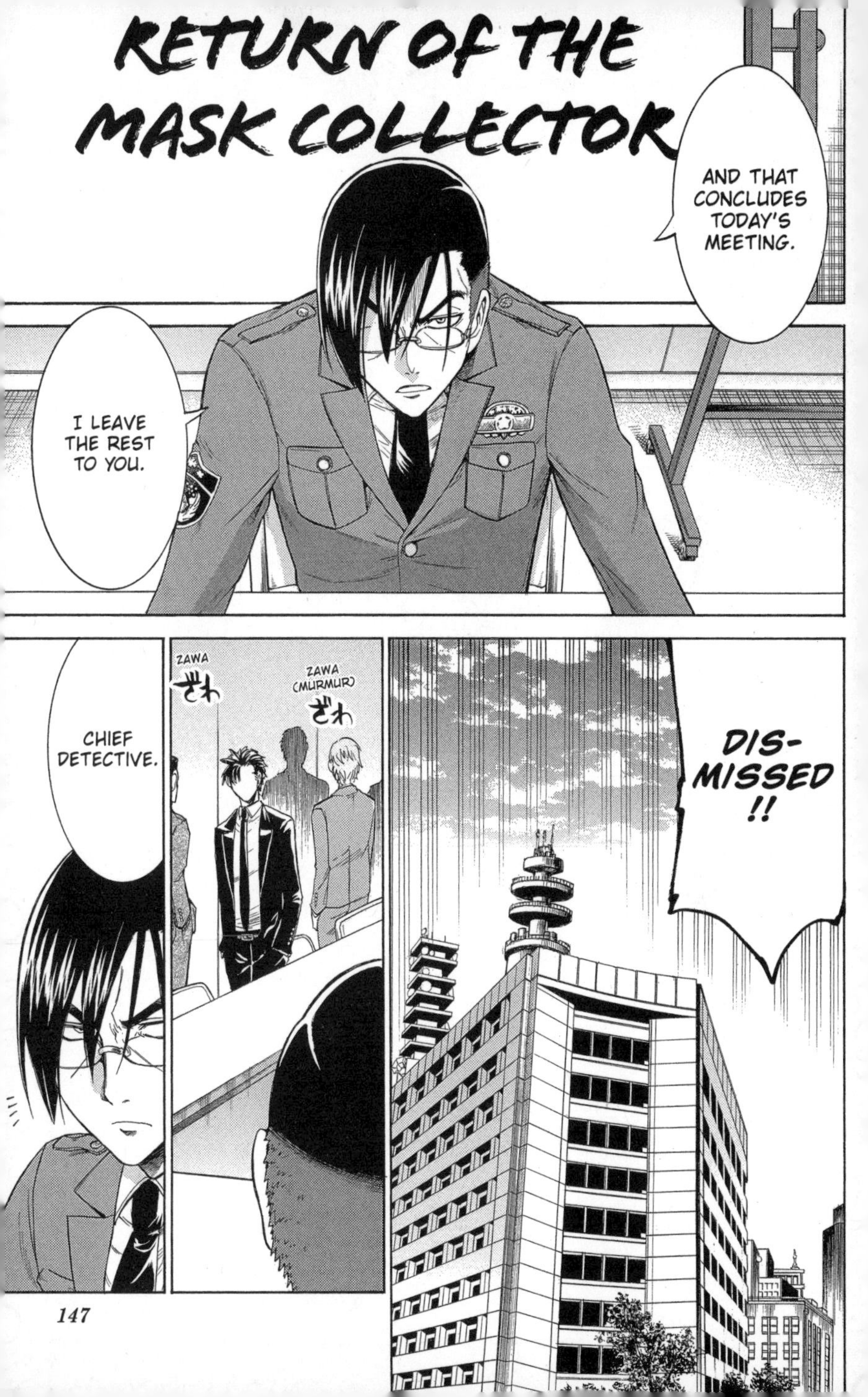
RETURN OF THE MASK COLLECTOR
AND THAT CONCLUDES TODAY'S MEETING.
I LEAVE THE REST TO YOU.
DIS-MISSED!!
ZAWA ざわ
ZAWA (MURMUR) ざわ
CHIEF DETECTIVE.

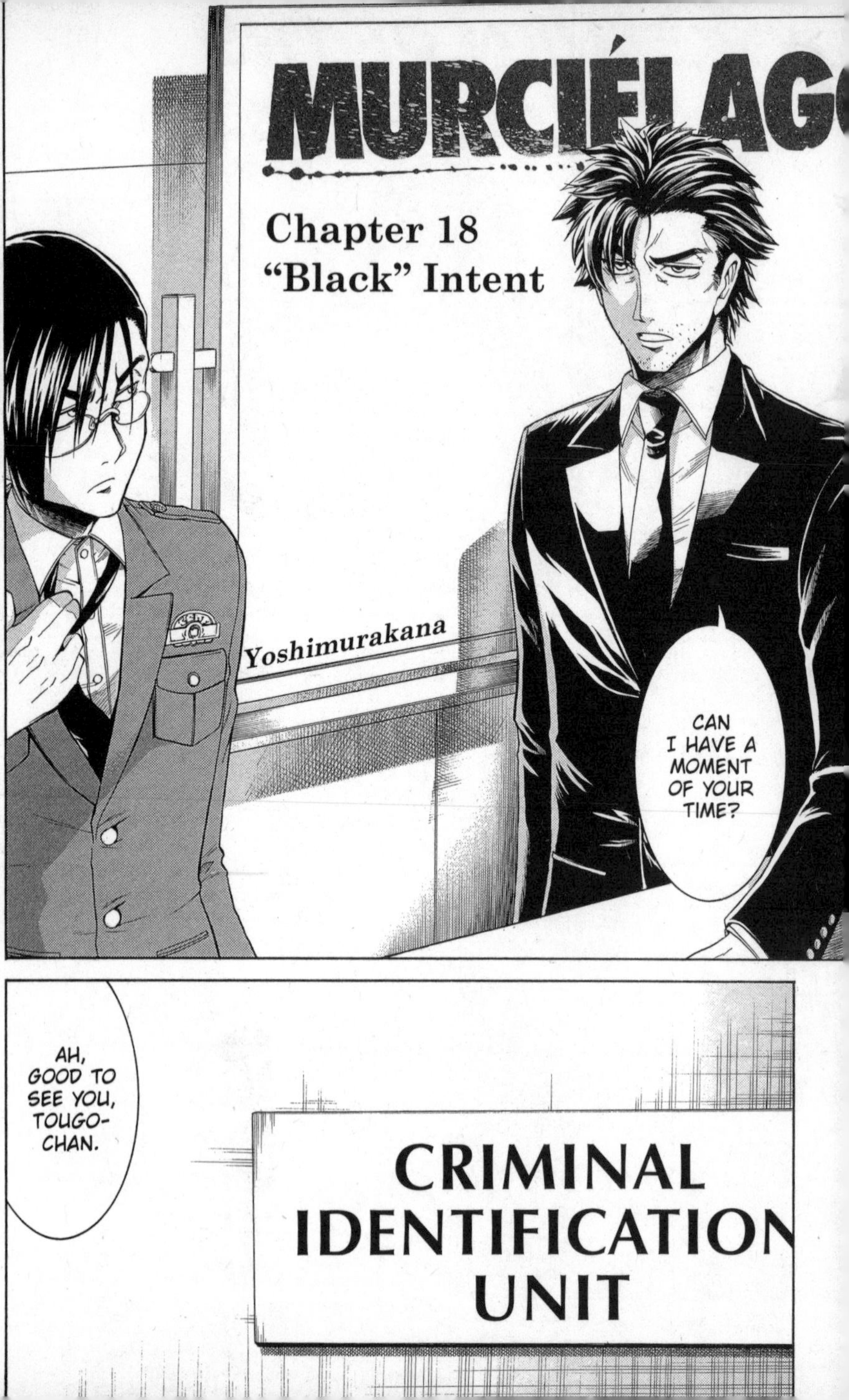

MURCIÉLAG
Chapter 18
"Black" Intent
Yoshimurakana
CAN I HAVE A MOMENT OF YOUR TIME?
AH, GOOD TO SEE YOU, TOUGO-CHAN.
CRIMINAL IDENTIFICATION UNIT

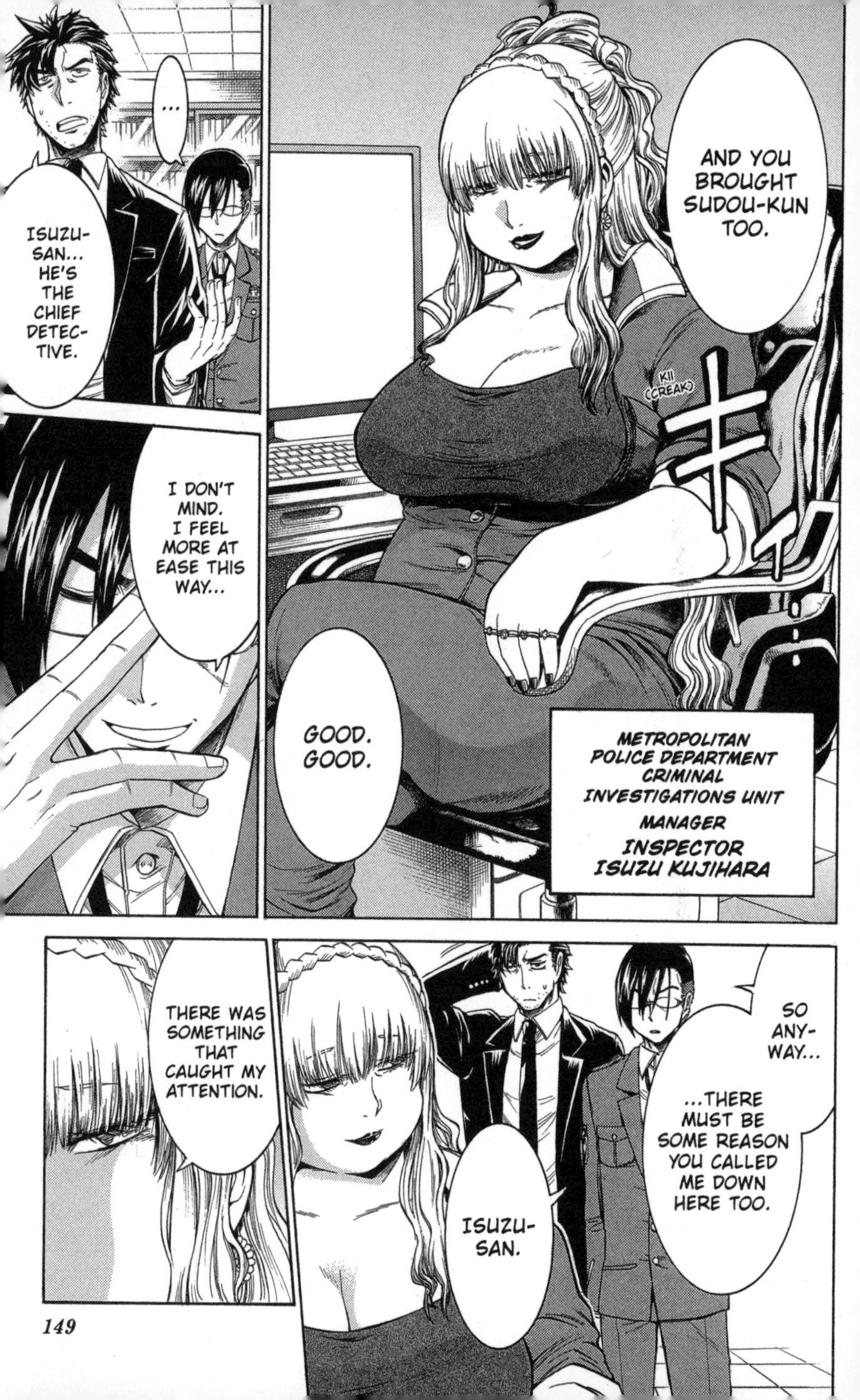
AND YOU BROUGHT SUDOU-KUN TOO.
KII (CREAK)
GOOD. GOOD.
METROPOLITAN POLICE DEPARTMENT CRIMINAL INVESTIGATIONS UNIT MANAGER INSPECTOR ISUZU KUJIHARA
...
ISUZU-SAN... HE'S THE CHIEF DETECTIVE.
I DON'T MIND. I FEEL MORE AT EASE THIS WAY...
...
SO ANYWAY...
...THERE MUST BE SOME REASON YOU CALLED ME DOWN HERE TOO.
ISUZU-SAN.
THERE WAS SOMETHING THAT CAUGHT MY ATTENTION.

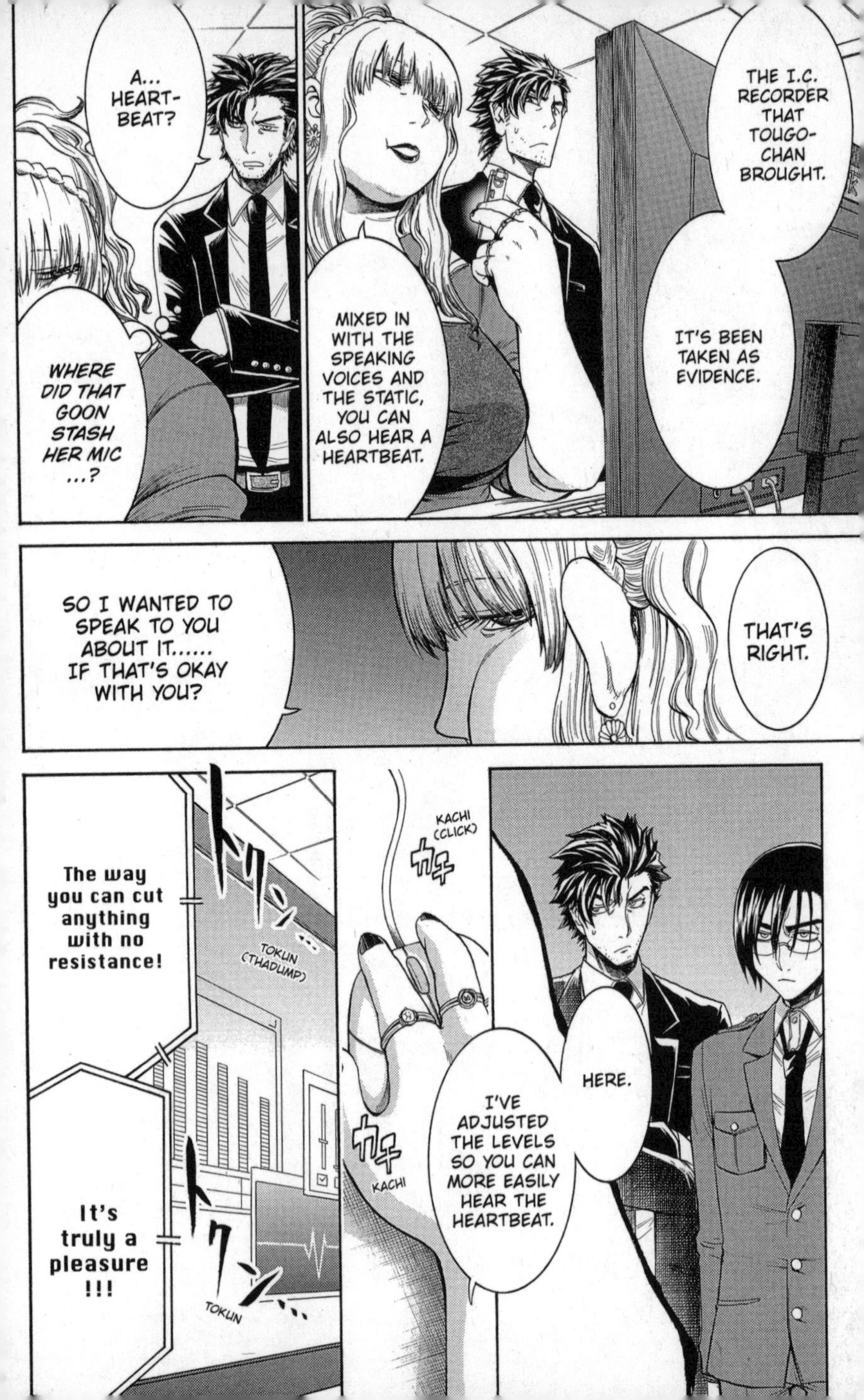
THE I.C. RECORDER THAT TOUGO-CHAN BROUGHT.
IT'S BEEN TAKEN AS EVIDENCE.
MIXED IN WITH THE SPEAKING VOICES AND THE STATIC, YOU CAN ALSO HEAR A HEARTBEAT.
A... HEART-BEAT?
WHERE DID THAT GOON STASH HER MIC ...?
THAT'S RIGHT.
SO I WANTED TO SPEAK TO YOU ABOUT IT...... IF THAT'S OKAY WITH YOU?
HERE.
KACHI (CLICK)
I'VE ADJUSTED THE LEVELS SO YOU CAN MORE EASILY HEAR THE HEARTBEAT.
KACHI
TOKUN (THADUMP)
The way you can cut anything with no resistance!
It's truly a pleasure !!!
TOKUN

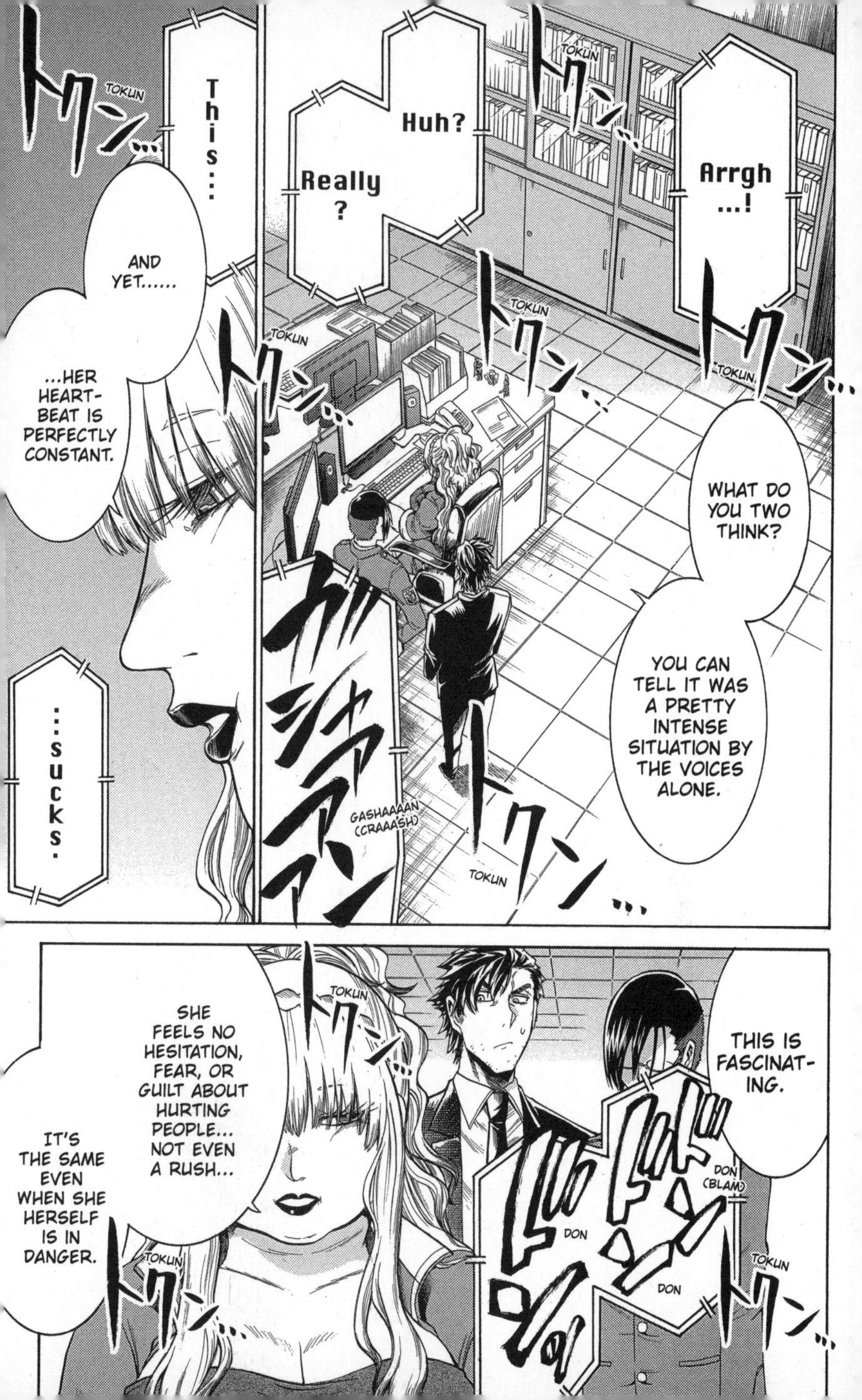
TOKUN
Arrgh ...!
Huh?
Really ?
TOKUN
TOKUN
TOKUN
WHAT DO YOU TWO THINK?
YOU CAN TELL IT WAS A PRETTY INTENSE SITUATION BY THE VOICES ALONE.
GASHAAAAN (CRAAASH)
TOKUN
TOKUN
This...
AND YET......
...HER HEARTBEAT IS PERFECTLY CONSTANT.
...sucks.
THIS IS FASCINATING.
DON (BLAM)
DON
DON
TOKUN
TOKUN
SHE FEELS NO HESITATION, FEAR, OR GUILT ABOUT HURTING PEOPLE... NOT EVEN A RUSH...
IT'S THE SAME EVEN WHEN SHE HERSELF IS IN DANGER.
TOKUN

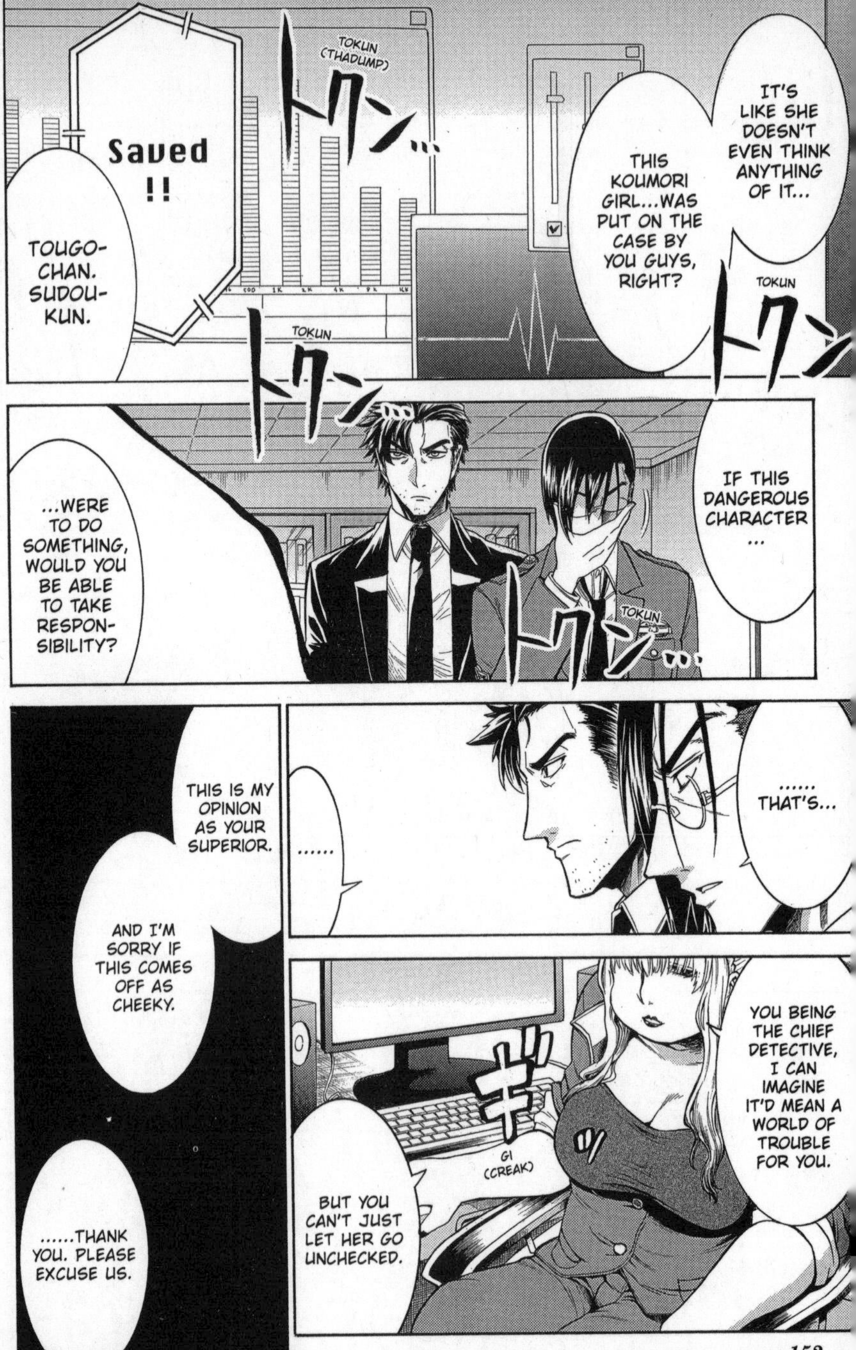
IT'S LIKE SHE DOESN'T EVEN THINK ANYTHING OF IT...
TOKUN
THIS KOUMORI GIRL...WAS PUT ON THE CASE BY YOU GUYS, RIGHT?
TOKUN (THADUMP)
Saved !!
TOKUN
TOUGO-CHAN. SUDOU-KUN.
IF THIS DANGEROUS CHARACTER ...
TOKUN
...WERE TO DO SOMETHING, WOULD YOU BE ABLE TO TAKE RESPONSIBILITY?
...... THAT'S...
......
YOU BEING THE CHIEF DETECTIVE, I CAN IMAGINE IT'D MEAN A WORLD OF TROUBLE FOR YOU.
GI (CREAK)
BUT YOU CAN'T JUST LET HER GO UNCHECKED.
THIS IS MY OPINION AS YOUR SUPERIOR.
AND I'M SORRY IF THIS COMES OFF AS CHEEKY.
......THANK YOU. PLEASE EXCUSE US.

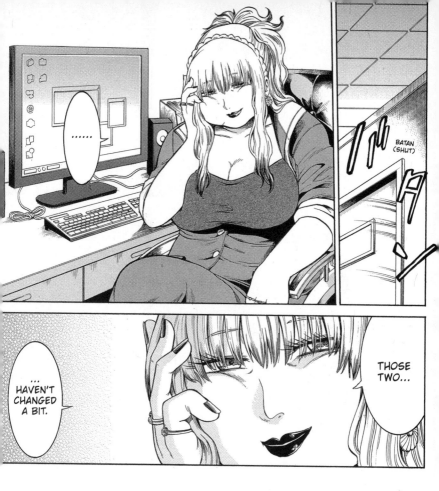

......

BATAN
(SHUT)

THOSE
TWO...

... HAVEN'T
CHANGED
A BIT.

......

PHEW.

KO
(CLIK)

KO

KO

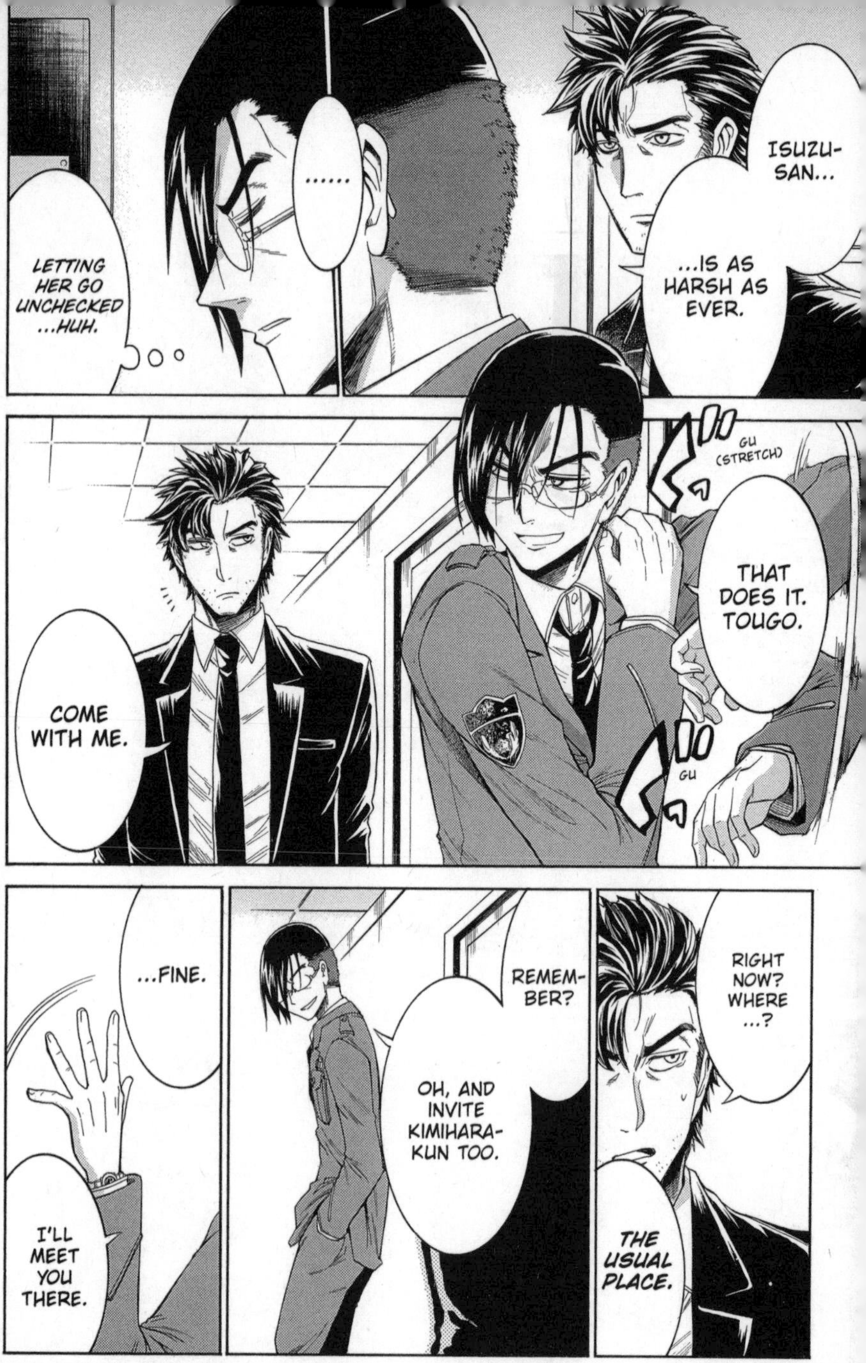
ISUZU-SAN...
...IS AS HARSH AS EVER.
......
LETTING HER GO UNCHECKED ...HUH.
GU (STRETCH)
THAT DOES IT. TOUGO.
GU
COME WITH ME.
RIGHT NOW? WHERE ...?
THE USUAL PLACE.
REMEM-BER?
OH, AND INVITE KIMIHARA-KUN TOO.
...FINE.
I'LL MEET YOU THERE.

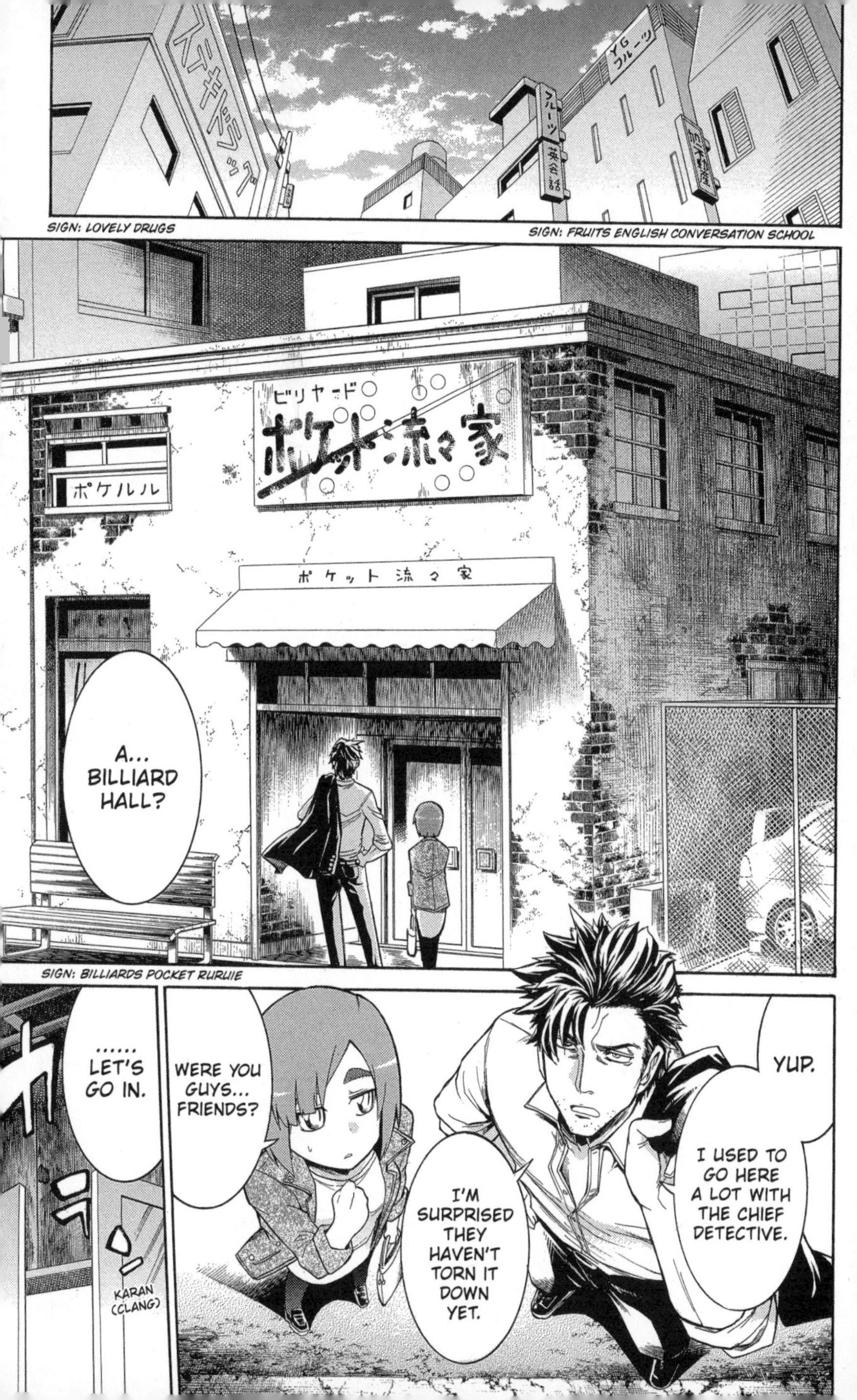
SIGN: FRUITS ENGLISH CONVERSATION SCHOOL
SIGN: LOVELY DRUGS
ビリヤード
ポケット流々家
ポケルル
A... BILLIARD HALL?
SIGN: BILLIARDS POCKET RURUIE
YUP.
I USED TO GO HERE A LOT WITH THE CHIEF DETECTIVE.
I'M SURPRISED THEY HAVEN'T TORN IT DOWN YET.
WERE YOU GUYS... FRIENDS?
...... LET'S GO IN.
KARAN (CLANG)

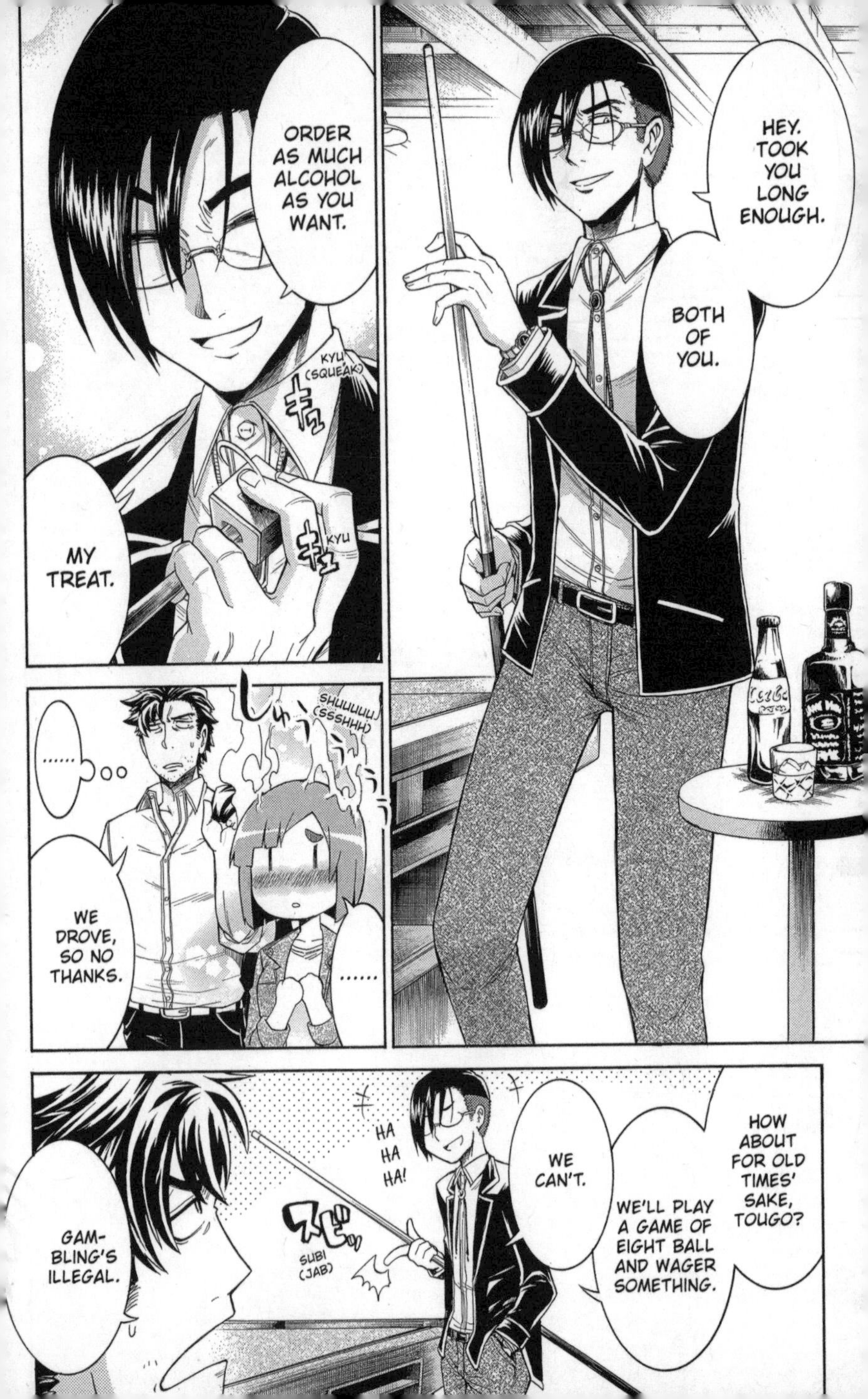
HEY. TOOK YOU LONG ENOUGH.
BOTH OF YOU.
ORDER AS MUCH ALCOHOL AS YOU WANT.
KYU (SQUEAK)
KYU
MY TREAT.
SHUUUUU (SSSHHH)
......
......
WE DROVE, SO NO THANKS.
HOW ABOUT FOR OLD TIMES' SAKE, TOUGO?
WE'LL PLAY A GAME OF EIGHT BALL AND WAGER SOMETHING.
WE CAN'T.
HA HA HA!
SUBI (JAB)
GAM-BLING'S ILLEGAL.

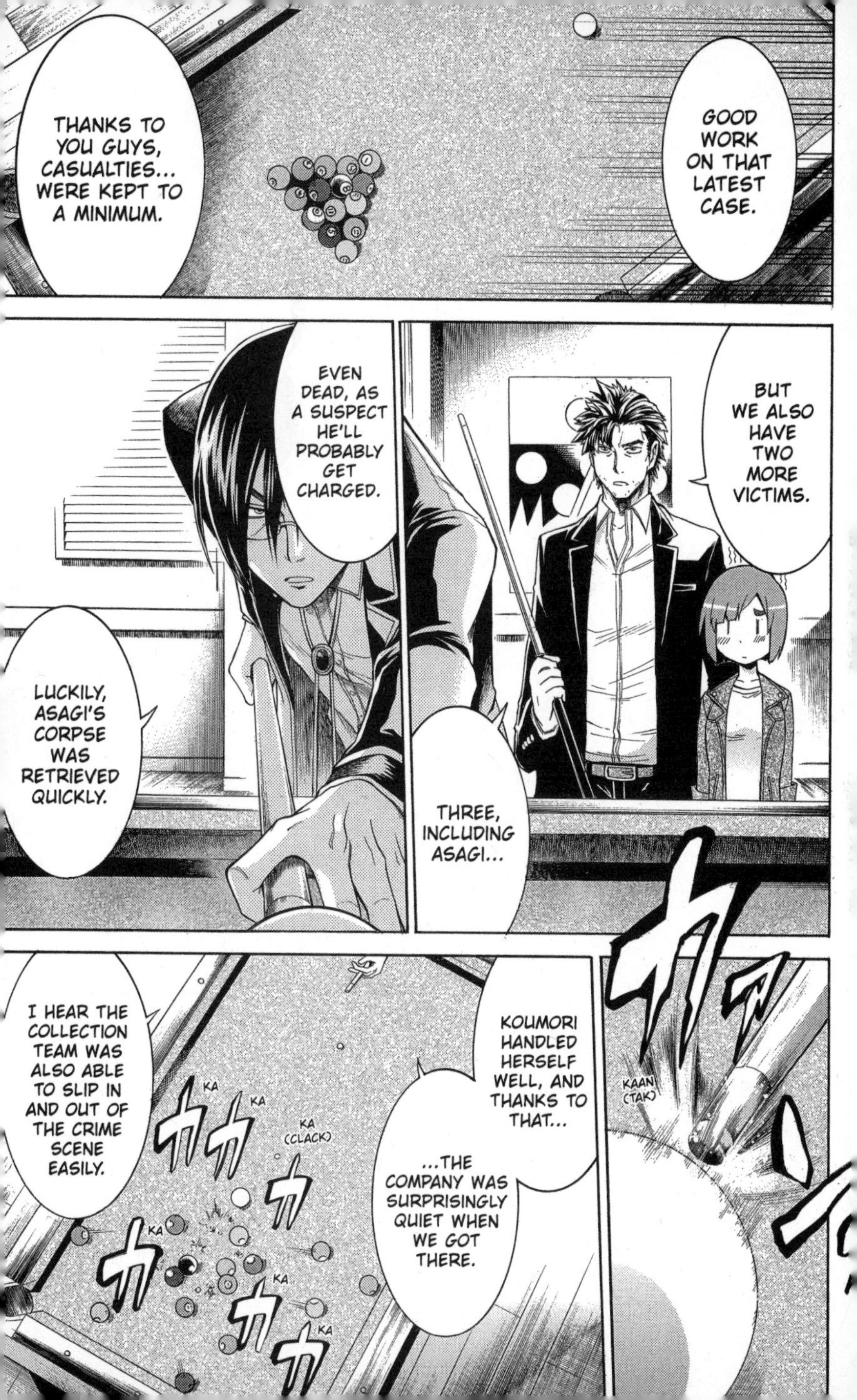
GOOD WORK ON THAT LATEST CASE.
THANKS TO YOU GUYS, CASUALTIES... WERE KEPT TO A MINIMUM.
BUT WE ALSO HAVE TWO MORE VICTIMS.
THREE, INCLUDING ASAGI...
EVEN DEAD, AS A SUSPECT HE'LL PROBABLY GET CHARGED.
LUCKILY, ASAGI'S CORPSE WAS RETRIEVED QUICKLY.
KAAN (TAK)
KOUMORI HANDLED HERSELF WELL, AND THANKS TO THAT...
...THE COMPANY WAS SURPRISINGLY QUIET WHEN WE GOT THERE.
KA
KA
KA (CLACK)
KA
KA
KA
I HEAR THE COLLECTION TEAM WAS ALSO ABLE TO SLIP IN AND OUT OF THE CRIME SCENE EASILY.

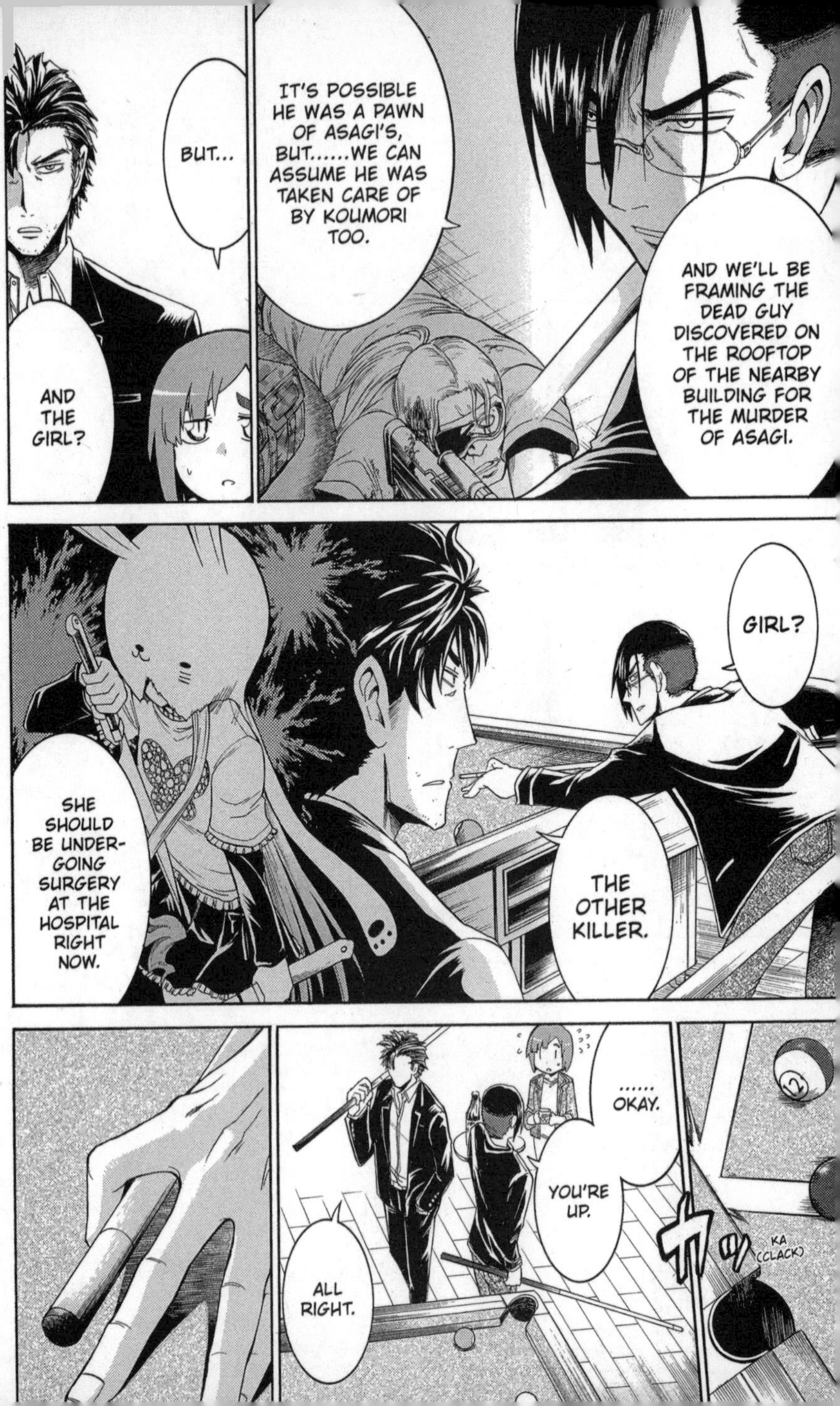
IT'S POSSIBLE HE WAS A PAWN OF ASAGI'S, BUT......WE CAN ASSUME HE WAS TAKEN CARE OF BY KOUMORI TOO.
AND WE'LL BE FRAMING THE DEAD GUY DISCOVERED ON THE ROOFTOP OF THE NEARBY BUILDING FOR THE MURDER OF ASAGI.
BUT...
AND THE GIRL?
GIRL?
THE OTHER KILLER.
SHE SHOULD BE UNDER-GOING SURGERY AT THE HOSPITAL RIGHT NOW.
KA (CLACK)
......OKAY.
YOU'RE UP.
ALL RIGHT.

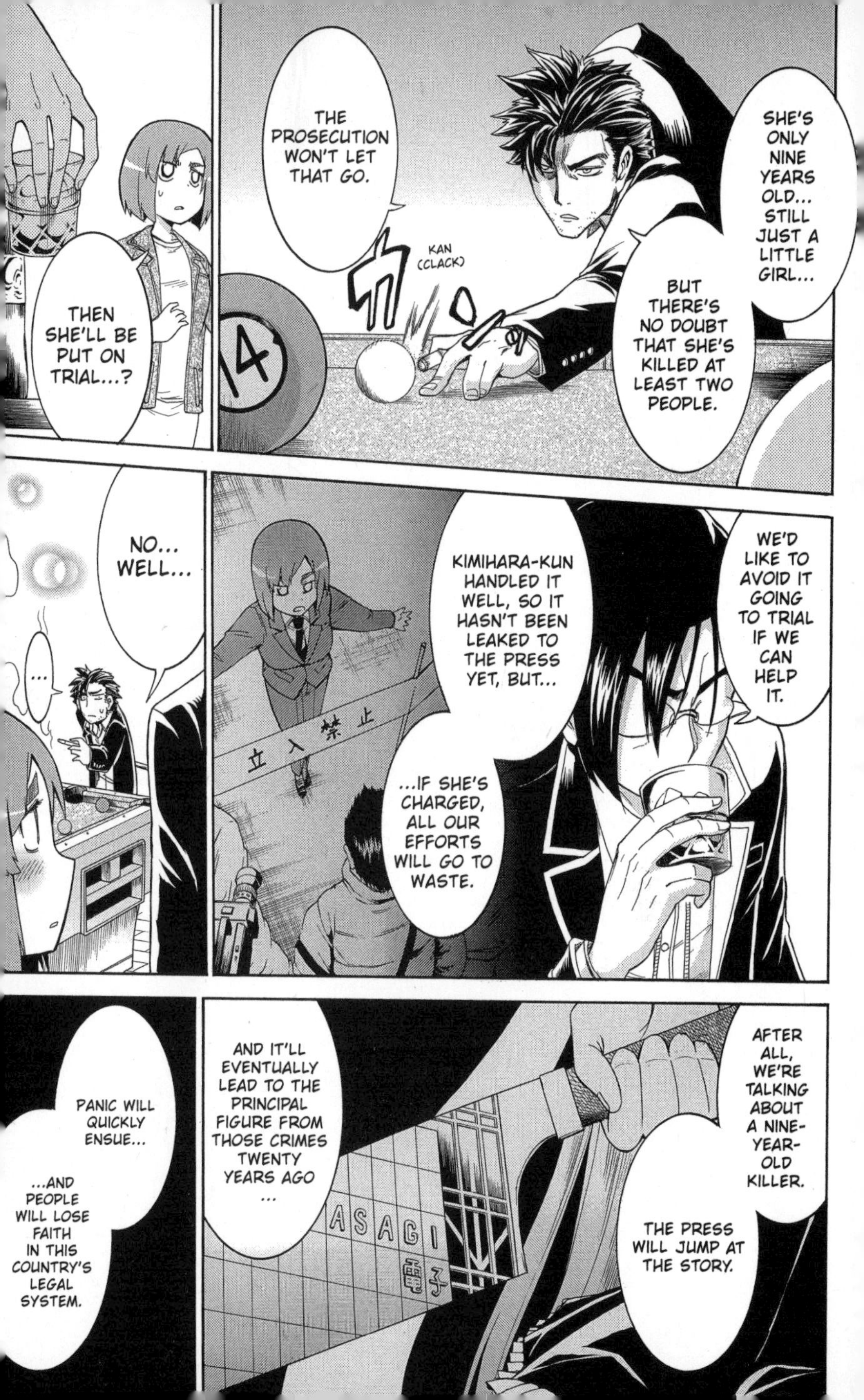
SHE'S ONLY NINE YEARS OLD... STILL JUST A LITTLE GIRL...
BUT THERE'S NO DOUBT THAT SHE'S KILLED AT LEAST TWO PEOPLE.
KAN (CLACK)
THE PROSECUTION WON'T LET THAT GO.
THEN SHE'LL BE PUT ON TRIAL...?
WE'D LIKE TO AVOID IT GOING TO TRIAL IF WE CAN HELP IT.
KIMIHARA-KUN HANDLED IT WELL, SO IT HASN'T BEEN LEAKED TO THE PRESS YET, BUT...
立入禁止
...IF SHE'S CHARGED, ALL OUR EFFORTS WILL GO TO WASTE.
NO... WELL...
...
AFTER ALL, WE'RE TALKING ABOUT A NINE-YEAR-OLD KILLER.
THE PRESS WILL JUMP AT THE STORY.
AND IT'LL EVENTUALLY LEAD TO THE PRINCIPAL FIGURE FROM THOSE CRIMES TWENTY YEARS AGO...
ASAGI
電子
PANIC WILL QUICKLY ENSUE...
...AND PEOPLE WILL LOSE FAITH IN THIS COUNTRY'S LEGAL SYSTEM.

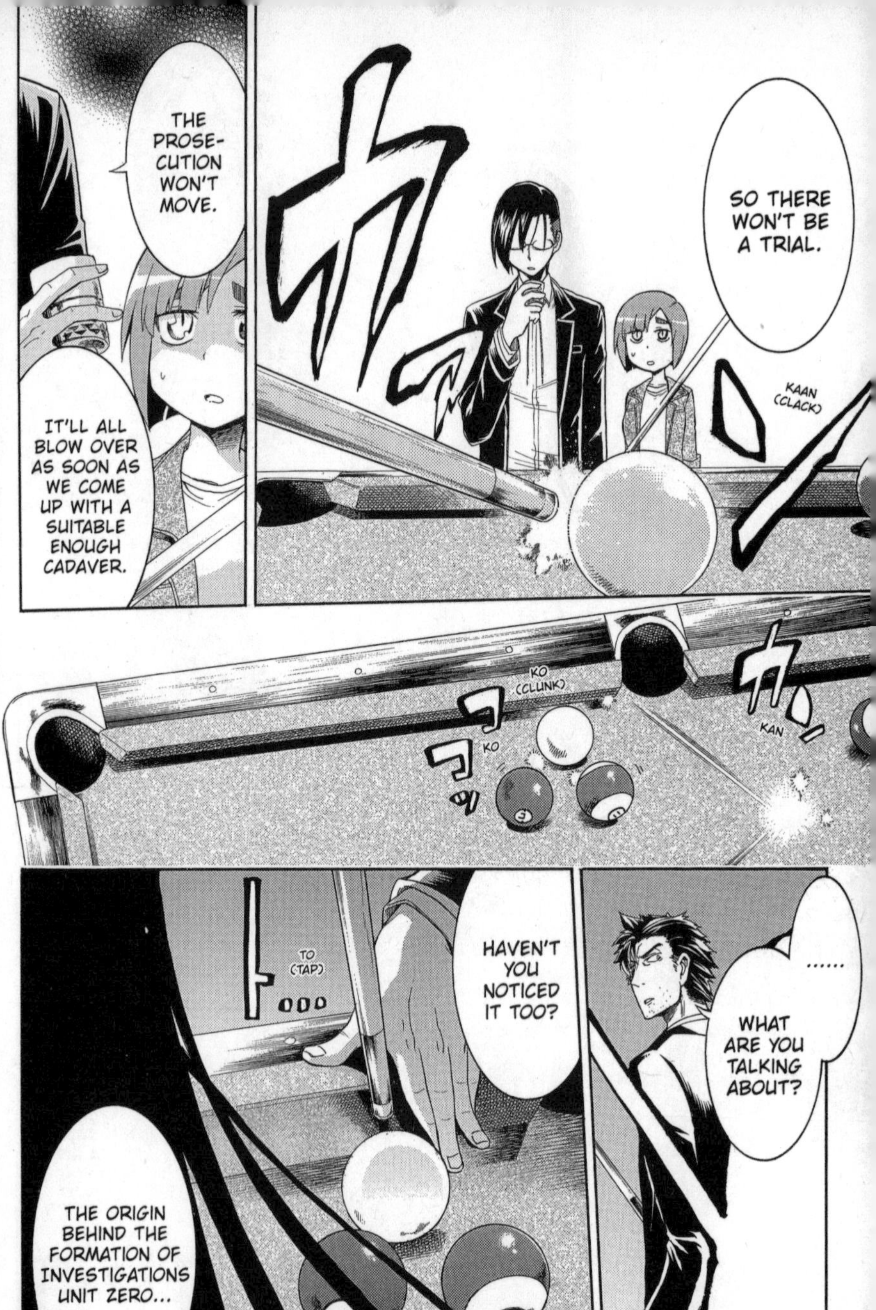
SO THERE WON'T BE A TRIAL.
KAAN (CLACK)
THE PROSE-CUTION WON'T MOVE.
IT'LL ALL BLOW OVER AS SOON AS WE COME UP WITH A SUITABLE ENOUGH CADAVER.
KAN
KO (CLUNK)
KO
......
WHAT ARE YOU TALKING ABOUT?
HAVEN'T YOU NOTICED IT TOO?
TO (TAP)
THE ORIGIN BEHIND THE FORMATION OF INVESTIGATIONS UNIT ZERO...

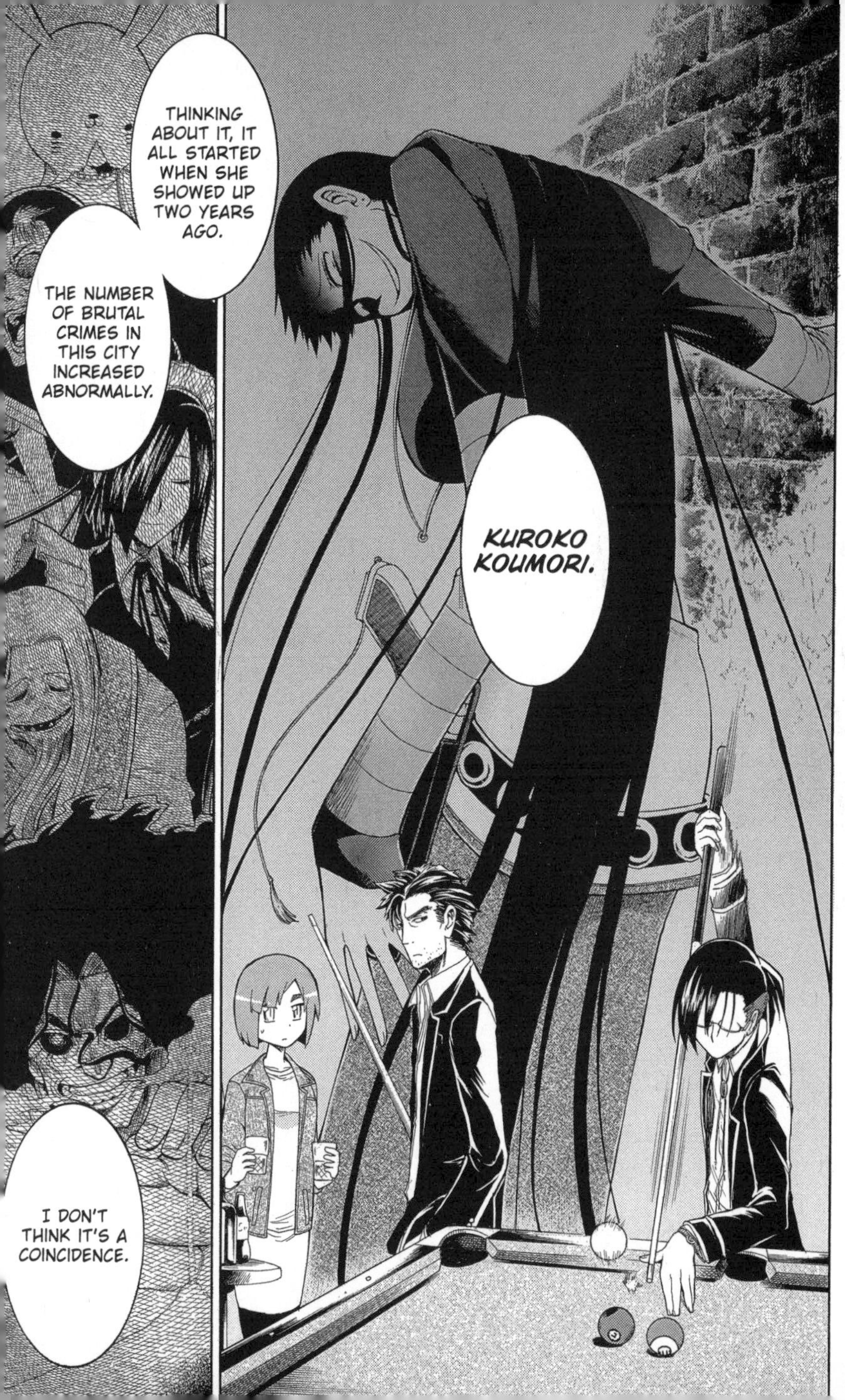
KUROKO KOUMORI.
THINKING ABOUT IT, IT ALL STARTED WHEN SHE SHOWED UP TWO YEARS AGO.
THE NUMBER OF BRUTAL CRIMES IN THIS CITY INCREASED ABNORMALLY.
I DON'T THINK IT'S A COINCIDENCE.

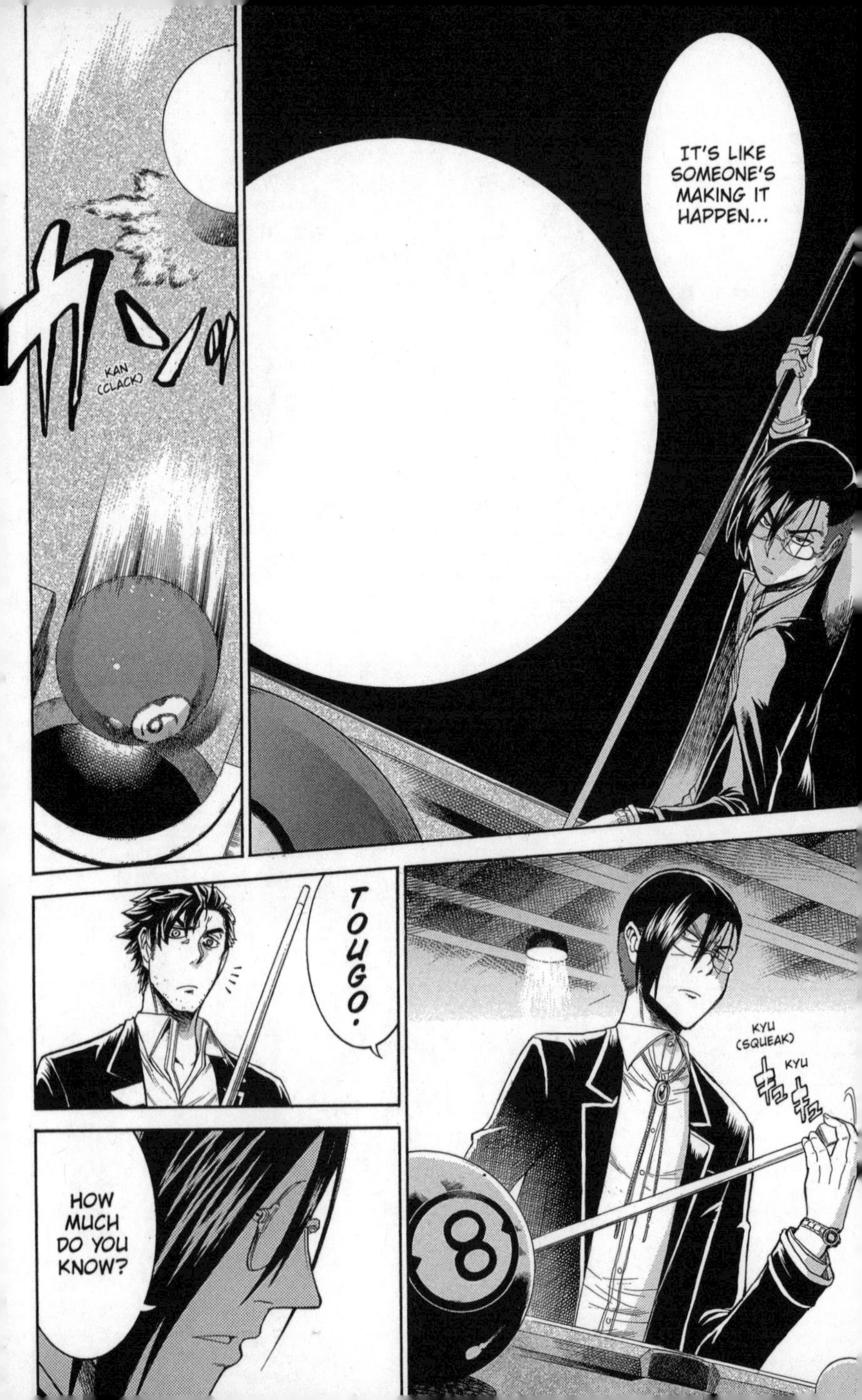
IT'S LIKE SOMEONE'S MAKING IT HAPPEN...
KAN (CLACK)
KYU (SQUEAK) KYU
TOUGO.
HOW MUCH DO YOU KNOW?

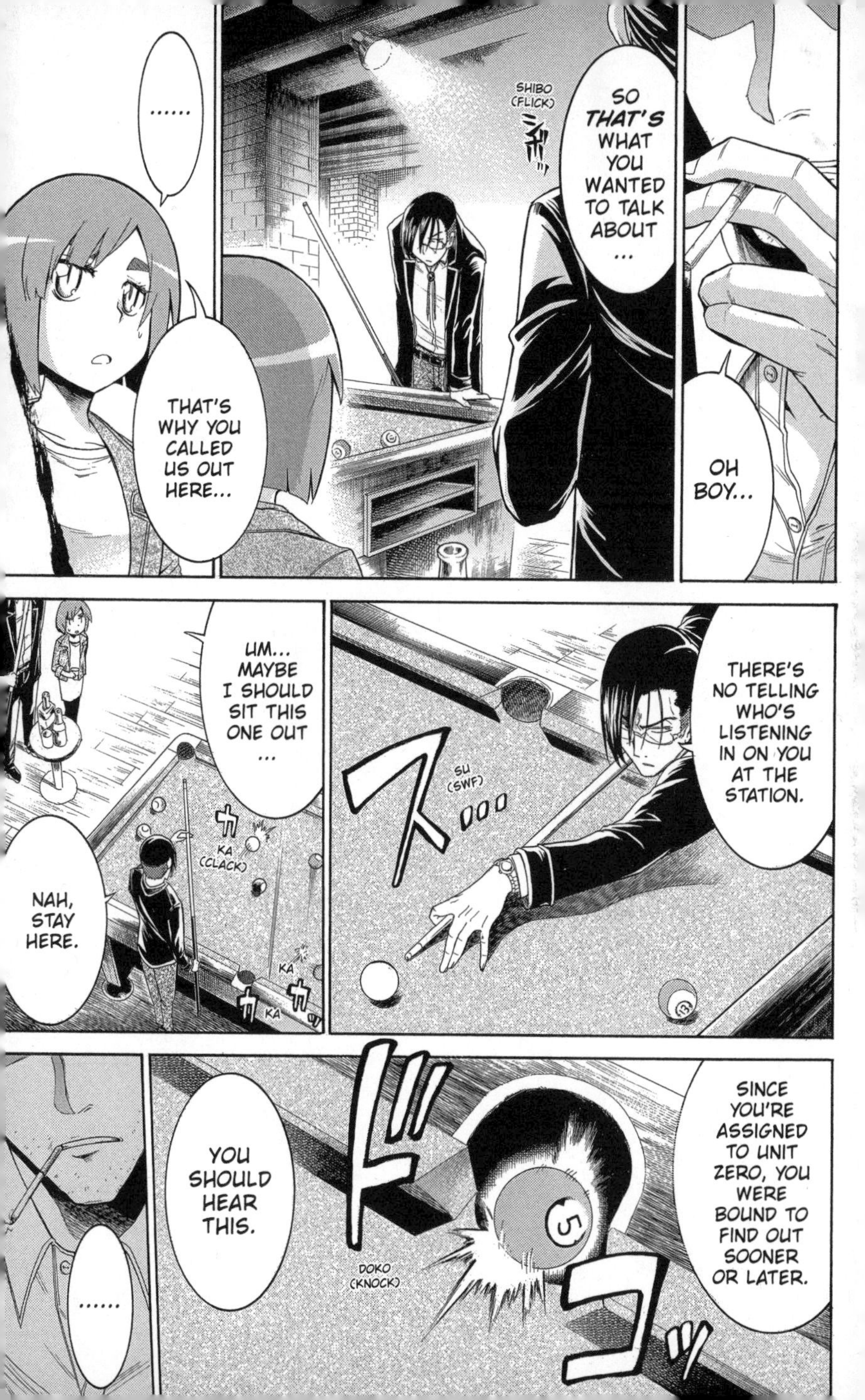
SO THAT'S WHAT YOU WANTED TO TALK ABOUT ...
SHIBO (FLICK)
OH BOY...
......
THAT'S WHY YOU CALLED US OUT HERE...
THERE'S NO TELLING WHO'S LISTENING IN ON YOU AT THE STATION.
SU (SWF)
UM... MAYBE I SHOULD SIT THIS ONE OUT ...
KA (CLACK)
NAH, STAY HERE.
KA
KA
SINCE YOU'RE ASSIGNED TO UNIT ZERO, YOU WERE BOUND TO FIND OUT SOONER OR LATER.
YOU SHOULD HEAR THIS.
DOKO (KNOCK)
......

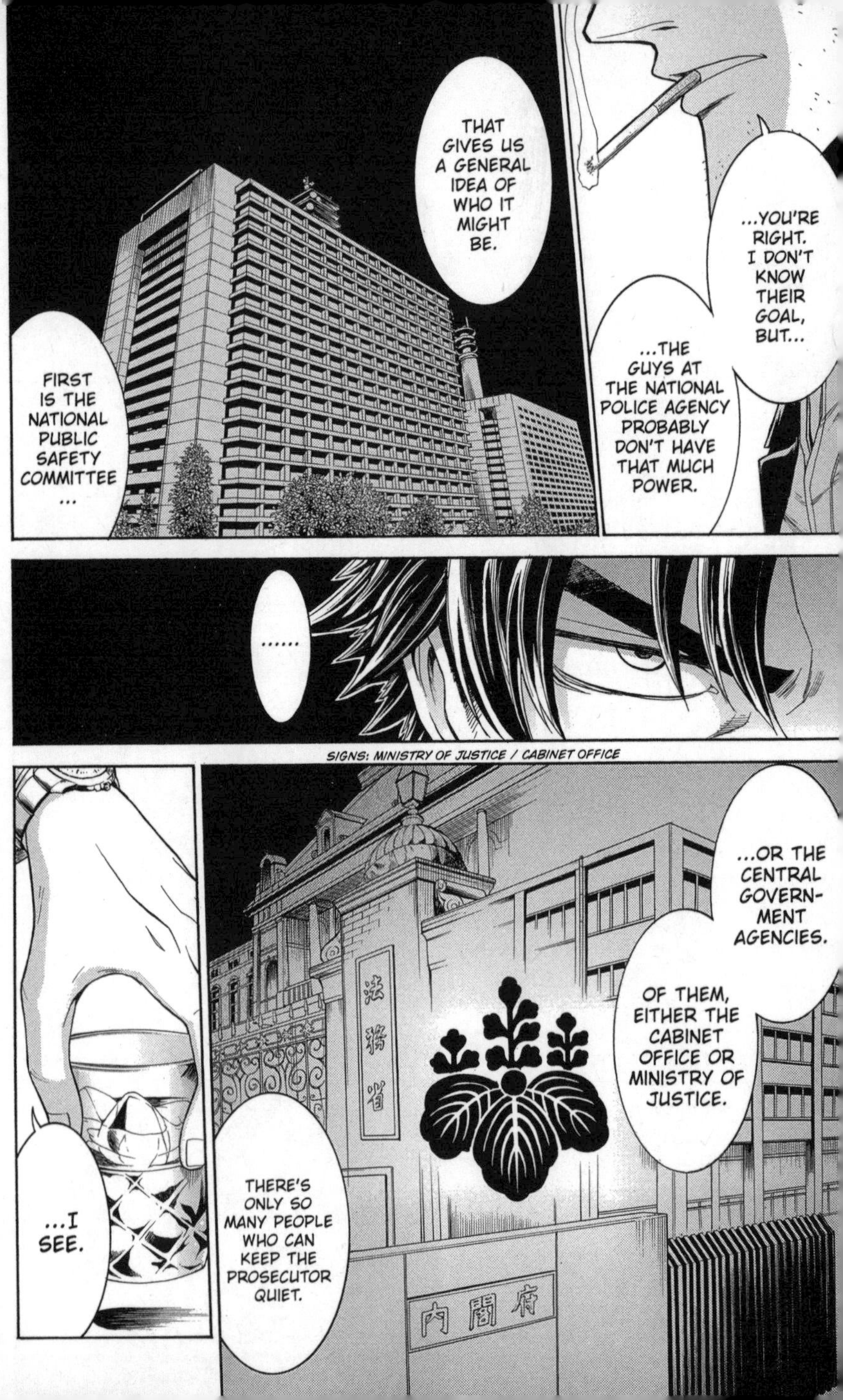
...YOU'RE RIGHT. I DON'T KNOW THEIR GOAL, BUT...
...THE GUYS AT THE NATIONAL POLICE AGENCY PROBABLY DON'T HAVE THAT MUCH POWER.
THAT GIVES US A GENERAL IDEA OF WHO IT MIGHT BE.
FIRST IS THE NATIONAL PUBLIC SAFETY COMMITTEE...
......
SIGNS: MINISTRY OF JUSTICE / CABINET OFFICE
...OR THE CENTRAL GOVERN-MENT AGENCIES.
OF THEM, EITHER THE CABINET OFFICE OR MINISTRY OF JUSTICE.
法務省
THERE'S ONLY SO MANY PEOPLE WHO CAN KEEP THE PROSECUTOR QUIET.
内閣府
...I SEE.

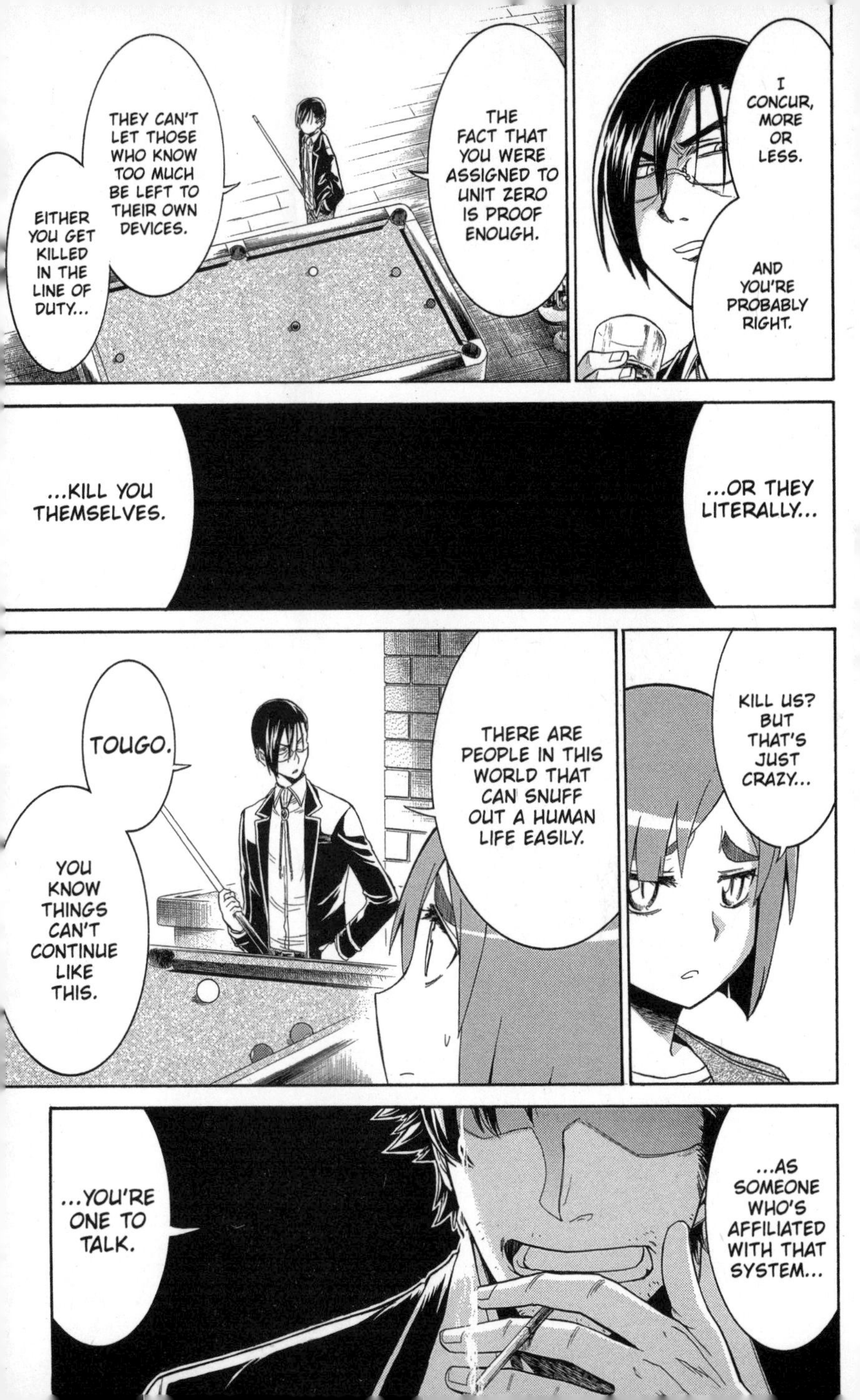
I CONCUR, MORE OR LESS.
AND YOU'RE PROBABLY RIGHT.
THE FACT THAT YOU WERE ASSIGNED TO UNIT ZERO IS PROOF ENOUGH.
THEY CAN'T LET THOSE WHO KNOW TOO MUCH BE LEFT TO THEIR OWN DEVICES.
EITHER YOU GET KILLED IN THE LINE OF DUTY...
...OR THEY LITERALLY...
...KILL YOU THEMSELVES.
KILL US? BUT THAT'S JUST CRAZY...
THERE ARE PEOPLE IN THIS WORLD THAT CAN SNUFF OUT A HUMAN LIFE EASILY.
TOUGO.
YOU KNOW THINGS CAN'T CONTINUE LIKE THIS.
...AS SOMEONE WHO'S AFFILIATED WITH THAT SYSTEM...
...YOU'RE ONE TO TALK.

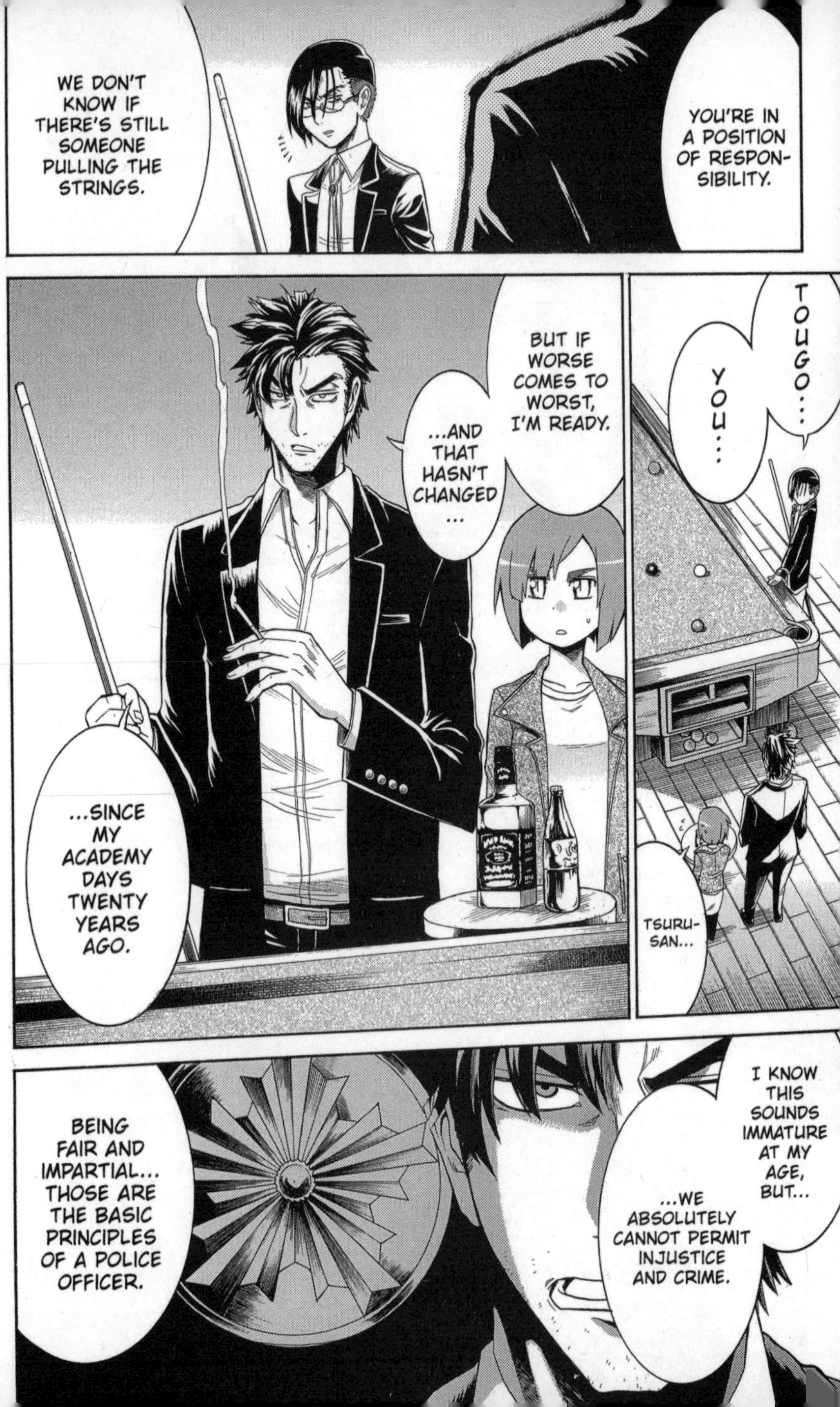
YOU'RE IN A POSITION OF RESPONSIBILITY.
WE DON'T KNOW IF THERE'S STILL SOMEONE PULLING THE STRINGS.
TOUGO...
YOU...
TSURU-SAN...
BUT IF WORSE COMES TO WORST, I'M READY.
...AND THAT HASN'T CHANGED...
...SINCE MY ACADEMY DAYS TWENTY YEARS AGO.
I KNOW THIS SOUNDS IMMATURE AT MY AGE, BUT...
...WE ABSOLUTELY CANNOT PERMIT INJUSTICE AND CRIME.
BEING FAIR AND IMPARTIAL... THOSE ARE THE BASIC PRINCIPLES OF A POLICE OFFICER.

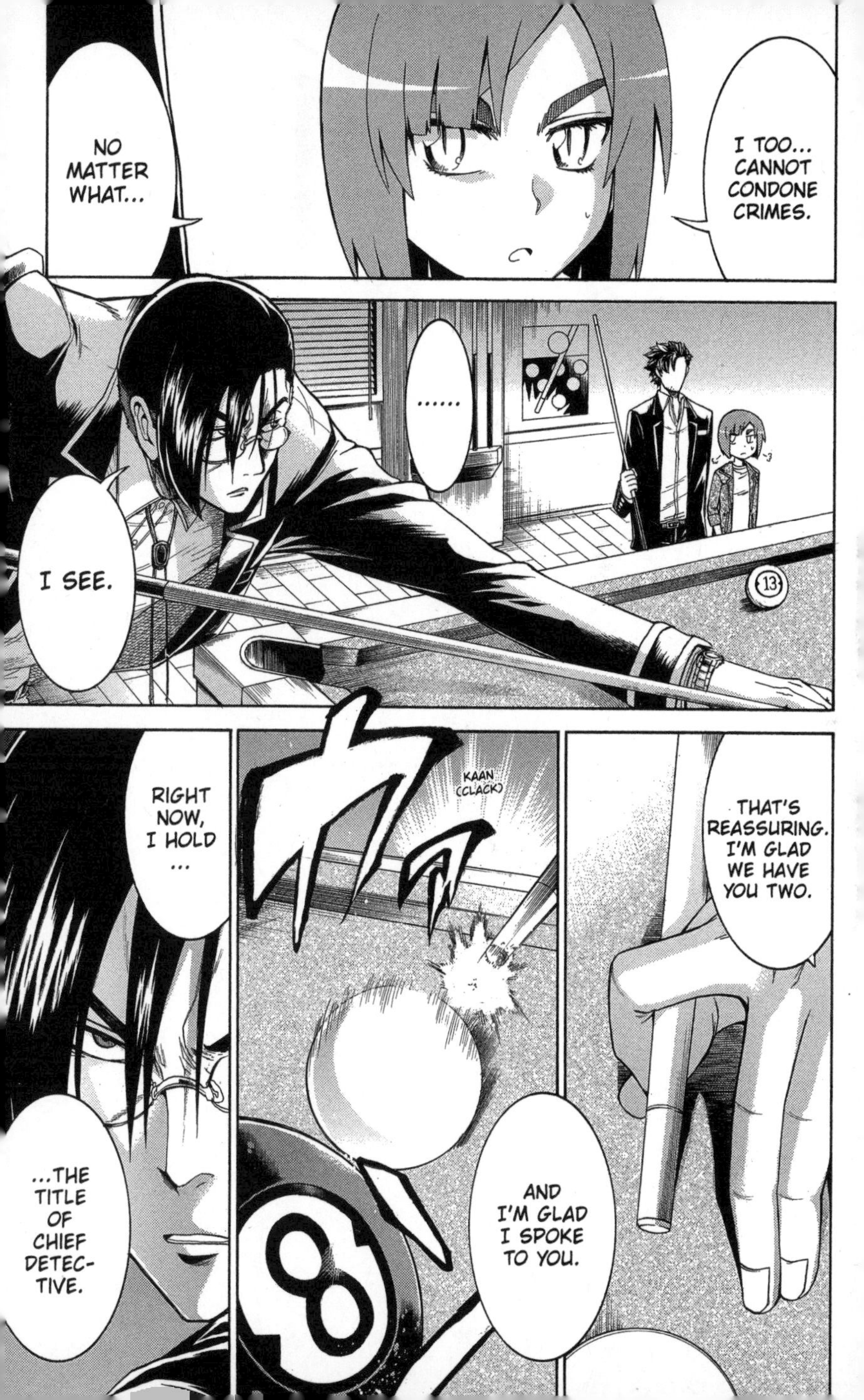
I TOO... CANNOT CONDONE CRIMES.
NO MATTER WHAT...
......
I SEE.
THAT'S REASSURING. I'M GLAD WE HAVE YOU TWO.
KAAN (CLACK)
AND I'M GLAD I SPOKE TO YOU.
RIGHT NOW, I HOLD ...
...THE TITLE OF CHIEF DETECTIVE.

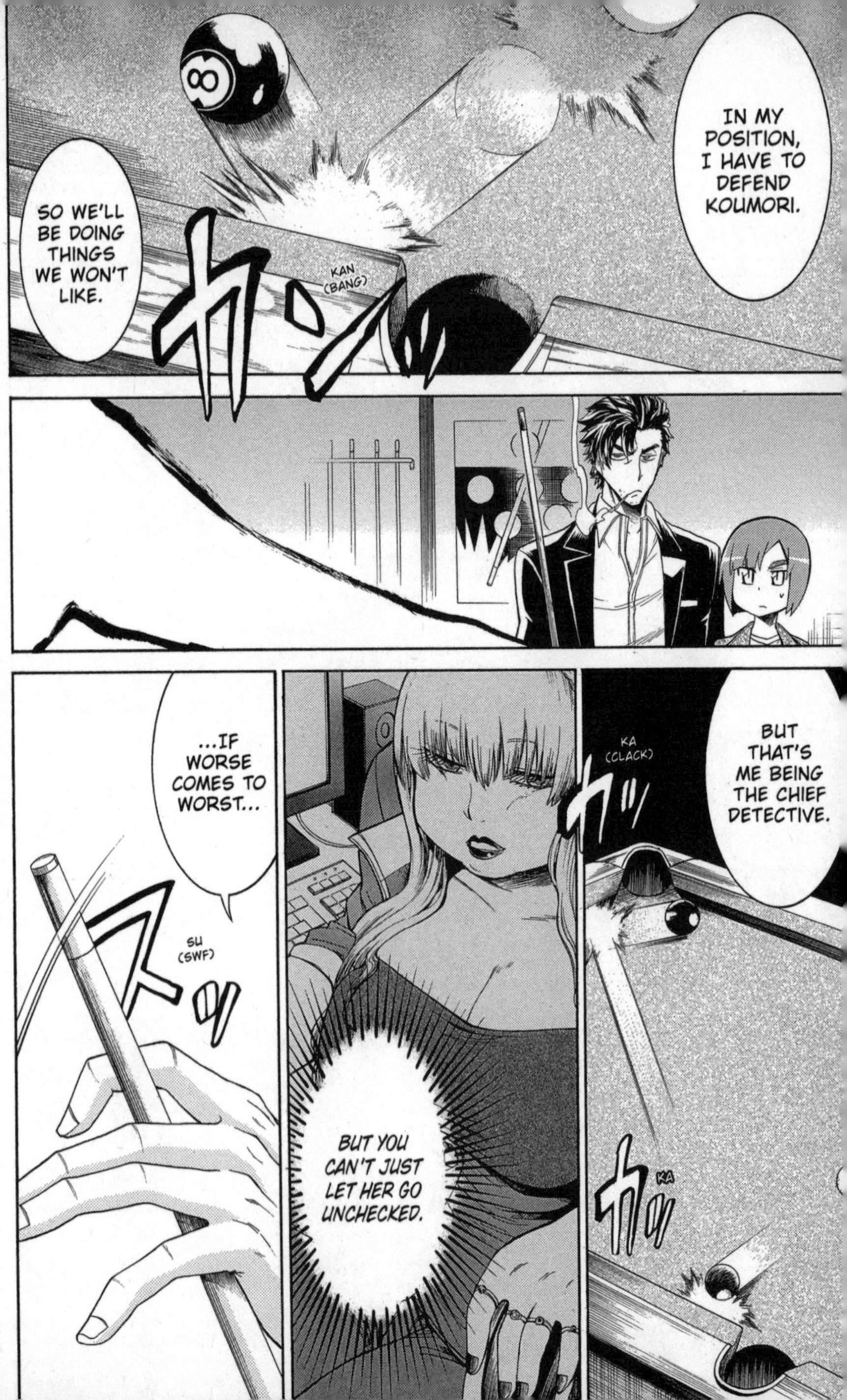
IN MY POSITION, I HAVE TO DEFEND KOUMORI.
KAN (BANG)
SO WE'LL BE DOING THINGS WE WON'T LIKE.
BUT THAT'S ME BEING THE CHIEF DETECTIVE.
KA (CLACK)
KA
BUT YOU CAN'T JUST LET HER GO UNCHECKED.
...IF WORSE COMES TO WORST...
SU (SWF)

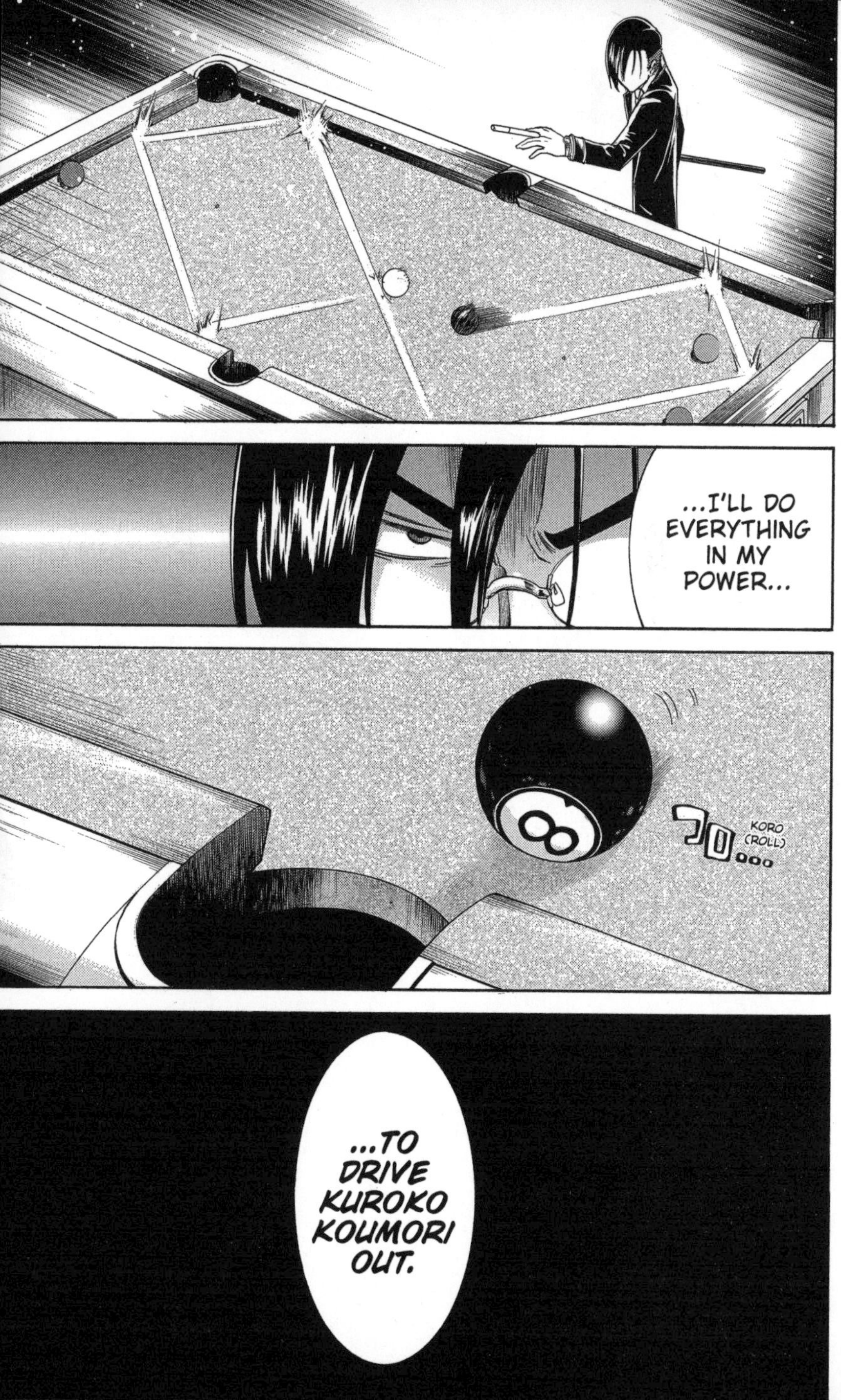
...I'LL DO EVERYTHING IN MY POWER...
KORO (ROLL)
...TO DRIVE KUROKO KOUMORI OUT.

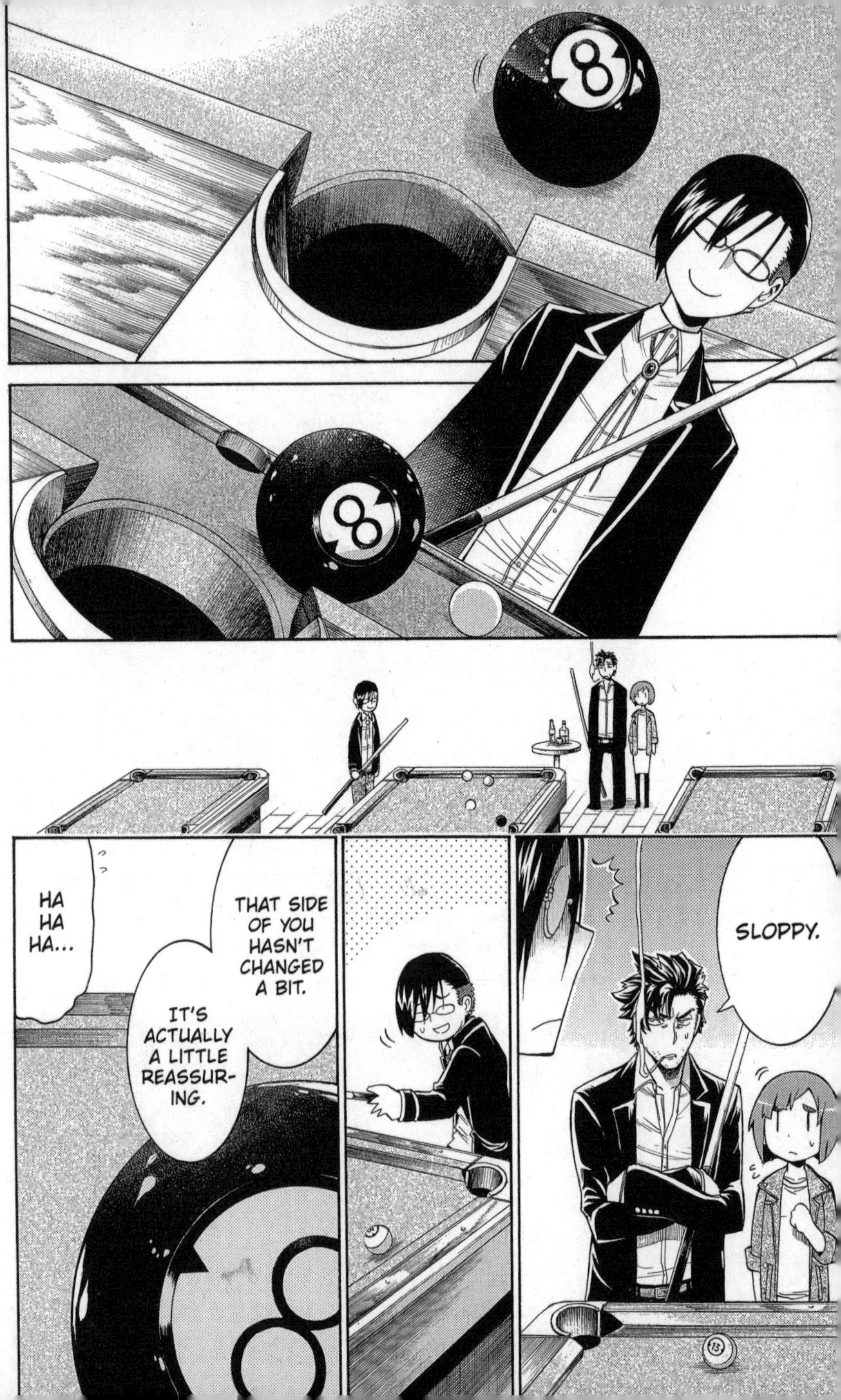
SLOPPY.
THAT SIDE OF YOU HASN'T CHANGED A BIT.
IT'S ACTUALLY A LITTLE REASSURING.
HA HA HA...

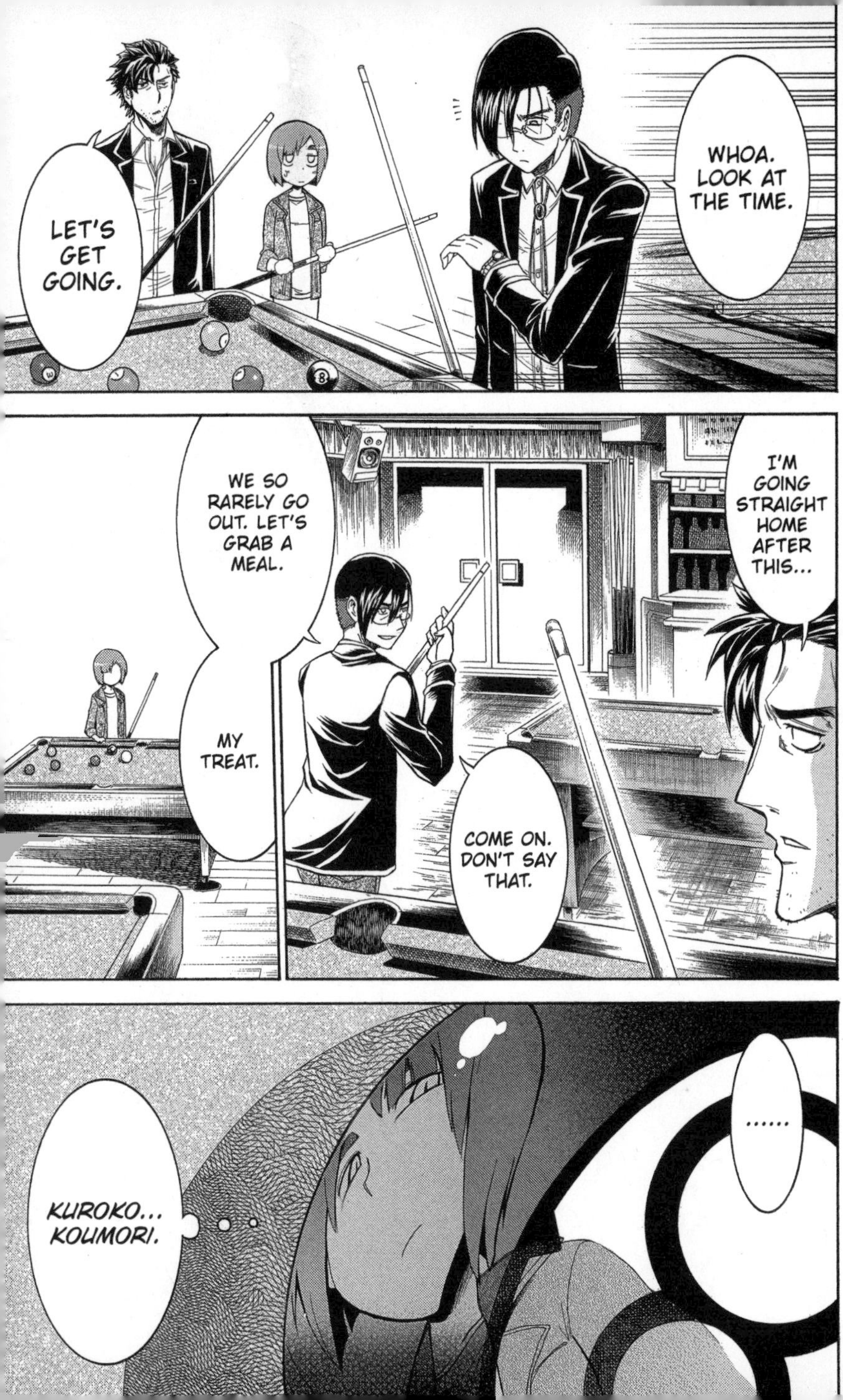
WHOA. LOOK AT THE TIME.
LET'S GET GOING.
I'M GOING STRAIGHT HOME AFTER THIS...
COME ON. DON'T SAY THAT.
WE SO RARELY GO OUT. LET'S GRAB A MEAL.
MY TREAT.
......
KUROKO... KOUMORI.

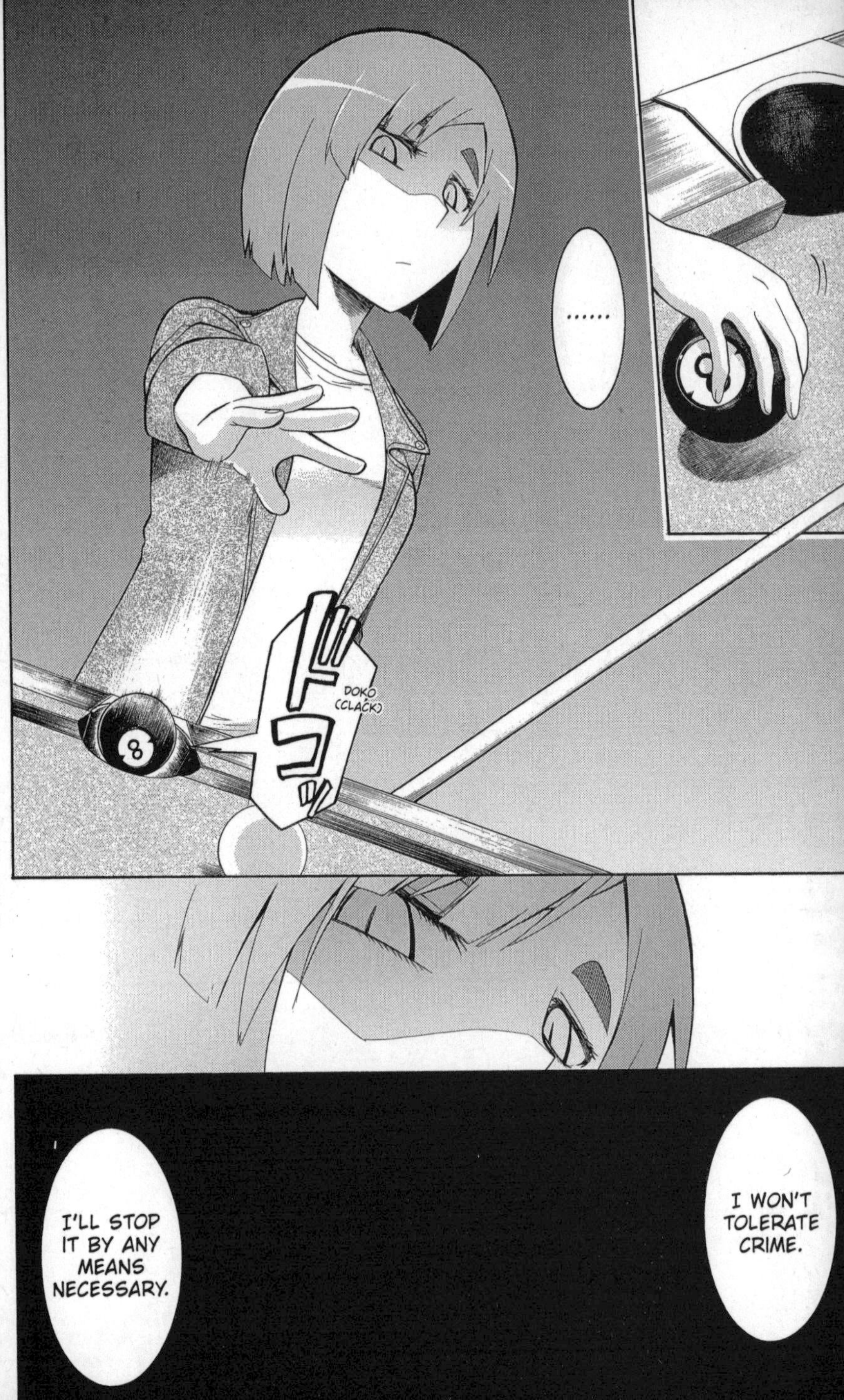
......
ドコッ
DOKO (CLACK)
I WON'T TOLERATE CRIME.
I'LL STOP IT BY ANY MEANS NECESSARY.

MURCIÉLAGO

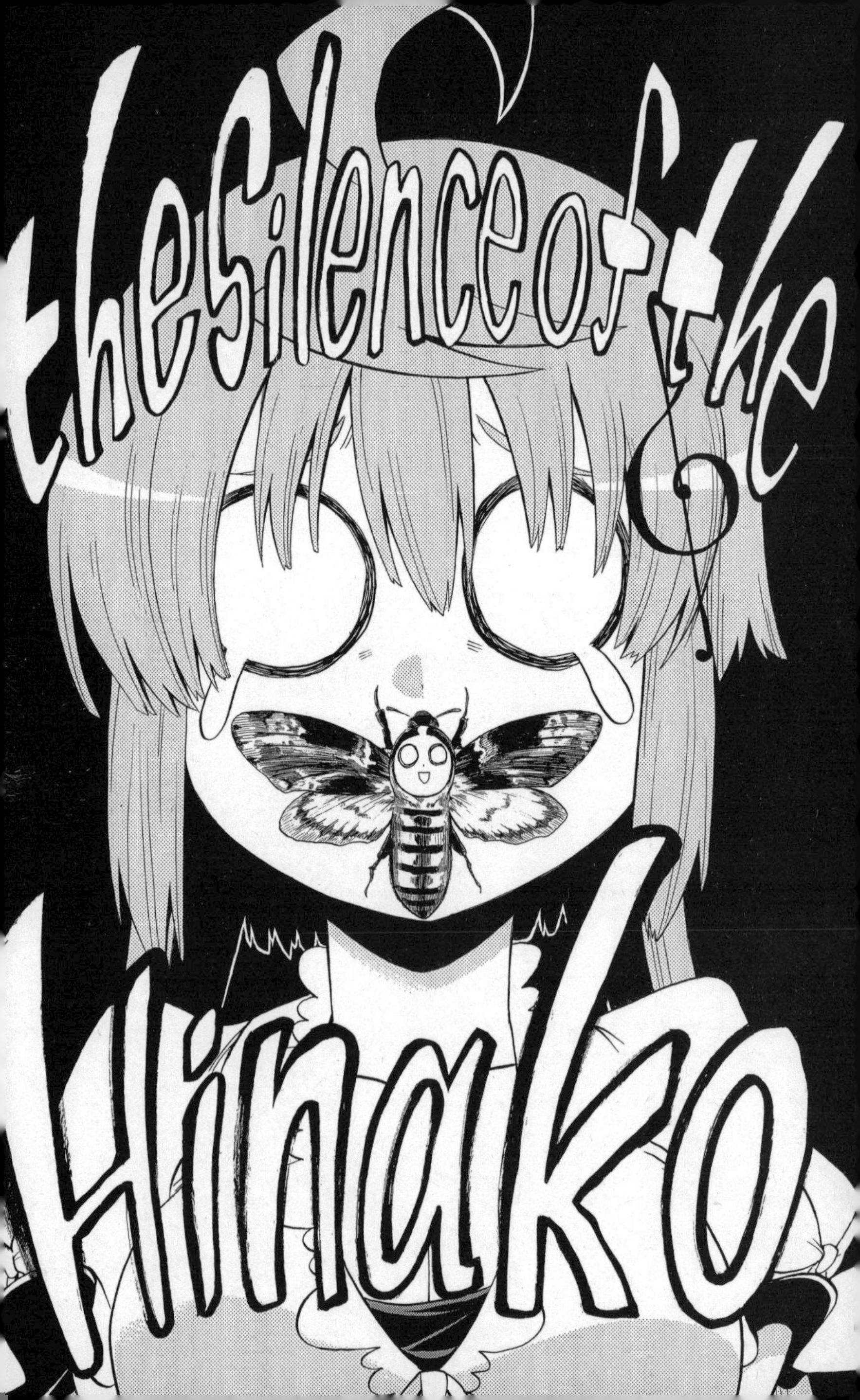

The Silence of the
Hinako

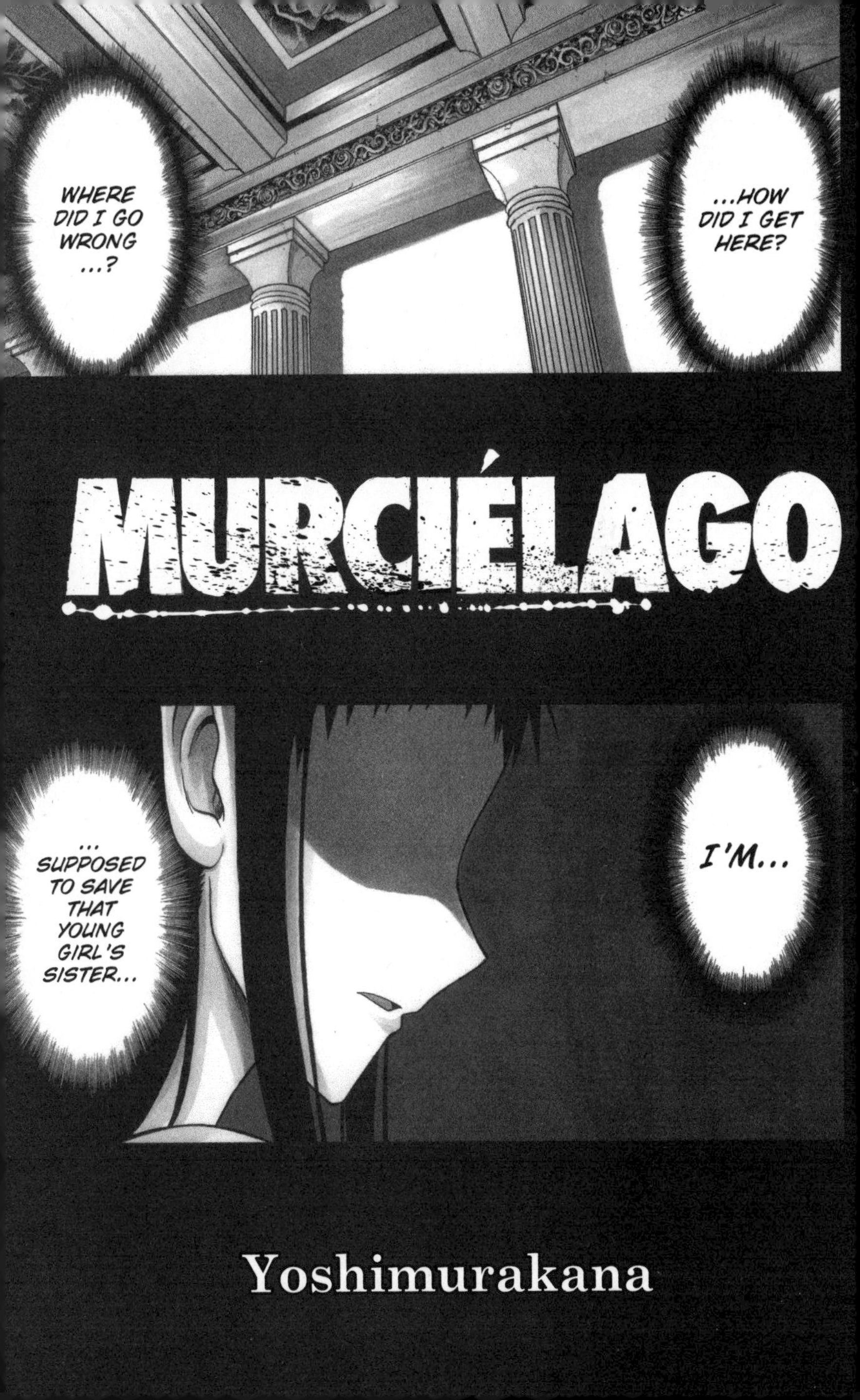
...HOW DID I GET HERE?
WHERE DID I GO WRONG ...?
MURCIÉLAGO
I'M...
... SUPPOSED TO SAVE THAT YOUNG GIRL'S SISTER...
Yoshimurakana

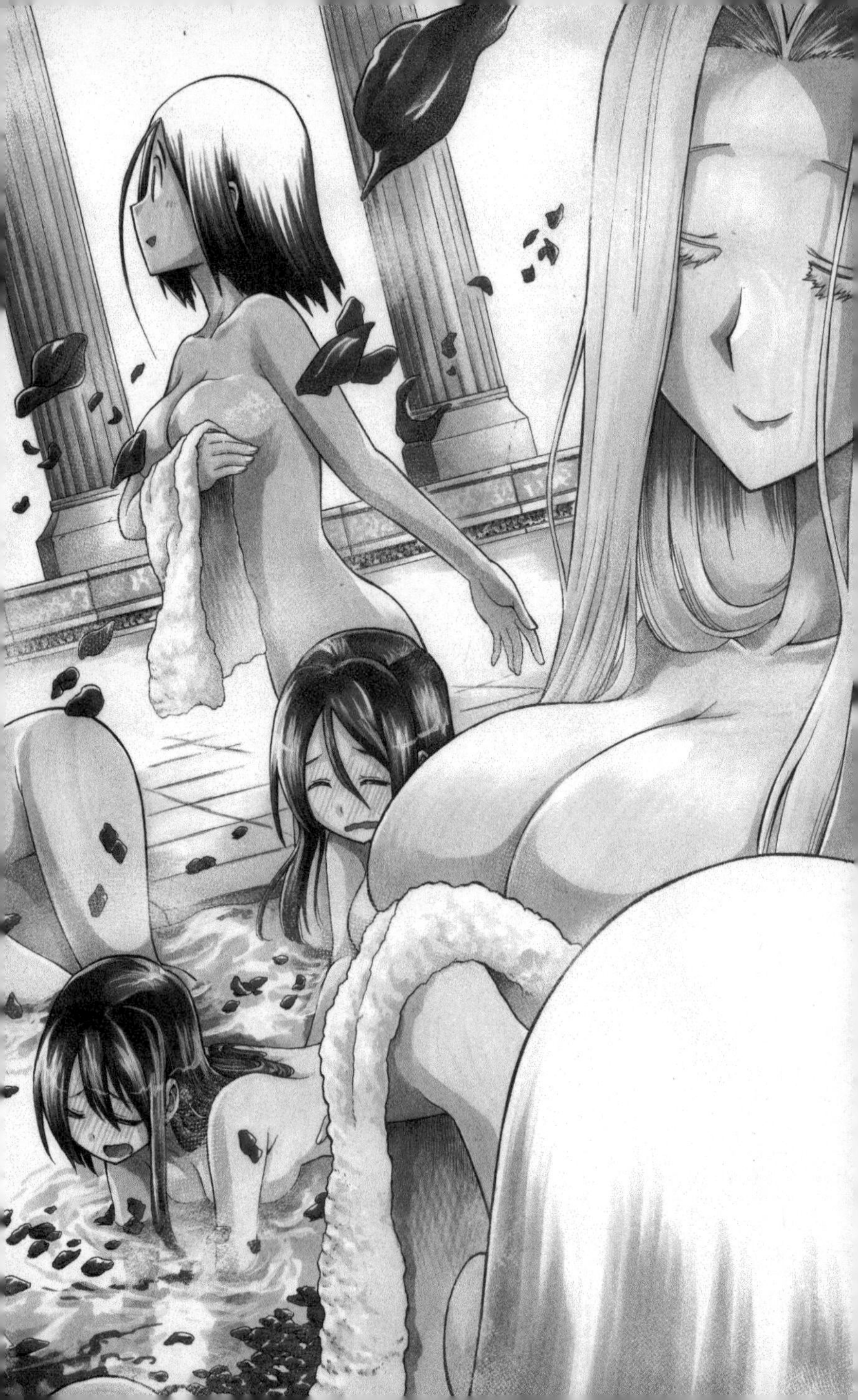

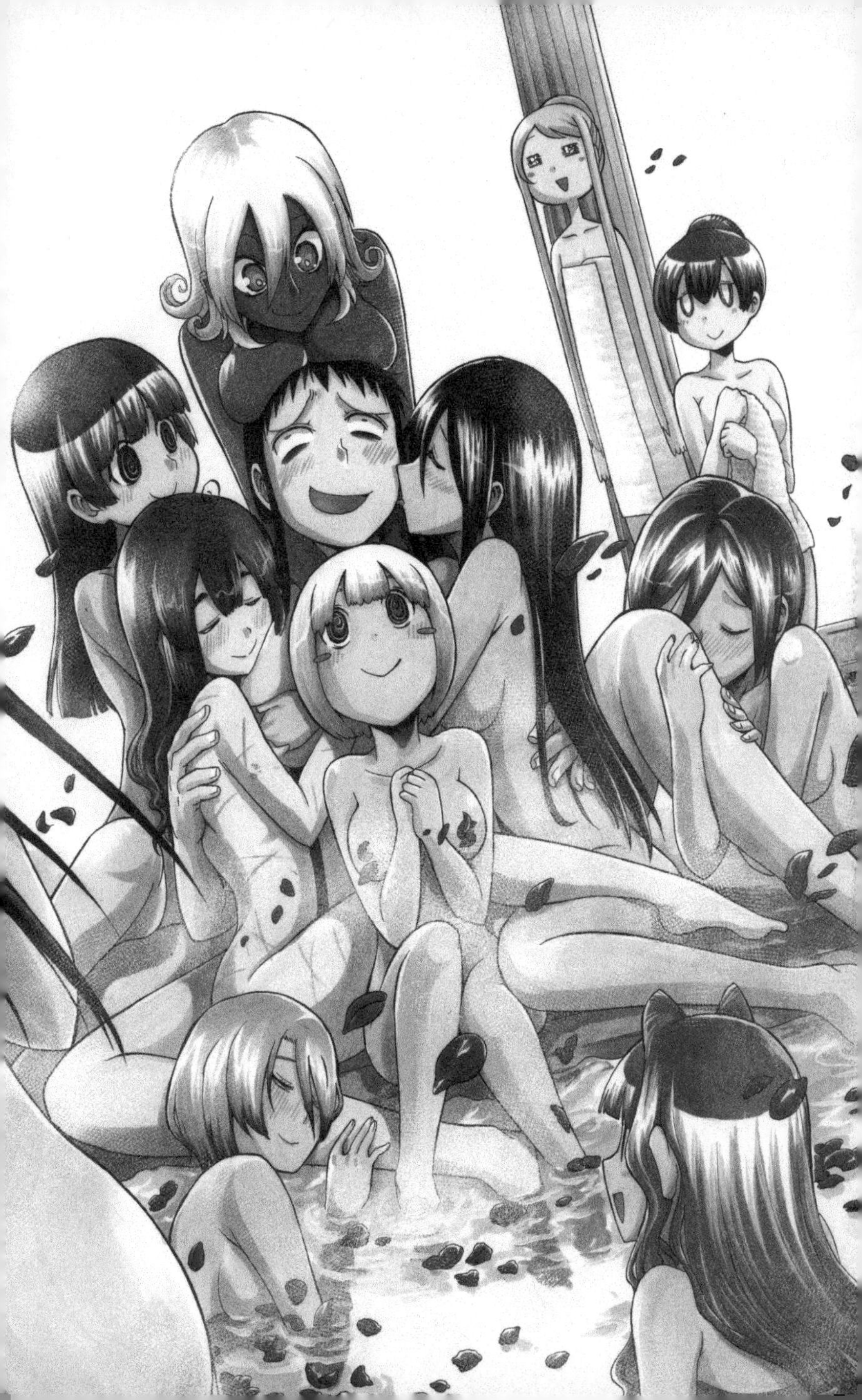

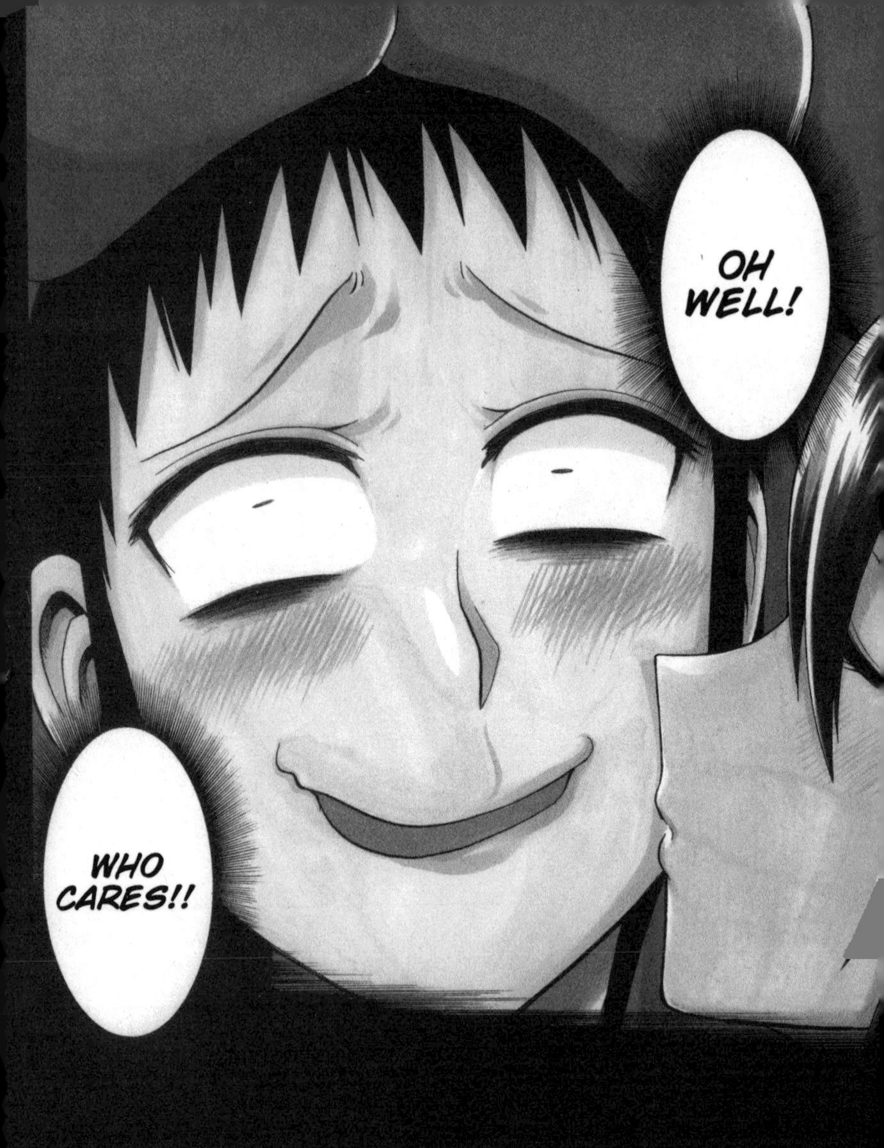
OH WELL!
WHO CARES!!

Chapter 19
Rose-Colored Prison

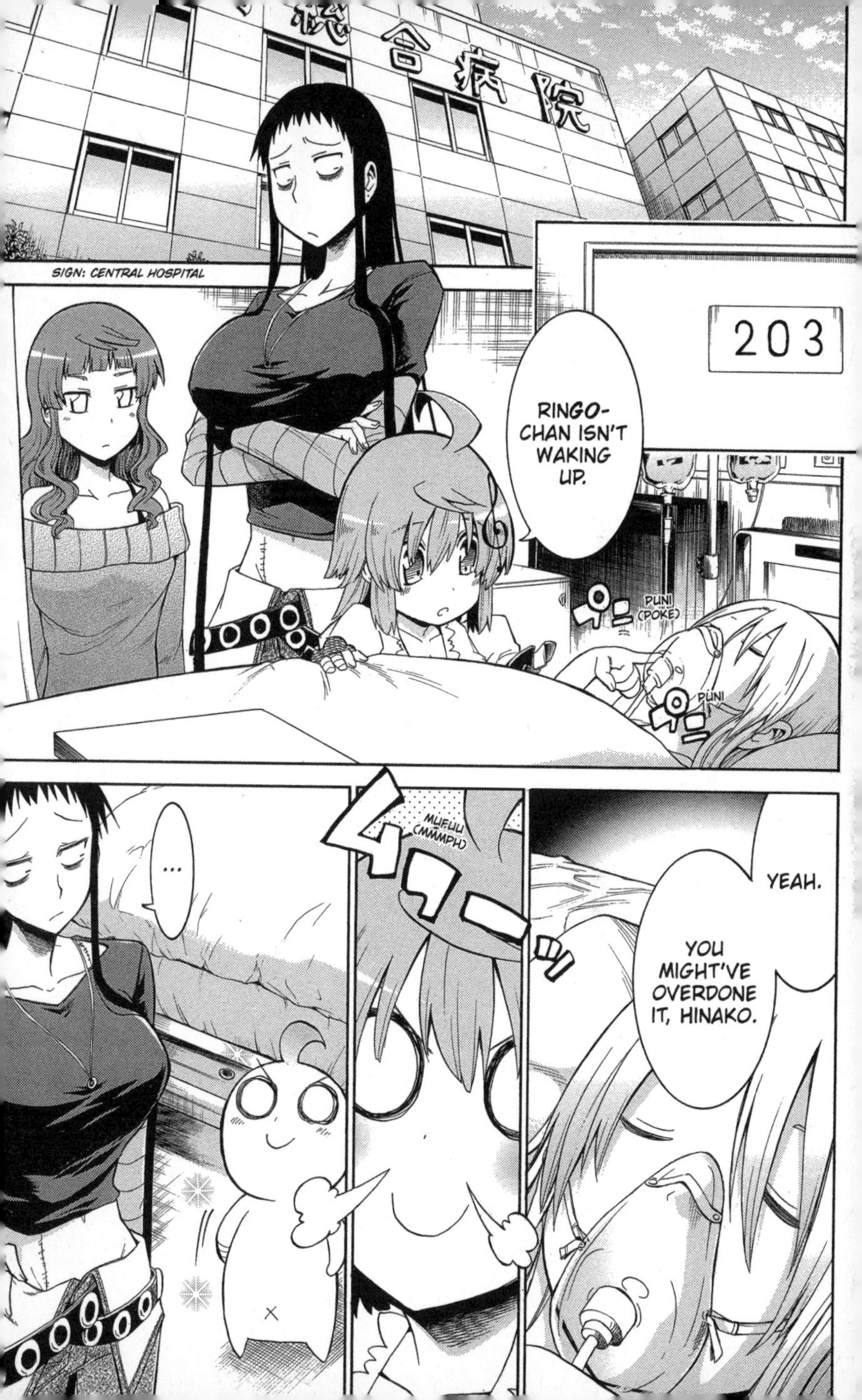
SIGN: CENTRAL HOSPITAL
203
RINGO-CHAN ISN'T WAKING UP.
PUNI (POKE)
PUNI
YEAH.
YOU MIGHT'VE OVERDONE IT, HINAKO.
MUFUU (MMMPH)
...

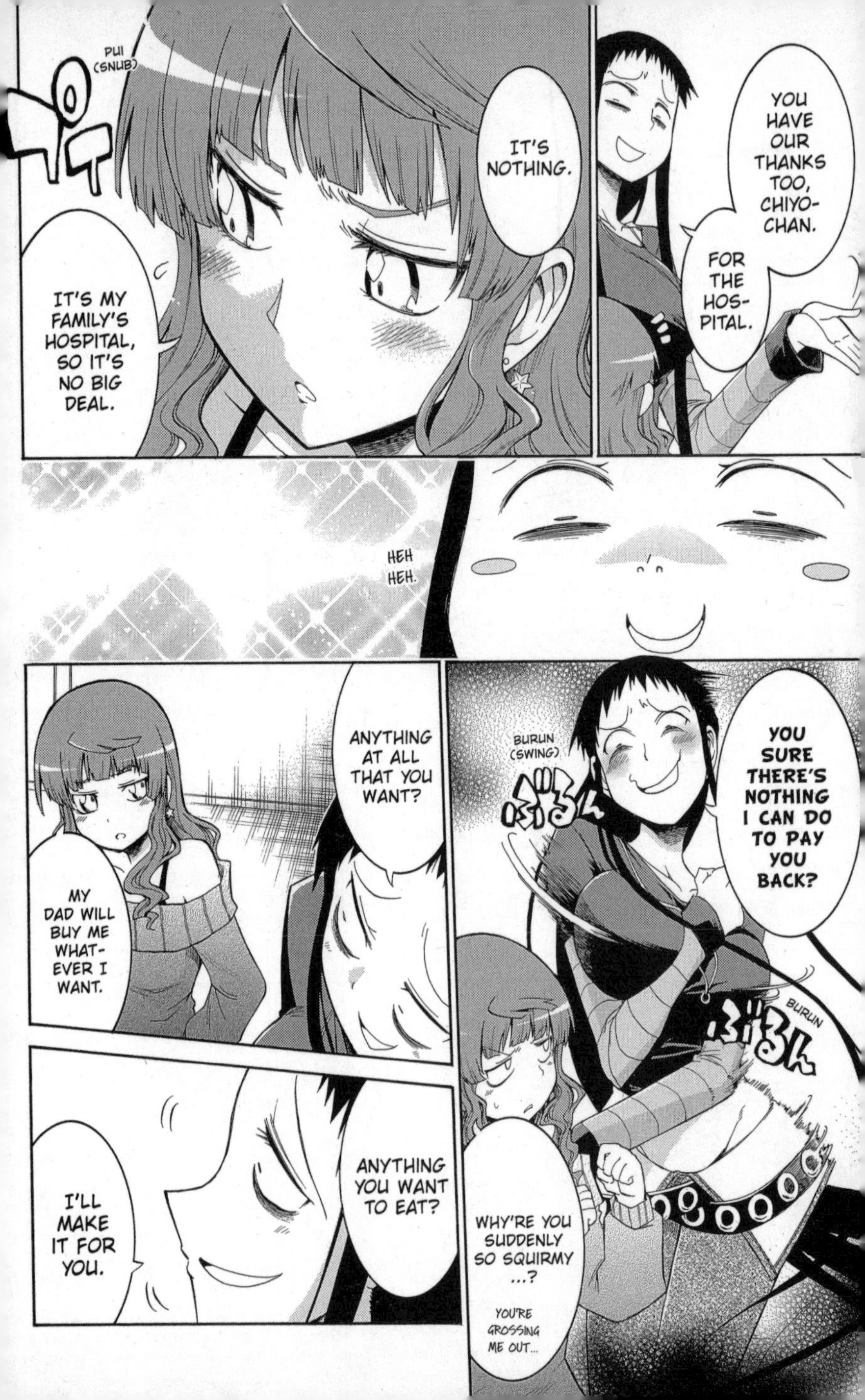
YOU HAVE OUR THANKS TOO, CHIYO-CHAN.
FOR THE HOS-PITAL.
IT'S NOTHING.
PUI (SNUB)
IT'S MY FAMILY'S HOSPITAL, SO IT'S NO BIG DEAL.
HEH HEH.
YOU SURE THERE'S NOTHING I CAN DO TO PAY YOU BACK?
BURUN (SWING)
BURUN
WHY'RE YOU SUDDENLY SO SQUIRMY ...?
YOU'RE GROSSING ME OUT...
ANYTHING AT ALL THAT YOU WANT?
MY DAD WILL BUY ME WHAT-EVER I WANT.
ANYTHING YOU WANT TO EAT?
I'LL MAKE IT FOR YOU.

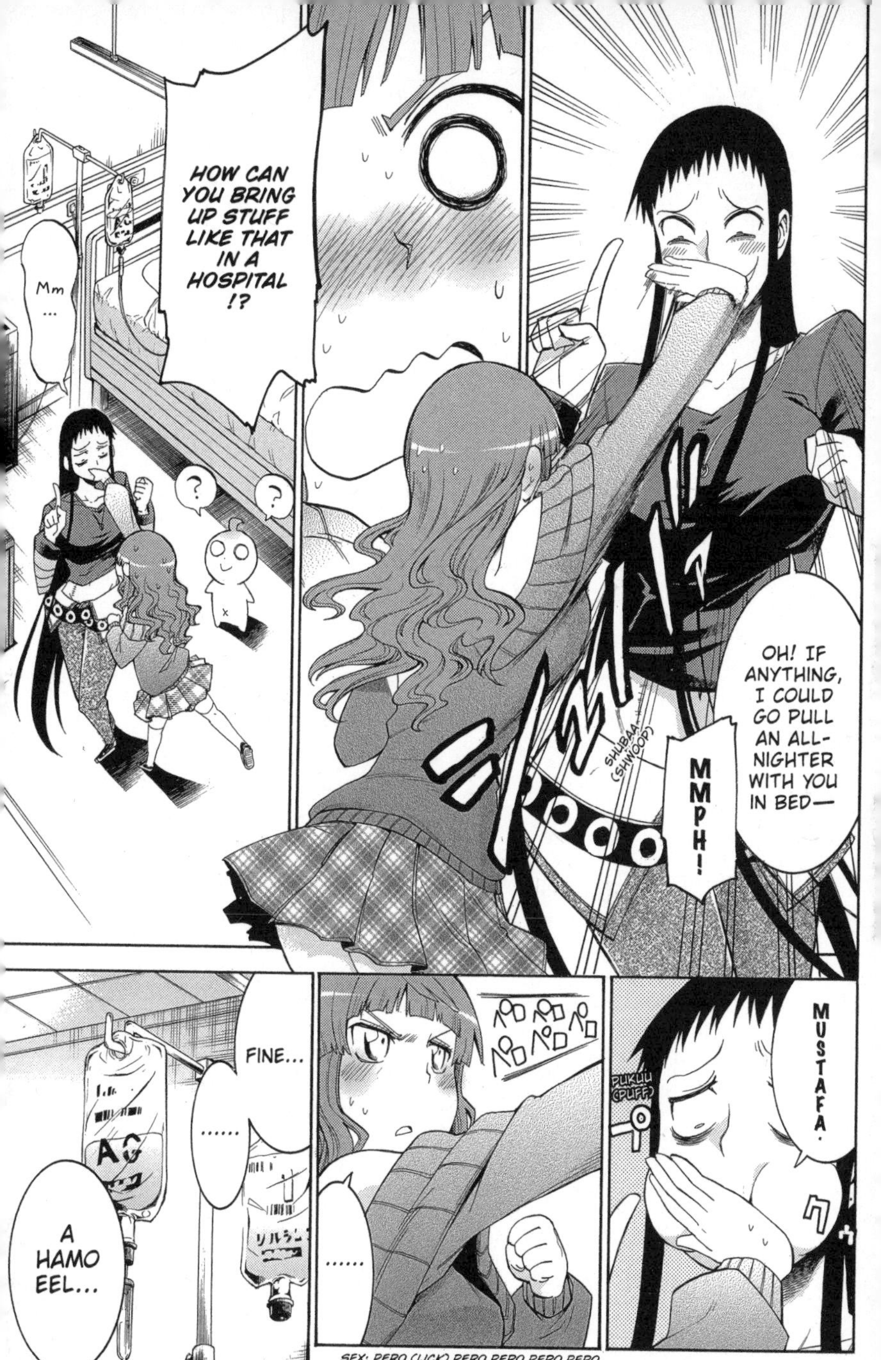
OH! IF ANYTHING, I COULD GO PULL AN ALL-NIGHTER WITH YOU IN BED—
MMPH!
SHUBAA (SHWOOP)
HOW CAN YOU BRING UP STUFF LIKE THAT IN A HOSPITAL !?
Mm ...
?
?
MUSTAFA.
PUKUU (PUFF)
FINE...
......
......
A HAMO EEL...

SFX: PERO (LICK) PERO PERO PERO PERO

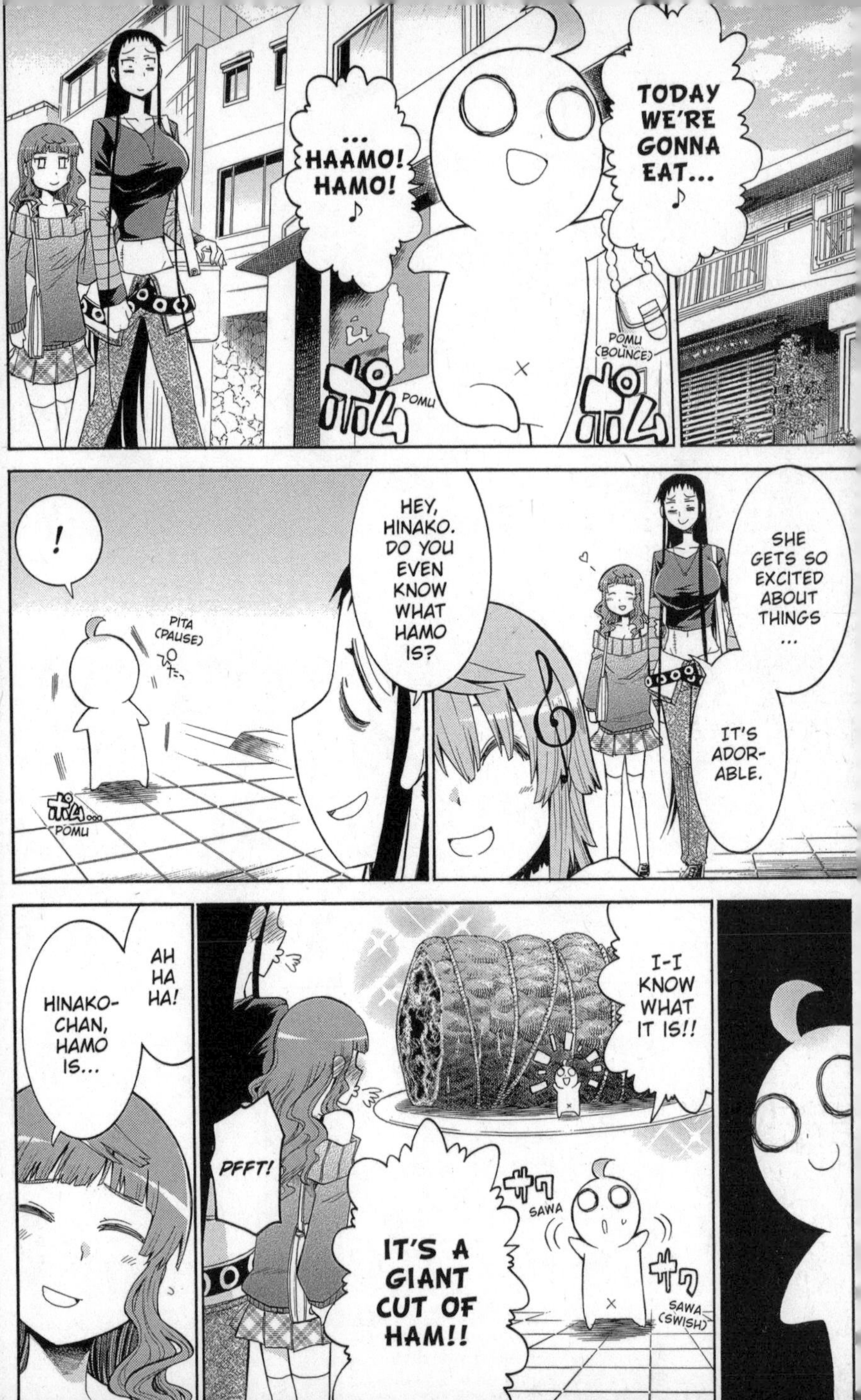
TODAY WE'RE GONNA EAT... ♪
POMU (BOUNCE)
... HAAMO! HAMO! ♪
POMU
SHE GETS SO EXCITED ABOUT THINGS...
IT'S ADORABLE.
HEY, HINAKO. DO YOU EVEN KNOW WHAT HAMO IS?
!
PITA (PAUSE)
POMU
I-I KNOW WHAT IT IS!!
SAWA
SAWA (SWISH)
IT'S A GIANT CUT OF HAM!!
PFFT!
AH HA HA!
HINAKO-CHAN, HAMO IS...

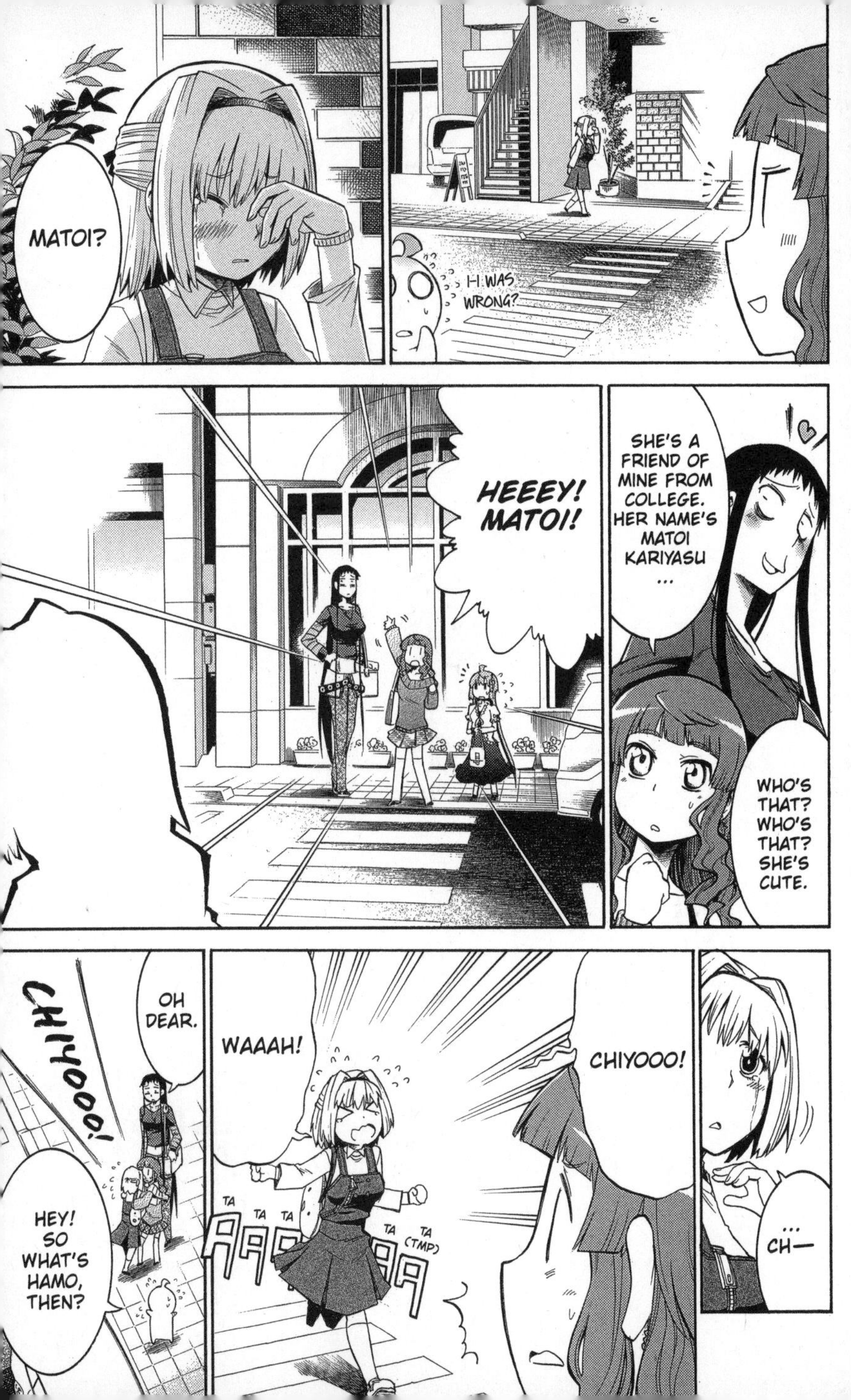
I-I WAS WRONG?
MATOI?
SHE'S A FRIEND OF MINE FROM COLLEGE. HER NAME'S MATOI KARIYASU ...
WHO'S THAT? WHO'S THAT? SHE'S CUTE.
HEEEY! MATOI!
... CH—
CHIYOOO!
WAAAH!
TA TA TA TA TA (TMP)
OH DEAR.
CHIYOOO!
HEY! SO WHAT'S HAMO, THEN?

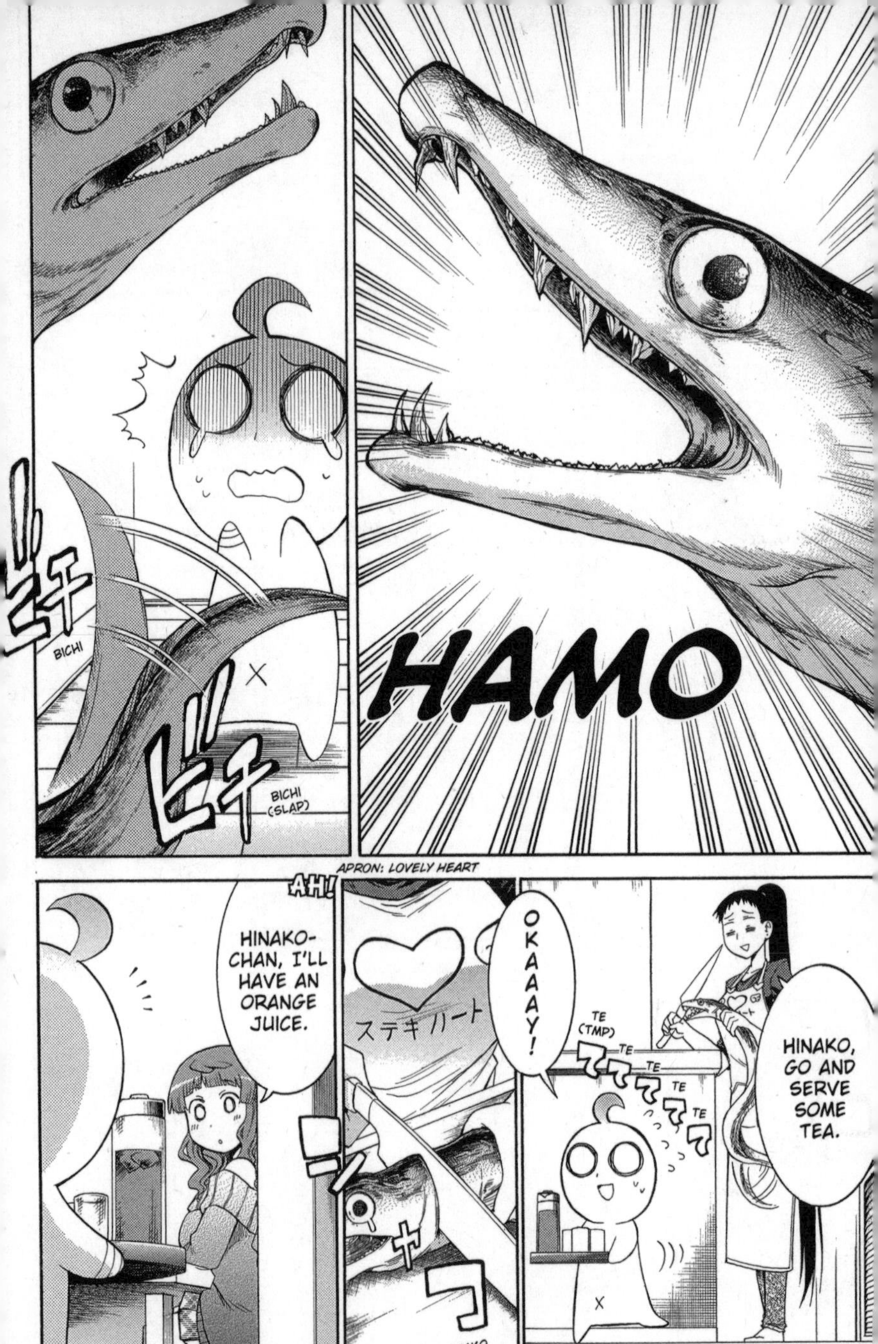
HAMO
ビチ
BICHI
ビチ
BICHI (SLAP)
APRON: LOVELY HEART
HINAKO, GO AND SERVE SOME TEA.
TE (TMP)
TE
TE
TE
TE
OKAAAY!
ステキハート
SHAKO (SLICE)
AH!
HINAKO-CHAN, I'LL HAVE AN ORANGE JUICE.

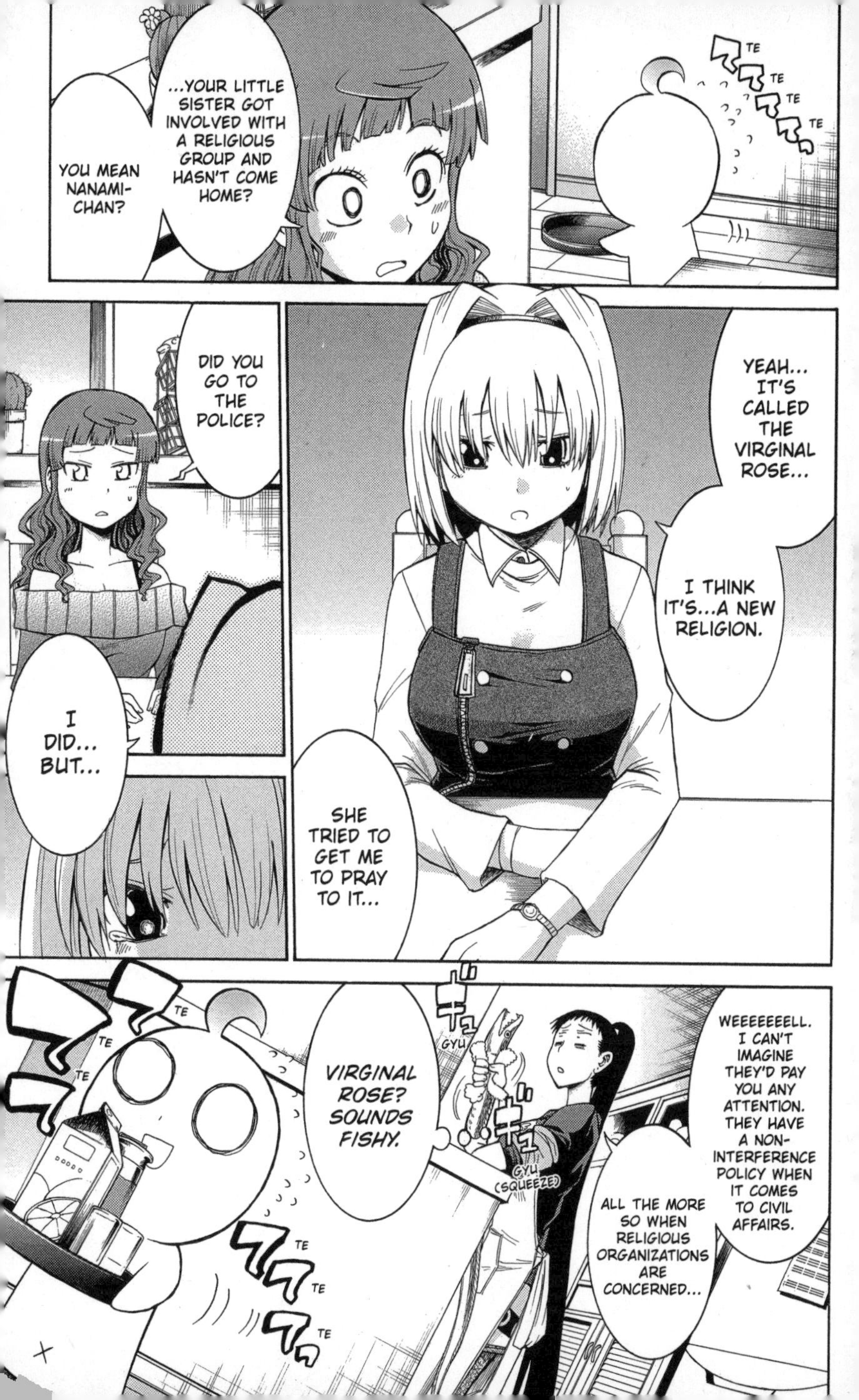
TE
TE
TE
TE
...YOUR LITTLE SISTER GOT INVOLVED WITH A RELIGIOUS GROUP AND HASN'T COME HOME?
YOU MEAN NANAMI-CHAN?
YEAH... IT'S CALLED THE VIRGINAL ROSE...
I THINK IT'S...A NEW RELIGION.
SHE TRIED TO GET ME TO PRAY TO IT...
DID YOU GO TO THE POLICE?
I DID... BUT...
WEEEEEEELL. I CAN'T IMAGINE THEY'D PAY YOU ANY ATTENTION. THEY HAVE A NON-INTERFERENCE POLICY WHEN IT COMES TO CIVIL AFFAIRS.
ALL THE MORE SO WHEN RELIGIOUS ORGANIZATIONS ARE CONCERNED...
GYU
GYU (SQUEEZE)
VIRGINAL ROSE? SOUNDS FISHY.
TE
TE
TE
TE
TE
TE

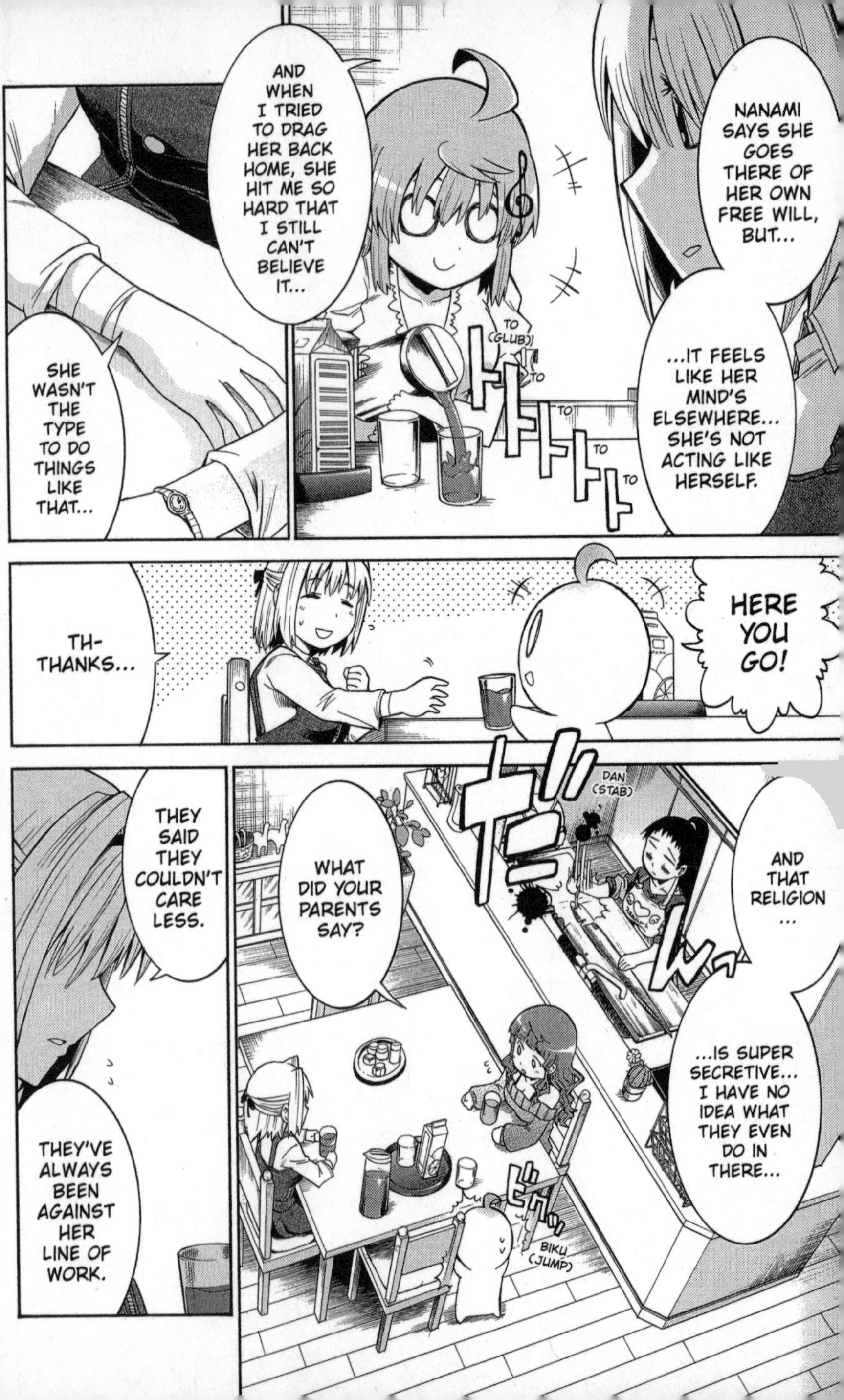
NANAMI SAYS SHE GOES THERE OF HER OWN FREE WILL, BUT...
...IT FEELS LIKE HER MIND'S ELSEWHERE... SHE'S NOT ACTING LIKE HERSELF.
AND WHEN I TRIED TO DRAG HER BACK HOME, SHE HIT ME SO HARD THAT I STILL CAN'T BELIEVE IT...
TO (GLUB)
TO
TO
TO
TO
SHE WASN'T THE TYPE TO DO THINGS LIKE THAT...
HERE YOU GO!
TH-THANKS...
AND THAT RELIGION...
...IS SUPER SECRETIVE... I HAVE NO IDEA WHAT THEY EVEN DO IN THERE...
DAN (STAB)
WHAT DID YOUR PARENTS SAY?
BIKU (JUMP)
THEY SAID THEY COULDN'T CARE LESS.
THEY'VE ALWAYS BEEN AGAINST HER LINE OF WORK.

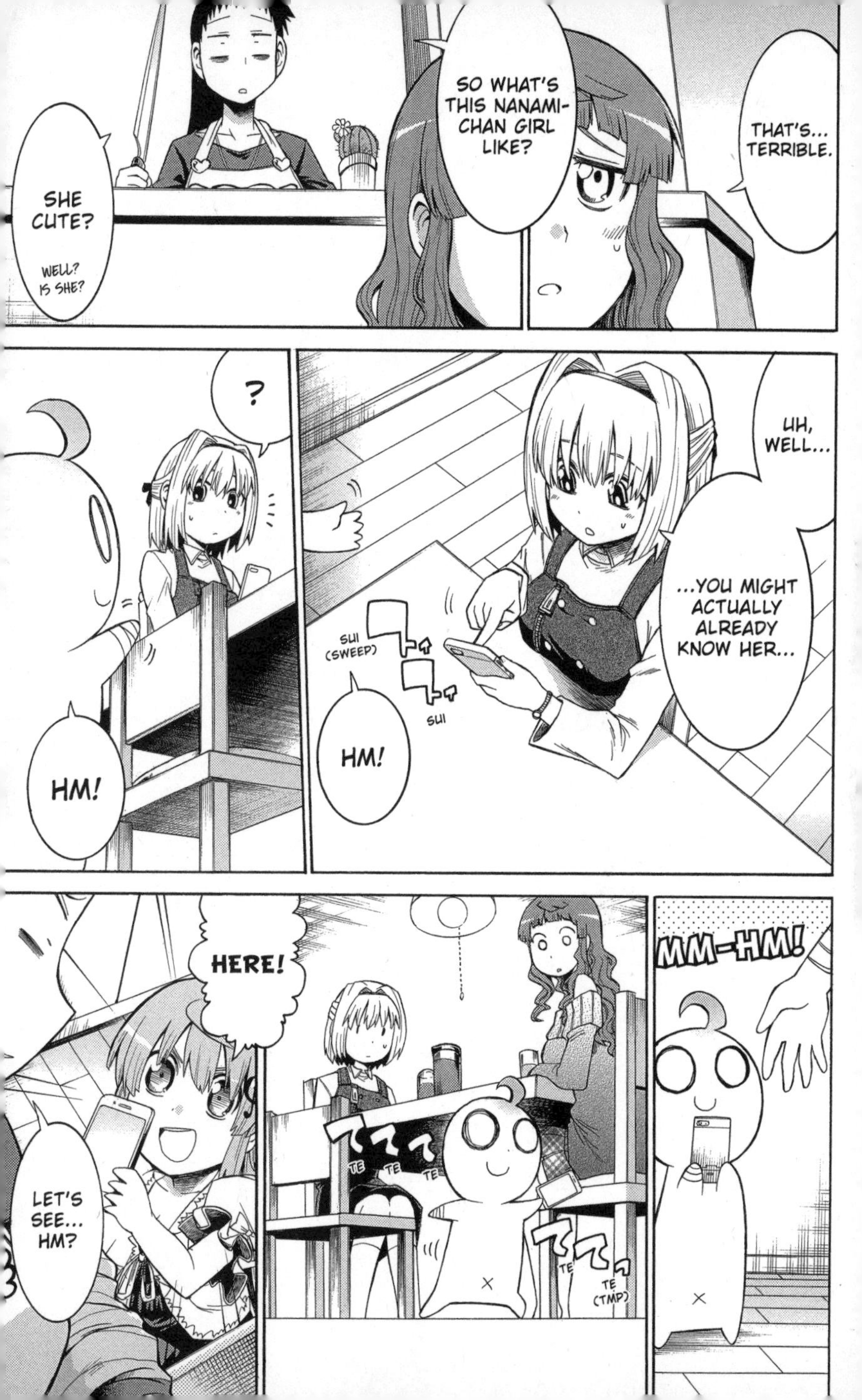
THAT'S... TERRIBLE.
SO WHAT'S THIS NANAMI-CHAN GIRL LIKE?
SHE CUTE?
WELL? IS SHE?
UH, WELL...
...YOU MIGHT ACTUALLY ALREADY KNOW HER...
SUI (SWEEP)
SUI
HM!
?
HM!
MM-HM!
TE TE TE
TE TE (TMP)
HERE!
LET'S SEE... HM?

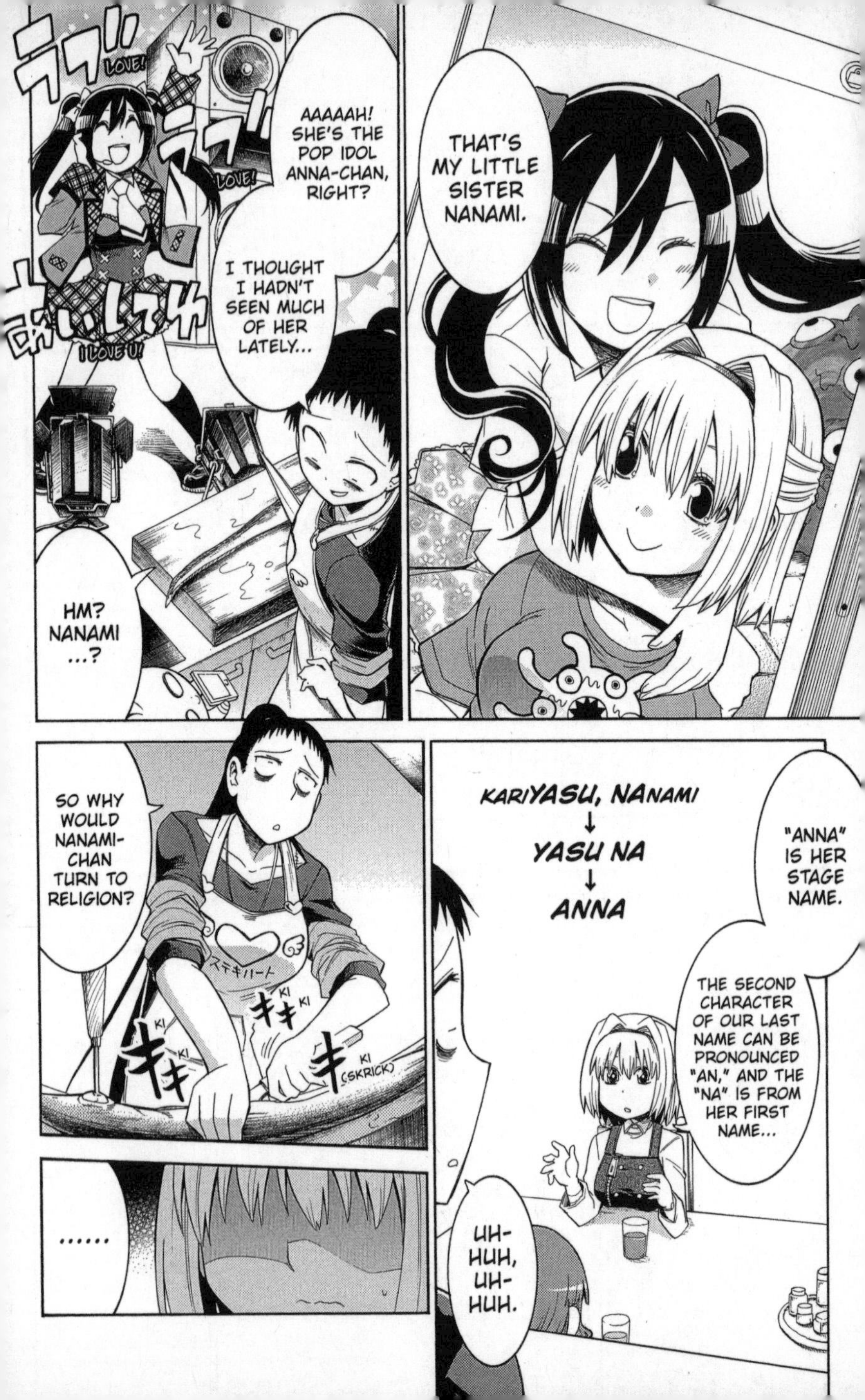
THAT'S MY LITTLE SISTER NANAMI.
AAAAAH! SHE'S THE POP IDOL ANNA-CHAN, RIGHT?
LOVE!
LOVE!
I LOVE U!
I THOUGHT I HADN'T SEEN MUCH OF HER LATELY...
HM? NANAMI ...?
KARIYASU, NANAMI
↓
YASU NA
↓
ANNA
"ANNA" IS HER STAGE NAME.
THE SECOND CHARACTER OF OUR LAST NAME CAN BE PRONOUNCED "AN," AND THE "NA" IS FROM HER FIRST NAME...
UH-HUH, UH-HUH.
SO WHY WOULD NANAMI-CHAN TURN TO RELIGION?
KI KI KI KI KI (SKRICK)
......

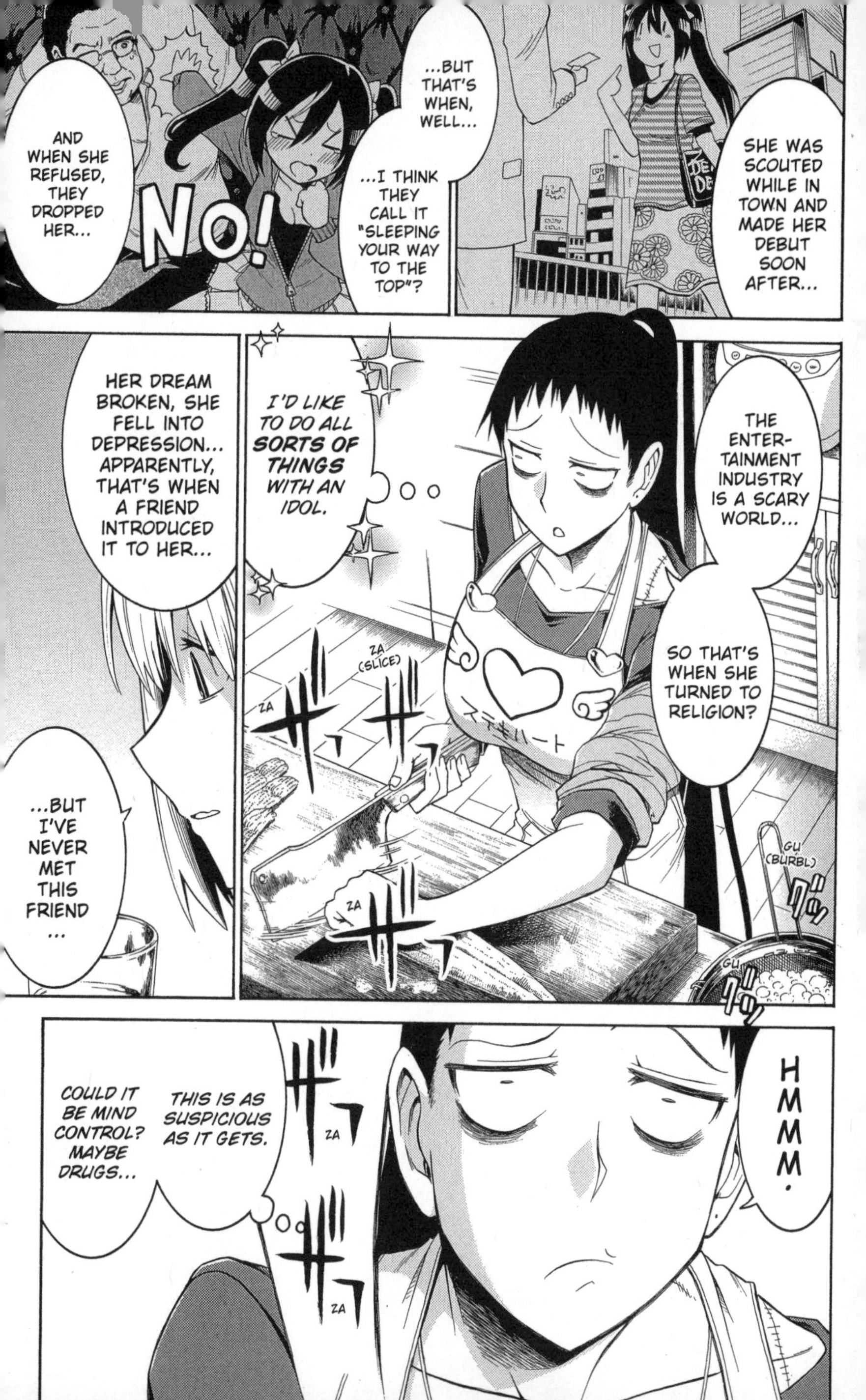
SHE WAS SCOUTED WHILE IN TOWN AND MADE HER DEBUT SOON AFTER...
...BUT THAT'S WHEN, WELL...
...I THINK THEY CALL IT "SLEEPING YOUR WAY TO THE TOP"?
AND WHEN SHE REFUSED, THEY DROPPED HER...
NO!
THE ENTER-TAINMENT INDUSTRY IS A SCARY WORLD...
I'D LIKE TO DO ALL SORTS OF THINGS WITH AN IDOL.
SO THAT'S WHEN SHE TURNED TO RELIGION?
ZA (SLICE)
ZA
ZA
GU (BURBL)
GU
HER DREAM BROKEN, SHE FELL INTO DEPRESSION... APPARENTLY, THAT'S WHEN A FRIEND INTRODUCED IT TO HER...
...BUT I'VE NEVER MET THIS FRIEND...
HMMM.
THIS IS AS SUSPICIOUS AS IT GETS.
COULD IT BE MIND CONTROL? MAYBE DRUGS...
ZA
ZA

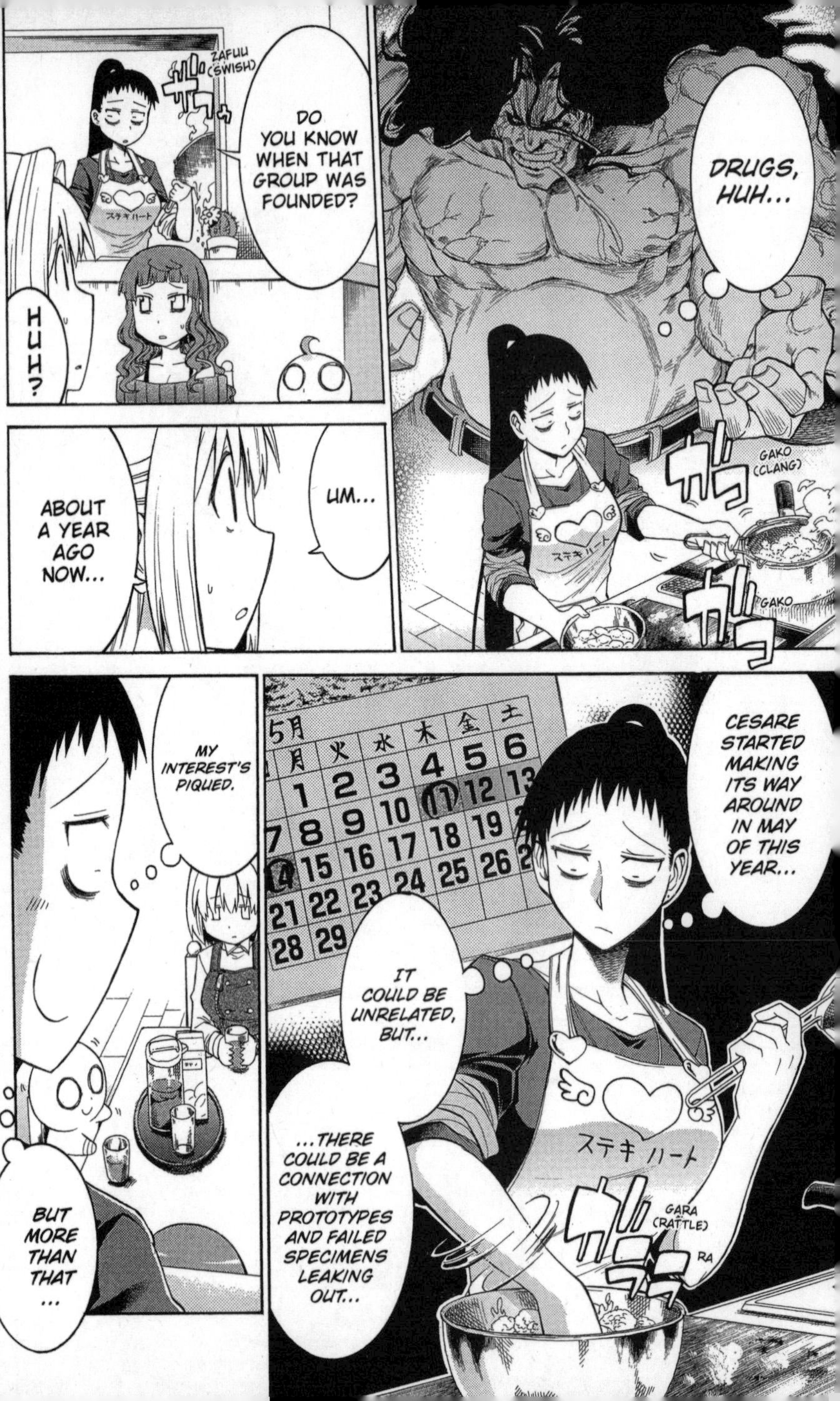

DRUGS, HUH...
GAKO (CLANG)
GAKO
ZAFUU (SWISH)
DO YOU KNOW WHEN THAT GROUP WAS FOUNDED?
HUH?
UM...
ABOUT A YEAR AGO NOW...
CESARE STARTED MAKING ITS WAY AROUND IN MAY OF THIS YEAR...
IT COULD BE UNRELATED, BUT...
...THERE COULD BE A CONNECTION WITH PROTOTYPES AND FAILED SPECIMENS LEAKING OUT...
GARA (RATTLE)
RA
MY INTEREST'S PIQUED.
BUT MORE THAN THAT...

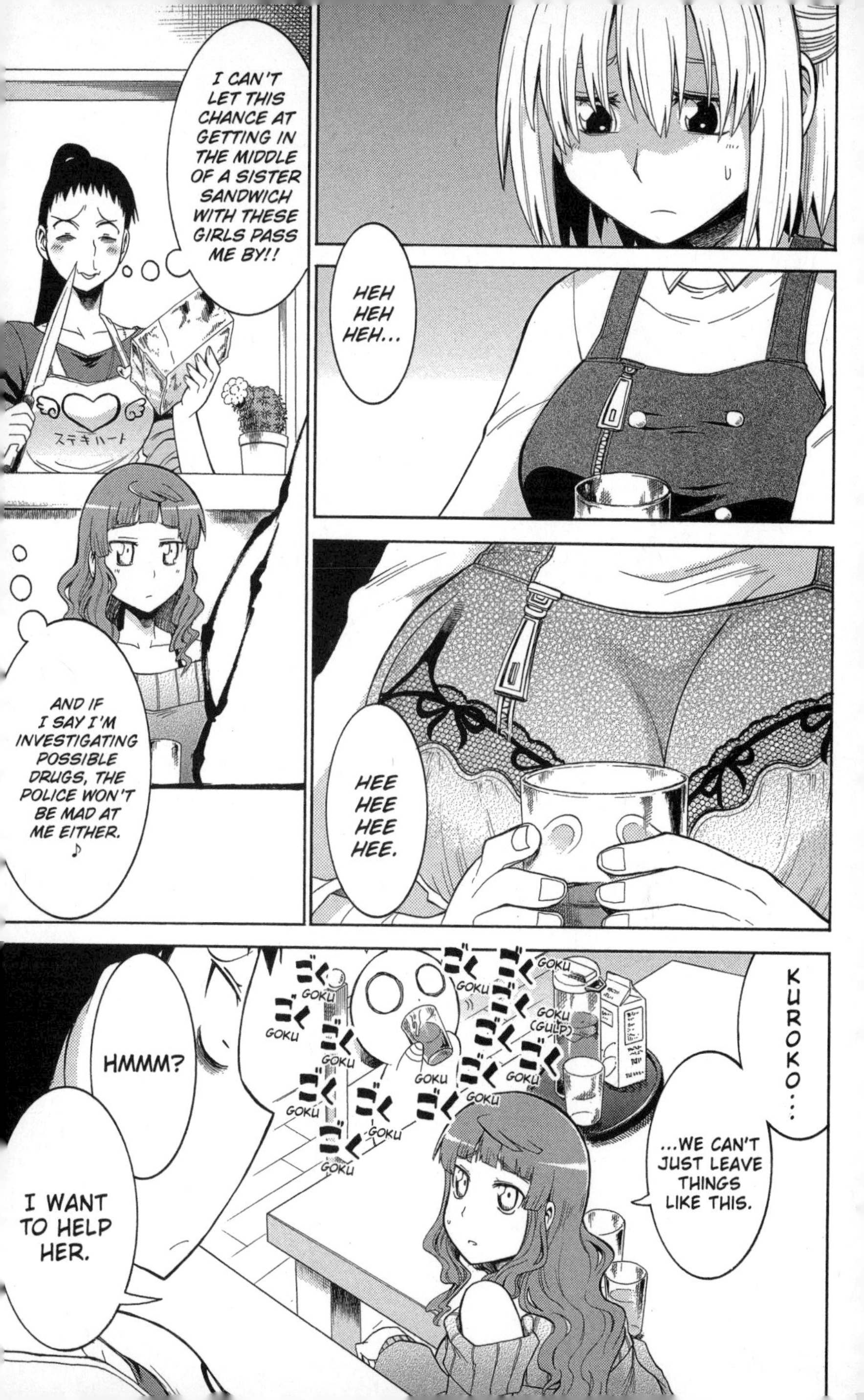
HEH HEH HEH...
HEE HEE HEE HEE.
I CAN'T LET THIS CHANCE AT GETTING IN THE MIDDLE OF A SISTER SANDWICH WITH THESE GIRLS PASS ME BY!!
ステキハート
AND IF I SAY I'M INVESTIGATING POSSIBLE DRUGS, THE POLICE WON'T BE MAD AT ME EITHER. ♪
KUROKO...
...WE CAN'T JUST LEAVE THINGS LIKE THIS.
GOKU GOKU GOKU (GULP) GOKU GOKU GOKU GOKU GOKU GOKU GOKU GOKU
HMMM?
I WANT TO HELP HER.

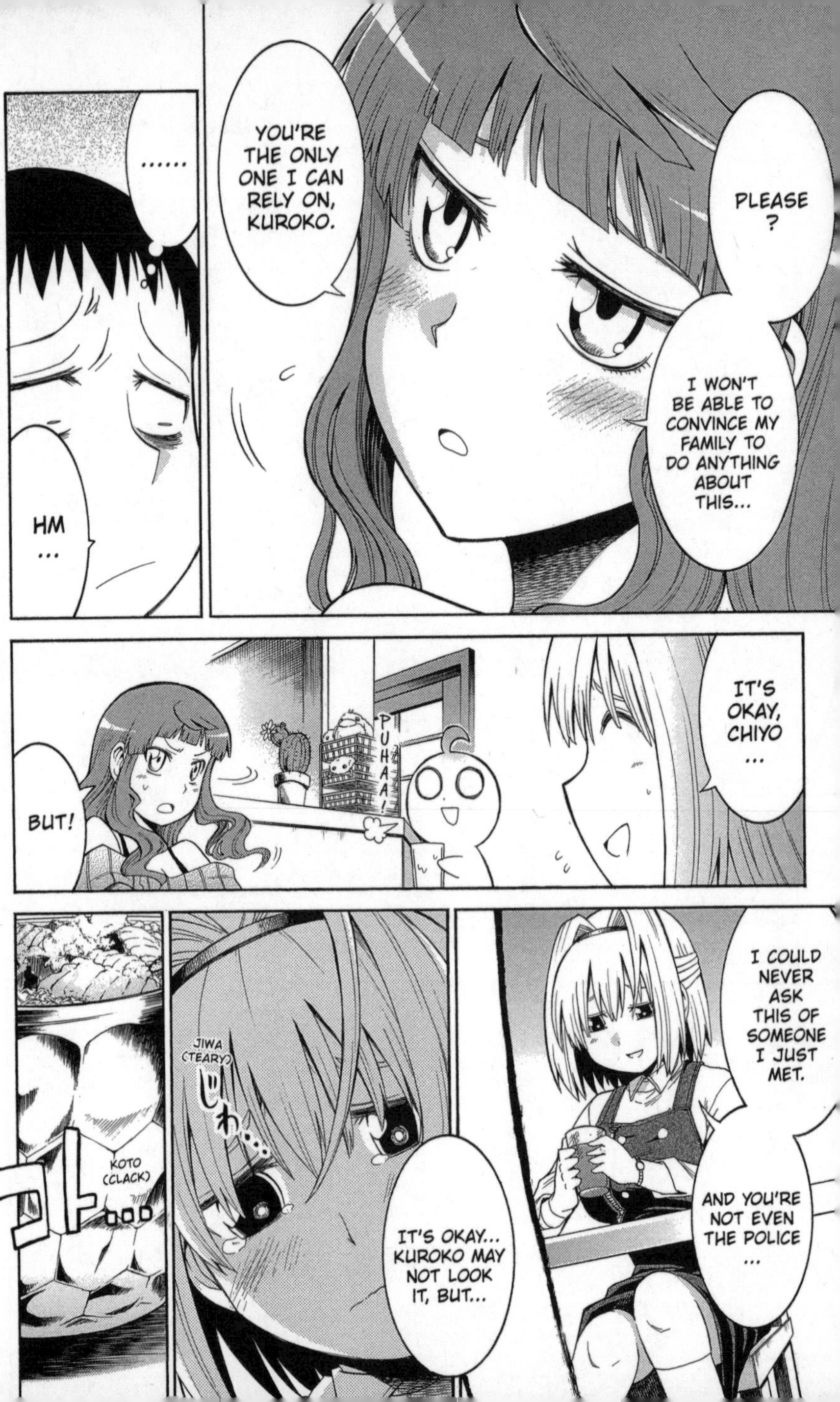
PLEASE?
I WON'T BE ABLE TO CONVINCE MY FAMILY TO DO ANYTHING ABOUT THIS...
YOU'RE THE ONLY ONE I CAN RELY ON, KUROKO.
......
HM...
IT'S OKAY, CHIYO...
PUHAAA!
BUT!
I COULD NEVER ASK THIS OF SOMEONE I JUST MET.
AND YOU'RE NOT EVEN THE POLICE...
JIWA (TEARY)
IT'S OKAY... KUROKO MAY NOT LOOK IT, BUT...
KOTO (CLACK)

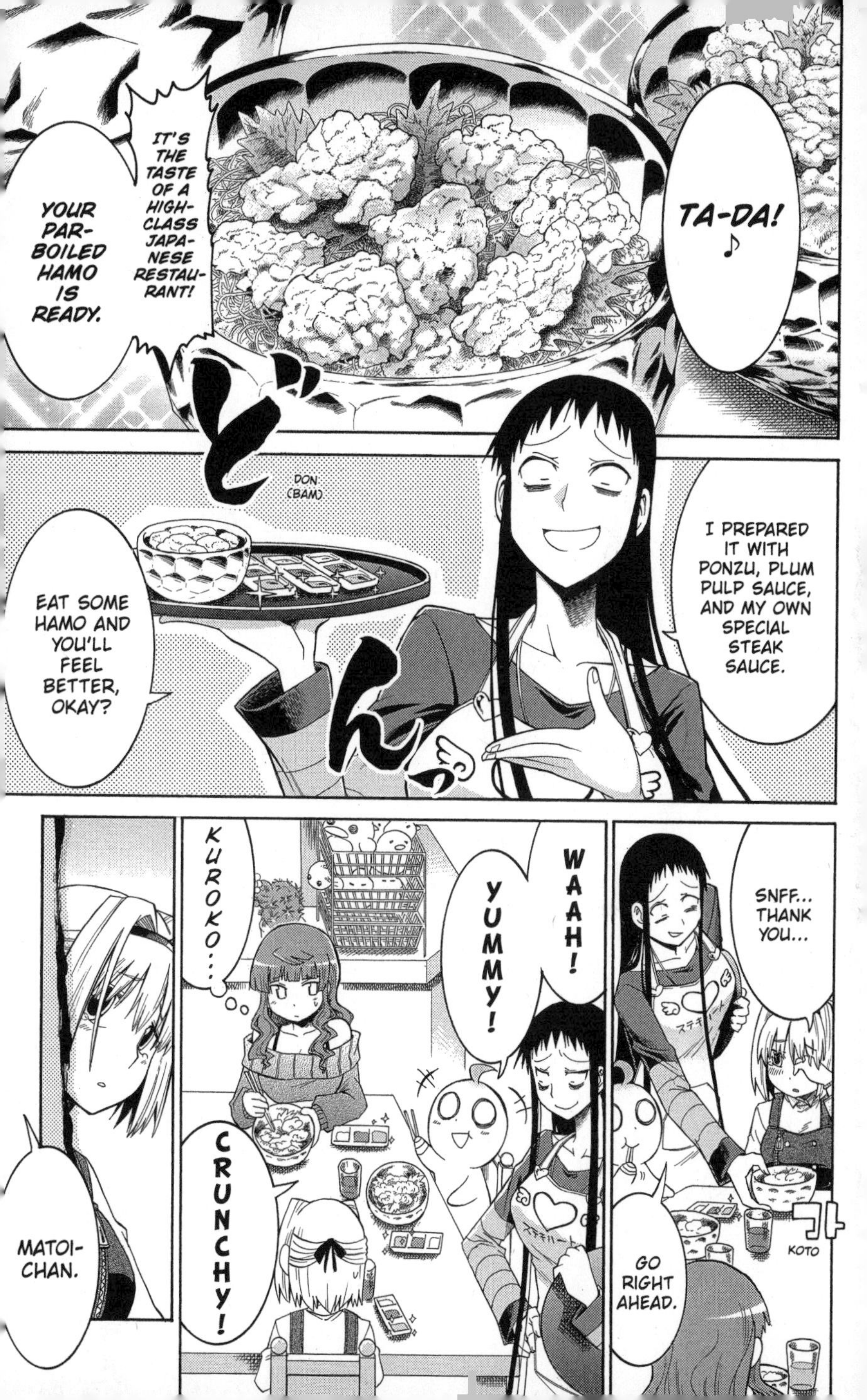
TA-DA! ♪
IT'S THE TASTE OF A HIGH-CLASS JAPANESE RESTAURANT!
YOUR PARBOILED HAMO IS READY.
DON (BAM)
I PREPARED IT WITH PONZU, PLUM PULP SAUCE, AND MY OWN SPECIAL STEAK SAUCE.
EAT SOME HAMO AND YOU'LL FEEL BETTER, OKAY?
SNFF... THANK YOU...
KOTO
GO RIGHT AHEAD.
WAAH!
YUMMY!
KUROKO...
CRUNCHY!
MATOI-CHAN.

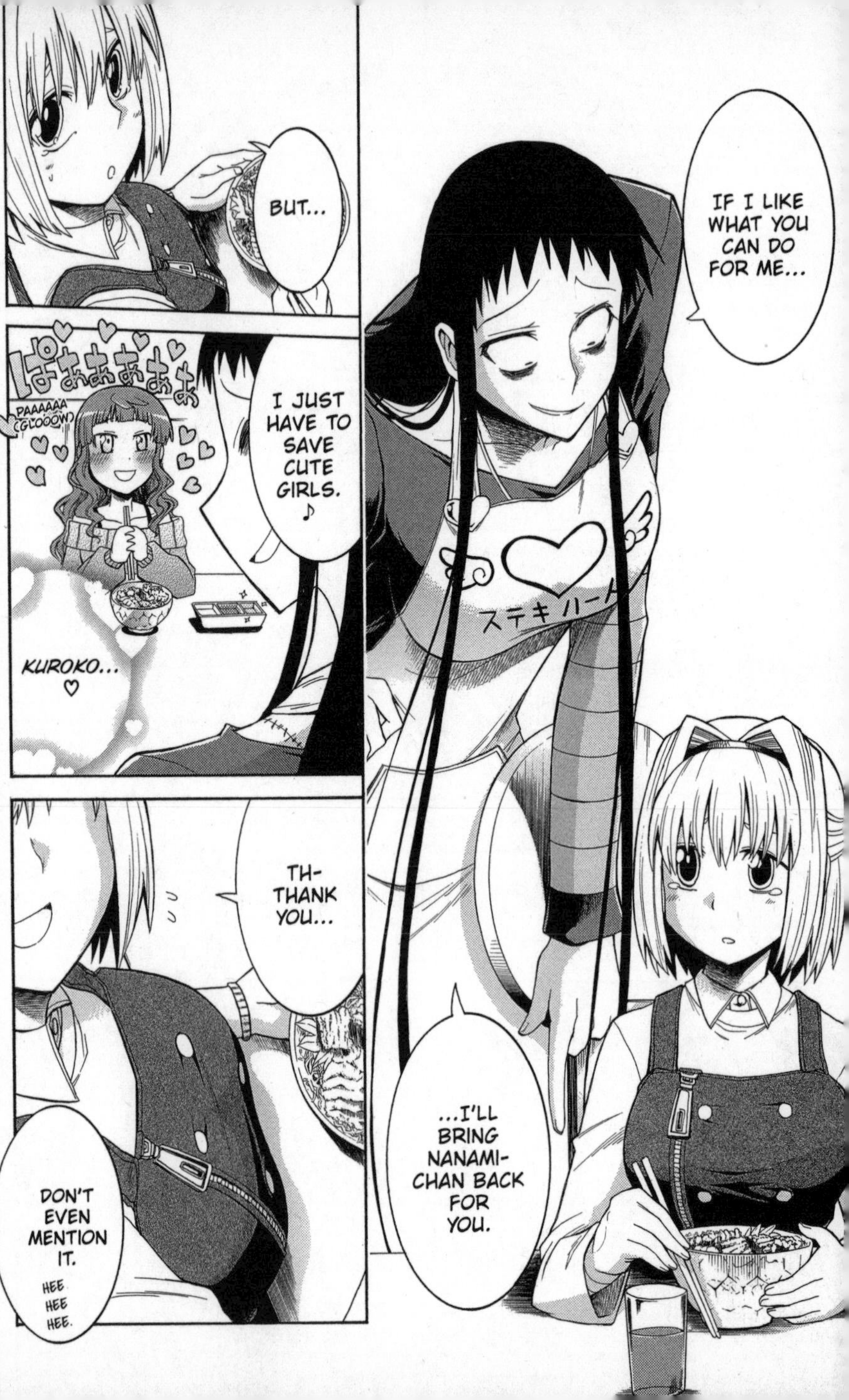
IF I LIKE WHAT YOU CAN DO FOR ME...
...I'LL BRING NANAMI-CHAN BACK FOR YOU.
BUT...
I JUST HAVE TO SAVE CUTE GIRLS. ♪
ぱあああああ
PAAAAAA (GLOOOW)
KUROKO... ♡
TH-THANK YOU...
DON'T EVEN MENTION IT.
HEE HEE HEE.

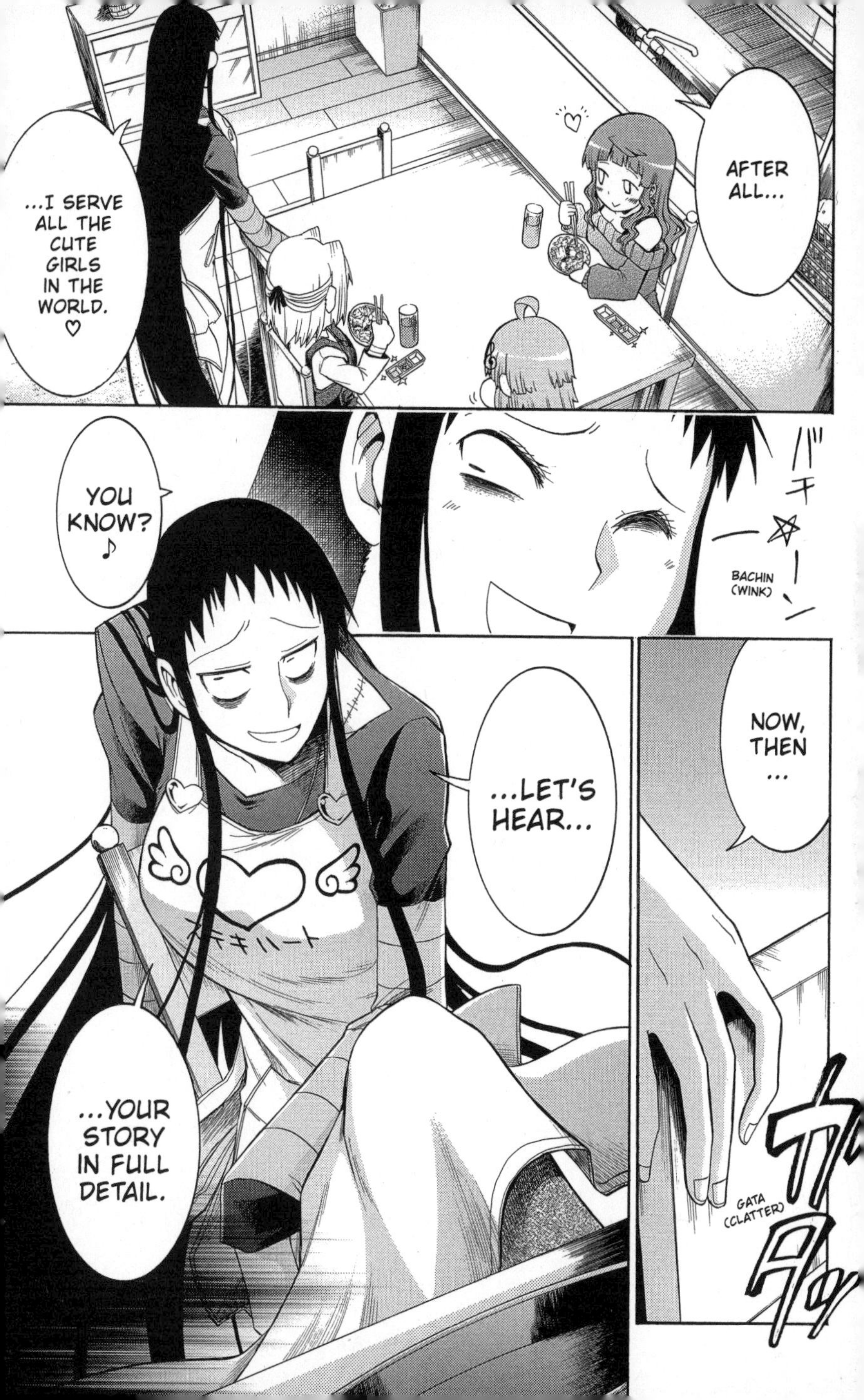
AFTER ALL...
...I SERVE ALL THE CUTE GIRLS IN THE WORLD. ♡
YOU KNOW? ♪
BACHIN (WINK)
NOW, THEN...
GATA (CLATTER)
...LET'S HEAR...
...YOUR STORY IN FULL DETAIL.

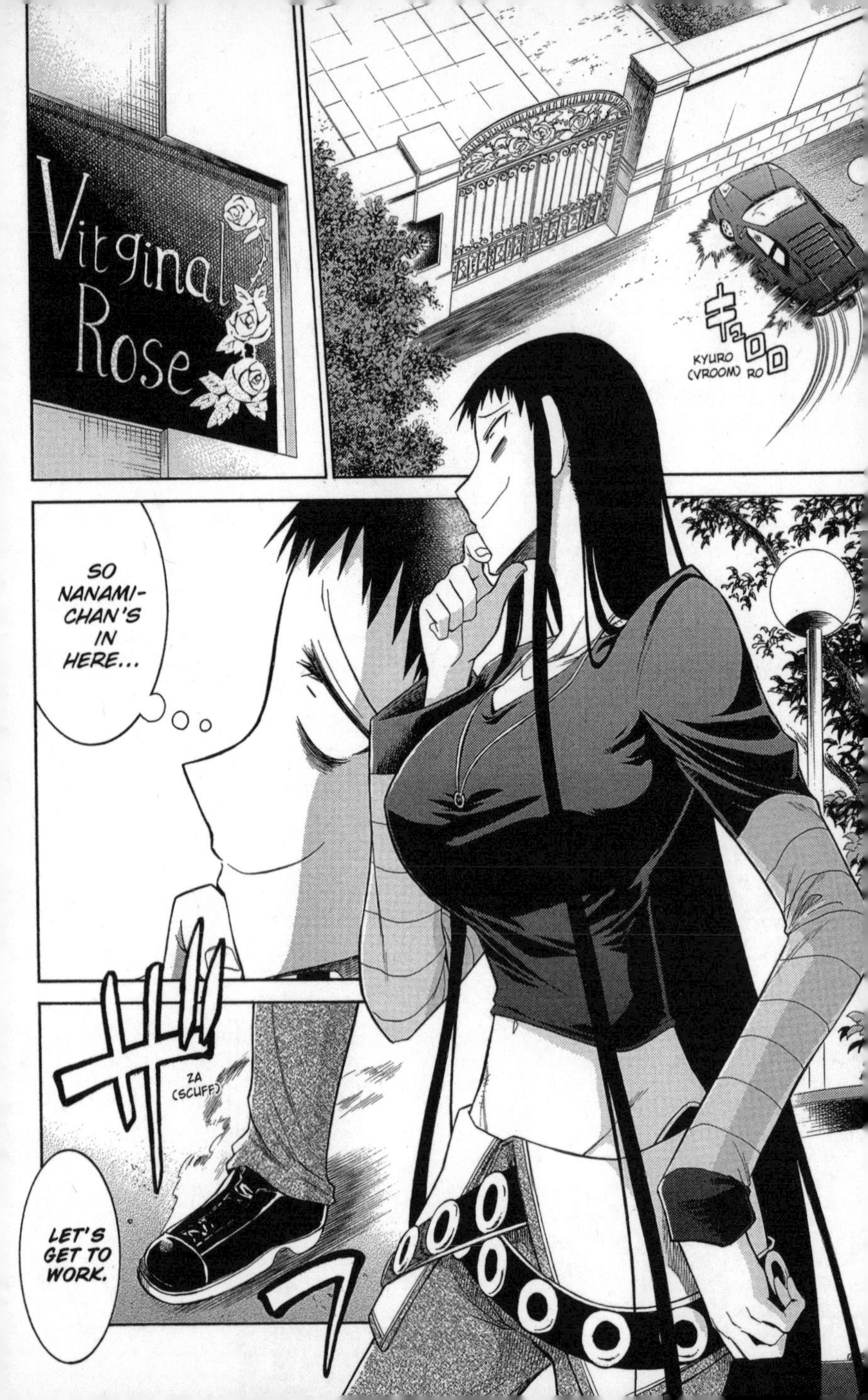
KYURO (VROOM) RO
Virginal Rose
SO NANAMI-CHAN'S IN HERE...
ZA (SCUFF)
LET'S GET TO WORK.

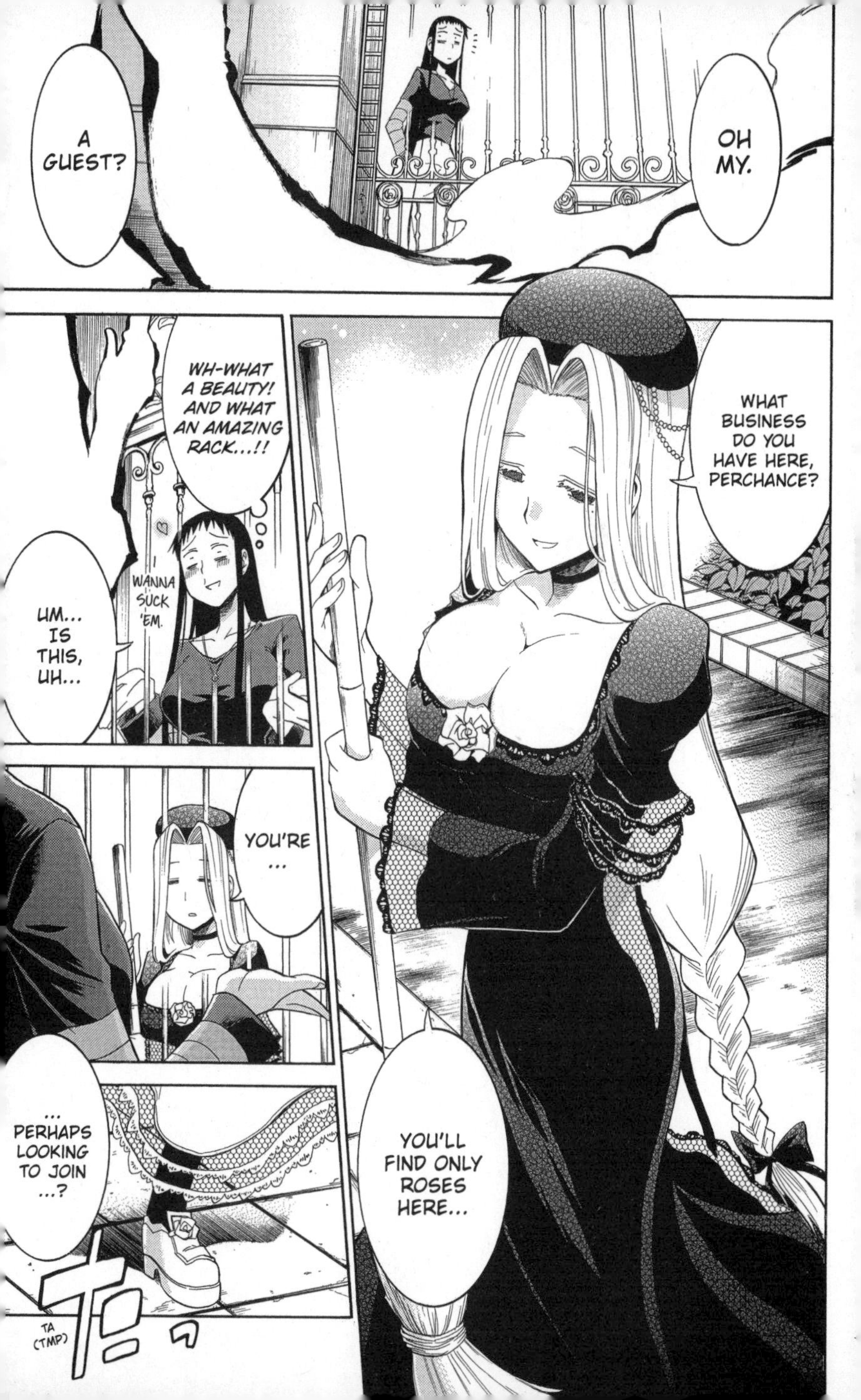
OH MY.
A GUEST?
WHAT BUSINESS DO YOU HAVE HERE, PERCHANCE?
YOU'LL FIND ONLY ROSES HERE...
WH-WHAT A BEAUTY! AND WHAT AN AMAZING RACK...!!
I WANNA SUCK 'EM.
UM... IS THIS, UH...
YOU'RE ...
... PERHAPS LOOKING TO JOIN ...?
TA (TMP)

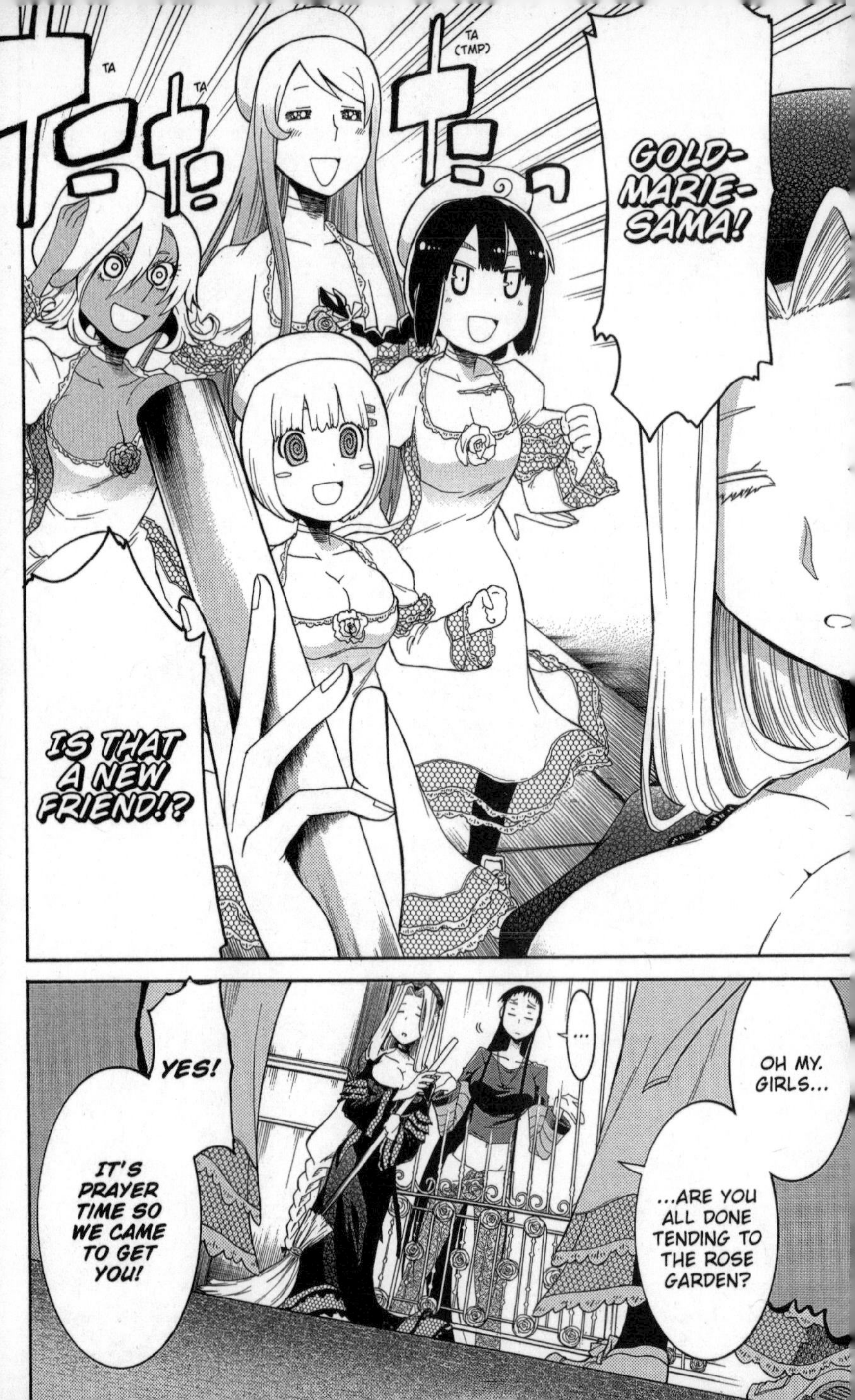
GOLD-MARIE-SAMA!
TA (TMP)
TA
TA
IS THAT A NEW FRIEND!?
OH MY. GIRLS...
...ARE YOU ALL DONE TENDING TO THE ROSE GARDEN?
...
YES!
IT'S PRAYER TIME SO WE CAME TO GET YOU!

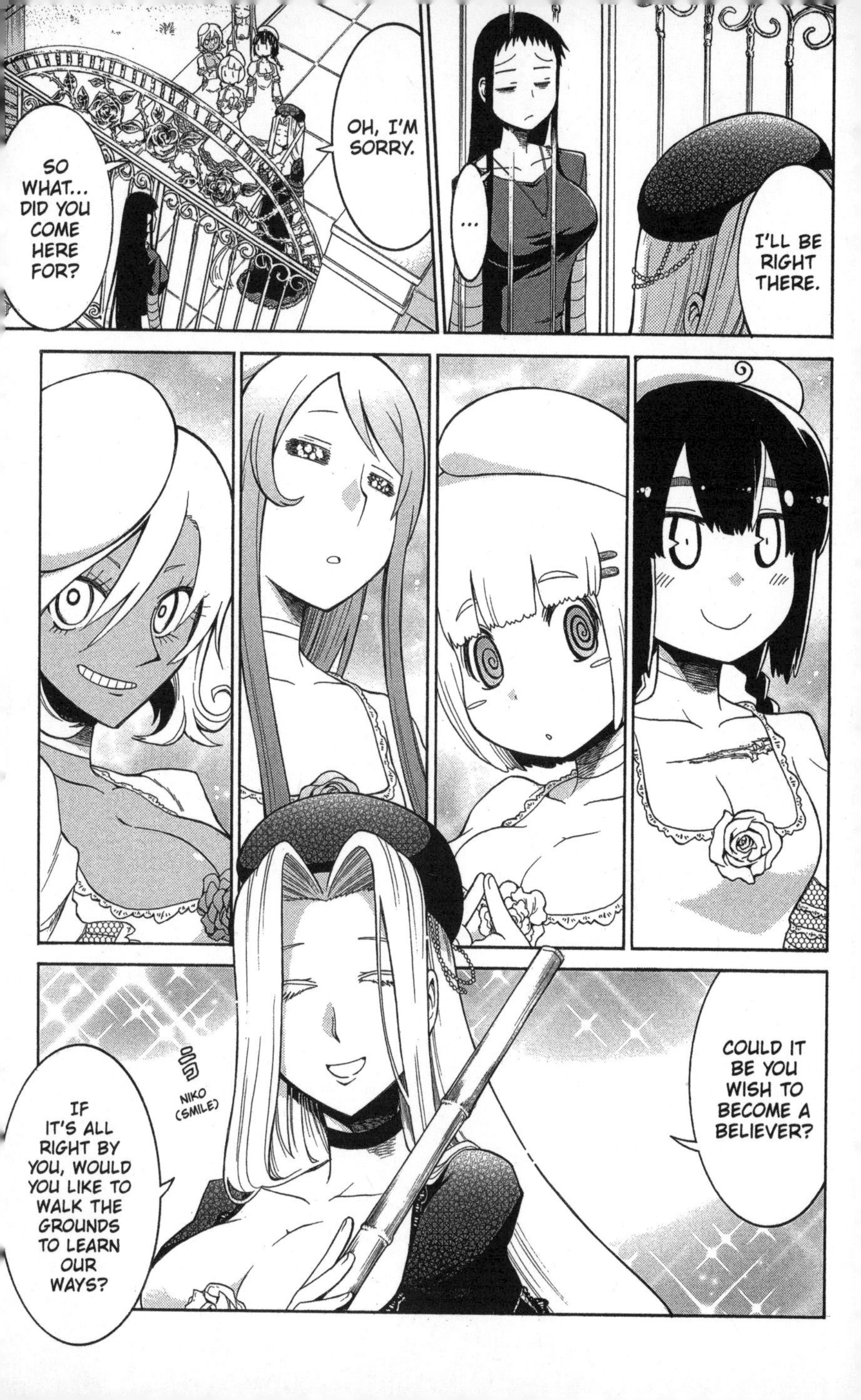
I'LL BE RIGHT THERE.
...
OH, I'M SORRY.
SO WHAT... DID YOU COME HERE FOR?
COULD IT BE YOU WISH TO BECOME A BELIEVER?
NIKO (SMILE)
IF IT'S ALL RIGHT BY YOU, WOULD YOU LIKE TO WALK THE GROUNDS TO LEARN OUR WAYS?

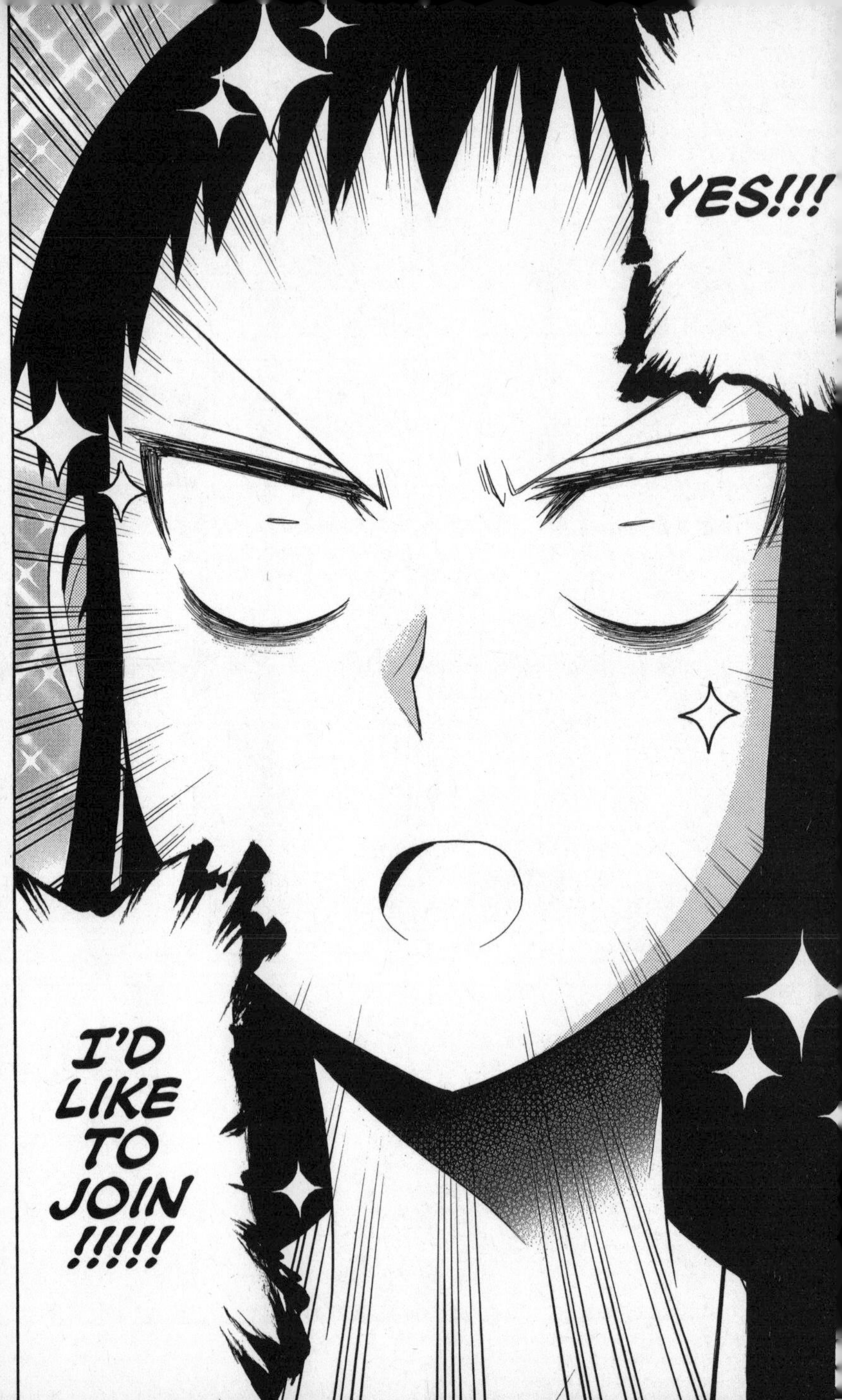
YES!!!
I'D LIKE TO JOIN !!!!!

MURCIÉLAGO

MYSTERIOUS CREATURE

Vol. 3 — Popular Manju Being (PMB)

Height: 10cm - 20cm

Weight: 200g - 1.2kg

Range: Kuroko and surrounding area

Likes: Girls, Honey

Dislikes: Fish

Excels as: Whispering, Seduction

Struggles with: Math

Skills: Lovely Sexy Body, floating in midair

Cry: "Kuh hee hee hee!" and "Ah-kyah-kyah-kyah-kyah!!"

DATA

"How can she possibly be so popular?" "She's the worst kind of person, so how...?" "What do people see in her exactly?" "But they're both girls..."
This is all the work of the Popular Manju Being.
She'll attach herself to a person on a whim and has the ability to make that person very popular.
It's a mystery as to what it subsists on, but it smiles when given honey.
They often will crowd in great numbers around "Kuroko Koumori," but are invisible to the human eye.
The reason why it physically resembles "Kuroko Koumori" is currently being investigated.
It's highly poisonous and will kill even an Indian elephant if consumed.

BONUS CONTENT

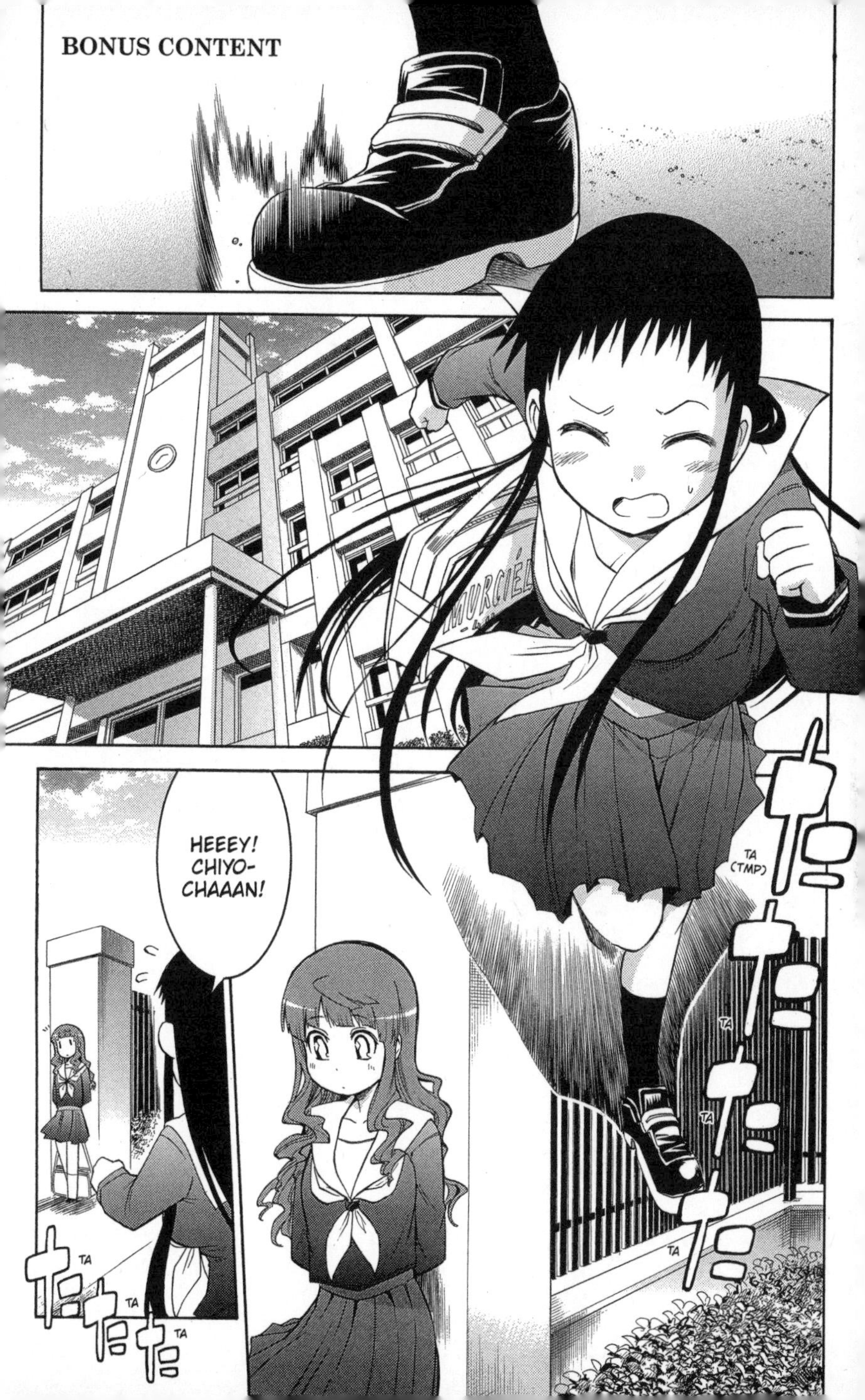
TA
(TMP)
TA
TA
TA
HEEEY! CHIYO-CHAAAN!
TA
TA
TA

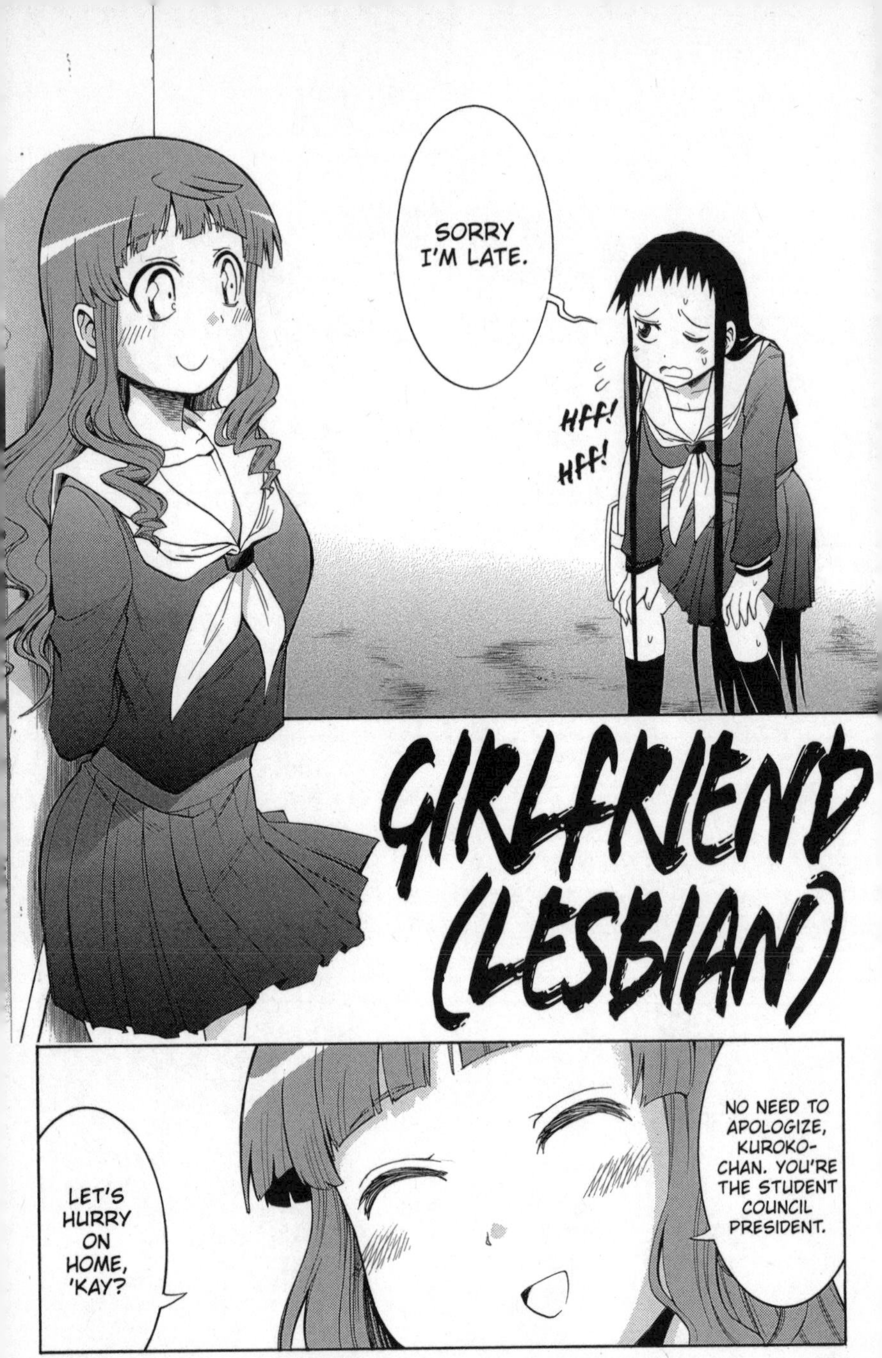
SORRY I'M LATE.
HFF! HFF!
GIRLFRIEND (LESBIAN)
NO NEED TO APOLOGIZE, KUROKO-CHAN. YOU'RE THE STUDENT COUNCIL PRESIDENT.
LET'S HURRY ON HOME, 'KAY?

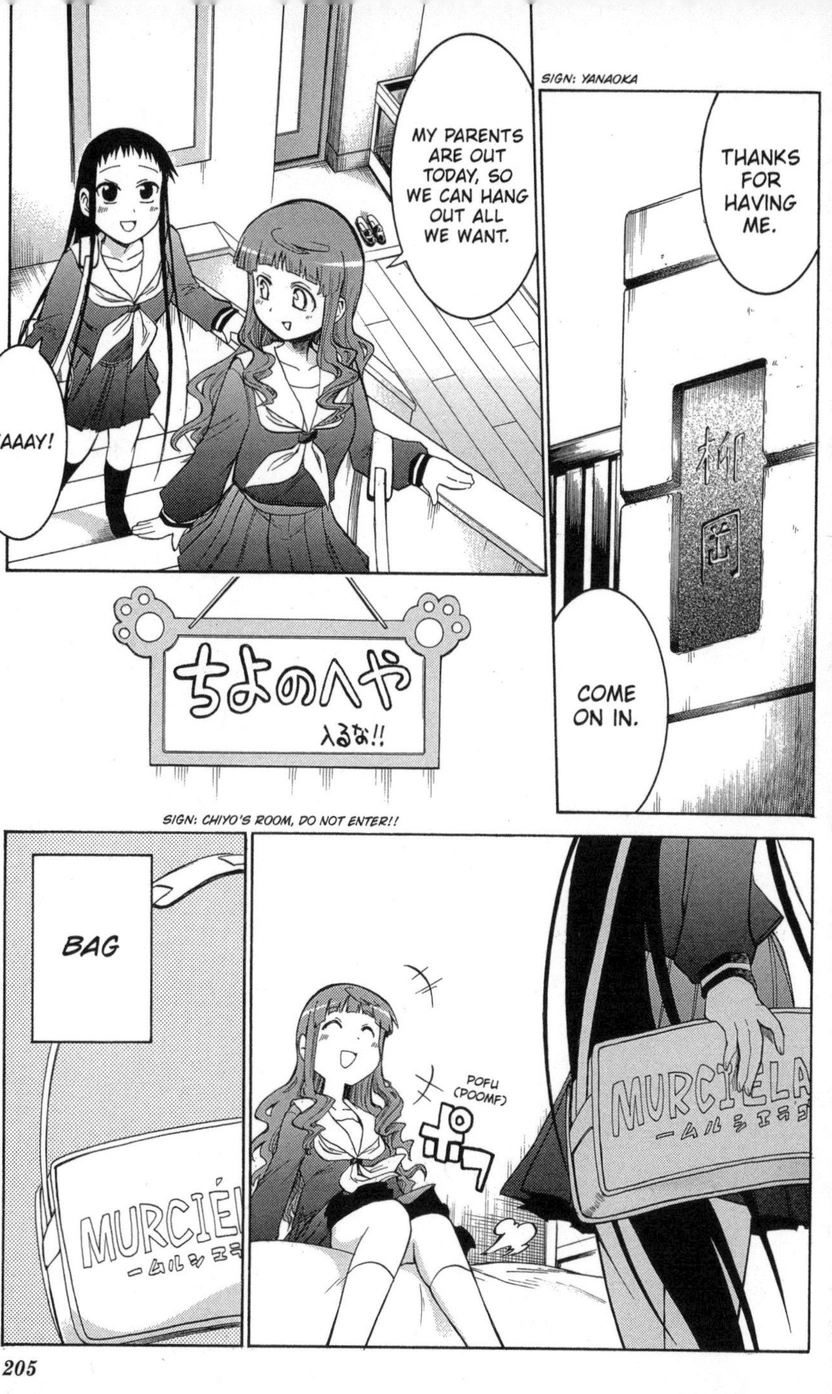
SIGN: YANAOKA
THANKS FOR HAVING ME.
柳岡
COME ON IN.
MY PARENTS ARE OUT TODAY, SO WE CAN HANG OUT ALL WE WANT.
YAAAY!
ちよのへや
入るな!!
SIGN: CHIYO'S ROOM, DO NOT ENTER!!
POFU (POOMF)
ポフ
BAG

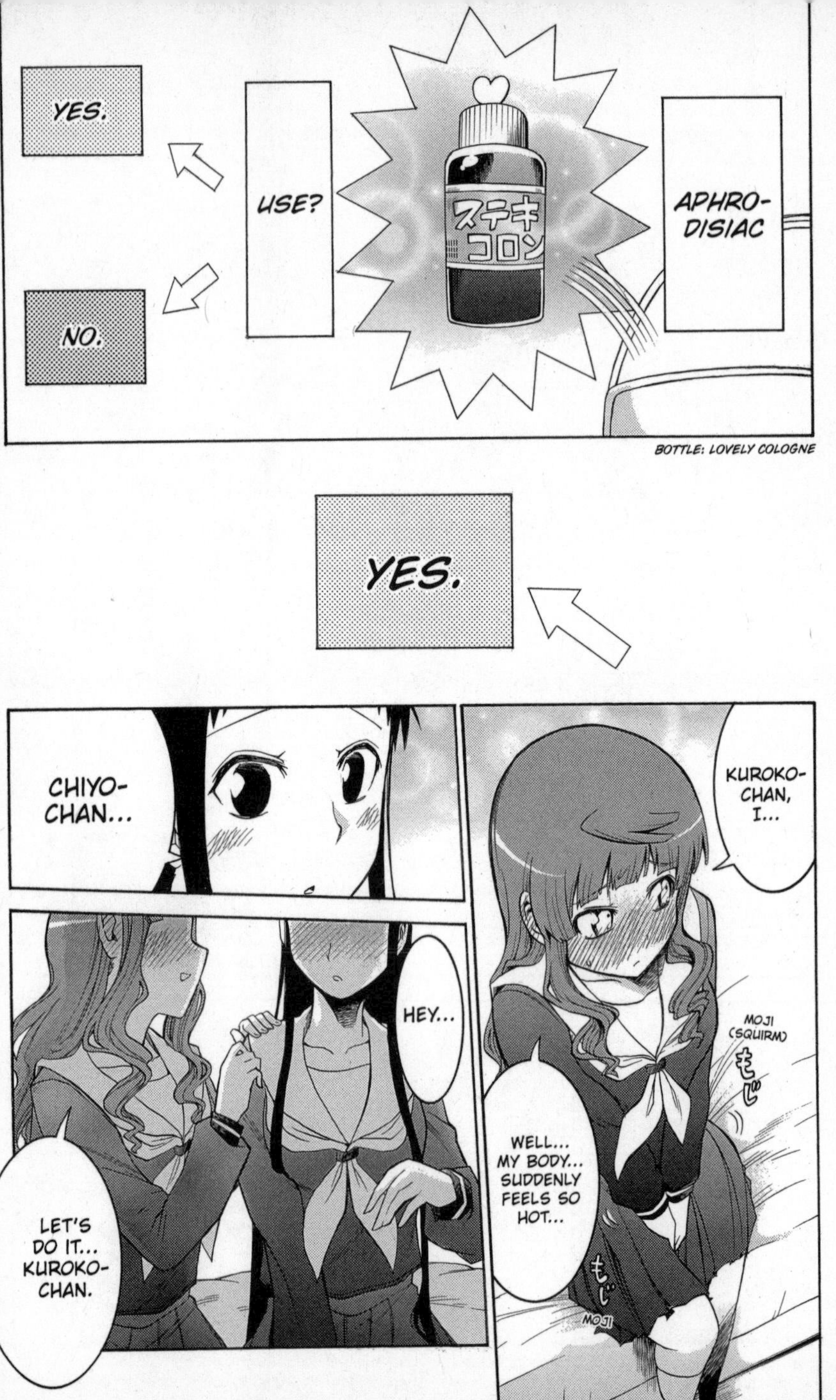
APHRO-DISIAC
ステキコロン
USE?
YES.
NO.
BOTTLE: LOVELY COLOGNE
YES.
KUROKO-CHAN, I...
MOJI (SQUIRM)
もじ
WELL... MY BODY... SUDDENLY FEELS SO HOT...
もじ
MOJI
CHIYO-CHAN...
HEY...
LET'S DO IT... KUROKO-CHAN.

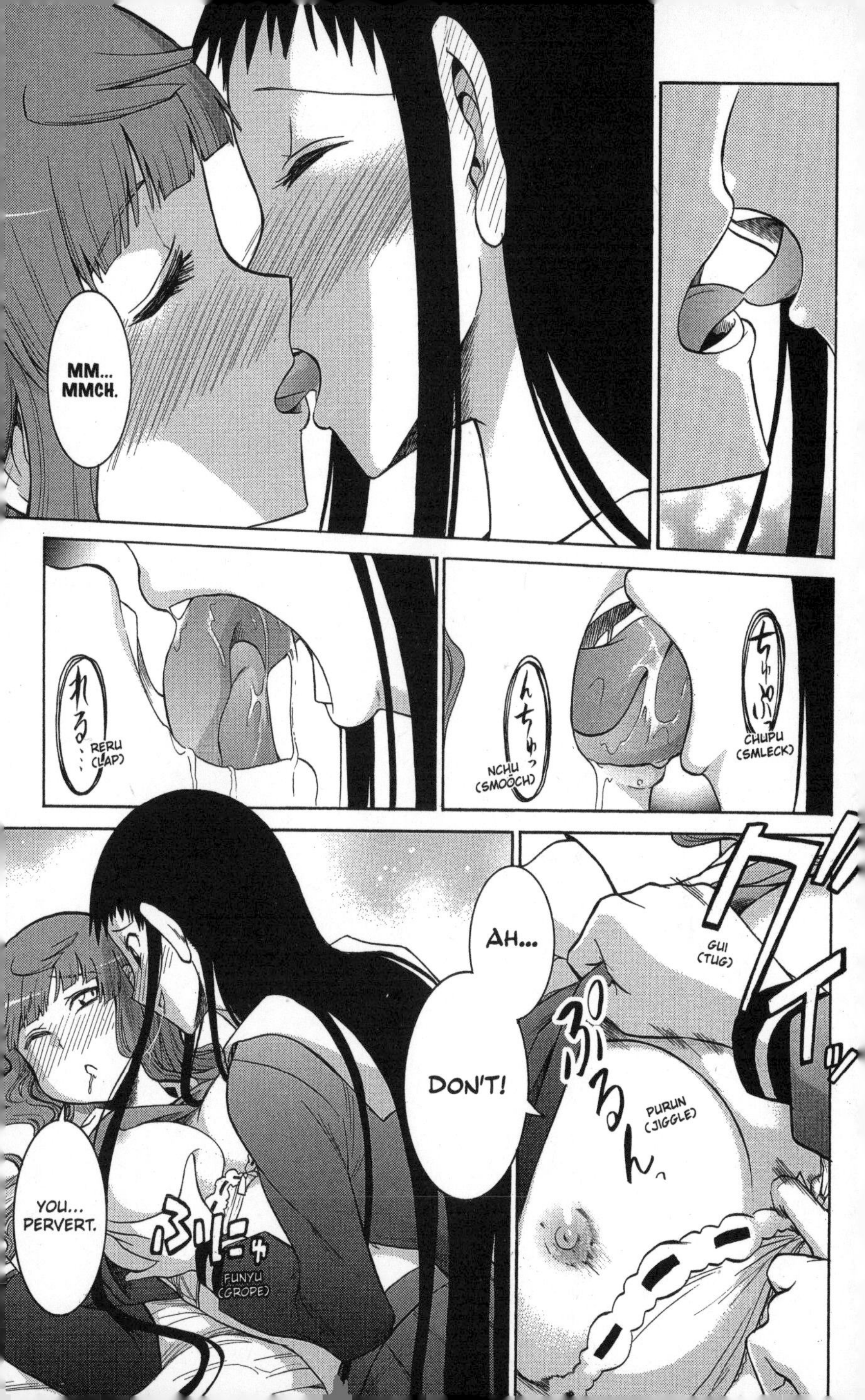
MM... MMCH.
ちゅぷ
CHUPU (SMLECK)
んちゅっ
NCHU (SMOOCH)
れる…
RERU (LAP)
グイッ
GUI (TUG)
AH...
DON'T!
ぷるんっ
PURUN (JIGGLE)
YOU... PERVERT.
ふにゅ
FUNYU (GROPE)

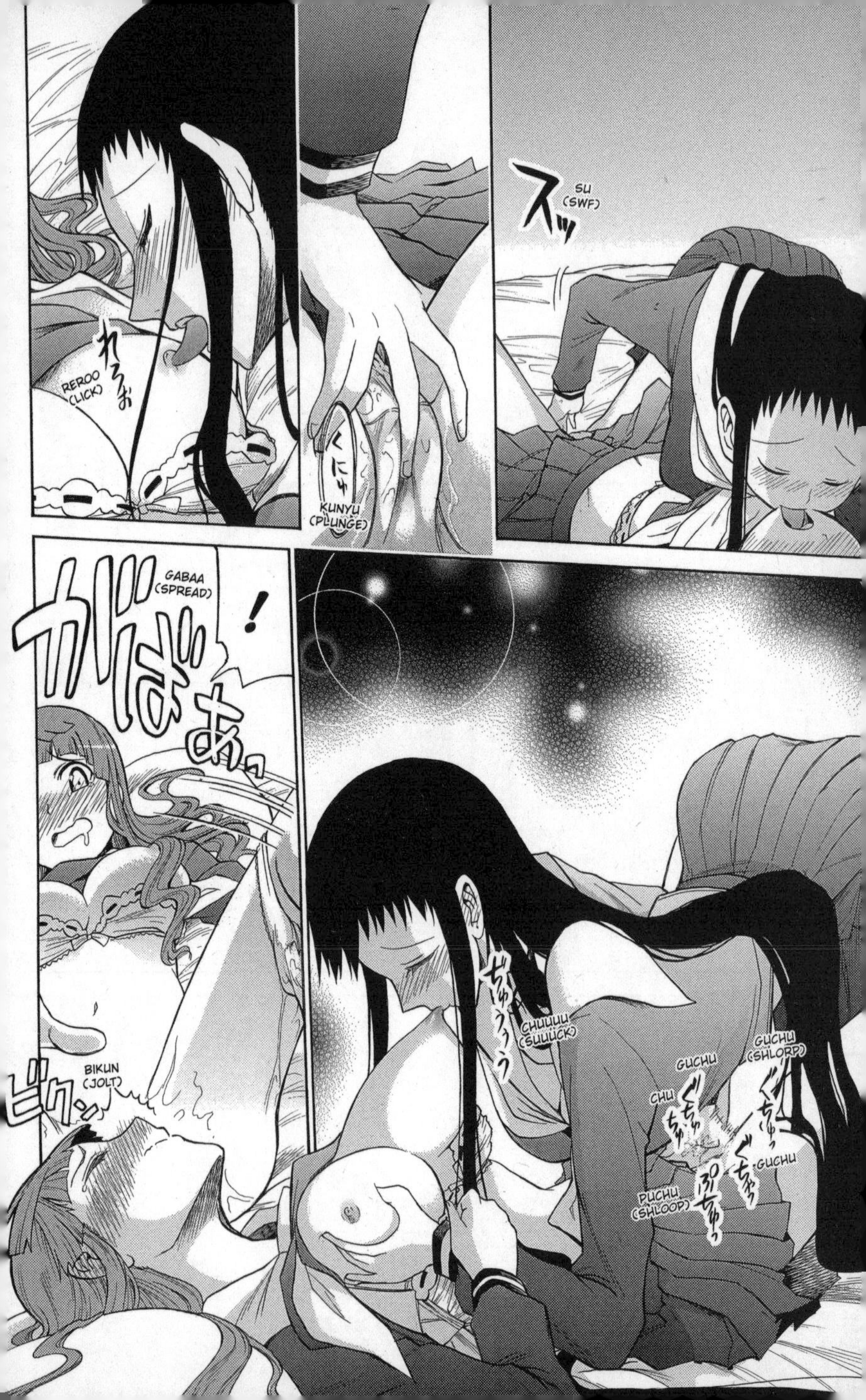

スッ
SU (SWF)
くにゅ
KUNYU (PLUNGE)
れろぉ
REROO (LICK)
ぐちゅっ
GUCHU (SHLORP)
ぐちゅっ
GUCHU
ぷちゅっ
PUCHU (SHLOOP)
ぐちゅ
GUCHU
ちゅ
CHU
ぢゅううう
CHUUUUU (SUUUCK)
がばぁっ
GABAA (SPREAD)
!
ビクンッ
BIKUN (JOLT)

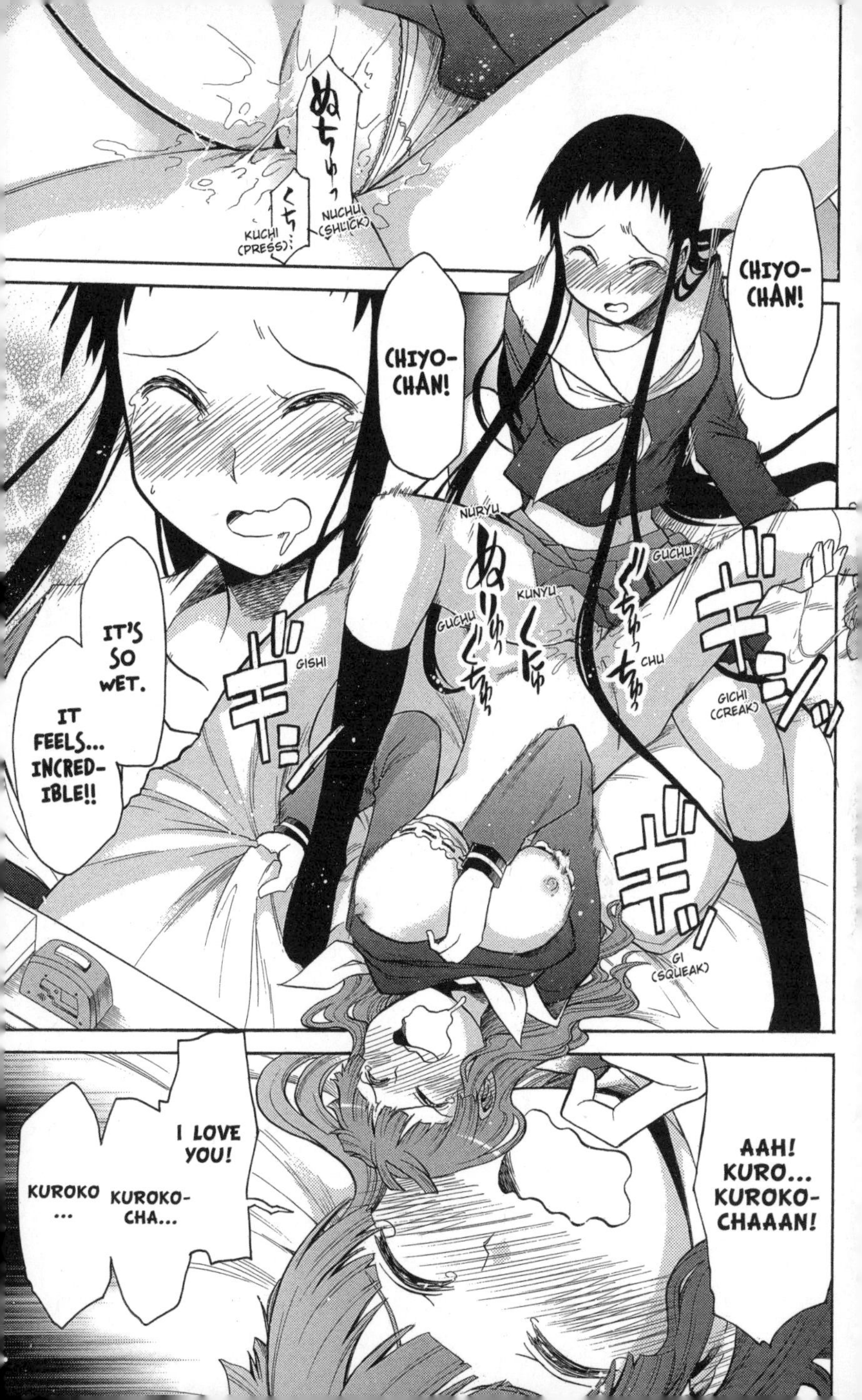
ぬちゅっ
NUCHU (SHLICK)
くち
KUCHI (PRESS)
CHIYO-CHAN!
CHIYO-CHAN!
GICHI (CREAK)
GUCHU
CHU
KUNYU
NURYU
GUCHU
GI (SQUEAK)
GISHI
IT'S SO WET.
IT FEELS... INCREDIBLE!!
AAH! KURO... KUROKO-CHAAAN!
I LOVE YOU!
KUROKO-CHA...
KUROKO ...

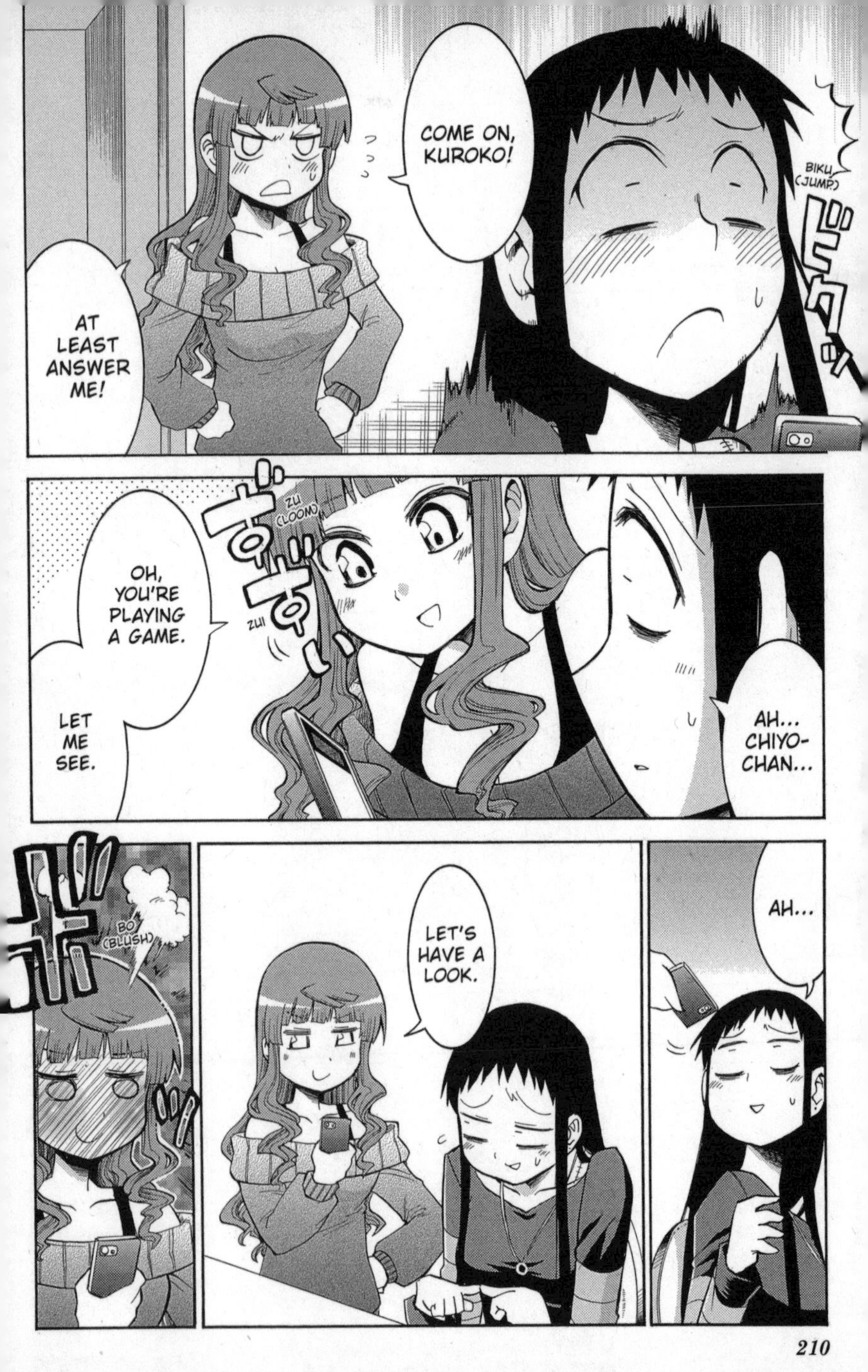
BIKU (JUMP)
COME ON, KUROKO!
AT LEAST ANSWER ME!
AH... CHIYO-CHAN...
ZU (LOOM)
ZUI
OH, YOU'RE PLAYING A GAME.
LET ME SEE.
AH...
LET'S HAVE A LOOK.
BO (BLUSH)

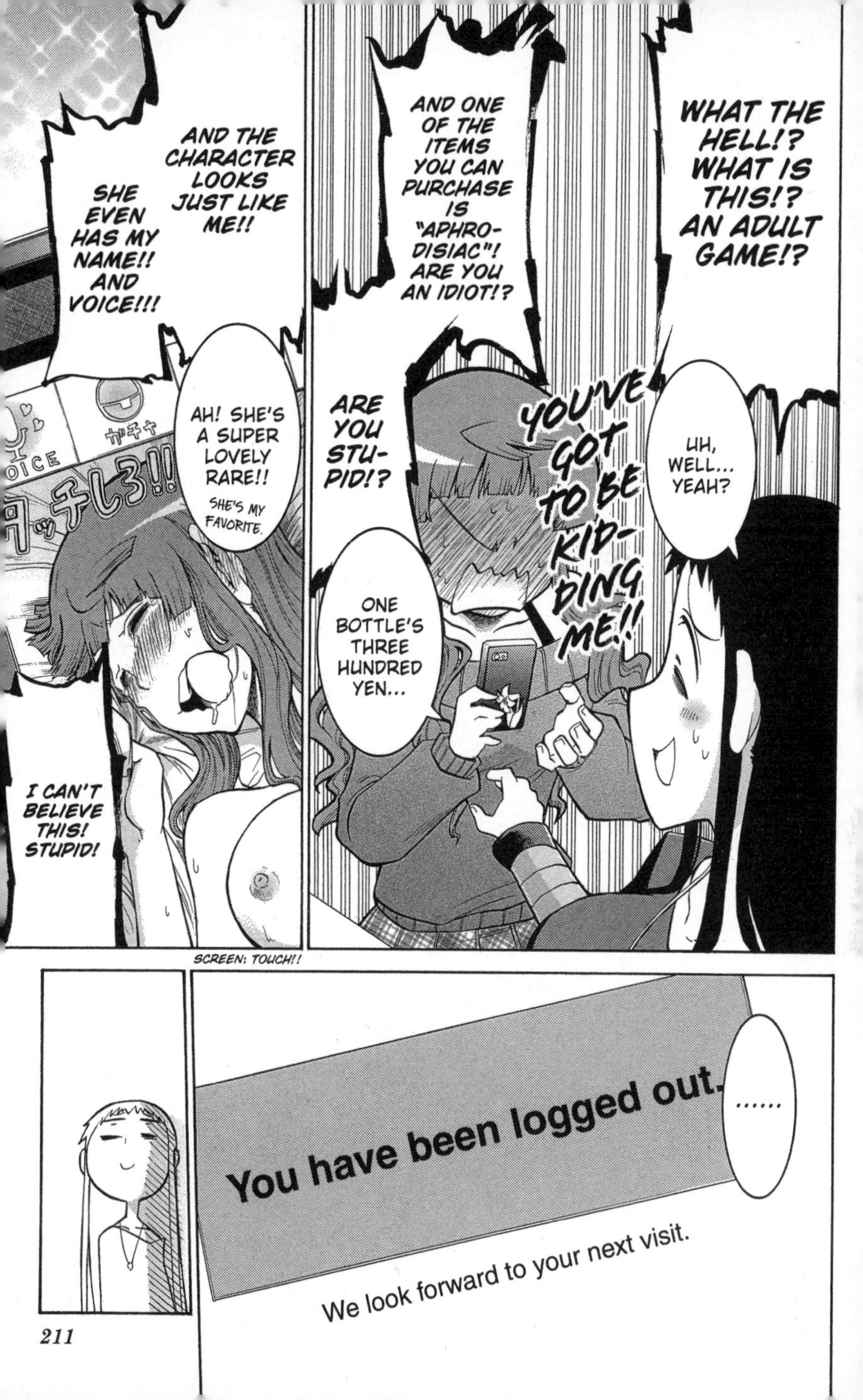
WHAT THE HELL!? WHAT IS THIS!? AN ADULT GAME!?
AND ONE OF THE ITEMS YOU CAN PURCHASE IS "APHRODISIAC"! ARE YOU AN IDIOT!?
UH, WELL... YEAH?
YOU'VE GOT TO BE KIDDING ME!!
ARE YOU STUPID!?
ONE BOTTLE'S THREE HUNDRED YEN...
AND THE CHARACTER LOOKS JUST LIKE ME!!
SHE EVEN HAS MY NAME!! AND VOICE!!!
AH! SHE'S A SUPER LOVELY RARE!!
SHE'S MY FAVORITE.
OICE
ガチャ
ッチしろ!!
I CAN'T BELIEVE THIS! STUPID!
SCREEN: TOUCH!!
You have been logged out.
......
We look forward to your next visit.

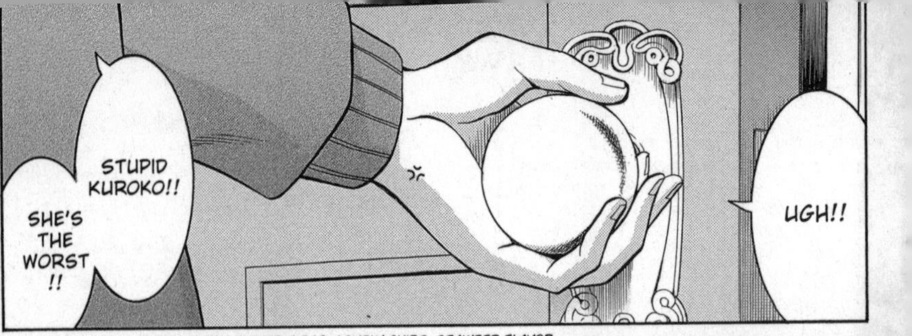
UGH!!
STUPID KUROKO!!
SHE'S THE WORST !!

BOTTLE: LOVELY JUICE, LOVELY FLAVOR / BAG: LOVELY CHIPS, SEAWEED FLAVOR

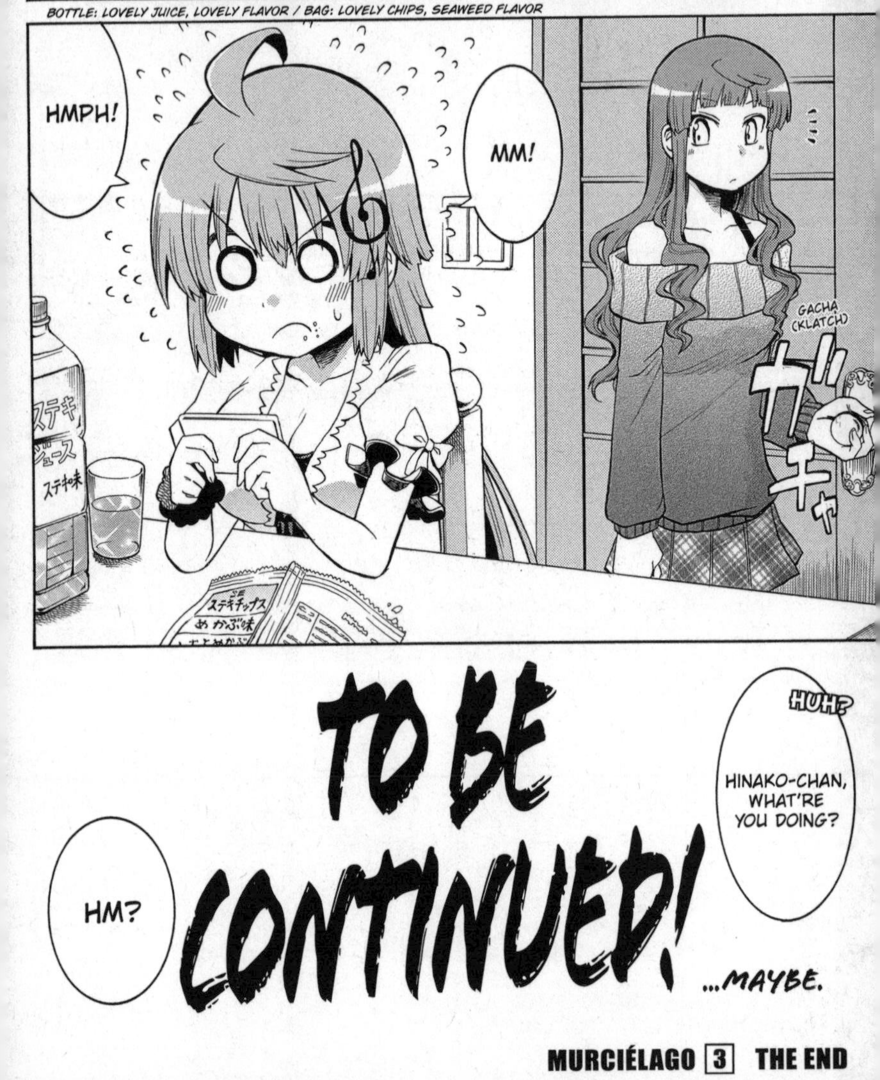
GACHA (KLATCH)
MM!
HMPH!

HUH?

HINAKO-CHAN, WHAT'RE YOU DOING?

TO BE CONTINUED!

HM?

...MAYBE.

MURCIÉLAGO 3 THE END

lo nonoriic. indicates familiarity or closeness. If used without permission or reason, addressing omeone in this manner would constitute an insult.

san: The Japanese equivalent of Mr./Mrs./Miss. If a situation calls for politeness, this is the ail-safe honorific.

sama: Conveys great respect; may also indicate that the social status of the speaker is lower han that of the addressee.

kun: Used most often when referring to boys, this indicates affection or familiarity. Occasionally used by older men among their peers, but it may also be used by anyone referring to a person of lower standing.

chan: An affectionate honorific indicating familiarity used mostly in reference to girls; also used in reference to cute persons or animals of either gender.

senpai: A suffix used to address upperclassmen or more experienced coworkers.

sensei: A respectful term for teachers, artists, or high-level professionals.

General

Murciélago is Spanish for "bat."

Kuroko means "black lake" in Japanese, and is a Cthulhu Mythos reference to the Lake of Hali, where the Dark God Hastur dwells.

Page 3

Nkai refers to N'kai, a cavern in the Cthulhu Mythos where the Great Old One Tsathoggua resides.

Page 15

Baiakuhe comes from Byakhee, insectoid aliens capable of interstellar travel in the Cthulhu Mythos.

Page 18

The city of **Ruruie** is a reference to R'lyeh, a fictional lost city in the Cthulhu Mythos.

Page 20

On Kuroko's badge, **"Komori"** is written with the Japanese characters for "small" and "forest." "Koumori" is written with "red" and "guard." Note that her badge name is "Kurako" with an a.

Page 30

ekeli-li is the sound made by Shoggoths, shape-shifting creatures in the Cthulhu Mythos.

Shoggo-tan is a cute mascot version of Shoggoth.

Page 39

The Deep Ones are Cthulhu Mythos ocean creatures who mate with humans.

Page 41

Dainagon is a large type of *azuki* red bean, a common ingredient in Japanese sweets.

Page 57

Ya got good goods, yah?" (*"Ii mon monjanjon"* in Japanese) is a line from the manga *Crayon Shin-chan,* which is about a potty-mouthed, little boy. The phrase is intentionally awkward-sounding.

Page 95

Kutaato refers to Cthäat, the shape-shifting Dark Water God from the Cthulhu Mythos.

Page 104

In the Cthulhyu Mythos, **Daoloths** are dimension-traveling creatures whose shape is so complex and indescribable that the sight of one is said to drive a person mad.

MURCIÉLAGO

MURCIÉLAGO

Yoshimurakana

Translation: Christine Dashiell ✦ Lettering: Alexis Eckerman

MURCIÉLAGO vol. 3
© 2014 Yoshimurakana / SQUARE ENIX CO., LTD.
First published in Japan in 2014 by SQUARE ENIX CO., LTD.
English translation rights arranged with SQUARE ENIX CO., LTD. and Yen Press, LLC
through Tuttle-Mori Agency, Inc.

English translation © 2017 by SQUARE ENIX CO., LTD.

Yen Press
1290 Avenue of the Americas
New York, NY 10104

Visit us at yenpress.com
facebook.com/yenpress
twitter.com/yenpress
yenpress.tumblr.com
instagram.com/yenpress

Yen Press is an imprint of Yen Press, LLC.
The Yen Press name and logo are trademarks of Yen Press, LLC.

First Yen Press Edition: August 2017

Library of Congress Control Number: 2016958266

ISBNs: 978-0-316-47318-7 (paperback)
978-0-316-47324-8 (ebook)

10 9 8 7 6 5 4 3 2 1

BVG

Printed in the United States of America